ESSAYS

PHILOLOGICAL AND CRITICAL

SELECTED FROM THE PAPERS

OF

JAMES HADLEY, LL.D.

Professor of Greek in Yale College; President of the American Oriental Society; Vice-President of the American Philological Association; Member of the National Academy of Sciences, etc., etc.

NEW YORK
HOLT & WILLIAMS
1873

POOLE & MACLAUCHLAN,
PRINTERS AND BOOKBINDERS,
205–213 *East Twelfth St.*,
NEW YORK.

PREFACE.

THE articles contained in this volume have been selected from among the papers, published and unpublished, left by Professor Hadley, and are put forth by his family and friends. He died on the 14th of November, 1872, in the fifty-second year of his age. He had been for twenty-seven years an instructor in Yale College, entering its service as tutor in 1845, being appointed assistant professor of Greek in 1848, and succeeding President Woolsey in the principal charge of that department in 1851. A sketch of his life, with an estimate of his character as a man and as a scholar, is given by President Porter in the New Englander for January, 1873, and has also been issued as a pamphlet, accompanied by an account of his early studies, drawn up by himself many years ago, and by a nearly complete list of his literary productions, with the times and places of their composition and publication.

Of the papers here given, the following have already appeared: Art. I., on the Ionian Migration (first part), in the Journal of the American Oriental Society, vol. v., 1856; Art. IV., on Bekker's Digammated Homer, in the Transactions of the Connecticut Academy, vol. i., 1866; Arts. VI. and VII., on Greek Accent and Greek Pronunciation in the tenth century, and Art. XV., on English Vowel Quantity, in the Transactions of the American Philological Association, 1869–72; Art. XIV., on Ellis's Early English Pronunciation, in the North American Review, vol. cx., 1870; Arts. XVI. and XVII., on Tennyson's Princess and the Number Seven, in the New Englander, vols. vii., 1849, and xvi., 1858; and Art. XX., on the Language of Palestine at the Time of Christ, in Messrs. Hackett and Abbot's edition of Smith's Bible Dictionary, vol. ii., 1868. Thanks are due, and are here publicly given, to the proprietors of the several works named, for kindly permitting the republications made in this volume. Art. VI., it may be added, has been reproduced, in German translation, in Professor G. Curtius's *Studien zur Griechischen und Lateinischen Grammatik*, vol. v., 1872. To Art. XV., on English Vowel Quantity, there is added in the original a "list of all the words, not already noticed, which appear in the Ormulum with the same vowel quantity which they have in modern English," occupying twelve pages; this list it was thought better to omit here.

Of the remaining essays, the larger number (together with some of the preceding) were prepared for the American Oriental Society, and read at its meetings; such are Arts. I. (second part), II., III., VIII., IX., X., XIII., and XIX.; others—namely, Arts. V. and XII.—were presented to the Classical and Philological Society of Yale College; and one, Art. XI., was brought before the Connecticut Academy, but at a meeting of which the record is lost; its precise date is therefore uncertain. The XVIIIth article, the Class Decisions, calls for a word of explanation. As one of the College instructors and officers, Professor Hadley was accustomed to preside at weekly "disputes" in the Junior class—the reading of essays upon selected questions—and to review and sum up the arguments brought forward, giving his own opinions on the subject discussed. In preparation for this exercise, it was his habit often to write out beforehand his views, not for reading to the class, but as part of the groundwork of his "decision;" and of such written arguments he has left a considerable mass (about a hundred and fifty in number). These exercises were always greatly enjoyed by the class; and it is partly in response to wishes warmly expressed from various quarters that a selection from the decisions is here included. They must be taken for what they are—thoroughly off-hand productions, written *currente calamo* and without special preparation, and in no case revised or corrected. Their author, doubtless, would never have thought of such a thing as making any of them public; but it seemed highly proper that, in a volume intended as a memorial and illustration of his scholarly life, they should not be passed over. They will show, on the one hand, the zeal and devotion with which he performed his College duties, and, on the other, the rapidity and precision with which he thought and wrote; they will be valued especially by his numerous pupils, and by all the graduates and friends of Yale College.

There are perhaps other essays in the volume which their author might not himself have chosen to publish. There are certainly some which he would not have let pass from his hands without a thorough revision. This is especially true of the essays in comparative philology (Arts. II. and IX.–XI.); the progress of investigation and deduction in this department is so rapid that no one's views can remain long absolutely unmodified. But although these essays need not be taken as representing in every item Professor Hadley's final opinions, it has not been thought worth while to alter or annotate them; as popular summaries they are authoritative, and by the special student who shall criticise them in detail they need only to have their date duly considered.

The plan of arrangement of the volume has been to put first the Greek articles, next those in general philology, then those upon English, and last the more miscellaneous and lighter papers; each division being arranged nearly chronologically. Taken together, they will measurably illustrate the wide range and varied direction of their author's studies—but with the exception, especially, of three departments: mathematics, where he early displayed an ability that bade fair, if he had continued his devotion to it, to place him among the foremost men of the day in that branch of science; Celtic philology, in which he was a proficient; and the Roman Law, his academical lectures on which are published in a separate volume, simultaneously with this.

And yet it may also be said with truth that the specimens of his work here presented are far from fully exhibiting his powers and acquirements. He was a man who put a larger share of himself into his personal teachings, and a smaller into what he gave to the world at large, than most others. He was absolutely without the desire to shine, and he needed the impulse of a more imperative call than he ever received to draw him fully out of his modest retirement. It is no proper place here to extol his abilities before the wider public which will, as it has the right to do, judge them by his recorded work, and which will do them justice ; and yet I cannot close this preface without a word of recognition of them, of appreciation of his worth and sorrow at his loss. In extent and accuracy of knowledge, in retentiveness and readiness of memory, in penetration and justness of judgment, I have never met his equal. Whatever others may have done, he was, in the opinion of all who knew him most fully, America's best and soundest philologist, and his death, in the maturity and highest activity of his powers, is a national calamity, a calamity to the world of scholars. Especially painful and irreparable to me has been the loss of a fellow-student to whom I had for twenty-three years looked up as a teacher, a colleague and friend whose counsel and sympathy I had so long enjoyed, and the purity and elevation of whose character had been to me a model of human excellence; and I have found it a very sad pleasure to assist his family in arranging and publishing this memorial of his high and varied scholarship.

W. D. WHITNEY.

YALE COLLEGE, NEW HAVEN, *April*, 1873.

CONTENTS.

I.

THE IONIANS BEFORE THE IONIAN MIGRATION.*

1856.

THE name of Ernst Curtius is well known to American scholars from his excellent volumes on the geography of Peloponnesus, as well as several smaller works. His essay, published last year under the title above given, presents novel and interesting views in regard to the earliest times of Greece. I propose in this article to give a brief statement of those views, with some criticism of the arguments by which they are supported. It will appear, as I proceed, that the subject, though belonging to Greek history, is one which has its claims upon the attention of an Oriental Society.

At the outset of authentic Greek history, we find the western coast of Asia Minor, with the neighboring islands, occupied by Greeks, undoubted members of the Hellenic body. Of these the largest portion, extending on the mainland from the mouth of the Hermus to that of the Mæander, and holding the important islands of Chios and Samos, called themselves Ionians—a name which belonged to them in common with the inhabitants of Attica and Eubœa on the west of the Ægean, as well as the island group of the Cyclades in the centre of that sea. The Asiatic Ionians, after passing through a long career of independence and prosperity, were incorporated about 550 B. C. into the kingdom of the Lydian Crœsus, along with which they came only a few years later into the more comprehensive and permanent empire of the Persian Cyrus. This was the close of their independent existence. For its commencement we must go back to the mythic period —at least to a period lying on the debatable ground between history and mythus. In the traditions of the Greeks as to their own early times, we find the origin of the Asiatic Io-

* *Die Ionier vor der Ionischen Wanderung, von Ernst Curtius.* Berlin, 1855. 8vo. pp. 56.

nians traced up to an ancient colonization from the west, by emigrants who came from European Greece. This emigration is represented as one consequence, among many, of the great event which stands on the threshold of Greek history, itself obscurely seen, but sufficiently recognized as the cause or occasion of almost all we see in early Greece—the invasion and conquest of Peloponnesus by the Dorians. The story is briefly this: I condense from Grote. "A multitude of refugees from various parts of Greece, fleeing before the Dorian invaders, sought shelter in Attica. Alarmed by the growing population of that territory, the Dorians of Peloponnesus marched against it with a powerful army; but finding that victory had been assured to the Athenians by the generous self-devotion of their king Codrus, they gave up the enterprise and returned home. The Athenians on the death of Codrus abolished the kingship; but his descendants for several generations held the supreme power as archons for life. His two sons, Medon and Neileus, having quarreled about the succession, the Delphian oracle decided in favor of the former; whereupon the latter, affronted at the preference, resolved to seek a new home. There were at this moment many dispossessed sections of Greeks, and an adventitious population, accumulated in Athens, who were anxious for settlements beyond sea. The expeditions which now set forth to cross the Ægean, chiefly under the conduct of members of the Codrid family, composed collectively the memorable Ionic Emigration, of which the Ionians, recently expelled from Peloponnesus, formed only a part; for we hear of many quite distinct races, some renowned in legend, who withdrew from Greece amidst this assemblage of colonists. The Kadmeians, the Minyæ of Orchomenus, the Abantes of Eubœa, the Dryopes; the Molossi, the Phokians, the Bœotians, the Arcadian Pelasgians, and even the Dorians of Epidaurus—are represented as furnishing each a proportion of the crews of those emigrant vessels. At the same time other mythic families beside the Codrids, the lineage of Neleus and Nestor, took part in the expedition. Herodotus mentions Lykian chiefs, descendants of Glaukus, and Pausanias tells us of Philotas a descendant of Peneleos, who went at the head of a body of

Thebans. Prokles, the chief who conducted the Ionic emigrants from Epidaurus to Samos, was said to be of the lineage of Ion son of Xuthus. The results were not unworthy of this great gathering of chiefs and races. The Cyclades were colonized, as also the large islands of Samos and Chios near the Asiatic shore, while ten different cities on the coast of Asia Minor, from Miletus on the south to Phokæa on the north, were founded, and all adopted the Ionic name. Athens was the metropolis or mother city of all of them: Androklus and Neileus, the Œkists of Ephesus and Miletus, and probably other Œkists also, started from the Prytaneium at Athens with those solemnities, religious and political, which usually marked the departure of a swarm of Grecian colonists." Such is the traditional account. The main fact contained in it may be regarded as certain—that after the Dorian conquest of southern Greece, and in consequence of that event, large bodies of Greeks, the most important part of them Ionians, set forth, chiefly from the coast of Attica, to cross the Ægean Sea. The time of this migration may be set down by a loose approximation at 1000 years before our era.

Now the principal thesis of Curtius in his Essay is this: that in the migration just described, the Ionians of Greece were going home, to their own country and kindred. It was the returning emigration to a land from which, ages before, their fathers had passed over into Greece—and not only that, but a land which had never ceased to be occupied by the same race, by a people of Ionian name and lineage. They found, on arriving in Asia, not only Dardanians, Carians, Lycians, and other tribes, which Curtius regards as differing not very widely from Ionians in language and culture: but they found there Ionians, identified with themselves by virtue of the common name, origin, and traditions. They found in fact *the* Ionians—the principal branch as well as the elder of their race—who in these Asiatic seats had risen to a height of achievement and reputation not yet equalled by any Greeks of Europe. Let us, however, trace the theory more in detail, going back to its remote starting-point in the past, beyond the reach of history, beyond the reach even of mythus, where only ethnographic science can furnish any glimmering of light.

The primitive Aryan colonization, flowing westward from Armenia into Asia Minor, filled the elevated plateaux of that peninsula with Phrygian races. Here the Greeks, long identified with the Phrygian stock, first begin to be distinguished as Greeks, with a stamp and nationality of their own. Here they develop what must be considered as the common type of Hellenism in language and character. But almost from the beginning they divide themselves into two great sections. The one is that afterwards known in history as the Ionian. The other includes the remaining fractions of the Greek nation: we might call it Hellenic in a narrower sense, as being first to assume the Hellenic name: it is sometimes called Æolo-Dorian, from the designations of its leading members in the historic period. After a time these sections part company. The latter or Hellenic section break up from Asia, cross the Hellespont and Propontis, and find new seats in the mountains of Thrace and Macedonia. Here they remain in isolated Alpine valleys, forming their separate local constitutions, until, dislodged by new movements of population, and pressed southward, they make their appearance in different masses, as Æolians, Dorians, Achæans, in Northern Greece. Here again in the course of time new causes arise, which carry portions at least of these tribes still further in the same direction, into Central and Southern Greece. Hence the occupation of Peloponnesus by the Achæans, whom the Homeric poems represent to us as seated in that territory and exercising full ascendancy. And hence too the later and far more important conquest of the same territory by the Dorians and their auxiliaries.

The Ionians meanwhile remain in Asia Minor, but no longer in the highlands of the interior. Descending gradually along the great river-valleys, they at length reach the Ægean sea, and then, spreading themselves northward and southward, occupy the whole western coast—possessing thus a territory distinguished alike for the richness of its soil and the genial beauty of its climate. They are closely connected here by proximity and by intercourse with other tribes, such as the Dardanians, Lycians, Carians, Leleges, from whom in fact they are not separated by any broad lines of ethnical distinction. Under these circumstances they enter upon a career of activity and culture, which appears to have received its impulse from the Phœnicians, and to have been shared in, more or less, by the other tribes just mentioned. Visited at first by the Phœnicians for the purposes of trade, they soon learned from them the art of navigation, and set up business on their own account, as the rivals of their late masters. Associated with the Phœnicians in many parts of the Ægean, and supplanting them in others, they have become inextricably confused with them in the traditions of the Greeks. The Ionian myth which represents Byblus, one of the oldest Phœnician cities, as the daughter of Miletus, shows perhaps that the Ionians gained a foothold even on the coast of Syria; at any rate, it is a proof of close connection between these two maritime peoples. There is clearer evidence to show that the Ionians visited the coast of Egypt, and even established settlements, more or less permanent, in the marshy Delta of the Nile. This was regarded by the Egyptians themselves almost as foreign territory; since we find that Psammetichus—the same prince, who, perhaps a thousand years later, opened the whole country to the Greeks—when banished from Egypt, took refuge in the Delta. And the men of brass who were announccd to Psammetichus, while there, as having just made their appearance, and who proved to be a party of Ionian rovers recently landed, were but a specimen of their own countrymen, who, a thousand years earlier, made repeated descents upon the same coast for the mingled purposes of traffic and plunder. But the attention of the Ionians was naturally directed more to the west. Crossing the Ægean Sea, they occupy first the Cyclades, and then Eubœa and Attica. They establish their settlements on the Pagasæan Gulf, and on both sides of the Euripus. Traces of them are found along the whole eastern coast of Peloponnesus, in Corinth, Epidaurus, Trœzen, Argos, and even in the island of Cythera. Passing over the Isthmus, they appear in the Corinthian Gulf, where we find them in southern Phocis, and much more in northern Peloponnesus, in the district afterward called Achaia. From thence they spread southward over Elis and Messene in western Peloponnesus;

and having thus reached the Ionian Sea, they occupy the Ithacan islands, and extend themselves northward to the island of Corcyra, and the coasts of Epirus and Illyria. More than this: in the mythic wanderings of Æneas, Curtius would recognize a traditionary representation of Ionian settlement, which must then have stretched along the western coast of Italy from Eryx to the mouth of the Tiber. Even in Sardinia, he considers the name of a people called the Iolæans, and of their founder Iolaos, as giving evidence of early Ionian colonization.

Throughout the course of these migrations, the Ionians carry with them the culture of the vine and the worship of the wine-god Dionysus. Everywhere we find them settling along the coasts, and showing an especial preference for the rich, though marshy, alluvium at the mouth of rivers. Occasionally, however, they follow up a river-valley quite into the interior of a district, as in Bœotia, where the Asopus leads them to the inland city of Thebes. Everywhere wandering in ships, they wander without women; and hence their colonization appears as the establishment of a few foreign settlers among a native population, whom they do not attempt to dispossess, but exercise over them the natural ascendancy of superior ability and civilization. Thus in Attica there is no change of population: the primitive people, whom Greek tradition names Pelasgi, remain in their old seats, unchanged except as they are civilized, Ionized by the foreigners from Asia. The Egyptian Cecrops, the mythic author of civilization in Attica, is no proper Egyptian, but an Ionian, who had become domiciled in Egypt. A similar view is taken of Danaus the Egyptian founder of Argos. These traditions of early connections between Egypt and Greece are, in the view of Curtius, too deeply rooted and too widely ramified to have sprung up, as K. O. Müller assumed, after the comparatively recent period when the Egyptians under Psammetichus came into closer relations with the Greeks. Yet, on the other hand, it seems equally evident that no influence strictly and properly Egyptian could have had a leading part in moulding the civilization, substantially homogeneous and independent, of early Greece. The difficulty finds its solution in the view that these

Egyptian settlers, who figure in tradition, were Ionians, who had found a residence in Egypt and came from thence to Greece. The Phœnician Cadmus and his colonization of Thebes are treated in the same way. Curtius does not deny, indeed, that there were in Greece, to a greater or less extent, ancient settlements of native Phœnicians; but he maintains confidently that no such alien Semitic settlers could have gained historic importance as founders of royal or sacerdotal families. It is of course still easier to connect the Phrygian Pelops, and his immigration into the peninsula which took his name, with the colonial extension of the Ionian race. The Argonautic expedition is a story of Ionian adventure. Its leader, who comes into Thessaly an unknown wanderer, bears a name, Jason (Ἰάσων), which stamps him as Ionian; and its Thessalian starting-point, Iolcos or Iaolcos, is with great probability explained as meaning 'the naval station of the Ionians.'

Here on the coast of Thessaly the Ionians are again brought into contact with their brethren of Æolo-Dorian descent. After a local separation of generations and centuries, these long-sundered sections of the Grecian people are brought once more into local connection. The most conspicuous result is the formation of the celebrated Amphictyonic League, the oldest and largest and most influential of the Grecian Amphictyonies. It is a religious association of Thessalian tribes (neighbors to one another, Ἀμφικτίονες) for the common worship of the god Apollo. The Ionians, after being for a long time worshippers preëminently of the god Poseidon, of whom the western Greeks at that time knew as little as of the element he ruled, had in their eastern home received the Apollo-worship—a new religion, as Curtius calls it, which everywhere exercised a transforming and inspiring influence on its converts. Zealously devoted to its propagation, they introduced it among their brethren of Thessaly. Thus in the Amphictyonic deity we find a proof of Ionian influence; which appears further in the frequently-recurring Ionian number twelve, as that of the confederate tribes. The Amphictyonic League, though primarily a religious organization, expressed political aspirations, and worked toward political results. It produced a feeling of closer union and of common brotherhood among its members, which led to the adoption of the Hellenic name as a common designation for the united Amphictyonic people. Hellen in the myths is either father or brother of Amphictyon. Hence the tribes of Macedonia and Epirus, however closely resembling the Hellenes, never received the Hellenic name, which belongs only to the Amphictyonic tribes and the districts which come under their control or influence.

Although Ionian influence, as we have seen, was predominant in the origin of the Delphic Amphictyony, that first reunion and organization of the Greek races, yet the relative weight of parties did not always remain the same. A reaction at length commenced—a reaction of the older tribes in the interior against the newer occupants of the sea-board—of the western Greeks against their emigrant brethren from the east. The ruder tribes of Thessaly, receiving the imported civilization of the Ionians, come at length to feel themselves the equals of their late instructors, and can no longer brook the ascendancy to which they at first submitted. Hence a decided revolution in the political state of Greece, proceeding from Thessaly, and having for its ultimate result the almost complete expulsion of the Ionians from European Greece. But this revolution is the work of ages, and has its different epochs, according to the different races who successively appear to carry it forward.

First, the Æolians, who are represented in the traditions as arising from a mixture of the inland tribes with the maritime population of the sea-board. Though in fact supplanting the Ionians, they do not appear as their opponents or even as their rivals. The Æolids are themselves bearers of Ionian cultivation and the worship of Poseidon; their royal seats, as Iolcos and Corinth, are stations of Ionian colonization; their mythic heroes, as Jason and Sisyphus, are representatives of Asiatic culture.

Second, the Achæans are likewise in many ways closely connected with the Ionians, as the mythus intimates, when it makes both Ion and Achæus sons of Apollo. Yet the military exaltation of the Achæans is the first great blow to Ionian preponderance in Greece. While the Achæans of Phthiotis press on toward the sea-coast of Thessaly, the other branch of that people conquer the Peloponnesus, form new states there hostile to the Ionians, whom they expel from Trœzen and other parts of Argolis, and with fleets of their own begin those struggles with the tribes of Asia Minor which are commemorated in the legends of the Trojan war—a war in which the Ionian peoples, as the Athenians, take scarcely any part, while heroes akin to the Ionians, as Palamedes and Odysseus, enter into it with reluctance.

Third, the Dorians, a people much more alien to the Ionians and much more independent of their influence; a people who adhere with tenacity to their original peculiarities of life and character; in them was first seen the full native vigor of the mountain tribes. Breaking up from their seats in Mt. Œta, they cross the Corinthian Gulf, by a gradual conquest overthrow the Achæan power, and make themselves masters of nearly all Peloponnesus. As they advance, the Ionians everywhere lose ground; on all sides they are driven back to their ships: and now begins a great retreat of the Ionians from their settlements in the west; a great return to their mother country on the east of the Ægean Sea. Only in Attica do they at last succeed in making an effectual stand: thus maintaining a foothold in European Greece, and preventing Hellenic history from being again divided, as it had been, ages before, between two distinct races upon opposite sides of the Ægean. Even in Asia Minor they are not by themselves. Achæan and Dorian colonies reproduce there the collisions of western Greece, keeping up a restless activity of mind, by which Ionian art is stimulated to a rapid development, until it puts forth its fairest blossom in the Homeric Epos. Still, in the Dorian and Æolian districts of Asia Minor, the basis of population remained essentially Ionian: and in the Ionian revolt, as it is called, the whole people of the western coast, from Lycia to the Propontis, rose as one people against the barbarian conqueror.

Such is the theory of this ingenious and strikingly written essay. Before taking up any points in the argument on which it rests, we must observe that this idea of Ionians in Asia previous to the Ionian Migration is wholly foreign to the mythic or semi-historical traditions of the Greeks themselves. It may be shown, perhaps, that in those traditions there are statements which imply the existence of a primitive Ionian people in that region; statements which cannot be explained on any other supposition. But it is confessedly true that the traditions conveyed no such idea to the ancient Greeks who had them; certainly not, after they had assumed the forms in which they have come down to us.

In looking at the evidence on which our author relies, to sustain a proposition of which no memory is found in the most ancient literature and tradition of Greece, it is natural to inquire, first, whether any testimony can be gleaned from early Oriental sources. Here Curtius finds a confirmation of his views in the name given to the Greeks by all the ancient nations of the East. It is well known that the common form *Ἴωνες* is made by a contraction of the earlier *Ἰάονες*; and there is great reason to believe that this latter form had originally a medial digamma, and was pronounced *Ἰάϝονες*, sing. *Ἰαϝων*. Now the Greeks are called by the Indians Javanas, by the Hebrews Javan, by the Persians Juna or Jauna, in Aramaic Jaunojo, in Arabic Jaunâni, in Armenian Juin, and in Coptic Uinin. It can hardly be doubted that these are all forms of one and the same name; and that this is no other than *Ἰάϝων* or *Ἰάϝονες*, the special name of the Ionian Greeks. We may not unreasonably suppose that it was the Phœnicians who first applied this name as a common designation for the whole Greek people, and that the widely-extended commerce of the Phœnicians was the means of its diffusion throughout Asia. It is further probable that the Phœnicians had the name in this use of it before the time of the Ionian Migration. We find it in the tenth chapter of the book of Genesis, in the list of Noachids, where it undoubtedly refers, not to a part of the Greeks, but to the whole people. This document, if of Mosaic origin, is at least thirteen centuries older than the Christian era: while, even among those who deny its Mosaic origin, it is allowed by all the sounder critics to be older than the division of the Hebrew monarchy. But this occurred about 1000 B. C., perhaps at the same time with the Ionian

Migration, probably not later than that event. What shall we conclude, then, from this early use of the Ionian name as a designation for the whole Hellenic people? Curtius replies —the fact is inexplicable unless we assume that, of all the Grecian tribes, the Ionian was the first which became known to the Orientals; it must have existed as their neighbor and carried on intercourse with them by land and water, not simply as early or a little earlier than Æolians and Dorians, but long before all other Greeks. It appears to me that this language overstates the case. On the coast of Syria at the present day all Europeans are Franks. Yet other nations of Europe beside the French were represented in the first crusade, and still more in the second, which followed only a half century later. On the other hand, the Europeans have given the common name of Tartars to the nomadic tribes east of the Caspian Sea. Yet it is certain that even the first invading hordes, which entered Europe under the successors of Genghiz Khan, were not composed wholly or principally of Tartars properly so called. Because the French give the name of Allemands to all the Germans, it surely does not follow that their ancestors for a long time were acquainted with no Germans except those included in the Alemannic confederacy. As to the case in hand, we can only say (assuming that the Phœnicians were the first who used Ionian for Greek) that either the Ionians were the first Greeks known to the Phœnicians, or they were somehow, from greater proximity, or closer intercourse, or some one of many other possible reasons, more prominently present to the view of the Phœnicians, when this use of the name originated.

A second testimony is supposed to be furnished by early Egyptian records. On the celebrated Rosetta stone, and on other monuments of the Macedonian and Roman periods, the idea 'Greek' is represented by a hieroglyphic group consisting, first, of three papyrus plants standing side by side, and secondly, of three baskets placed one above another. These elements, it is said, give the meaning 'Lords of the North.' The pronunciation of the group, as determined by a comparison of the demotic characters in the Rosetta inscription, is said to be unquestionably *Uinen*, which we have just seen to be the Coptic name for the Greeks. Now the same hieroglyphic group is found upon a series of monuments belonging to the early Pharaohs, and always in reference to a people described as subject to the kings of Egypt. Of these kings, some—as Amenophis II, Sethos I or Sesonchis I—belong to the great heroic dynasties of Thebes, the eighteenth and nineteenth dynasties, in the fifteenth and fourteenth centuries: others to the twenty-second dynasty and the tenth century, as Sesonchis, the Shishak of the Old Testament, the conqueror of Jerusalem. It would seem, therefore, that several of the early Egyptian sovereigns claimed to be masters of the Uinen, Ionians or Greeks. Curtius does not suppose, what indeed would be in the highest degree improbable, that these records refer to expeditions by sea or land sent out from Egypt to the western border of Asia Minor, and there subduing or pretending to subdue the Ionian population of the country. He considers them as referring to Ionians of Egypt, settled in the Delta of the Nile, who may at various times have been attacked and perhaps reduced to submission, more or less complete, by native sovereigns of the country. It appears from the researches of Lepsius that this name belongs to a group containing nine names of nations, which recur in the same fixed order, the supposed Uinen standing first among them, and Egypt itself, upper and lower, being included in the series. That all the others beside Egypt belong to foreign nations is inferred from the fact that in a Theban tomb the bearers of the two Egyptian shields are plainly distinguished from the other seven by their red complexion and peculiar hair-dress. These are the statements. If they really prove that Ionian settlements were made in Egypt as early as fourteen or fifteen centuries before Christ, they doubtless serve to confirm the theory of Curtius. It does not appear, indeed, that the monuments give any direct indication as to what part of the world these Uinen (if they are rightly read so) come from. But it is certainly more probable that such Ionian settlements, if actually made in Egypt, should have been made from Asia Minor than from European Greece. But we seem to have here what may eventually turn out to be a good argument, rather than what we can now receive and rely upon as such. Even Curtius does not appear to expect that it will produce general conviction. "Every first attempt," he says, "to connect Greek and Egyptian history with one another, to supplement the beginnings of one by materials drawn from the other, must, however cautiously undertaken, encounter manifold objection, consisting either in a vague and general want of confidence, or in scientific doubts as to the correctness of the method and the certainty of the facts made use of." In the present case our suspicions are stronger from the obscurity which rests on other names of conquered nations found upon the monuments of these ancient Pharaohs; hardly two or three of them, it is said, have been identified with certainty. We must add, however, that Lepsius accepts without hesitation the views of Curtius upon this point: he has no doubt that the name in question refers to Ionian Greeks settled in Egypt, "so that, as early as the sixteenth and fifteenth centuries, Ionians—that is, at least a part, a considerable colony of that people—were dependent on the Egyptian sovereigns."

We turn now from Oriental testimonies to inquire how far the known facts of Grecian history support the theory in question. Curtius asserts that in particular localities on the coast of Asia and the neighboring islands there are traces of Ionian occupancy before the time of the Ionian Migration. It is to be regretted that he has not drawn out more at length this part of his argument. As it is, the few brief indications which he gives hardly suffice to make a definite and satisfactory impression. Miletus and Ephesus, he says, were even in name nothing but renewals of older settlements: and the same fact is expressly attested in regard to Erythræ, Chios, and Samos. Admitting now the correctness of these traditionary notices, granting that the places mentioned were inhabited before the Ionian Migration, are we authorized to assume, what is not contained in the traditions, that these earlier occupants were Ionians? What more natural than to find that, among the numerous places settled by these colonists from Europe, some had been previously occupied by the natives of the country, who may have abandoned them before the time of the Ionian colonization; or, in other instances, may have been dispossessed and driven out by the colonists themselves; or, again, may have remained where they were, submitting to the new-comers and fusing with them into one community.

Again, he urges that the worship of Apollo Didymæus in his sanctuary near Miletus—a worship common to all the Ionians—appears in tradition as older than the planting of the Ionian colony in Miletus. In like manner, the Delian sanctuary of Apollo was the Mother-sanctuary for all the stations of Apollo-worship in Greece, and must therefore have existed earlier than the Ionian Migration, though tradition very distinctly represents the island of Delos as having at that time received its Greek population in place of the Carians, its earlier inhabitants. I would not say there is no force in the argument derived from these facts. Yet the question must be raised: granting, in accordance with the tradition, the primitive antiquity of these places as stations of Apollo-worship, how far may we infer, what is not expressed in the tradition, that the primitive worshippers were Ionians? Curtius himself does not suppose that the worship of Apollo was confined to the Greeks: he will not venture to say that it originated with them; he believes it to have been extensively diffused among the non-Hellenic tribes of western Asia. There is no strong improbability against the supposition that the Ionians, instead of founding the establishments referred to, were only the successors of their founders. It is well known that the nations of antiquity regarded it as a point of great importance to keep up local rites of worship, even in conquered places. Curtius mentions that when the Ionians were driven out by the Achæans from northern Peloponnesus, some of their families were retained in Helice, in order to continue there the former worship of Poseidon. And, apart from this general feeling, the Ionians were little likely to neglect any old and celebrated sanctuary of Apollo, a divinity whom they honored with peculiar veneration.

For further proof of primitive Ionian occupancy, we find our author referring to the city of Iasus, situated on a small island near the coast of Caria. No tradition, he observes, was able to refer this Carian place to any settlement proceeding from the west; and yet Iasus, with its entire environment, was, in more than name alone, a genuine, primitive portion of Ionia. Now the Greek character of this place, and even its Ionian character, will be readily admitted. But we know not how to explain the statement that no tradition could refer it to a settlement proceeding from the west. For Polybius (xvi. 11), in a passage which we can imagine no reason for discrediting, tells us expressly that Iasus, according to the assertion of its people, was settled by a colony of Argives, though, having afterwards lost a considerable portion of its citizens in a war with the Carians, it received a large reinforcement from Miletus, headed by a son of Neileus, the Ionian founder of the latter city. Iasus, then, appears in the same class with other Greek cities of Asia, which referred their origin to European Greece: there can be no reason why it should be distinguished from the rest, as furnishing clearer evidence of a primitive Ionian population in western Asia.

Curtius argues from the immediate and great prosperity of the settlements established by the Ionian Migration that they could not have been planted among an alien people, on coasts before occupied only by barbarians. But the Greek cities of Sicily and Southern Italy were founded centuries later, in regions where the previous inhabitants were entirely and unquestionably barbarian: yet, notwithstanding this original disadvantage, such was their progress that, in the time of Xerxes, Hiero of Syracuse was the greatest power in the independent Grecian world, and perhaps a match for all others put together. And later, we find the Greeks of Sicily maintaining their ground, though with difficulty, in a long-continued struggle against the Carthaginians, a power which proved almost an overmatch for Rome, when mistress of all Italy. Our author evidently feels that this parallel progress of the Italiot Greeks tells against his argument; and, to weaken its force, asserts that the progress of the Asiatic Ionians was different and more remarkable in three particulars: 1. They established a confederacy of their cities. But the want of coöperation in the other case serves rather to increase the marvel. 2. They developed a civilization more purely Hellenic. This, however, may be accounted for by the fact, which probably all would admit, that the barbarians of western Asia Minor were much more like the Greeks than the barbarians of Southern Italy and Sicily ; so that the extraneous influences were more nearly Hellenic in the former case than in the latter. Nor does this general similarity of Carians, Lycians, Phrygians, etc., to the Greeks require us to suppose that they had been in previous uninterrupted communication with Greeks on the same shores, as our author assumes. He maintains, in fact, that the two sections of the Greek people preserved their essential identity notwithstanding a separation for centuries by the waters of the Ægean. 3. The Ionians of Asia made higher attainments in art and literature. True : but would the colonists of Sicily have gone higher in these respects, if on their first landing they had found the island half peopled by their countrymen ? Their attainments, in fact, if inferior to those of the Ionians, may compare with the attainments of Dorians and Æolians in Asia, though these latter, as Curtius supposes, had the advantage of settling among an old established population of their countrymen.

The strong point of this theory is the fact of its affording an explanation for the peculiar position which the Ionians appear to have had in early Greece. The argument may be stated thus. A people scattered far and wide along the seacoast, and found in the interior only where they might have come by following a river-course back from the sea—such a people are not likely to have reached their seats by an overland emigration. The Ionians in Greece, then, must have come there by sea, and in all probability from the east ; immediately from the Ægean islands, remotely from Asia Minor. But it is not likely that a whole people settled on the Asiatic coast would float over the sea in this way. Their wide diffusion in Greece makes it probable that there were successive expeditions, with a considerable interval of time from first to last. As they were thus established in large numbers and for a long time on the coast of Asia, it is likely that a numerous people remained there, after the last expedition set sail toward Greece ; enough to maintain themselves in that position until, after the lapse of centuries, they welcomed back their returning brethren from the west. I will not stop to criticize the probabilities in this argument. . But

I must not close without observing that, whatever advantages the theory under consideration may give us in explaining the early times of Greece, they are not gained without drawback: we encumber ourselves with some new and serious difficulties. One of these has been already alluded to; the complete forgetfulness of Greek tradition as to the existence of these primitive Ionians of Asia. If the tradition, as our author holds, has preserved some memory of their names and actions, it has at any rate forgotten that they were Ionians. This is the more strange, as the national pride of Ionians, living and flourishing in the same seats, might naturally have clung with more tenacity to the ancient renown of their ancestors. Why should they give up their own Cecrops and Danaus and Cadmus to the Egyptians and Phœnicians? Why should they remember so much about their early neighbors, and nothing about their early selves? Why should they remember so much about Dardanians, Phrygians, Lycians, Carians in western Asia, and nothing about Ionians there? Or why should they remember so much about Ionians in Attica and Peloponnesus, and nothing about that people in their own Asia Minor? Why should a people whose forefathers, born on the same soil, had run a career of wide-reaching activity and enterprise, forget its connection with those forefathers, and attach itself instead to the distant and less distinguished ancestors of a part only of its members? Athens, according to this view, was the daughter of an Asiatic mother. So long as there were Ionians in Asia, the Athenians must have looked to them as colonists to the inhabitants of the mother country, with feelings of respectful attachment, which were peculiarly strong in the ancient Greek mind. Why then should Athenians, returning to that mother country, forget the respect and attachment which they had before cherished? why should they forget their original connection with a country which had now become their own home? If in everything else the tradition lost its hold upon these primitive Ionians, we should expect that it would have retained them in connection with the Ionian Migration. How could it carry these wanderers across the Ægean, without remembering the capital circumstance that they went, not to aliens or enemies, but to their own friends, countrymen, and kindred? There is a singular unanimity in this forgetfulness. Among a large number of cities, scattered along a wide extent of sea-coast, we might have expected that some one at least would remember a fact so important in its early history. But there is no single exception to the general obliviousness. It has a greater extent, indeed, than we have yet noticed; the Cyclades share in it. If the view of Curtius be true, these islands must have received their Greek population from the East, from Asia Minor. But here again tradition is no less distinct and uniform in referring the beginnings of Greek occupancy to colonization from the West, from European Greece.

I will only notice further some particulars in the early Epic literature which seem inconsistent with this theory. Almost all critics are agreed now in referring the Homeric poems to a date earlier than the year 800. They were composed, then, within two centuries from the Ionian Migration, perhaps not more than a century after that event. If we were to put the Ionian Migration at about 950, and the composition of the Iliad and Odyssey at about 850, these dates would perhaps correspond as nearly to the collective probabilities of the case as any that could be assigned. Now the remarkable absence of allusions to Ionia, its places and people, in the Iliad and Odyssey, which does not seem to be fully accounted for by the Achæan subjects and Æolian scenes of those poems, is naturally explained by the recent arrival of the Ionians in that country. Their beginnings in Asia were still matters of historic recollection; there was still a conscious newness about their places and their doings, which interposed a wide gulf between them and the ancient traditions of Achæans and Dardans. But the theory of Curtius supplies an immemorial past for the Ionians in Asia, and thus renders the phenomenon in question far more difficult of explanation. Again, a people who had for centuries followed the Phœnicians in a career of maritime enterprise, competing with them and in many places supplanting them as traders, must have become familiar with the use of letters: and this, if true, would render still more unaccountable the fact, already sufficiently perplexing, that these two long poems, with their innumerable references to everything in the public and private life of the Homeric age, contain but one disputed and doubtful allusion to the art of writing. And once more, a people who had wandered for ages almost around the Mediterranean must have acquired a stock of geographical information more extensive and accurate than that represented in the poems of Homer. If, for instance, the Ionians were conversant with the Delta of the Nile for several centuries, and as late as the time of Shishak, about 950, how could the author of the Odyssey place the island of Pharos, which stood close to the Egyptian coast, a full day's sail away from it? And what shall we say of the "*speciosa miracula*" which Horace admires, "*Antiphaten, Scyllamque, et cum Cyclope Charybdin?*" How could such notions prevail among a people who had colonized western Sicily and western Italy as far up as the Tiber, and even the remoter island of Sardinia?

We are aware that the foregoing discussion does very imperfect justice to a theory, the strength of which, in its author's own view, lies not in a few decisive arguments, but in the simple, natural connection which it gives to many scattered facts. We wish, also, to acknowledge, in the fullest manner, the ability and learning with which it is supported. We admit that it throws light upon important points in Greek antiquity. We cannot, however, help feeling that the case is not yet made out in its favor, and that it would be unsafe to accept it, until further discussion and the progress of knowledge shall have weakened the objections which now present themselves, and set the evidence for it in a clearer light. It is just to add, that this theory is propounded by its author with all becoming modesty. He recognizes the obscurities and perplexities which environ his subject, and declares that his object in publishing his views is to determine, from the discussion they call out, how far he can himself hold fast to them as established truth. His views may be imperfectly supported by the evidence; but they are not put forward with that offensive dogmatism which is perhaps nowhere more common than in fields like this, where hardly anything whatever can be known with certainty.

2. RECENT DISCUSSION AND OPINION CONCERNING THE IONIAN MIGRATION.

1863.

The dissertation of Curtius on the Ionian Migration appeared in 1855. In 1856 came out the third and fourth volumes of Max Duncker's (Prof. Extr. at Halle) excellent *Geschichte des Alterthums*. The author, in a note to vol. iii., p. 242, alludes to the new theory, "that the Ionians, prior to the Ionian Migration, occupied the coast of Anatolia, and setting out from thence, planted colonies in Greece, from which colonies at a much later period some noble families wandered back again to Asia Minor. The only sure way (he adds) of establishing this theory would be to show that ancient Oriental sources prove, in opposition to the Greek tradition, the settlement of the Ionians on this coast prior to B. C. 1000. The proofs which Curtius endeavors to draw from the name of the Ionians on monuments of Sethos and Ramses can convince no one who is aware of the fact that, among the names of nations whom the Pharaohs profess to have vanquished, hardly two or three have yet been made out with certainty. If the name Yavana occurs in the Laws of Manu and the Epos of the Hindus, this circumstance may probably be used to determine the age of those works, but not that of the Ionian settlements. The mention of Javan in the lists of Genesis, 10th chapter, proves nothing against the Greek tradition, as the composition of that document falls into the 10th century, into the times after Solomon. The theory in question is further contradicted by the unanimous testimony of Greek authorities, Herodotus and Thucydides at the head, declaring that the inhabitants of the Ægean islands, before the Greeks occupied them, were Carian or Phœnician. If the Ionians had come from Asia Minor to Greece, they must have taken previous possession of these islands." This last argument is somewhat obscurely stated. It may be expressed in this way. According to Curtius, the Ionians, at an immemorial period, crossed the Ægean from Asia to Greece. But we cannot suppose them to have done this without occupying the Ægean Islands which lay in their way. Those islands, then, must have been occupied from an immemorial period by Greek inhabitants. But the universal opinion of the Greeks in the historical period was to the contrary of this--that those islands, down to a comparatively recent time, were occupied by barbarians, Carian and Phœnician.

The essay of Curtius was reviewed in Jahn's *Jahrbücher*, early in 1856, by J. Classen of Frankfort. The reviewer adopts in the main the views of his author, declaring that "he cannot escape from their internal evidence and their clearly-established connection," and avowing his belief that "in them is found the key to one of the most difficult enigmas of ancient history." He specifies four particulars in the argument of Curtius which have made the strongest impression on his own mind. 1. There are no traditions which refer the Ionians of Greece, like other Greek tribes, to any primitive home in the interior of the country; while their earliest habitations in scattered localities along the sea-coast "show plainly that they are settlements of a sea-faring people, who never feel themselves at home except when they can breathe the air of the sea-coast." 2. On the coast of Asia Minor, from the Hermus to the Mæander, we find the Ionians in a compact and united body, such as they show nowhere else; so that, comparing their position here with that which they had in Greece, we cannot doubt that they were only colonists in Greece, but had their proper home in Asia. 3. The wide diffusion of the Ionian name at an early period among the nations of the East is only to be accounted for by assuming that this race was in closer proximity and more intimate intercourse with the Oriental nations than were the other Greek races. 4. This theory furnishes the only plausible explanation for the stories of Cecrops, Cadmus, and the rest, whom we cannot regard as wholly alien to the Greeks, but may well believe to have been men of Ionian descent, who came to Greece from settlements in the East, and were therefore represented in the myths as Egyptians, Phœnicians, etc.

But, while he adopts the theory of Curtius, Classen calls attention to some points in which his views are defective and unsatisfactory. He complains particularly of the vagueness of Curtius in reference to the connection between the Greeks and their neighbor-tribes in Asia Minor, the Dardanians, Phrygians, Lycians, and Carians. Curtius often speaks of these as if he regarded them as having a very close affinity with the Greeks in race and language, so as not to be really a foreign population, but to coalesce readily with Greeks whenever they are brought together, and to form with them a homogeneous union. And yet he does not expressly affirm that they have this character; and indeed an affinity so close is not only inconsistent (in appearance, at least) with various indications, historical and philological, but, if it were true, would make the theory of Curtius unnecessary; for the facts which he seeks to explain by his primitive Ionians might then be explained by the agency of Phrygians, Lycians, etc.

In regard to the Ionian name, Classen makes an ingenious suggestion, which has since been adopted by a number of inquirers, and even by Curtius himself. May it not be, he says, that the name Ionians (whatever was its primitive meaning) was not at the outset applied to themselves by the Greek population of Asia, but applied to them by the nations of the Orient, and used as a collective designation, embracing the sea-coast tribes of Dardanians, Mæonians, Carians, and Lycians? May not this name have been carried into European Greece by the Phœnicians, who everywhere preceded and served as pioneers for the wanderings of the Ionian tribes? May it not have been received in Greece under a Grecized form, and applied to the wanderers from Asia Minor who settled on the Greek coasts and became fused with the earlier population? And when the counter movement began from Greece to Asia Minor, may not the wanderers (or rather, a part of them) have carried with them the Ionian name, as a domestic designation, which became established on the coast between that of Æolian on the north and that of Dorian on the south, the application being determined by the fact that the leaders of emigration to these regions were Ionian, Æolian, and Dorian respectively?

Classen suggests, also, that the name Leleges may have been used from a very early period by the Greeks of Asia as a general designation for themselves—that is, for all who could speak their language, in opposition to the βάρβαροι—that is, the collective tribes whose speech was unintelligible to them. This, too, is a very ingenious thought, and has since been reasserted by various other writers.

The views of Curtius were discussed about the same time by a more distinguished scholar, G. F. Schömann, of Greifswald, in a paper entitled *Animadversiones de Ionibus*. Schömann is ready to admit that there were Ionians in Asia Minor long before the Ionian Migration. But he objects strongly to the proposition that the Ionians of Attica were derived from these Asiatic Ionians by colonies crossing over to the western coasts of the Ægean and there establishing themselves among a non-Ionian people. He sees no reason to believe that there ever was a non-Ionian people in Attica. And he sees no reason for supposing that the Ionians came into Greece at a different time or in a different way from the other Greeks. If the Ionians are found only on the sea-coast, the same may be said of their brethren in Asia; and in both cases they may have been driven down by the pressure of other tribes from an earlier home in the interior to these maritime abodes. He goes into a somewhat lengthened examination of the legends concerning Ion and his father Xuthus, to show that they present no trace of a colonization from beyond the sea. This result, indeed, is of inferior importance, as he proceeds to prove that the legends in question are of no very high antiquity, but must have arisen after the great Dorian invasion and the new relations which this established in Central and Southern Greece. The derivation of the name *Ion*, from εἶμι, 'to go,' which Curtius had spoken of with some favor, making the Ionians to be 'wanderers' in name as well as in fact, Schömann proves to be improbable on etymological grounds. In regard to Cecrops, Cadmus, and other leaders of colonies from the Oriental world, he avows that, if it be forbidden to consign them to the realm of fable, he would rather accept them for Ionians than for Phœnicians and Egyptians. He remarks, however, that by the treatment of Curtius great vagueness is given to the designation of "Ionians," which comes to be like that of Franks in the modern Orient. So that when, in this theory, a multitude of things are ascribed to the Ionians—wanderings, settlements, establishment of religious worships and festivals, communications of the most various arts and industries—it becomes a question in each case to what Ionians they are attributed. And though many things thus ascribed to the Ionians are not improbable in themselves, he denies that they are more certain than what we believed before, and holds that such conjectures can avail nothing at all toward a more accurate knowledge of the Ionian race.

To the objections of Schömann, Curtius replied at once in the *Göttinger Gelehrte Anzeigen* for 1856. I regret that I have been unable to obtain a sight both of this article and of another by the same author, which appeared in 1859 in the same periodical. In 1857, Curtius published the first volume of his elaborate and attractive History of Greece. He here brings out in a popular form the views developed in his essay, and defended in his reply to Schömann. He does not, indeed, put them forward as ascertained historic truths, established by documentary evidence, and entitled to unquestioning assent. He speaks of them as an attempt to connect the Hellenic people with the Indo-European family of nations, and to make intelligible their wanderings in the earliest period. But he makes them the basis of his whole treatment of the primitive Greek history, and thus gives them a position which no hypothesis should receive unless it is pretty clearly required by the known facts of history. His work being of a popular character, he naturally abstains from polemical discussions. He does, however, vindicate his theory from the objection that it is at variance with the tradition of the Greeks. To this he replies, first, that his view is not opposed to any positive statement of Greek tradition; for in reference to the primitive diffusion of the Ionian race the ancients tell us nothing: they are simply silent on the subject. And, second, if his view is not attested by any positive statement of Greek tradition, it is easy to assign reasons for this fact. "The Greeks were so proud a people that they regarded their land as the central land, the point of departure for the important affinities of nations. And when, in Asia, the barbarians had pressed on to the borders of the Archipelago, it became, under

Athenian influence, a general feeling that European Greece, still free and independent, was the proper land of the Hellenes. Athens itself was assumed to be the metropolis of all Ionians. Under this influence all opposing traditions were more and more thrust into the background, or with haughty boldness set aside altogether. Even of the Carians it was maintained that they had been driven to Asia from Europe, while, according to their own well-established belief, they were at home in Asia. The Lycians, in like manner, were supposed to have come from Attica to Lycia. Nay, the entire connection of the Greeks with the races of Asia Minor was completely reversed, and the consciousness of an original affinity of the Greeks with the Phrygians and Armenians was so expressed that the Phrygians were represented as having migrated from Europe to Asia, and the Armenians, again, as having derived their origin from the Phrygians."

This answer, it appears to me, gives undue weight to the Athenian influence, at least for the earlier times of Grecian history. The prominence of Athens in the political world of Greece dates from the Persian wars, long after the beginnings of literary production and documentary record. We have a multitude of notices, of a historical or traditionary character, which were composed in the sixth and seventh centuries before our era; and some, doubtless, of even older date. But in those times the Greek cities of Asia were independent and prosperous. Miletus and Ephesus were then more splendid and powerful than Athens, and were not inferior to her in literary culture. Why should the Greeks of those cities surrender the honorable consciousness of their own ancient subsistence on the same sites, and be content to trace the origin of their political being to a colonization, not then very ancient, from a less powerful city on the other side of the Ægean? In the literature of the sixth, seventh, and eighth centuries before Christ, we find many legends in regard to things that befell in Thebes and Argos and Sparta prior to the Ionian Migration. Why do we find none such for Ephesus and Miletus, which Curtius supposes to have had a long history as Greek cities prior to the same event? It is certainly quite conceivable that cities should have existed on the sites of Miletus and

Ephesus at the time when the colonists from Attica landed on the coast of Asia. But I see not how we could then account for the obliteration of all legends relating to earlier personages and fortunes of those cities, without supposing that their old population was viewed as an alien race, so that a wholly new order of things, a wholly new nationality for these cities, was regarded as commencing with the colonization from Attica.

An appendix to vol. i. of Curtius's History contained remarks by Lepsius in defence of his belief that the Ionian name is to be recognized on Egyptian monuments of the fifteenth and fourteenth centuries B.C., among the nations described as subject to the great Pharaohs of the 18th and 19th dynasties. There is no doubt that such monuments contain a group identical in form with that used for the Ionians, or rather the Greeks, in the period of the Ptolemies. But De Rougé had, some years previous, proposed a different interpretation for the group as found on the earlier monuments. He noticed that it occurs generally in the first place among a list of given nations; and the ideographic value of the signs composing it appeared to give the meaning 'the Northerners all,' *i. e.* 'all the tribes of the North;' which would thus be a general designation for the eight tribes enumerated after it. This view appeared to be confirmed by the fact that in some instances the nine names are followed by another series beginning with Kesh (*i. e.* Cush) and containing apparently the names of southern tribes. It was supposed further that, after the Greeks or Macedonians became masters of Egypt, the group was held to signify 'the northern lords,' and applied as a flattering designation to the now dominant people.

Bunsen, in the last part of his *Aegyptens Stelle in der Weltgeschichte*, had taken up this view of De Rougé's, and maintained it in opposition to that of Lepsius. In doing so, he was uninfluenced by any prepossession against the new Ionian theory; for to this, in the same place and in the fullest terms, he signified his own adhesion. Lepsius, in the appendix referred to, brings forward objections to the interpretation of De Rougé and Bunsen, and reiterates his clear conviction that the group in question can only refer to the Greeks of the islands and coasts of the Ægean. He thinks it probable, too, from the monumental evidence, that some of this people had formed permanent settlements in northern Egypt, on the Delta of the Nile. The force of his arguments can hardly be appreciated by any but professed Egyptologists ; and Curtius himself admits that, as matters now stand, the evidence from this source is not such as to demand the full confidence of scholars in general.

Conrad Bursian, since known as a zealous student of Greek geography, published in 1857 a dissertation entitled *Quæstionum Euboicarum Capita Selecta*, in which he came forward as an adherent of the Ionian theory; and not long afterwards, reviewing Duncker's History in Jahn's *Jahrbücher*, he censured that writer for his skepticism in reference to it. To the objection of Duncker, already noticed—that if the Ionians at an immemorial period had crossed the Ægean from Asia to Greece, they would at the same time have occupied the islands on their way, whereas Greek tradition represents these islands as occupied down to a much later period by Phœnicians and Carians—he replies, that the Ionians passed by these islands without taking possession, for the very reason that they found them already held by the Phœnicians. This answer is hardly in accordance with the spirit of the theory, which makes a previous Phœnician occupancy to be everywhere the condition and occasion of Ionian settlement; and in fact, Curtius, in a subsequent article (which we shall notice further on), gives a different reply. The latter asserts, first, that the barbarians might be supposed, without improbability, to have thrust themselves into these islands after they had been settled by the Ionians; second, that there is good reason for believing that these islands, long prior to the Ionian Migration, were not wholly in barbarian possession, but were occupied, at least in part, by a Greek population; and third, that the Carians themselves were closely akin to the Greeks, and perhaps originally spoke Greek, but were afterwards barbarized—Semitized—by communication with the Phœnicians.

The Ionian theory was further discussed, in 1857, by Alfred von Gutschmid, in his *Beiträge zur Geschichte des alten Orients.* This work was an extended and far from favorable critique of the fourth and fifth volumes of Bunsen's Egypt. But, as Bunsen in his closing volume had taken up the Ionian theory, Gutschmid also was naturally led to take notice of it. His remarks are very interesting, though not free from a tone of dogmatism, and an asperity towards those from whom he differs, which appear too often in the writings of this learned and able scholar. He denies, as my own article had already done, that the great and rapid progress in wealth, power, and literary culture, made by the Ionian cities of Asia Minor after the colonization from Athens, is any proof that those colonies were not planted among an alien people. He brings forward many examples to show that such a progress, surpassing that of the mother country in the same time, is a frequent phenomenon in the history of colonization. He refers especially to North America, and the uncommonly rapid increase of population and the growth of new states which have been witnessed here. To the great argument of Curtius, founded on the position of the Ionians in Greece, he replies as follows:

"The assertion that the Ionians in Greece nowhere appear in a compact mass is of a subjective nature. On both sides of the Isthmus, we find them in connected seats: in the South they form the population of all Achaia and the northern coast of Argolis; in the North they have Attica, Southern Bœotia and the neighboring parts of Phocis, and Eubœa. What is most important—in this region, beside the towns on the coast, those of the interior also are Ionic, which is not the case in Asiatic Ionia. The fact which Curtius notices (p. 4), that just here no trace is found of migrations made by the Ionians from one habitation to another, might be regarded as an indication of their primitive settlement in this region. But if these seats appear to any one insufficient to be the home of so great a race, let him hold to the statement of Herodotus—a statement oftener evaded than really refuted—that the Ionians were originally Pelasgians. Curtius himself has taken a step in this direction, by claiming for his Ionians the names Argos and Larissa, which have been universally regarded as Pelasgian. True, he conceives the relation between the Ionians and Pelasgians to be this, that the former came by sea in single parties, that they connected themselves with the native inhabitants, and especially the Pelasgians, and became gradually so lost in the general mass as to be no longer distinguishable from it. Still, there is nothing to forbid our regarding the Ionians as a name which at a more recent period separated itself from the Pelasgian. To show how far Curtius is warranted in his hypothesis concerning the home of the Ionians, I will bring forward an analogy from a time of authentic history, in which we have the advantage of documentary data. I refer to the Malays, who, as a people of coasts and islands, are well adapted to the comparison, and who have, in common with the Ionians, not only a decided capacity for the sea, and a free restless nature, but also the fact that in the diffusion of Islam they have been the carriers of culture in the Indian Archipelago, just as the Ionians were, according to Curtius, in the Greek Archipelago, by transporting the ancient civilization of the East. The Malays—the name is said to mean the same thing as that of the Parthians, viz. μετανάσται, 'emigrants'—are spread over all the Indian islands, but only the smaller belong wholly to them; the larger are occupied in their interior by primitive inhabitants, who are of the Ethiopian race. Whence the Malays came, nobody can say; it appears inconceivable that one of the islands should have been their home. On the continent there is but one land where the Malays are found in large masses, the peninsula of Malacca, which has its name from them, as Ionia has from the Ionians. Nowhere do the Malays form states to the same extent as here (precisely what Curtius insists on in reference to the Asiatic Ionians). For here was the seat of the most powerful Malay kingdom, that of Singhapura, Malacca, and Gohor; here are still found numerous Malay states, while, *e.g.* in Java, the most important of the Indian islands, the older states were founded by Brahman wanderers from Further India, and that of Bantam by Arab Sayyids. If now we should apply the argument of Curtius to this case, we must infer that Malacca was the primitive seat of the Malays, and that from thence they occupied the coasts of the islands. But history teaches us that in the year 1160 A.D., the Malays, under their king Çrî Tribhuvana, first passed over from Sumatra to the mainland, and founded Singhapura; that in 1253, under their fifth king, Çrî Skandar, they founded Malacca; that in 1511, under their twelfth king, Sultan Mahmud Shâh, they founded Gohor: while we have similar exact dates for the successive diffusion of the Malays on the peninsula. This example may teach us the necessity for caution, in cases where we have no authentic history to depend upon."

In his celebrated essay on the Book of Nabathæan Agriculture (*Ztschft. d. deutschen morgenl. Ges.* vol. xv., 1861), Gutschmid again found occasion to speak of the Ionian theory, which Chwolson had laid hold of to account for the amazing fact that a Babylonian author, twenty-five centuries before Christ, should combat the botanical opinions of Greek or Ionian writers. He does not here enter upon any formal discussion of the theory. He only says: "Chwolson, as was to be expected, tries to make out of the universal Ionians a little capital for his client Qût'âmî;" and then, after quoting a passage in which Chwolson thanks heaven "that the old naïve chronology of primary schools, with its dates of 1697 for Phoroneus, 1377 for Deucalion, etc., has passed away forever," he adds: "The fact is just the other way, that the Asiatic and Egyptian wanderers Pelops, Danaus, Cecrops, Peteos, Erectheus, whom one had thought to have passed away forever, have been dragged by Curtius out of the rubbish-hole, and turned to profitable account as Orientalized Ionians or Ionized Orientals. The lofty air with which the author of the hypothesis warns off objectors, preferring this course to an attempt at refuting their objections, and the eagerness with which enthusiastic philologs in Jahn's *Jahrbücher* claim the admiration of their readers for E. Curtius's studies on the older Greek history, may certainly lead outsiders to suppose that they have here a made-out fact, to which only personal enmity refuses its due acknowledgment. But in truth, the very persons who are most competent to judge, historians and geographers (I mention only Duncker, in his Greek History, and Kiepert, in his Researches on the Genealogical List of Nations in Genesis), have declared themselves very decidedly against the Ionian hypothesis, and this is pretty generally regarded as a thing gone by. In reference to every hypothesis, the first question must be, not 'is it good,' but 'is it necessary?' 'is it on the whole the most satisfactory solution of existing difficulties?'" He then maintains that the only positive fact alleged in support of the theory (if fact it be)—the appearance of the Ionian name on the early Egyptian monuments—is not really explained by it, the occurrence of Ionians in Egypt at that remote period being about equally marvellous whether you suppose them to have come there from the eastern or the western shores of the Ægean.

Among "the enthusiastic philologs of Jahn's *Jahrbücher*," Gutschmid must have included August Baumeister, who in 1860 reviewed the Greek History of E. Curtius, and spoke particularly of the Ionian theory in the warmest terms of commendation.

The same question was treated, with greater thoroughness, in another work which appeared in 1860—a gymnasial program by H. Dondorff, entitled the Ionians in Eubœa. Dondorff agrees with Curtius in recognizing the existence of Ionians (so called) in Asia, and their wide-spread activity as a seafaring people long prior to the Ionian Migration. But he does not therefore accept the theory of Curtius, against which he acknowledges the force of the objections raised by Duncker and Gutschmid. He holds that the early Ionians of Asia and the Ægean were not the same people as the Ionians of Attica: the latter were a Hellenic tribe, while the former, he thinks, were wholly or mainly Semitic barbarians, including Carians, Cypriots, and even Philistines. The connection between these and the Ionians of Greece is nothing but a coincidence in name.

This description of Dondorff's views I give, having never seen his dissertation, on the faith of Curtius himself, who reviewed it in Jahn's *Jahrbücher* for 1861. The review, as might be expected, is mainly occupied with a vindication of the Ionian theory against the objections of dissenting critics. It is evidently prompted in part by the sarcastic remarks of Gutschmid in the essay on the Nabathæan Agriculture, although that essay is nowhere mentioned. Curtius refers to his own former articles as proof that he has not shunned a discussion of the subject: he may have refused the challenge of an overbearing and contemptuous polemic, but he has been always ready to meet candid and courteous opposition. He takes pains to show that his views have not failed to commend themselves to a number of well qualified judges. "Leonhard Schmitz," he says, "even before the appearance of my History, had made this view the basis of his own. I find my own view again fully set forth in Lorenz Diefenbach, *Orig. Europ.*, p. 78, and if he has come to it independently (for he makes no mention of me), this is only the more welcome guaranty for the truth of my hypothesis. W. Vischer, in his *Erinnerungen aus Griechenland*, p. 301, agrees with me entirely as to the Ionizing of Argos; and more recently, in the *Schweizerisches Museum*, he expresses only a wish that the inferences drawn from the hypothesis might be kept within narrower limits."

It is evident from this article of Curtius that three arguments which, as we have already seen, were used in the essay of 1855 to support his theory, are now no longer relied on for that purpose. These are: 1. the wide diffusion of the Ionian name throughout the East as a designation for the Greeks; 2. the mention of Ionians on the old Egyptian monuments of the fifteenth and fourteenth centuries; and 3. the rapid progress of the cities which the colonists from Attica, in the so-called Ionian Migration, were said to have planted on the coast of Asia Minor. These arguments, which were all objected to as unreliable in my previous communication on this subject, are now practically abandoned: it may be said that they are withdrawn, and no longer form part of the case. Curtius now rests his cause mainly on two points. These are: 1. the position of the Ionians in Greece, confined from the earliest time to certain scattered localities on the seacoast: this he still maintains against the opposition of Schömann and Gutschmid; 2. the traditions in reference to the colonists from Attica in the Ionian Migration: these he examines in some detail, to show that they imply a close affinity between the new-comers in Asia and the previous inhabitants of the places where they settled. In this examination, I must think that he relies too much on the fullness and authenticity of the traditional accounts, and thus draws from them conclusions which have no sufficient vouchers.

As to the first point, which I have always regarded as the stronghold of the Ionian theory, its strength, it seems to me, is in a measure compromised by the new views which our author has taken up in reference to the Ionian name. I translate the highly interesting paragraph which relates to this subject. "As regards the history of the name Ionians, I am quite ready," he says, "to adopt the same points of view as Dondorff, and to recognize in it a collective name, which gradually came to be restricted, and to assume a more definite application. That view was proposed by Classen, and defended with much penetration in this Journal, as far back as 1856, and I have never ventured to maintain an opposite position. According to this view, we should have to assume some three principal epochs in the history of the name: 1. the name *Yavanim*, as diffused among Aryans and Semites through the whole Eastern world, embraces all the seafaring tribes of the Ægean except the Phœnicians, including both pure Greeks and various tribes of mixed origin, Carians, Citians, Philistines, etc. It is a name which may correspond somewhat to that of the Leleges, an aggregate name, which does not, any more than that of Franks in the modern East, designate a whole connected by community of language, a definite *ethnos*. This name, first brought by the Phœnicians to the European Greeks, was adopted by the latter to designate their kinsmen who were gradually settling on their seacoast, whom they became acquainted with first as intermixed with Phœnicians, and afterwards in their purer nationality. Thus, 2. the foreign name *Yavanim*, adapted to the Greek mouth as Ἰάονες or Ἴωνες, became established on the soil of Europe, and especially in Attica and Ægialeia. Here Ionian history first develops itself. Here, therefore, the name also first obtains a historical significance, which causes the prior existence of the people, their transmarine origin, to be wholly forgotten. Then follows the περαίωσις τῶν Ἰώνων εἰς Ἀσίαν (the Ionian Migration). And now, 3. the name fixes itself in Asia Minor, where the Carians, barbarized kinsmen of the Greeks, are overcome, the nobler germs existing among the Greeks who had remained in their primitive home on the Asiatic coasts are roused to new life, and a city-culture established, which, under influences from the Asiatics of the interior, soon takes such a direction that the Athenians disclaimed the very name of Ionians."

Curtius is careful to mark these views as relating only to the name "Ionian:" yet it is plain that they are of no little importance with reference to his whole theory. On the one hand, they appear to weaken in some measure the foundations on which it rests. Evidently they destroy whatever residue of weight any one might recognize in the diffusion of the Ionian name through the Eastern world, and in the supposed mention of Ionians on the ancient Egyptian monuments. But further than this: if it is admitted that the Ionian Greeks received that name in Greece itself, having previously been otherwise designated, then the confinement of that name to certain limited localities becomes a matter of less consequence, for it does not necessarily imply that the race was confined to the same localities: it is quite conceivable that the race itself may have had a much wider extension in Greece, and that only a particular part, which in some way came to be distinguished from the rest, received the name of Ionians. Yet, on the other hand, these new views give some aid to the theory. They help to account for the fact that no traditions represent the Ionians in Greece as having come there either from the opposite coast of Asia or from the islands of the Ægean. They also help to account for the fact that no traditions represent the Ionian emigrants from Attica to Asia as having settled there among a population whom they regarded as kinsmen and brethren. This last point I have alluded to before, and it is one which I look upon as of great consequence. It is not at all improbable that the Attic settlers in Ephesus and Miletus may have found in those regions a population not widely diverse from themselves in language and ethnical affinities. But there is no convincing reason to believe—there is much reason for declining to believe—that they found a population which they recognized as having the same nationality with themselves, as standing in a relation to themselves similar to that of the Achæans, Dorians, or Æolians. There is no reason for supposing that the earlier inhabitants of the land were any nearer to the Greeks in origin and language than were the Pelasgians. Curtius, in his History, describes the Pelasgians as an earlier wave of population which streamed over from Asia to Europe, just in advance of that which brought the Hellenes to their Grecian home. He describes them as distinct from the Greeks, yet closely resembling them, and readily coalescing with them. That a population of this kind, whether called Pelasgic or designated by other names—a population standing in this sort of relation to the Greeks—may have existed in Asia Minor long before the Ionian Migration, is certainly not improbable. That the Lycians and Phrygians stood thus near to the Greeks, I cannot believe. The language of the Lycian monuments is so far from resembling the Greek that some have doubted whether it was even Indo-European. As for the Phrygians, we have in Homer the proper names of Dardanians or Trojans, a people of the Phrygian stock. George Curtius has shown that many of these names imply a language different from the Greek. In regard to the Carians, though the Semitic origin often asserted for them is not sufficiently proved, we yet see, from the Homeric epithet, *βαρβαρόφωνοι*, applied to them, that their language was unintelligible to the Greek ear. But we hear of Pelasgians in Asia Minor, and yet more of Leleges, whom we may believe to have stood in a near relation to the Greeks. While, therefore, we hold it improbable that the colonists of the Ionian Migration found on the Asiatic coast any people whom they felt to be so near them as the Ionians or even the Dorians and Æolians of their own land, we think it not indeed a historic certainty, but by no means improbable, that they found populations who seemed as near to them as the Pelasgians in Europe. And we think it still less a historic certainty, yet also not improbable, that these populations of the Asiatic coast may in earlier centuries have had communication with the western shores of the Ægean, and that the development of the Ionian character and name in Greece may be somehow connected with such communications. So much as this we should, according to our present lights, consider to be the net result of the discussions which have been set on foot by the dissertation of E. Curtius. But it seems highly important that these conclusions should not be invested with more of certainty than properly belongs to them—that they should be recognized as historic speculations rather than historic verities, as probabilities or possibilities rather than facts.

Curtius insists that we must have some theory which shall enable us to comprehend the facts that lie on the threshold of Hellenic history. Such a theory he has labored to construct, and he claims the right to maintain it until a better one is offered him. It is unquestionably right that he should show his theory to be superior to any other which has been proposed: but it is quite conceivable that he should succeed in this without thereby proving it to be true. There are many problems in history, and especially in ancient history, of which the solution is more to be desired than looked for; many in which the deficiency or uncertainty of the data is such as almost to preclude the hope of a satisfactory solution. It may be that the problem which Curtius has discussed with so much ingenuity and learning, and with no less candor and courtesy, will have to be ranked in this category.

II.

THE ROOT *PRACH* IN THE GREEK LANGUAGE.

1855.

THE Sanskrit language has a root *prach*, in very common use, signifying 'to ask a question.' This radical appears to have been preserved in all the great subdivisions of the Indo-European class. We find it in the Gothic *frah*, 'he asked,' A. S. *fregnan*, modern German *fragen*. Bopp, in his Sanskrit Glossary s. v., gives a Lithuanian *praszau*, 'rogo, precor,' and *perszu*, 'procus sum, uxorem mihi deposco:' a Russian *pros'u*, 'rogo, precor:' an Irish *fiafrach*, 'inquisitive,' which Bopp explains by a supposed reduplication—which, however, is more probably to be explained as a compound of the root with the old preposition *fia*, 'before:' so '*fiafraighe*, 'question,' *fiafruighim*, 'I inquire, ask.' In Latin we find the verb *precor*, 'to pray,' and the noun *procus*, 'a suitor,' both certain derivatives of this root. Bopp also refers to it the verb *posco*, as if for *prosco*, supposing that *r* is omitted, as in the Greek preposition ποτί for προτί. προτί or πρός is a derivative from πρό: its ρ therefore is original, and the form ποτί is a corruption, as also the corresponding Latin form *pot*, which never indeed occurs as a separate word, but appears as a prefix in *possideo* (=*pot*+*sedeo*), *porrigo* (=*pot*+*rego*), and other compounds. Bopp further adds the Latin *rogo*, as if for *progo*, and the comparison is certainly plausible; but I am not able to produce any fully satisfactory analogy for this assumed loss of the initial *p* before a following *r*.

As to the Sanskrit *prach* itself, Pott has explained it as a compound, made up of the prefix *pra*, 'before,' and the root *ich*, 'to desire,' which appears only in the special tenses (corresponding to the Greek present and imperfect in the different modes). It is a curious fact that this compound of *pra* and *ich* does really occur in Greek, with a distinctness which excludes all doubt as to its nature and origin. The Sanskrit *pra* is the Greek *πρό*, and the Greek equivalent of *ich* would naturally be *ικ*, as the Sanskrit palatals are for the most part degenerate gutturals. Hence *pra+ich=προϊκ*, which we find already in the Homeric *προΐκτης*, 'a beggar.' See Odyssey xvii. 352, where Ulysses, appearing at the banquet of the suitors in the garb of a beggar, is thus addressed by the swineherd Eumæus, who brings him bread and meat from Telemachus :—

> *Τηλέμαχός τοι, ξεῖνε, διδοῖ τάδε, καί σε κελεύει*
> *αἰτίζειν μάλα πάντας ἐποιχόμενον μνηστῆρας*
> *αἰδῶ δ' οὐκ ἀγαθήν φησ' ἔμμεναι ἀνδρὶ προΐκτῃ.*

The corresponding verb *προΐσσομαι*, fut. *προΐξομαι*, 'to beg,' is found in Archilochus, and in the compound *καταπροίσσομαι* occurs with considerable frequency. We have likewise the noun *προΐξ*, Attic *προῖξ*, 'a free gift, gratuity' (literally, 'obtained by begging, had for the asking'), the genitive of which, *προικός*, and the accusative, *προῖκα*, are used very commonly to signify 'as a free gift, gratis.'

Now the Sanskrit *prach* is not by any means so clearly the compound of *pra* and *ich* as is the Greek *προΐκ*. According to the constant law of Sanskrit euphony, *pra+ich* ought to give us *prech* and not *prach*. There is therefore room to doubt whether the form *prach* is really a compound. At all events, if it be so, it has undergone such change as to assume the appearance of a simple root—it has completely lost the consciousness of its composition, has passed as an uncompounded radical through the whole class of Indo-European languages, and has received thus an extension far wider than the simple *ich*, from which it is perhaps derived. We have seen it already in the Latin, the Slavonic, the Lithuanian, the Teutonic, and the Celtic languages. Does it occur also in Greek? Does this language furnish us, besides the distinct compound of *pra* with *ich*, which we have been considering, with any representative for the more common and extensive *prach*, which is perhaps only the result of their fusion? My belief is that it does so, in the noun *θεοπρόπος*. This word occurs frequently in Homer, and signifies 'one who prophesies, a diviner or soothsayer.' In Herodotus we find a different meaning, that of 'a public envoy sent to consult an oracle.' We might give examples of the word in both these uses; but this is not necessary. I suppose it to be a compound of θεός with the root *prach*, and to signify, according to its etymology, 'one who asks a god or the gods.'

This derivation explains perfectly the two meanings which we have just mentioned as belonging to the word. The prophet who pre-announces the events of the future does so, not of himself, not from his own stores of knowledge, but from information which he seeks and obtains of a divinity—he professes himself and is understood by others to be 'a questioner of the gods.' And the propriety of the term is no less clear in its application to the public envoy sent to consult an oracle: it is his office 'to interrogate the god.'

This derivation is equally satisfactory as regards the form of the word. The Sanskrit palatals, as already intimated, correspond generally to gutturals in the cognate languages, and the interchange of gutturals and labials is one of the most familiar phonetic phenomena. No one could hesitate about accepting the Latin *procus* as a derivative of the Sanskrit *prach*, and there is as little difficulty in admitting a Greek πρόπος as the equivalent of the Latin *procus*. A case exactly analogous may be found in the Sanskrit *vac*, 'to speak:' from which root we have the Latin *vox*, *vocis*, *vocare*, and the Greek ὄψ, ὀπός (originally ϝοπς, ϝοπος, compare ϝέπος, ϝειπεῖν). The compound name καλλιοπη, 'beautifully speaking,' bears the same relation to the Latin *vox* and Sanskrit *vac*, that θεοπρόπος, according to our view, bears to the Latin *procus* and the Sanskrit *prach*.

Let it not be thought strange that in προΐκτης, 'a beggar,' the Greek should retain the primitive κ, and yet in προπος, 'an asker,' coming perhaps from the same ultimate theme, should change it to the labial π. The language vacillates between these sounds in one and the same word, as in the Ionic κοῖος, κόσος, κότε, κῶς, etc., which present the primitive guttural, while the common Greek has ποῖος, πόσος, πότε, πῶς, etc., with the labial. So in the root which signifies 'to see,'

Sanskrit *îksh*, perhaps originally *aksh*, from which come *aksha* and *akshi*, 'eye,' Latin dim. *oculus*, *ocellus*. In Greek the corresponding radical is **οπ**, found in **ὄψομαι**, 'I shall see,' **ὄπωπα**, 'I have seen,' **ὀφθαλμός**, 'eye,' etc., and yet we find **ὄσσε**, 'the two eyes,' which presupposes a form **ὀκιε**, while the Bœotian **ὄκταλλος**, 'eye,' gives us the primitive guttural without change.

The etymology here proposed has the advantage of accounting perfectly for the accent of the word. It is a well-known rule for compounds of the second declension, such as **παιδοκτονος**, in which the second part (**κτονος**) is a verbal of two syllables with short penult—that if this verbal has a transitive relation to the first part of the compound, the accent is on the penult; thus, *παιδοκτόνος*, 'son-killing, murderer of a son;' but if the verbal is intransitive or passive in its relation to the other part, the accent goes back to the antepenult; thus *παιδόκτονος*, 'son-killed, killed by a son.' According to this rule *θεοπρόπος*, derived from *prach* and accented on the penult, could only have the sense of 'questioning the gods (or a god)'—a sense which, as we have seen, accounts perfectly for the actual uses of the word.

The arguments in favor of this derivation will gain additional force, if we look at the other attempts which have been made to assign the etymology of the word. The old established traditional method makes the **πρόπος** a compound of **πρό** with the root of **ἔπος**, **εἰπεῖν**, as though **πρόπος** were for *πρόϝοπος*. As a transitive compound, this would signify 'foretelling the gods,' which, of course, could hardly have an intelligible meaning. As an intransitive compound, it would signify 'foretold by the gods,' a meaning intelligible enough, but wholly inapplicable here. To account for its actual use, we should have to render it 'foretelling *from* the gods,' *i. e.* 'by communications derived from them,' or 'foretelling *by* the gods,' *i. e.* 'by their counsel or assistance.' Now there is some latitude in regard to the relations expressed by compound words, and it is not unlikely that instances might be found which would go to support the rendering just given. Still, they are inconsistent with the general analogy which prevails in the composition of words, and ought not, of course, to be adopted without clear and convincing evidence. But the form of the word supplies an insuperable objection to this etymology. The primitive form, as we have seen, would have been πρόϝοπος. To make προπος out of this, we must suppose that the weak letter ϝ fell away, and that the *ο* of the preposition was then elided before the *ο* of the root. Now there are two circumstances which render this elision in the highest degree improbable: 1. that in other compounds of this root the Homeric language holds on with marked tenacity to the ϝ, allowing no elision to take place before it: so in the compound with ἀπό, which occurs very frequently, but always as ἀποειπεῖν, never as ἀπειπεῖν: so in ἁμαρτοεπής, not ἁμαρτεπής; ἀμετροεπής, not ἀμετρεπής;—and, 2. that even before words which began with an original vowel, the preposition πρό always retains its *ο*, suffering it indeed to be contracted with the following vowel, but never surrendering it altogether: thus φρουρός, 'a guard,' from πρό and ὁράω, not φρορός. So strong are these reasons that, since Buttmann in his Lexilogus declared himself against this derivation, it has been generally abandoned: and it is matter of surprise that Benfey in his *Wurzellexikon* should not only have retained it, but retained it without the slightest expression of doubt, without intimating that it either had been or could be called in question.

Buttmann himself proposed to take the word from θεός and πρέπω. This etymology would account well for the form, which would thus correspond (for instance) to θεολόγος from θεός and λέγω. How is it as regards the meaning? In its Homeric use, πρέπω signifies 'to be prominent or conspicuous, to appear.' It is said of things that strike the eye, and by later poets is occasionally applied to objects that impress other senses—the hearing or even the smelling. From this idea of 'appearing,' the word came to mean, 1. 'to appear as something, be like it;' 2. 'to appear well, be seemly or becoming'—which in later writers is by far the most frequent use of the word. But neither of these uses is to be found in Homer: and, of course, neither of them can well be relied upon for the explanation of θεοπρόπος. For this purpose, we must go back to the first meaning, 'to be conspicuous, to appear.' But this meaning is intransitive, and hence unsuited to the accent of *θεοπρόπος*, which, as we have seen, indicates a transitive compound. Buttmann indeed suggests that *πρέπω* may have been originally transitive, 'to make conspicuous, to make appear, to show,' and he finds an instance of this earlier use preserved in a line of Euripides (Alcestis, 515, *τί χρῆμα τῇδε τῇ κουρᾷ πρέπεις*); but his explanation of the line, as President Woolsey has remarked in his note on the passage, is not only inconsistent with the settled usage of the tragic poets, but at variance even with the immediate context. It must, however, be admitted as a thing altogether possible, that a word which in its separate use is constantly intransitive may appear as transitive in a compound. This, if we assume it in the present case, would give us for *θεοπρόπος* the meaning 'one who makes a god appear, manifests or reveals a god.' Such a designation for the diviner, though certainly quite conceivable, would belong rather to the style of rhetorical description than to the simpler and more obvious views of ordinary etymology. He is a revealer of the will, purpose, or knowledge of the divinity; but to call him 'a revealer of the divinity, one who makes the god appear to men,' seems unnatural and overstrained. Nor does Buttmann himself appear to have understood the origin of the term in this way. After explaining the primitive use of *πρέπω*, according to his view of it, as meaning to 'make a thing appear, show it,' he goes on to say that "probably the old expression was *θεός πρέπει*, 'a god sends a sign' (causes an appearance)—the sign sent was called *θεοπρόπιον* and the interpreter of it *θεοπρόπος*." In this explanation, it would seem, he takes *θεοπρόπιον*, the neuter noun, directly from *θεός* and *πρέπω*, with the meaning 'that which a God shews,' 'the sign or omen' (a meaning, by the way, which the word appears not to have in actual use); and then, from this *θεοπρόπιον*, derives the masculine *θεοπρόπος*, as if it were 'one who deals in *θεοπρόπια*.' It is hardly necessary to say that such a procedure is wholly inadmissible, being in fact the reverse of the real one: *θεοπρόπιον*, instead of coming before *θεοπρόπος*, must be formed from it, so as to mean 'that which belongs to a *θεοπρόπος*, his utterance or oracle.' Compare *μαντεῖον* (*μαντήϊον*), formed from *μαντεύς*, 'a prophet,' with the meaning 'prophecy or oracle.'

It is hardly worth while even to mention a third explanation of the word, according to which it would mean 'one who speaks things *θεῷ πρέποντα*, 'fitting for a god.'

It is certainly a curious fact that a root so widely extended in the cognate languages, and so fully represented in the Latin, should be confined in Greek to a single compound, a compound evidently formed after the language had assumed its distinctive character, and yet one which may be referred with probability to the earliest period of the language, and which even in the classic time of Athenian literature had become an antique expression. Perhaps the accidental coincidence of sound between *πρεπω*, 'to ask,' and *πρέπω*, 'to appear,' may have had something to do with the early disappearance of the former. At all events, we have a somewhat similar phenomenon in the Celtic languages. The Irish retains the root, but only in composition with a proper Irish prefix—a compound, therefore, which must have been formed after the language had assumed its distinctive character. From the Welsh it seems to have disappeared altogether.

III.

THE GREEK GENITIVE AS AN ABLATIVE CASE.

1858.

IT is well known that some eminent grammarians have regarded the Greek genitive as primarily a *from*-case, and have therefore sought to explain its various uses as being all of them at bottom *from*-relations. Thus Kühner, in his largest Greek Grammar (*ausführliche Grammatik der griechischen Sprache*), commencing the discussion of this case, says: "The Genitive expresses, 1. in *local* relation, the proceeding *from* an object, or removal and separation from it, inasmuch as it assigns the object or the point *from* which goes out the action of the verb: *χάζεσθαι κελεύθου*, 'to retire from the way;' 2. in *causal* relation, the cause, origin, author, in general the object which calls forth the action of the verb, produces it (*gignit*, hence the significant name *genitivus*),* excites it, occasions it: *ἐπιθυμῶ τῆς ἀρετῆς*, 'I have a desire for virtue (a desire awakened by virtue).' As both in the local and the causal relation the direction *whence* lies at the basis, the genitive may be named also the *whence*-case." Thus Kühner, who, in accordance with this exordium, proceeds to develop the uses of the case as follows: (I beg leave to present a brief outline of his development, and to solicit attention to it, though the detail, I am afraid, may appear a little tedious) A. In LOCAL relation, with words which express more or less distinctly the ideas of separation and removal: to these Kühner adds verbs of beginning, but with questionable propriety; *ὑπάρχειν ἀδικῶν ἔργων* is not 'to begin *from* unjust actions,' as a starting-point, but rather 'to make a beginning

* Kühner perhaps means only that the term genitive is *capable* of bearing this significance: not that those who first used it understood it thus. With them the *nominative* case (*ἡ ὀνομαστική*) was the one used to *name* a person; the *genitive* (*ἡ γενική*), the one used to express his *γένος*, 'family connection, origin, or descent:' thus *Ἀλέξανδρος ὁ Φιλίππου*, 'Alexander the son of Philip.'

of, *in* unjust actions;' the special relation here would seem to be partitive more than separative. Then B. In CAUSAL relation, which is drawn out to much greater length than the local, and is arranged under three principal heads, according as the cause is conceived to be an *efficient*, an *occasioning*, or a *conditioning* cause. Under *efficient* cause comes, 1. Genitive of *origin* and *author;* 2. Genitive of *possessor*—the owner being regarded as in a manner producing what he posses-ses, making his money, making his property, as we phrase it; certainly, making it his own; 3. Genitive of *the whole* or genitive *partitive*—the whole being conceived as in a sense giving rise to its parts, producing them from itself; 4. Genitive of *place* (where) and *time* (when)—the action being regarded as evolved from and by the place and time of its occurrence; 5. Genitive of *material*—either the material which makes, composes something, as *a house of stone;* or the material which makes a fullness of something, as *full of corn: i. e.* genitive of plenty. Under this head Kühner puts constructions such as ἐσθίειν κρεῶν, 'to eat of flesh-meat,' as if the meat were the material which makes the eating (where Prof. Crosby, with better reason, recognizes a partitive relation); also ἀκούειν θορύβου, 'to hear a noise,' as if the noise were the material of the sensation (which again is explained differently, and, as it seems to me, better by Prof. Crosby): τοῦ κασιγνήτου τί φῄς; 'what say you of your brother?' (where, however, the genitive seems really to depend upon the pronoun—'what report, what account of your brother do you give?') etc., etc. So much for the efficient cause. Next the occasioning cause: this occurs, 1. with words of emotion: ἐμῶν ἐμπάζεο μυθῶν, 'be heedful of my sayings'—the sayings themselves are to serve as a cause, an occasion for heedfulness; 2. with words of punishment, accusation, condemnation—these being consequences occasioned by the crimes to which they relate; 3. in some other connections, among which we find ὡς ποδῶν εἶχον, '(as they were in respect of feet, *i. e.*) according to their swiftness of foot,' the feet being looked upon as occasioning the state of swiftness, more or less, which they happen to be in. Third and last, the conditioning cause. This is used especially for expressing mutual relations, the existence of the relation on the one side being a necessary condition to its existence on the other. Thus, 1. Genitive of *superiority* and *inferiority:* Τισσαφέρνης ἄρχει τῶν πόλεων, 'Tissaphernes governs the cities'—to a governor subjects are an indispensable condition; 2. Genitive *with comparatives:* μείζων τοῦ ἀδελφοῦ, 'greater than his brother'—to any greater a something less is an indispensable condition. This, however, Prof. Crosby explains more probably as a genitive of distinction, *i. e.* greater (in distinction) from his brother; 3. Genitive of *price, value, merit*—the price of a commodity being the condition of its sale; 4. Genitive *with substantives,* to express almost any mutual relation: Φίλιππος ὁ πατὴρ Ἀλεξάνδρου, 'Philip the father of Alexander'—Alexander here is the conditioning cause of Philip's paternity.

Such is Kühner's theory of the Greek genitive. Our distinguished countryman and associate, Prof. Crosby, adopts the same leading view, but develops it in his own way, with characteristic ingenuity and elegance, with much more simplicity and naturalness than the German grammarian—with all the simplicity and naturalness, I believe, which the necessities of his theory admit of—without the Beckerite tendency, too frequently apparent in Kühner, to impose a meaning on language rather than educe the meaning out of it.

I propose to offer some remarks on this theory of the Greek genitive, which regards it as always a *from*-case, and finds in the idea of departure or derivation its primary and pervading significance. That the Greek genitive is *a* from-case, in frequent use as such, is conceded at the outset: the question will be, whether this was its primitive and universal character. This question might be discussed from the standpoint of philosophy—if philosophy has any point that stands; float-point would perhaps be the more proper word. I propose, however, to treat it as a question of history; to inquire whether in point of fact the uses of the case had the genesis ascribed to them. It is only the possibility of treating it thus in a historical way that makes it proper for me to bring it before the notice of the Oriental Society: it is the historical aspect of the subject that looks toward the Orient.

The Greek language, as all know, has not preserved the complete case-system of the Indo-European class. In this respect it is inferior to the Latin, which, in addition to the five cases of the Greek, has an *ablative*, and, to some extent, a *locative:* while the Latin is inferior to the Zend and Sanskrit, which have a *locative* throughout, and besides that an eighth case, the *instrumental*. It will be observed that this full system of cases includes both a *genitive* and an *ablative;* and that these are clearly distinguished from each other both in form and meaning. The ablative singular in Sanskrit is made by adding *t* or *d* to the stem: the rules of euphony in reference to final consonants are such in that language as to leave it uncertain whether the proper affix was *t* or *d*. But a comparison of the Zend makes it probable that the original form was *t*. In Latin the ablative singular ended in *d*. This ending, it is true, does not appear in the classical Latin: but in the oldest monuments of the language, such as the inscriptions of the *Columna rostrata* (260 B. C.), and the *Senatus-Consultum de Bacchanalibus* (186 B. C.), it is found as the regular and constant ending: thus we find *præda-d, senatu-d* as ablatives of *præda, senatus; in altod marid = in alto mari; præsented, dictatored*, from *præsens, dictator*. The Oscan inscriptions show the same ending *d* through all the declensions: *e. g. dolud mallud*, corresponding to Old Latin *dolod malod*, later Latin *dolo malo*, 'with evil art, fraud.' The ablative plural in all these languages coincides with the dative plural, and has in all of them substantially the same ending: in Sanskrit *bhyas*, Zend *byô* (with *ô* for *as* by a regular euphonic law), Latin *bus*. If now we look at the meaning of the case thus formed, we find it to be, what the name we give it imports, a *from*-case. It is appropriately used in expressing removal, separation, or distinction. It is used in a transferred or metaphorical sense to express cause—not cause in the all-comprehending extension given to that idea by the theory just described—but cause that *is* cause (if I may be allowed the expression), in which the character of origin, procession, derivation, is obvious and palpable. As it may thus express not only the producing cause, but also the means, it encroaches on the borders of the instrumental: in Latin, indeed, which has lost the instrumental form, the whole domain of that case has been seized upon and appropriated by the ablative. Still further, the Latin ablative covers in a great measure the ground of the original locative, and is thus much broader in its extension, and more various in its character, than the corresponding case in Zend and Sanskrit. Still it remains the fact, that in all these languages the ablative is the *from*-case, the proper case for expressing a *from*, whether literally in space-relation, or metaphorically in those relations which most distinctly and unequivocally imply a *from*-idea.

From the endings of the ablative, as just given, those of the genitive are widely different. The Sanskrit genitive singular adds *s* to the stem, often with a connecting-vowel *a*, making *as*, Zend *ô*, Greek ος, Latin *is*. But to stems in short *a* the Sanskrit adds *sya:* thus *vrikă*, 'wolf,' Nom. *vrika-s*, Gen. *vrika-sya*. To this corresponds the Homeric genitive λύκο-ιο (for λυκο-σιο) in which the σ is dropped; in the common form ι is also dropped and the two ο's contracted: λυκο-ο, λύκου. In Latin the *jus* of *hu-jus*, *cu-jus*, *e-jus*, perhaps corresponds to the same ending *sya*. In the genitive plural, the Sanskrit has *âm*, Greek ων, Latin *um*. Some of the pronouns in Sanskrit have *sâm* instead of *âm;* thus from *ka*, interrogative, come Gen. Plur. *ke-shâm*, fem. *kâ-sâm*. These reappear in Latin, with the usual change of *s* to *r*, as *quô-rum*, *quâ-rum*. The Latin even extends this formation (in *rum*) to all words of the first, second, and fifth declensions. The genitive is the only case of the eight which remains to us in English (leaving out of view the pronouns); and it is not at all unlikely that the meaning indicated by our common name for it, the *possessive*, was in fact the primitive meaning of the form. If, however, we look at the general range of its use in the languages that have it, we may describe it as the case of *appurtenance*, which means belonging to something, pertaining to it. Its most frequent use, and by far the most important, is with substantives, to mark one thing as in some way belonging to, or connected with another. When used with verbs, it represents the action of the verb as belonging to or connected with the object, rather than as falling directly upon it: as, in English, *I know of the man* differs from *I know the man*.

Now in these simple facts we have the materials for an

argument, the grounds for a probable conclusion. The Sanskrit, Greek, and Latin have a case common to all the three, formed by all in the same way, by the same additions to the stem, and employed by all in the same way (as regards its leading use), *i. e.* as a case of *appurtenance*. The Sanskrit and Latin have another case, common to both, formed alike in both, and employed alike in both (as regards its leading use), *i. e.* as a case of departure, a *from*-case. This latter case is wanting in Greek, its meaning being expressed by the one before described. What is the natural inference? Is it not, that the primary use of the genitive in Greek is that which belongs to the same form in the other languages, and that its ablative use has been superadded to this, through the loss or abandonment of a proper ablative form? If so, then, instead of explaining those uses of the Greek genitive in which it coincides with the Sanskrit and Latin by its ablative use, we ought rather to reverse the process, to show how the ablative use can be explained from that of the proper genitive.

The only way, perhaps, of escaping from this conclusion, would be to set up a hypothesis of extremely hypothetical character, something like the following: "That the ablative form as distinct from the genitive is a later thing in the history of the Indo-European languages; that the primitive stock had but one form, the genitive; that this form was used originally in the meaning of an ablative, but in process of time developed from that a great variety of uses, such as we find in the Greek genitive; that afterwards, for the sake of distinctness or for some other reason, a new form was invented, an ablative form; and that a portion of the uses of the genitive, in fact its most original uses, were set off to this new ablative case."

It is hardly necessary to point out the assumptions involved in this hypothesis. If the ablative form is of later origin than the genitive, it does not follow that its meaning was before expressed by the genitive. If before the invention of an ablative form its meaning was expressed by the genitive, it does not follow, nor is there evidence to prove, that this ablative meaning was the primitive use of the genitive, out of which all its other uses were developed. But it is far from certain that the ablative form is actually more recent than the genitive. It is true that the ablative singular in *t* or *d* does not occur, so far as we know, in the languages of Europe, with the exception of the Latin and its Italican kindred. But the non-appearance of a case-form in particular languages does not prove that they never had it. Our vernacular has in nouns but one inflected case, the genitive ; but our ancestors a thousand years ago had a nominative, dative, accusative, and vocative. In pronouns they had the trace of an instrumental. Could we make out the Teutonic as it was a thousand years earlier, we might perhaps find a complete instrumental form, with an ablative and a locative, the perfect apparatus of Indo-European noun-inflection. The ending of the dative and ablative plural (Sanskrit *bhyas*, Latin *bus*) lingers still on the extreme western verge of Indo-Europeanism, in the Irish *bh*. The case which has this ending is used in the Irish as a dative plural: that it was once used as an ablative is not unlikely, though we have no certain proof of the fact, since the *from*-relation is always expressed by means of prepositions ; and though these prepositions are regularly followed by the form in *bh*, yet nothing positive can be inferred from that, as other prepositions show the same construction. It must be confessed, however, that this discussion is somewhat irrelevant, with reference to our present object. For that, it matters little whether the genitive was or was not earlier in its origin than the ablative. Whether or not any members of the Indo-European family broke off from the common stock, carrying with them a genitive, before the ablative form had made its appearance, is of little consequence to us in this inquiry. For the Greeks, it is quite certain, did nothing of the kind. On that point the Latin ablative is an unequivocal and unimpeachable witness. The Italican languages may have assumed a distinct existence about the same time with the Greek: that they are not of later origin than the Greek, will be admitted on all hands. As they have a genitive and ablative completely distinct from each other, we are forced to believe that the distinction of these two cases in form and meaning existed in the common language before the separation of the Greek, and was not the result of any later development. It follows that the Greeks must have given up an existing and established ablative form, transferring its functions to the genitive. Why they did so, it may not be possible for us to ascertain. We should find it equally difficult to show why they gave up the instrumental form, which is found in the Slavonic, the Lithuanian, and to some extent even in the Teutonic idioms; or why they gave up the dative form, which is almost as widely retained among the languages of Europe as the genitive, while they transferred its functions to the locative. It is important, however, to observe, in regard to the ablative, that the Sanskrit, even in its earlier Vedic form, shows us to some extent the same condition which we find in Greek. The ablative singular in *t*, already described, belongs to only one class of Sanskrit nouns, though a most numerous and important class—words which have stems in short *a*, corresponding to the Greek and Latin substantives and adjectives of the second declension. For all other nouns in Sanskrit, the form of the genitive singular is used also as an ablative, precisely as in Greek; though in the other numbers the Sanskrit invariably distinguishes the two cases. The Greek, then, only carries out consistently, through all words and all numbers, a tendency which the Sanskrit shows in most classes of words in the singular number. Bopp conjectures that the use of the genitive for the ablative in Sanskrit rests upon a merely phonetic interchange of consonant-sounds; he supposes that *nâus*, 'ship' (for instance), stem *nâu* or *nâv*, made originally an ablative *nâv-at*, and that this by a sibilation of the *t* became *nâv-as*, like the genitive. Now the assumed mutation of *t* to *s* is perhaps hardly borne out for the Sanskrit by the euphonic analogies of that language. But for the Greek there is no difficulty in such an assumption; the euphonic law of the language proscribes the final τ; and as we have πρός for προτί or προτ, and λελυκός for λελυκοτ, Gen. λελυκότ-ος, so we might have νᾶος, νᾶϝος for an earlier νᾶϝοτ. The identity thus arising between the genitive and ablative forms in most singular words would naturally contribute much to bring about a universal substitution of the one case for the other. According to a plausible conjecture of Bopp's, the same change of τ to ς has occurred even in adjectives of the second declension, producing the adverbs in ως (for ωτ); thus κακῶς, 'badly,' would be for κακωτ, an original ablative of κακός, 'bad,' though used in an instrumental rather than a proper ablative meaning: compare Sanskrit *pâpa*, 'evil,' Nom. *pâpas*, Abl. *pâpât*, 'from evil, by evil means, in evil manner.'

I think it must be evident, from these considerations, that there is no historical reason for regarding those uses of the Greek genitive in which it coincides with the common use of that case through the other Indo-European languages as arising from the idea of the ablative; but, on the contrary, that there are historical probabilities of considerable force against such a supposition. In the view of comparative philology, the theory of Kühner, who deduces the idea of appurtenance from that of departure, is less warranted than Madvig's, who takes the idea of appurtenance as the proper meaning of the case, and deduces from that the idea of departure; since departure (he says), removal, separation, imply a previous connection or appurtenance. Thus the first idea of the genitive would be 'in connection with;' the second idea, 'out of connection with.' Why the genitive should not equally have come to mean 'into connection with,' it might be hard to explain. In fact, this view of Madvig's seems scarcely tenable, and he himself does not insist upon it, or attempt to give it that completeness of development which Kühner and Crosby have given to the opposite view. The truth appears to be, that the Greek genitive combines in itself the functions of two cases originally distinct, functions associated in Greek not so much from any perceived internal connection between them, as from accidents affecting the outward forms of inflection. The Greek language itself furnishes another and more striking instance of this accumulation of offices, originally distinct, in one form. The Greek dative, it is well known, both in singular and plural, has the form of a locative case, denoting the place where or in which; but, as actually used, it combines, with the meaning of a locative, those of the dative and the instrumental. These, in the full system of the Indo-European languages, make three distinct cases. In this instance, Prof. Crosby, guided by his finer appreciation for language, has recognized the diversities of meaning as fundamental, and abstained from any attempt to connect the locative and instrumental uses with the proper dative. Kühner, on the other hand, whether that his sensibility to language was less delicate from the first, or because it was blunted by his Beckerite philosophy, or for both reasons together, has been less abstinent; he makes no scruple to identify all these uses. The fundamental use of the case (he says) is the locative, to express the *where*: from this comes, on the one hand, the proper dative, the *whither*, and on the other, the instrumental, the *whence*. With equal propriety, as the genitive and dative have but one form in the Greek dual, he might for that number derive all the uses of the genitive also from what he recognizes as the fundamental idea of the dative. This could give him no difficulty: for as the locative *where* of that case has developed an instrumental *whence*, and as all the relations of the genitive are in his view *whence*-relations, they could easily be connected with the instrumental dative. To a grammarian whose *where* by natural evolution develops a *whither* and a *whence*—that is, gives at once all possible space-relations—it cannot be difficult from any given relation to derive all other possible relations. If the genitive were not only a genitive and ablative, as it is in the Greek singular and plural, and to a great extent in the Sanskrit singular, but a genitive and locative, as it is in the Sanskrit dual, or a genitive, locative, dative, instrumental and ablative, as it is in the Greek dual—and even if to all these it superadded the offices of nominative and accusative—such modes of explanation would be quite sufficient to demonstrate the fundamental identity of all these uses.

Let me not be misunderstood. I do not regard it as absurd in itself (however unhistorical it may be) to derive all the uses of the Greek genitive from a single root—the one idea of departure. If the historical argument were as strong in its favor as it actually is against it, I should not reject it as a thing incredible. The historical analogies sometimes brought up in its support have, as it seems to me, but little force. It is said that the Greek genitive can almost always be represented by the English 'of,' and that *of* means 'from,' so that *father of Alexander* must have meant originally 'father *from* Alexander,' *house of Miltiades* must have meant 'house *from* Miltiades,' and so in all those uses where the from-idea seems at first view most alien from the proper meaning of the genitive. Similarly the French genitive is made by the preposition *de*, the original meaning of which is 'from.' But the original meaning of a preposition is not of necessity to be regarded as having once belonged to it in every phrase or class of phrases which contains it. Compare the English preposition *to*, as used with the infinitive. There can be no doubt that this preposition originally meant 'towards.' There can be no doubt that, when first used with the infinitive, it was in this sense of direction or tendency. But it is equally certain that with the infinitive, when used as the subject of a sentence, it has not, and never could have had, such a meaning. *To err is human* never meant, or could have meant, 'toward erring is human.' One who should attempt to derive this use of the preposition by internal connection from its original meaning would have to subject language to unwarrantable force. The *to* was, no doubt, first used with the infinitive in cases where the meaning 'towards' was appropriate—either literally, *I sent him to do it*, *i. e.* 'toward doing it,' or metaphorically, *I exhorted*, *commanded*, *requested him to do it*. In this way it extended its use, until it came to be regarded as the proper concomitant or exponent of the infinitive, without reference to its origin: and only then, when its original force had vanished, when it had taken on a wholly different character, could it be used in such expressions as *to err is human*. Now something like this may have been true in reference to the genitive in *of* or *de*. The preposition was perhaps applied first in those cases of the genitive which may without violence be regarded as ablatives: as *John of Salisbury* (where we may say either 'belonging to,' or 'arising from Salisbury'), *one of the peers* (one belonging to, or one taken from the peers), *the son of Alfred* (belonging to him, or springing from him, as his son), etc. Having thus established itself in these and similar cases as an equivalent for the genitive, the form with *of* may then have been extended, without reference to its proper meaning, so as to represent the genitive in its other uses. If this course of things be admitted as probable, or even possible, it cannot be asserted that all the uses of the genitive in *of* or *de* were ever actually thought of as *from*-relations, in any development or modification of the *from*-idea. And of course the English and French constructions cannot be relied on as parallel cases to support the theory which makes all uses of the Greek genitive to be *from*-relations, developments or modifications of the *from*-idea.

It may be thought, however, that there is some practical advantage in making the student refer all uses of the same form, even if originally distinct, to one common root; that the one form and one universal meaning will thus stand together in his mind, mutually supporting and supported, and the phenomena of the language present a unity and harmony which must be lost under a different treatment. Whatever advantages may be gained in this way are perhaps hardly an equivalent for the sacrifice of truth, at least of historic probability, which this method involves. But there is another point to be considered—a question of pedagogical ethics—is there not some danger of blunting the philological conscience of the student? While I admit the abstract possibility of deducing all uses of the genitive from this single root, I cannot help believing, and my brief analysis of Kühner's scheme may bear me out in the belief, that the process can hardly be accomplished without a good deal of straining and forcing. It cannot be well for the learner that he should be accustomed, in the first stadium of his grammatical course, to subject the facts of language to a process of screwing and twisting; that he should be taught to desert the simple, obvious, natural interpretation of language for that which is constrained or arbitrary.

IV.

ON BEKKER'S DIGAMMATED TEXT OF HOMER.

1863.

IT is more than forty years since Richard Payne Knight published in 1820 his famous digammated Iliad—or rather Vilviad—of Homer. The book has taken its place among the curiosities of literature. Its author was an ingenious and elegant scholar; but he had his hobby, and he rode it unmercifully. The horse of Phidippides, the spendthrift son in Aristophanes' Clouds, was marked with a **Κόππα** (κοππατίας). Payne Knight's hobby was branded with another lost letter of the primitive Greek alphabet, the Digamma: wherever he goes, he bears the digamma with him.

It is one of the most remarkable circumstances about Payne Knight's Iliad, that, more than twenty years after its publication, a distinguished American scholar should have thought it worth while to reproduce three books of it on this side the ocean (see Anthon's Homer, New York, 1844). A page or two by way of specimen might have been amusing at least, even if uninstructive: but to take up in this way more than fifty pages of a school-book was to make the joke somewhat ponderous.

It might have been expected that the example of Payne Knight would deter succeeding editors from repeating an experiment which in his hands had turned out in a way at once so unfortunate and so ludicrous. But Immanuel Bekker, the Coryphæus of recent textual criticism, has not shrunk from the hazard. In 1858 he brought out an Iliad and Odyssey in which the lost letter is admitted to a place in the Homeric text. This work embodies the results of many years' minute and laborious study. In 1809, after the appearance of Wolf's Homer in its third edition, Bekker, then a young man, reviewed it in the Jena *Litteratur-Zeitung*. The review is said to have shown great mastery of the subject, and great aptitude for those critical labors which were to form the life-work of its author. In 1843 he published a new recension of the Homeric text, which was immediately and universally recognized as a marked advance on that of Wolf. For the last five or six years, he has been giving out in the *Monatsberichte* of the Berlin Academy a highly remarkable series of observations and researches in reference to Homer. With great ingenuity and acuteness, they evince an amount of patient labor which is absolutely marvellous. Thus, he goes through the whole extent of the poems to note and collect the verses in which the third foot is without a cæsura. In the 15,694 verses of the Iliad, he finds only 185 which have no cæsura in the third foot; in the 12,101 of the Odyssey, only 71. Again, he goes through the whole extent of the poems to mark the cases of bucolic cæsura, and observe whether the fourth foot, the one which precedes the cæsura, is a dactyl or a spondee. Thus, in the fifth book of the Iliad he finds 531 bucolic cæsuras, of which 470 are preceded by dactyls, 61 by spondees; in the eleventh book, 575 bucolic cæsuras, 478 preceded by dactyls, 97 by spondees; and so on for the other books. These are only specimens of the tasks which this conscientious and indefatigable critic has imposed upon himself. The results of these protracted investigations appear in his last edition of the Iliad and Odyssey, that of 1858. This edition shows a great advance upon his first, of 1843. It is, in fact, constructed on a different principle, and aims at a different object. The aim of Bekker in his first edition, like that of Wolf before him, was in general to reproduce the Homeric text as it was settled by the great critic Aristarchus, about two centuries before Christ, and handed down without intentional variation by subsequent copyists. It was the rule with Wolf, and with Bekker in his first edition, to give the readings which certainly or probably belonged to Aristarchus, except in occasional instances where there was unequivocal evidence to show the priority of a different reading. But in his second edition Bekker has taken a wider range. He has adopted as his guide the principle of analogy, and by the help of it has sought to go back beyond Aristarchus. Relying on analogies presented by a careful study of the Homeric poems, he has departed in many cases from the readings of the manuscripts, even where these could be traced with more or less certainty to Aristarchus himself. The general propriety of this method has been disputed in many quarters. It is, indeed, rather singular in a critic like Bekker, who strenuously maintains the fragmentary origin of the poems, and who finds evidence of such an origin in the varieties and inconsistencies which they show, both as to grammatical forms and as to the use of words. He expects departures from analogy; he regards them as having an *à priori* probability; and yet the tendency of his criticism is to sweep them away from the text, wherever this can be done by gentle means: for he abstains on principle from changes of a violent or extreme character; he does not treat his text with the despotic ingenuity of a Bentley.

But our object at present is to consider only one feature of the work—its introduction of the digamma. The objectors generally admit that the digamma-sound (the *v*, or rather, the *w*-sound) belonged originally to the Homeric poems, and that it is proper in commentaries and other philological works to point out the traces of its existence and to discuss the extent of its use. But they object to a digammated text. They maintain with much plausibility that the poems from their first reduction to writing have never shown this letter; and that the attempt to go back, not only beyond the first manuscripts that we have, but beyond the first that ever existed, can have no reasonable hope of success. At any rate, they say, the case is not yet ripe for a digammated text. In regard to many words, it is still uncertain whether they were or were not sounded with a digamma in the Homeric time; and in regard to many which certainly were so, it is doubtful whether they were uniformly sounded with this letter, or whether it was not sometimes omitted in pronunciation. If we take words which certainly had a digamma in the Homeric language, and attempt to represent them uniformly with this letter, we must make many violent and arbitrary changes of the text. If we adopt the principle of giving them with digamma wherever it can be done without such changes, we have to draw an uncertain line between changes which are violent and changes which are not so. And whichever of these courses we take, we can have no assurance that we are reproducing the genuine Homeric usage. It is impossible to deny the force of these objections. But their force would be much greater, if by the decree of fate the world were restricted to one printed text of Homer, just this and no more. In that case, we should say without hesitation, give us a text which comes as nearly as possible to that which Aristarchus—following, as we know that he did, with great soberness and caution, the testimony of the best manuscripts that he could find —fixed upon as the true one; or, if you depart from that, do so only when there is decisive evidence to warrant the departure. As a basis for Homeric study, as a standard for general use and reference, a text thus constituted is the best that we can have. But we are by no means restricted to a single text. For general purposes, we may continue to use Bekker's first edition, or we may take, what differs very little from it, the text of Dindorf in Teubner's Bibliotheca, or any better one which we can find constructed on the same principles. But Bekker's second edition will still have its value as a tentative, to show how far the principle of analogy, in the hands of a consummate critic, will serve to correct and improve the text of Homer which has come down to us by tradition from the ancient Alexandrine editors. And especially with reference to the digamma it will have a value of this kind, as showing what results can be secured by an intelligent, moderate, and cautious attempt to reinstate the long-lost Homeric letter. On this point the editor himself says, in his brief and pithy preface : "The Æolic letter, after it had disappeared through time and negligence, was by the marvellous sagacity of Bentley reclaimed from oblivion ; but lay thus for a long time, ridiculed by wits, by scholars invidiously assailed or unintelligently defended [the last evidently a hit at Payne Knight]. By Heyne it was admitted, at least into his commentary. The indispensable uses of this letter I could no longer treat with contempt. I have therefore restored the digamma, but so far only as I had the power and right to do, proceeding cautiously and with moderated step : I have restored it to its own place, as indicated by manifest traces, not by eager wishes or by hasty assumptions of my own."

This language is fully borne out by an inspection of the book. The carefulness and conscientiousness of the editor are everywhere apparent. In deciding what words are to be regarded as having the digamma, he relies mainly on the indications of the Homeric verse. From this it follows as a natural consequence that he recognizes only an *initial* digamma. Thus he writes *Διός*, 'of Zeus,' *κληΐς*, 'key,' *ὄϊς*, 'sheep,' not *ΔιϝόϚ*, *κληϝίς*, *ὄϝις*, though there is strong reason, derived from inscriptions or from later dialects or from cognate tongues, for believing that these words had digamma in the Homeric language. He does not, however, reject the initial digamma of a word when it is brought by a prefix or by composition into the middle. Thus the digamma of *ϝείκοσι*, 'twenty,' is retained in *ἐϝείκοσι*, that of *ϝάγνυμι*, 'to break,' in *ἐϝάγη*, 'was broken,' that of *ϝέλπομαι*, 'to hope,' in *ϝέϝολπα*, 'I hope,' that of *ϝιδεῖν*, 'to see,' in *Ἀϝίδης*, 'unseen god, Hades,' that of *ϝηδύς*, 'sweet,' in *μελιϝηδής*, *μελιϝηδέα ϝοῖνον*, 'honey-sweet wine.' He rejects all combinations of digamma with another consonant. Thus *δήν*, 'long,' which in numerous passages has the appearance of beginning with two consonants, and has been supposed by many to have the digamma-sound after the δ (δϝήν), is by Bekker always written with a simple δ. In *δείδια*, 'I fear,' many, since Buttmann, have recognized a Homeric *δέδϝια*; in *ἔδδεισα*, 'I feared,' a Homeric *ἔδϝεισα*: but Bekker always writes them according to the traditional way, only omitting one δ from *ἔδδεισα*. Nor does he recognize any lost letters beside digamma. Curtius, in the second part of his Principles of Greek Etymology, has endeavored to show that a consonant *y*-sound has in some instances given rise to the same appearances in the Homeric verse as those occasioned by the *v*- or *w*-sound (the digamma). But the words which are thus supposed to show traces of initial *y* Bekker either writes with digamma, or leaves them with a vowel-initial. We shall refer again to this point before closing.

We have said that, in determining what words had initial digamma in the Homeric language, our editor relies mainly on the indications of the Homeric verse. Having satisfied himself in the case of any particular word that it did have the digamma, he proceeds to write the word, as also its derivatives and compounds, with that character: and this he does, not only where metrical reasons favor or require the introduction of a consonant, but wherever metrical reasons do not absolutely forbid the introduction of a consonant. In very many instances where the verse as we have it in our traditional text will not allow the digamma to come in, the difficulty can be removed by changes of the text which are more or less obvious. Bekker's principle, it is evident, has been to write the word with digamma, whenever this is consistent with the verse as it stands in the ordinary text, or can be made so consistent by some slight and easy change of reading. He shows his judgment and moderation as a critic by refusing (at least, in general, with only rare exceptions) to make any considerable or arbitrary change of reading for the sake of getting in his digamma. Rather than do this, he will allow the word to appear in a particular case without the initial consonant which usually belongs to it. I may illustrate his mode of procedure by a more particular statement of what he has done in the first book of the Iliad. In the 611 lines of which it consists, there are found, if I have counted right, 162 which show the digamma. But some of these contain it more than once, so that 184 words are written with this character. In 36 of these, it is found, not at the absolute beginning of the word, but after a preposition or other prefix. Of the 184 words there are only 31, or about a sixth, in which the introduction of the diagamma has required any further change of text; and in 18 of these 31, the only change required has been the omission of a movable *ν* from the end of a preceding word. Thus in verses—

14.	στέμματ᾽ ἔχων ἐν χερσὶν ἑκηβόλου Ἀπόλλωνος.	B. χερσὶ Ϝεκ.
96.	τοὔνεκ᾽ ἄρ᾽ ἄλγε᾽ ἔδωκεν ἑκηβόλος ἠδ᾽ ἔτι δώσει.	ἔδωκε Ϝεκ.
294.	εἰ δὴ σοὶ πᾶν ἔργον ὑπείξομαι, ὅττι κεν εἴπῃς.	ὅττι κε Ϝείπῃς.

In 8 instances, a slight change has been made in the grammatical form of the preceding word, though in 2 out of the 8 the change was not necessary in order to the introduction of the digamma. The other six are as follows:—

21. ἀζόμενοι Διὸς υἱὸν ἑκηβόλον Ἀπόλλωνα. B. υἷα Fεκ.
230. δῶρ' ἀποαιρεῖσθαι, ὅς τις σέθεν ἀντίον εἴπῃ. ἀντία Fείπῃ.
288. πάντων μὲν κρατέειν ἐθέλει, πὰντεσσι δ' ἀνάσσειν. πᾶσιν δὲ Fαν.
365. οἶσθα· τίη τοι ταῦτ' εἰδυίῃ πάντ' ἀγορεύω. ταῦτα Fιδυίῃ.
482. στείρῃ πορφύρεον μεγάλ' ἴαχε νηὸς ἰούσης. μέγα Fίαχε.
576. ἐσθλῆς ἔσσεται ἦδος, ἐπεὶ τὰ χερείονα νικᾷ. ἔσται Fῆδος.

In three instances a particle which seemed unnecessary has been omitted to make room for the digamma :—

64. ὅς κ' εἴποι ὅτι τόσσον ἐχώσατο Φοῖβος Ἀπόλλων. B. ὅς Fείπῃ.
548. οὔτε θεῶν πρότερος τόνγ' εἴσεται οὔτ' ἀνθρώπων. τὸν Fείσ.
582. ἀλλὰ σὺ τόνγ' ἐπέεσσι καθάπτεσθαι μαλακοῖσιν. τὸν Fεπ.

In two instances one particle has been substituted for another :—

19. ἐκπέρσαι Πριάμοιο πόλιν εὖ δ' οἴκαδ' ἱκέσθαι. B. καὶ Fοίκαδ'.
395. ἢ ἔπει ὤνησας κραδίην Διὸς ἠὲ καὶ ἔργῳ. ἠέ τι Fέρλῳ.

I do not find in the first book any instance in which words are transposed for the sake of bringing in the digamma. I will add one or two instances from other parts of the poems :—

χ. 341. μεσσηγὺς κρητῆρος ἰδὲ θρόνου ἀργυροήλου. B. κρητῆρος μεσσηγὺ Fιδέ.
Ψ. 370. ἕστασαν ἐν δίφροισι· πάτασσε δὲ θυμὸς ἑκάστου.
θυμὸς δ' ἐπάτασσε Fεκ.

There are several instances in the first book where a word usually digammated is compelled by stress of metre to forego this addition. The lines which I have noted are—

216. χρὴ μὴν σφωΐτερόν γε, θεά, Fέπος εἰρύσσασθαι. not Fειρύσσασθαι.
239. πρὸς Διὸς εἰρύαται· ὁ δέ τοι μέγας ἔσσεται ὅρκος. Fειρύαται.
294. εἰ δὴ σοὶ πᾶν ἔργον ὑπείξομαι, ὅττι κε Fείπῃς. ὑποFείξομαι.
438. ἐκ δ' ἑκατόμβην βῆσαν ἑκηβόλῳ Ἀπόλλωνι, Fεκηβόλῳ.
555. νῦν δ' αἰνῶς δείδοικα κατὰ φρένα μή σε παρείπῃ. παραFείπῃ.

My search was a hasty one. It is most likely that careful looking would bring out a few more cases of this kind.

Before proceeding to notice and criticise the treatment of particular words, there are two remarks of a general nature which it seems important to premise. They relate to the evidence in favor of a digamma, and the evidence against a digamma, in the case of any particular word.

First, as to the evidence in favor, it must always be borne in mind that there are cases in which hiatus was more or less freely allowed in the epic verse, so that hiatus occurring in such cases furnishes little, if any, presumption for an initial digamma. In my Grammar (67 D) are mentioned three cases of this kind: 1. when the first of two words ends in a close vowel (*ι*, *υ*), and seldom or never suffers elision: this applies especially to the dative singular of the third declension, as *παιδὶ ὄπασσε*; 2. when the two words are separated by a clearly required mark of punctuation, as *κάθησο, ἐμῷ δ' ἐπιπείθεο μύθῳ*; 3. (the most important case) when the vowels which make hiatus are two short syllables of the third foot, or, in other words, at the feminine cæsura of the third foot, as *τῶν οἱ ἓξ ἐγένοντο ἐνὶ μεγάροισι γενέθλη*. In this place it has been proved that hiatus is allowed with much the same freedom as at the end of a verse. There is another case which ought to be added to these three—a case in which hiatus is easily excused, if not freely allowed—and that is, after a long vowel or diphthong in arsis, and particularly the arsis of the third or the fifth foot. The first line of the Iliad is an instance in point:—

1. μῆνιν ἄειδε, θεά, Πηληϊάδεω Ἀχιλῆος.

which shows hiatus after the arsis of the fifth foot: after the arsis of the third, we find it in *A*.—

24. ἀλλ' οὐκ Ἀτρεΐδῃ Ἀγαμέμνονι ἥνδανε θυμῷ.
42. τίσειαν Δαναοὶ ἐμὰ δάκρυα σοῖσι βέλεσσιν.

Here also, after the long arsis of the third foot, as well as in the feminine cæsura of that foot, we find something of the same freedom as at the end of a verse. This appears in such lines as *A*.—

153. δεῦρο μαχησόμενος, ἐπεὶ οὔ τί μοι αἴτιοί εἰσιν.

where *ος*, the last syallable of *μαχησόμενος*, stands in the third arsis before *ἐπεί*, which certainly did not begin with digamma.

The other remark relates to the negative evidence, that which goes to disprove a digamma. It is well known that, for every digammated word, even the best ascertained, there is some evidence of this character: there are some passages in the poems as we have them, in which the digamma cannot be written without violating the metre. It is obviously desirable that we should have some idea as to the range of these exceptional cases, their numerical ratio to the whole number of passages in which the word occurs. On this subject there are some good remarks in Kuhn's Zeitschrift, x. 60 ff., in an article by H. L. Ahrens on *ἕκαστος*, one of the words which Bekker has digammated. Ahrens enumerates all the instances, 110 in number, where this word occurs in the Iliad, and states that there are 44 of these in which the digamma could not be written into the traditional text without a violation of metre. But as 16 of the 44 can be made to admit the digamma by simply dropping a movable *ν* from the preceding word, they are left out of the count, which reduces the unconformable cases to 28 in 110, or about 25 per cent. This ratio, Ahrens says, is so large as to throw discredit on the initial digamma. To prove it so, he takes the word *ἄναξ* (originally *Fάναξ*), 'king,' which he finds to occur 151 times in the Iliad. Here, setting aside, as before, the cases in which only a movable *ν* stands in the way of the digamma, he makes 11 out of 151 to be the number of unconformable cases, or about 7⅓ per cent. He then proceeds to say that as to other words which have an unquestionable digamma, as *ἔργον*, *ἰδεῖν*, *οἶκος*, *οἶνος*, etc., any one may satisfy himself by his own observation that the percentage of unconformable cases is not larger, that it is rather smaller, than for *ἄναξ*. It could not justly be inferred from these observations of Ahrens that no words had the digamma in Homer for which the unconformable cases exceed 7 or 8 per cent.; but only that in such words the digamma must be regarded as more or less doubtful, and, if the proportion is very much greater, as improbable. It is also evident that the weight to be given to this test will depend somewhat on the absolute number of instances in which a word is found. If the word occurs but seldom, the ratio of conformable and unconformable cases may be in a measure accidental; but the influence of accident diminishes as the numbers we are dealing with increase.

We come now to some criticism of particular words, as written by Bekker with or without digamma. All the words which have been generally agreed upon as showing evidence of this initial receive it here. The list of digammated words given in my Grammar (23 D) was not designed to be complete, but only to include the most important roots in which traces of the consonant-initial have been generally recognized. It contains about 33 distinct roots; and in all these, without exception, Bekker has admitted the digamma. Besides these, he admits it in some 20 or 30 more, for I have not been able yet to make out an exact list. In many of these additional words, the real existence of the digamma is beyond all reasonable doubt. This is true, for instance, of ἔτος, 'year,' which connects itself naturally with Skt. *vatsara*, 'year,' Lat. *vetus*, 'old' (*i.e.* 'full of years, *annosus*'). Out of 19 Homeric passages which show the word, only two resist the introduction of the consonant, and these allow it if we only re-insert an elided vowel: thus, τοσσαῦτ' ἔτεα (*B*. 328) may be changed to τοσσαῦτα ϝέτεα, πόλλ' ἔτεα (*Υ*. 255) to πολλὰ ϝέτεα, the last two vowels of ϝέτεα being taken as one syllable by a frequent synizesis. But, as might have been expected, there are words written by Bekker with digamma in which there is room for doubt and for difference of opinion. A striking instance of this kind is found in the word ἕλωρ, 'prey,' which occurs 8 times, with the connected ἕλωρα and ἐλώρια, each of which occurs once (the last in *A*. 4). In three of these 10 passages (*P*. 667, *A*. 4, *E*. 684) there is a hiatus before the word, but it is at the feminine cæsura of the third foot, where hiatus has scarcely any weight in proving an initial consonant. In 5 passages (*E*. 488, *P*. 151, γ. 271, ε. 473, ω. 292), a ν movable precedes, which neither hinders us from assuming digamma, nor furnishes any proof of its existence. The remaining two passages give evidence of an initial vowel. In one, Πατρόκλοιο δ' ἕλωρα (*Σ*. 93), the ε of δέ is elided before *ἕλωρα*: in the other, *μή πώς μοι ἕλωρ* (*v.* 208), the diphthong of *μοι* is made short. In the first case, Bekker gets rid of the difficulty by reading *Πατρόκλου δὲ ϝέλωρα*; in the second, he yields to the difficulty, and writes *ἕλωρ* without digamma. We cannot here lay much stress on the proportion (20 per cent.) of unconformable passages, the whole number being so small. But as digamma is not required in any single passage of the 10, and is excluded by 2, it is certainly hazardous to assume it without other proof of its existence. Such proof one might perhaps find in its derivation. It is natural to take it from the root which appears in the second aorist of *αἱρέω*, infin. *ἑλεῖν*, indic. *εἷλον*, where the augment affords evidence of an original consonant initial. If *εἷλον* is for *εϝελον*, *ἑλεῖν* for *ϝελειν*, we might connect them with Latin *vello*, 'to pluck.' But the 2d aor. of *αἱρέω* is never written with digamma by Bekker, and it is quite clear that it was not digammated in the Homeric language. It furnishes, therefore, a very feeble presumption for the digamma of the substantives; and we cannot but conclude that it would have been the safer and wiser course to leave the substantives also without digamma.

Another word in which we must question the propriety of the digamma that Bekker gives it is the deponent verb *ἐρύομαι*, 'to watch, guard, preserve.' This verb, in many of its forms, is apparently identical with *ἐρύω*, 'to draw;' and it has been assumed almost universally that they come from the same root. Buttmann in his Lexilogus argues the question at length, maintaining their essential identity. Apart from the indications of a digamma, there are other reasons for separating the two verbs. Thus, as to form, *ἐρύω*, 'to draw,' shows *ει* only where it would arise from augment or reduplication; while *ἐρύομαι*, 'to guard,' shows *εἰρύσσονται* in the future, *εἰρύσσασθαι* in the aorist infinitive, and other like forms. Again, *ἐρύομαι*, 'to guard,' is sometimes inflected according to the *μι*-form, as in *ἔρυτο, εἴρυντο*, etc., which is never the case with *ἐρύω*, 'to draw.' And yet again, with *ἐρύομαι*, 'to guard,' there is a verb *ῥύομαι*, with initial *ρ*, which has the same meaning: with *ἐρύω*, 'to draw,' there is no such side-form. Of these points of difference, Buttmann does not notice the first two: as to the last, he says with much force that the substantive ῥυτήρ, 'pole of a wagon (drawer)' gives proof of a verb ῥύω=ἐρύω, 'to draw.' If we turn from the form to consider the meaning of these verbs, we find something of a step from 'drawing' to 'watching.' Buttmann, however, bridges over the gulf: from 'drawing to one's self' (the proper sense of the middle form) comes the idea of 'rescuing;' from 'rescuing' that of 'guarding:' from 'guarding' that of 'watching' and even of 'watching against.' The development is certainly possible, and, if it stopped at the point of 'rescuing,' we might regard it as probable: but from 'rescuing' to 'watching against, watching to injure,' there is still a long journey, which we cannot assume without hesitation. But these reasons for separating the words gain almost irresistible confirmation from a circumstance which Buttmann has not noticed—viz., that the indications of the Homeric verse show very clearly that ἐρύω, 'to draw,' began with a consonant, and almost as clearly that ἐρύομαι, 'to guard,' began with a vowel. I have collected the Homeric passages which show middle forms of ἐρύω, 'to draw:' I find 60 in all, many of which give strong proof of an initial consonant, while only 3 (*i. e.* 5 per cent. of the whole number) oppose its introduction. Of the deponent ἐρύομαι I find 43 instances in all, among which 23, or more than half, resist the introduction of a digamma. Forms which begin with ε followed by ρρ I of course do not reckon, as they obviously belong to ῥύομαι, not ἐρύομαι. It might be said, however, that some forms in which ε is followed by single ρ, such as ἔρυτο, 'was guarding,' ἐρύσσατο, 'guarded,' could also be taken from ῥύομαι, the ρ being left single after the augment, as often happens in the aorist of ῥέζω, 'to do.' Assuming this, we shall have in all 29 instances of ἐρύομαι, of which 12, or more than 40 per cent., will resist the introduction of digamma. Again, it might be said that such a form as εἰρύσσατο is to be explained from εϝερυσσατο, by omission of digamma and contraction of the vowels, so that we could not expect to see in εἰρύσσατο the digamma which belongs to the verb-root. If we admit the justice of this reasoning, we shall still further reduce the number of instances to be considered, bringing them down to 19; of which, however,

9, or nearly half, will still oppose the digamma. It is possible that two or three of the cases which I have regarded as middle forms of ἐρύω might be assigned to ἐρύομαι in the sense of 'rescuing;' but if we should transfer them accordingly, this would not materially affect the numerical relations just exhibited. Observe, then, that in the middle of ἐρύω only one twentieth of the instances resist the insertion of digamma, while in ἐρύομαι, 'to guard,' nearly or quite half of them resist it. This is a very great difference, and cannot possibly be imputed to accident. I hold, therefore, that Ahrens is fully justified in separating the two words, as he has done in his Grammar of 1852; and I regard as highly probable his conjecture that ἐρύομαι began originally with σ (compare the Greek ἁ conjunctive, which was originally *sa*), and that it is connected with Latin *servo*. The primitive sense may have been that of 'watching,' which we see in the compound *observo*, and from which we readily derive the ideas of 'guarding' and 'preserving.' But whether it once began with σ or not, we must in any case disapprove the procedure of Bekker in writing it, wherever he can, with digamma. There are in fact only 4 places out of more than 40 which give any sign of an initial consonant. Two of these are in the 23d book of the Odyssey (82, 229), which has in it much that is peculiar, while the others are in a line that occurs twice (ι. 194, κ. 444):—

αὐτοῦ πὰρ νηΐ τε μένειν καὶ νῆα ἔρυσθαι.

This shows another metrical irregularity, the short ι of νηΐ being used for a long syllable. Apparently it is only a variation of the perfectly regular verse—

αὐτοῦ πὰρ νήεσσι μένειν καὶ νῆας ἔρυσθαι (ξ. 260, ρ. 429).

the two plurals being changed to singulars, with little regard to metrical exactness.

In speaking of ἐρύομαι, I have touched incidentally upon the question whether digamma should be prefixed to the augmented forms of digammate verbs. Wherever the augment makes a syllable by itself, Bekker, no doubt with correctness, writes the digamma after it: thus ἐϝάγη, 'was broken,' from ϝάγνυμι; ἐϝάλη, 'was pressed,' from ϝείλω; ἔϝειπον, 'I said,' tense-stem ϝειπ, from ϝεϝεπ. But when the augment coalesces with the root in the same syllable, he places digamma at the beginning, and of course before the augment: thus he writes ϝεῖδον, 'I saw,' originally εϝιδον; ϝήνασσε, 'was ruling,' originally εϝανασσε; ϝήνδανε, 'was pleasing,' originally εϝανδανε. Now the temporal augment of ἤνασσε must either have come from a stem which had already lost the digamma, or it must have arisen from a stem with digamma, by dropping that consonant between ε and α, with contraction of these vowels. In either case, the augmented form should be without digamma, which could only appear by what must be regarded as an improbable transposition: εϝανασσε, ϝεανασσε, ϝήνασσε; εϝιδον, ϝεϊδον, ϝεῖδον. It is, at any rate, a transposition which we should not accept without clear indications in the Homeric verse. I must own that I have not looked up the evidence myself on this point. But a writer in Jahn's *Jahrbücher* (lxxxi. 681), Heinrich Rumpf, professes to have done so. He says, at least, that he has looked at all the 2d aorist forms of the root ιδ which by the augment begin with ει, also at the forms of ἀνάσσω, ἁνδάνω, and ἄγνυμι, which by the augment begin with η. The number of these, taken together, would be about 60, and there are 6 of them (ψ. 392, γ. 305, ι. 182, κ. 373, λ. 162, τ. 539) which resist an initial digamma. The proportion here is not decisive. But it is more important that he finds not a single case which requires digamma, and only one which on Bekker's principles can be regarded as yielding it any particular support. We must conclude, then, that there is no sufficient warrant for Bekker's writing of these forms.

In this connection I may speak of the form ἤϊκτο, a pluperfect middle of the stem ικ or εικ. It occurs four times in the Odyssey in the expression δέμας δ' ἤϊκτο γυναικί, which does not allow an initial digamma. Ἤϊκτο is most naturally explained as being equivalent to εϝεϝικτο, the first ε being the augment of the pluperfect, which after the loss of digamma is contracted with the ε of the reduplication: εϝεϝικτο, εεϊκτο, ἤϊκτο, like εϝανασσε, εανασσε, ἤνασσε. Now it is remarkable that the form ἔϊκτο, with ε instead of η, occurs once, in ψ. 107—καί μοι ἕκαστ' ἐπέτελλεν· ἔϊκτο δὲ θέσκελον αὐτῷ. This form is naturally explained as being for ϝεϝικτο, with the reduplication, but without the augment, of the pluperfect. It will be seen that the passage allows, though it does not require, an initial digamma. Bekker writes it without; in our judgment he should have inserted it: thus, καί μοι ἕκαστ' ἐπέτελλε· ϝέϝικτο δὲ θέσκελον αὐτῷ.

If we have complained of Bekker for prefixing digamma to the augmented forms of digammate verbs, we have to complain of him for omitting digamma in some instances from their reduplicated forms. The word just mentioned, in which he writes ἔϝικτο, not ϝέϝικτο, is a case in point. Another is seen in χ. 348:—

παντοίας ἐνέφυσεν· ἔϝοικα δέ τοι παραείδειν.

On first looking at this, I thought that perhaps the pause (colon) before ἔοικα might have had something to do with Bekker's retention of the preceding ν movable. But I found afterwards a passage (*I.* 70), which in this respect is exactly similar, but is differently treated by Bekker:—

δαίνυ δαῖτα γέρουσι· ϝέϝοικέ τοι, οὔ τοι ἀϝεικές.

This inconsistency, I suspect, must be the result of inadvertence. In all other cases, so far as I have observed, Bekker writes the perfect and pluperfect active of this verb with digamma, where the verse allows it. The number of instances is very large—125, if I have counted right—and the unconformable cases only 10, or about 8 per cent. The perfect of ἁνδάνω (root ϝαδ) occurs but twice (*I.* 173, σ. 422). Bekker both times writes πᾶσιν ἑϝαδότα. We hold that he should have written πᾶσι ϝεϝαδότα: the presumption is that the digamma was regularly repeated in the reduplication, as Bekker gives it in ϝέϝοικα. The perfect middle of εἴλω (root ϝελ) occurs four times, twice after ν movable, and twice after a hiatus, which however is at the feminine cæsura of the third root. Bekker everywhere writes ἐϝέλμεθα, ἐϝελμένος: we hold, as before, that he should have written ϝεϝέλμεθα, ϝεϝελμένος. The next case to be considered—that of ἔλπομαι (root ϝελπ), 'to hope'—is attended with more difficulty. The perfect *ἔολπα* and pluperfect *ἐώλπειν* occur twelve times in all: 3 times with hiatus, 4 times with *ν* movable before them: therefore 7 times where digamma is admissible; leaving 5 cases which resist it. This large proportion of unconformable cases might make us doubt whether we ought to recognize digamma at all in these forms. But the ϝ of the root is unquestionable, and gives a strong presumption for ϝ in the reduplication. And besides, the three cases of hiatus occur in a part of the verse (at fem. cæs. of 2d foot) where hiatus is inadmissible. We hold, therefore, that there is sufficient evidence of Homeric *ϝέϝολπα* and *ϝεϝώλπειν* (or *ϝεϝόλπειν*), and that these forms should have been given, according to Bekker's principle, wherever the verse allows them. He has in fact given them only in the 3 cases of hiatus, while in the 4 of *ν* movable he retains that letter, and writes *ἔϝολπα, ἐϝώλπειν*; thus contravening both his general method and his procedure in the parallel case of *ἔοικα, ἐῴκειν*. In *ἔοργα, ἐώργειν*, we find very much the same state of things—12 passages in all, of which 5 resist digamma. The *ν* movable, however, occurs here in only one case (ξ. 289):—

τρώκτης, ὃς δὴ πολλὰ κάκ' ἀνθρώποισιν ἐώργει.

Here, from the analogy of his procedure in reference to *ἐώλπειν*, we may presume that Bekker would have written *ἀνθρώποισιν ἐϝώργειν*, if he had not followed Voss in making a greater change, altering the dative to an accusative, in accordance with the usual construction of the verb, making *ἀνθρώπους εἰϝώργειν*. It might be questioned, however, whether we ought not in this case to have *ἠϝόργειν* for *εϝεϝοργειν*, in the same manner as *ἤϝικτο* for *εϝεϝικτο*. In the perfect middle of *ἔργω* (root *ϝεργ*), 'to shut,' we find a different state of things. Here we have *ἔρχαται* and *ἔρχατο* occurring 7 times. They are evidently forms without reduplication, like *οἶδα*, 'I know' (*i. e. ϝοῖδα*, not *ϝεϝοιδα*), *εἶμαι*, 'am clothed' (*i. e. ϝεσμαι*, not *ϝεϝεσμαι*); and, in stems beginning with other letters, *δέχαται*, 'have received' (for *δεδέχαται*), *ἄνωγα*, 'I command' (for *ἤνωγα*). Hence, when we find *ἐεργμέναι* and *ἐέρχατο* occurring each of them once, we must presume that the first ε is not part of a reduplication, but the same common prefix which we find, for instance, in ἐέλδομαι (*i. e.* εϝελδομαι) for ϝέλδομαι, 'to wish,' and the aorist participle ἐεισάμενος (*i. e.* εϝεισαμενος), 'having likened one's-self.' We shall not then be surprised to see that ἐϝεργμέναι and ἐϝέρχατο do not admit initial digamma.

We come now to consider the question whether our editor does right in recognizing only one lost consonant, the digamma, or whether he should not have recognized others as producing similar appearances in the Homeric verse. Curtius, in the concluding part of his Principles of Greek Etymology, maintains in the case of several words that the epic hiatus was occasioned by a consonant *y*-sound. He holds this to be true in reference to ἔοικα, ἐῴκειν, which we have just considered. He remarks that dialects and inscriptions give no evidence of digamma in this word; that no root *vik* in the sense of 'likeness' is to be found in the cognate languages; and that it is therefore very hazardous to write ϝέϝοικα, ϝεϝῴκειν, in the text of Homer. He observes that there are clear traces in Herodotus and elsewhere of a word δείκηλος or δείκελος having the sense of (ε)ἴκελος, 'like, similar.' He is therefore led to adopt the conjecture of Bopp, that the root of ἔοικα is formed from that of δείκνυμι, Lat. *dico*, Skt. *diç* (*i. e. dik*), 'to show.' He conceives that the δ assumed a parasitic *y*, and then dropped away itself—thus, *dik*, *dyik*, *yik*—and that from *yik* thus formed came by reduplication *y*ε*y*οικα, *y*ε*y*ῳκειν. I cannot think that there is much plausibility in this explanation. If the transition from *dik* to *yik* was made in the formative Indo-European period, we might expect to find a root *yik* having the sense of 'likeness' somewhere in the cognate languages, which Curtius does not pretend is the fact. It is evident, indeed, that he regards the evolution of *yik* from *dik* as taking place in the Greek, after the Indo-European time. We must think, then, of the root *dik* as already provided with inflection, making a reduplicated preterite δεδοικα, from which would come first, by adding *y* to both δ's, δ*y*εδ*y*οικα, and then, by dropping both the δ's, *y*ε*y*οικα. But the change from δ to *y* is confessedly a rare one in the Greek language; how hazardous then to assume that it has occurred twice in the same form! It might perhaps be said that the change occurred first in some such form as δικελος, meaning 'like,' which passed into *y*ικελος; that this gave the suggestion of a root *y*ικ, meaning 'to be like,' and that *y*ε*y*οικα was formed independently from this suggested root, and not by phonetic change from a pre-existing δεδοικα. This is indeed possible: but we should scarcely expect that a root arising at this comparatively late stage of linguistic development would take the more primitive formation seen in ἔοικα, with its interchange of ικ, εικ, οικ. For such reasons, the rise of ἔοικα from a root *dik* seems to me scarcely more than a possibility. It must be observed, too, that unless the connection of ἔοικα with a root *dik* is rendered probable, there is no more reason for writing it with *y* than with ϝ. And if no more reason, we may justly say that there is less reason for *y* than for ϝ, because the very regularity with which this word in the Homeric text gives evidence of a consonant initial is a circumstance in favor of ϝ. In this respect it ranks, as we have seen, among the most regular words, the unconformable cases being only 10 in 126, or about 8 per cent. If we consider how much earlier and more complete was the disappearance of *y* from the language when compared with that of ϝ, we shall be slow to believe that the former should maintain itself in the Homeric verse with the same constancy as the latter.

Another case in which Curtius recognizes traces of an initial *y* in Homer is the deponent ἵεμαι, 'to be eager, to desire, to long.' It occurs in 61 instances, of which 22 by hiatus give evidence of a consonant initial, and the unconformable cases are only 3, or about 5 per cent. Bekker writes it with digamma. To this Curtius objects, asserting that the verb ἵημι is a reduplicated form of the root *yâ*, which appears in Sanskrit, and is itself an extended form of the root *i*, 'to go.' Thus ἵημι=*yi-yâ-mi*, 'to cause to go, to send.' In the middle this would mean 'to send one's self,' and hence 'to hasten, to pursue eagerly, to aim at, to long for.' To this no objection can be made as regards the meaning. But it is a remarkable circumstance that ἵημι, 'to send,' shows no traces in Homer of anything but a vowel initial. Of simple forms in the present and imperfect—these I take for comparison because ἵεμαι, 'to desire,' is confined to those tenses—I find in the sense of 'sending' 29 (all active except *Δ*. 77, *M*. 274, χ. 304, which show the middle or passive); and of this 29, not less than 24, or more than 80 per cent., refuse to admit a consonant initial. Compound forms, such as ἀφίημι, μεθίημι, etc., I have not taken into the account: I believe, however, that all of them which are capable of furnishing any evidence on the point testify against a consonant initial for the simple verb. It may be regarded as perfectly certain that ἵημι, 'to send,' was sounded by Homer with an initial vowel, and ἵεμαι, 'to desire,' with an initial consonant. We have here a distinction of the same kind as that which we before proved to exist between ἐρύω, 'to draw,' and ἐρύομαι, 'to guard.' Now it might be said by one who maintained the original identity of ἵημι, 'to send,' and ἵεμαι, 'to desire,' that the *y* which once belonged to both alike was retained, and that with uniformity, in the sense of 'desiring,' after it had been lost, and that with uniformity, in the sense of 'sending.' That this is a possibility we admit, but it is nothing more. The probability is that the two words are radically distinct; and if so, then, for the same reason as before, the ϝ has more in its favor than the *y*. The fact that later dialects furnish no support to it is of little significance, as the deponent ἵεμαι belongs only to the early language.

The remaining case in which Curtius recognizes initial *y* as exercising the power of a consonant in the Homeric verse is the relative stem, which appears in ὅς, ἥ, ὅ, ὡς, οἷος, ὅσος, ὅπως, ὁποῖος, ὄφρα, ἦμος, ἵνα, ἕως, etc. Savelsberg, in the eighth volume of Kuhn's Zeitschrift, has given a series of citations from Homer showing traces of an initial consonant for this class of words. Unfortunately he has not furnished exact numerical data, by which we might see the comparative frequency or infrequency of the phenomenon. I have not myself had time to supply the deficiency. I have only run hastily through the first book of the Iliad, noting all words which show the relative stem—omitting, however, the relative adverb ὡς, which in this respect stands by itself. The whole number of instances noted was 72, of which 30, or about 42 per cent., testify against a consonant initial. Of the remaining instances, many were found at the beginning of a line, or in other indecisive positions; and in fact there are only 8, or one ninth of the whole number, which give any indication of a consonant initial. Even of these, the majority, either from the part of the verse which they occupy, or from the pause which precedes them, are of but little weight: only 2 or 3 give decided indications of an initial consonant. I strongly suspect that a more extended comparison would not essentially change the proportions derived from this first book. They seem barely sufficient to give plausibility to the conjecture that the relative stem did once begin with a consonant, but had nearly or quite lost it in the Homeric time. I say "nearly or *quite*:" for if the letter had wholly died out from common use shortly before Homer's time, the force of epic tradition would probably have caused some traces of it still to appear in his verse. But the adverb ὥς differs in this respect very remarkably from the other forms of the relative stem. According to Bekker, as cited by Curtius, the instances which indicate a consonant initial are three times more numerous than those which indicate a vowel initial. It can hardly be doubted that this word, as pronounced in the Homeric time, began frequently, if not generally, with a consonant.

It must be owned that our condition as regards the etymology of the Greek relative is an unsatisfactory one. We are less confident and comfortable than we were ten years ago. Then we had no hesitation about connecting it with the Skt. *yas*, *yâ*, *yat*, assuming a change of *y* to the rough breathing, as in ἧπαρ (*i. e.* ἥπαρτ), 'liver,' Skt. *yakṛt* (*i. e. yakart*). But now, if we do not surrender this conviction, our faith in it has become less full and sure. A Locrian inscription, published by L. Ross in 1854, presents the form **ϜOTI**, with digamma, for ὅτι. A digammated form of the relative stem is also seen in a gloss of Hesychius, quoted by Savelsberg: **Βαλικιώτης**, συνέφηβος, **Κρῆτες**—*i.e.* 'for "youthful companion" the Cretans use βαλικιώτης,' (*i.e.* ϝαλικιώτης, equivalent to ἡλικιώτης). To these testimonies, Savelsberg, in the article referred to, adds the indications of digamma in the Homeric verse, and concludes that the Greek relative was ϝός, ϝή, ϝό, or ϝός, ϝᾱ́, ϝότ. These he supposes to have been later forms of κϝος, κϝᾱ, κϝοτ, Latin *qui, quae, quod.* He thus identifies again the Greek and Latin relatives, though in a very different way from that of the old-fashioned etymology, which held that the original *h* of the Greek relative was in Latin hardened to a *k*-sound (*qu*). The omission of the *k*-sound in the Greek ϝός would be something like that in the Latin *ubi, unde,* for *cubi, cunde,* which remain in the compounds *sicubi, alicunde.* The stem *kva,* which would thus underlie the relatives of these two languages, Savelsberg supposes to have been developed out of *ka,* the stem of the Sanskrit interrogative. He goes yet further, and from the same origin derives even the Sanskrit relative: *ya,* he thinks, is for *kya;* and *kya,* like *kva,* is only an altered form of *ka.* But Schleicher and Curtius are not yet prepared to admit that the Greek relative-stem began with digamma, still less that it was ever *kva.* The former touches on the subject in his Compendium of Comparative Grammar, p. 180: the latter, more at length, in his Principles of Greek Etymology, ii. 177–8. In respect to the ***FOTI*** of the Locrian inscription, they say that, when the digamma-sound had nearly vanished from the Greek dialects, its sign was sometimes used improperly by scribes or grammarians for other spirants, and especially for the *y,* which had no sign of its own even in the earliest Greek alphabet; and they appeal to a Corcyræan inscription, which shows a genitive singular masculine of the first declension in *-AFO,* where all analogy would lead us to expect *-ayo* or *-ahyo,* Skt. *asya.* As regards the Homeric usage, they say that the phenomena which seem to indicate digamma could equally well be produced by *y.* In this there is no intrinsic improbability, though we should be glad to have the support of some parallel case which we could look upon as clear and certain. The parallels which Curtius brings forward are the verb ἵεμαι, 'to aim at, desire,' and the root of ἔοικα; neither of which, as we have seen, is much to be relied on. As to the derivation of a relative ϝος from κϝος by omission of κ, Curtius remarks that "the only phonetic analogy which could be called in to support it is that of the High

German *wer* (for *hwer*)=Gothic *hvas*, cf. Eng. *what.* But the loss of the feeble *h* proves little for that of *k;* and how improbable that of the two consonants the Greek would give up the perfectly familiar κ in favor of the unstable digamma, wavering even from the earliest time!" It may be observed, in passing, that Curtius' own derivation of ἔοικα from *dik, dyik, yik* is liable to the same objection: it makes the Greek give up the familiar δ in favor of the unstable and perishing *y.* "Still less," he continues, "can it be proved that Skt. *yas* has come from *kyas*, and that *ka*, with the secondary *kva, kya*, is the common root of all these widely ramified pronouns. Finally, the demonstrative meaning of the Greek ὅς in καὶ ὅς ἔφη speaks against this derivation, and recommends the assumption that the originally demonstrative stem *i*, with the secondary form *ya*, lies at the basis of the Greek relative." As the demonstrative use in καὶ ὃς ἔφη is confined to the nominative, while in the accusative we have καὶ τόν, it seems to me quite possible that the ὅς is for ὁ, by confusion of the two forms ὅς and ὁ, so much alike in appearance, though so diverse in origin. Curtius then adds, as Schleicher also does, that, if the Greek relative did really begin with ϝ, it would be preferable to explain it from a stem *sva*, which appears with relative force in Gothic *sve*, 'as,' whence the German *so* in its relative use. This relative stem *sva* was long ago recognized in Greek by Curtius himself (Kuhn's Zeitschrift, iii. 75, 76), though only in the merest relic, the adverb φή, 'as,' which the Alexandrine critic Zenodotus read in two passages of the Iliad (**B**. 144, **Ξ**. 499). Lottner afterwards, in Kuhn's Zeitschrift, ix. 320, proposed to derive all the forms of the Greek relative from this same stem. But the traces of a digamma in the Greek relative are much less frequent and decided than we should naturally expect to find them if this were its real derivation—much less so than in the forms of the possessive ὅς, ἥ, ὅν, 'his, her, its,' which come from a stem of the same sound, *sva*, though of widely different import. Possibly the fact which we have noticed, that the adverb ὥς differs so much from the other forms of the relative in the indications which it shows of a consonant initial, may warrant the conjecture that they are of different origin—that, in fact, ὡς came from the digammate stem *sva*, while ὅς, οἷος, ὅσος, and the rest, are akin to the Sanskrit *yas*, *yâ*, *yat*, and came from a stem with initial *y*-sound.

Ahrens, in Kuhn's Zeitschrift, x. 65 ff., has sought to show that appearances in the Homeric verse similar to those produced by digamma are in some instances to be ascribed to a lost sigma. An instance of this kind—in which, however, the initial σ is not lost, but retained in the written text—is presented by the word ὗς, 'hog.' The simple form of this word appears in 55 passages with initial σ, as σῦς, συός, etc. It occurs also in 21 passages where an initial consonant would be incompatible with the metre; and in all these places the σ is dropped; we have ὗς, ὑός, etc. In the later language, both forms of this word were in use, though the one with consonant initial was comparatively rare. If, when the poems were reduced to writing, the form with σ had been wholly lost from use, it is probable that our written text would have shown ὗς only, with initial vowel, in all the 76 passages, though in many of them the metre would have shown traces of a lost consonant. And it is quite conceivable that in other words this may actually have been the case. Such an occurrence Ahrens recognizes with no little plausibility in the words ὕλη, 'wood,' ἑός possessive, and ἕκαστος, 'each.' In regard to ὕλη, Lat. *silva*, it is certain that it began originally with σ, and equally certain that in Homer's language it usually began with a vowel. But there are two cases of a remarkable hiatus before the word (σείετο ὕλη, Ξ. 285, and ἐπεχεύατο ὕλην, ε 257, where ὕλη in each forms the sixth foot), which seem to show that the initial σ was not wholly forgotten in the Homeric time. The possessive ἑός, in its relation to ὅς, is explained by Ahrens in a way which has been quite generally received as probable. He assumes in the earlier period two forms, a fuller σεϝός, and a shorter σϝός: from σεϝός came regularly the ἑός, from σϝός the ὅς of our common text. This explanation is supported by the analogy of the possessive forms τεός and σός for the second person; of which, in all probability, τεός is for τεϝός, and σός for τϝός. Now in 92 instances of the pronoun ἑός, there are 52 which do not allow an initial consonant, and it is therefore certain that in the

Homeric time it generally began with a vowel. But there are 4 instances (*Α*. 533, *Ι*. 420, 687, *θ*. 524) of remarkable hiatus in the first foot, after the first short of a dactyl (Ζεὺς δὲ ἑόν, χεῖρα ἑήν, ὅςτε ἑῆς), which seem to present traces of the primitive initial σ. And moreover, this word makes hiatus 14 times in the feminine cæsura. We have seen that hiatus is readily allowed in that place; but its relative frequency is so great in the case of this word (three times greater than in the analogous case of ἐμός, 'my') as to warrant the suspicion that it arises from a peculiar cause, and is connected with the primitive initial σ. Bekker writes the pronoun, wherever he can, with initial ϝ: he appears to suppose that from ϝός came ἐϝός by a prefixed ε, and then, by transposition of digamma, ϝεός. But such a transposition is a more hazardous assumption than he seems to think; and the form ϝεός has little support, either in the Homeric text or in the suggestions of comparative philology.

It remains to speak of the pronoun ἕκαστος, 'each,' and the kindred adverb ἑκάτερθε, 'on each side:' the pronoun ἑκάτερος itself is incapable of appearing in the heroic hexameter. The derivation of ἑκάτερος and ἕκαστος is as yet far from certain. It is probable, however, that the -κατερος and -καστος are a comparative and superlative form from the interrogative stem κα—that they are, in fact, identical with the interrogatives πότερος and πόστος, which in their Ionic forms are κότερος and κόστος. It is probable also that the first syllable ἑ is the same as in the numeral ἑκατόν, Lat. *centum*, Skt. *çatam* (*i. e. katam*). If so, it is probably for ἕν, the root of the numeral εἷς, 'one:' thus, ἑκατόν='ONE hundred,' ἑκάτερος ='ONE which-more, one which of two.' Here now we stumble again upon an uncertainty: but of all the explanations proposed for the numeral εἷς, ἕν, the most probable is that which connects it with Skt. *sama*, our Eng. *same*, Lat. *semel*, *simplex*, *singuli*. It thus appears that σ may probably have been the primitive initial of ἑκάτερος, ἕκαστος. We have already observed that, according to Ahrens's enumeration, ἕκαστος occurs 110 times in the Iliad. Now 66 of these are cases of hiatus, some of them easily admissible, but many others giving strong indication of a consonant initial. It is not therefore surprising that Bekker should have written *ϝέκαστος* and *ϝεκάτερθε* wherever the verse allows it. Out of 28 unconformable cases, he makes 17 conformable by various conjectures, several of which belong to the most hazardous that he has ventured. In 11 cases he has left the initial vowel untouched. Here the proportion of unconformable cases, 25 per cent., throws suspicion on the digamma, which is much increased by the fact that comparative philology has no plausible explanation for the forms *ϝεκάτερος*, *ϝέκαστος*. Such forms as *σεκάτερος* and *σέκαστος* are much more probable on grounds of comparative philology. Practically, then, the case as to *ἕκαστος* stands in this way. It cannot well be doubted that the word, sometimes at least, began with a consonant in the Homeric language. If we assume that digamma is the only initial consonant of the Homeric language which has failed to appear in our text, then we must recognize a Homeric *ϝέκαστος*: such, doubtless, was the reasoning of Bekker. But the assumption is an unsafe one: there is reason for suspecting that other initial consonants of the Homeric language have had, though to a far less extent, the same fortune as digamma; and in this particular word there is reason for suspecting that it began with some other consonant. Yet we would by no means advise either that the relative-stem should be written in Homer with initial *y*, or that *ἕκαστος* and *ἑός* should be written with initial *σ*. A lost digamma manifests itself in the Homeric verse in many words with much clearness, and with considerable approach to uniformity: it may therefore with propriety be inserted in an edition having the character and aims of the one under review. But the case is widely different with a lost *y* and a lost *σ*: these, if we make the most of them, are only rare and doubtful.

V.

ON ANCIENT GREEK RHYTHM AND METRE.

1864.

RHYTHM consists in a regular succession of times—of proportional times—so marked off and distinguished that the proportionality of the times and the regularity of their succession shall be obvious to human sense. These times may be marked by movements of the body, as in dancing; by tones of various pitch and stress, as in music; by the syllables of uttered words, as in poetry. We have here the three principal applications of rhythm, three principal domains in which rhythm manifests its nature and power—dancing, music, poetry. They were recognized as such by ancient writers, as arts which are all alike under the sway of rhythm, in which the same principles of rhythm find application and illustration. These principles do not require words for their manifestation; they do not require even sounds: the silent art of orchestic has its arses and theses, its trochees and iambi, its dactyls and anapæsts, not less truly than music and poetry. In fact, the name *feet* for rhythmic elements, *arsis* (raising of the foot), *thesis* (setting down of the foot), have primary reference to orchestic. It is apparent from these remarks that rhythm may be treated in two different ways. Its principles may be set forth in a general, abstract manner: not without illustrations drawn from the concrete forms of dancing, music, or poetry; but in such a way as to give prominence to those abstract, general principles which pertain alike to these three arts. The subject thus treated is a true and proper rhythmic. But, on the other hand, a writer may take up one of the arts in which rhythm manifests itself, making it his leading aim to set forth the forms of that art as they have been developed under the influence of rhythm. If poetry, for instance, is subjected to this process, the result will be a system of metric. Metric is a description, a scientific description, of verse according to its rhythmical forms. Ancient literature had its works both of rhythmic and of metric, agreeably to the distinction which we have here traced. Those on metric were the more numerous, and have been more largely preserved. The most important is the *'Εγχειρίδιον*, or Manual, of Hephæstion, a grammarian who is supposed to have flourished about the middle of the second century after our era. Unfortunately these metrical writers had only an imperfect conception of the work which they were taking on themselves. In treating of metric, it was their business to point out in a systematic way everything pertaining to the rhythmic enunciation or delivery of verse; so that from a study of their writings one might form a distinct conception of the way in which an ode of Pindar or a chorus of Sophocles was actually intended to sound—I mean, as regards its rhythm. To do this it was not enough to note the succession of long and short syllables. It was necessary to mark also the rhythmic accent, and to distinguish a heavier accent from a lighter. It was necessary to note the cases in which rhythmic times were occupied by a prolongation of long syllables; for we know that these were sometimes so far prolonged as to become equal to three shorts, four shorts, or even five shorts. It was necessary to note the cases in which rhythmic times were occupied by pauses—intervals of silence, like the rests in music—for we know that such pauses were frequent, taking the time of one short, two shorts, three shorts, or even four shorts. It was necessary in treating of lyric compositions, such as Pindar's Odes, or the choruses of the dramatists, in which the verse changes from line to line, to point out the principles of symmetry and the laws of succession by which these changes were doubtless regulated and controlled: for we have the strongest reason to believe that here, as everywhere else, the Greeks exercised their prodigious power of invention in subordination to very definite canons of taste and beauty. Now of all this we find very little in the ancient writers on metric. They confine themselves, for the most part, to noting the succession of long and short syllables. It is true that they have something to say—though in a quite imperfect and unsatisfactory manner—on rhythmic accent, on thesis and arsis, the accented and unaccented parts of the foot. But beyond this they scarcely go. I may illustrate their deficiencies by a single instance. It is a fact that there were spondees in which each syllable had the length—not of two shorts, as usual—but of four. It is a fact known to us from other sources; but in the writings on metric now extant there is no hint of it whatever. This imperfection in the works on metric is not hard to account for. Their writers were mere grammarians: they were much interested in syllables, and their long and short quantity—but they had not the theoretical and practical knowledge of music which was indispensable to the proper execution of their task. I say that a theoretical and practical acquaintance with music was essential to a proper treatment of the ancient metric. It is a very important circumstance, and one that should never be lost sight of, that the ancient poetry was much more closely bound up with music than the modern. Even the simplest kinds of verse, the epic hexameter, the dramatic trimeter, were pronounced—they were intended to be pronounced—in a kind of recitative, a sort of semi-musical utterance, with musical accompaniment. But lyric compositions, such as the odes of Simonides and Timotheus, the choruses of Æschylus and Euripides, were designed to be sung. The poet was a musician also; his contemporaries were accustomed to think and speak of him as not only poet but musician. His musical characteristics formed an essential part of the critical judgment passed upon him by the public for whom he labored. The great variety and complexity of the rhythms which he used depends upon the fact that they were intended to be sung. Rhythmic structures so various and complex were not fitted for reading, and would never have been produced for it. They require musical utterance for the development and appreciation of the rhythm. German translators have often overlooked this fact. Hartung endeavors to reproduce the metres of Pindar line for line in his German version. It is impossible that an attempt so difficult and constraining should not operate disadvantageously on the force, aptness, and clearness of his translation. And what is the gain? No one could give the German verses their intended rhythm without a careful and painful scrutiny of the annexed metrical scheme. And when all is done, when with much effort you can accent the heavy German lines on the right syllables, the rhythmical result is one which Pindar himself would never have regarded as legitimate or desirable.

We may take yet another instance, an extreme case, to show how the writers on metric—some of them, at least—while counting longs and shorts, could overlook the most obvious facts of rhythm. The so-called elegiac pentameter, which in the elegiac distich alternates with the dactylic hexameter, is in fact only a variety of the hexameter—a hexameter in which the third and sixth feet are reduced to a single syllable, the remaining times in those feet being made up by pauses. If we take the first line of the Iliad—*Μῆνιν ἄειδε, θεά, Πηληϊάδεω Ἀχιλῆος*—and substitute a pause for the last half of the third and the sixth feet—*Μῆνιν ἄειδε, θεά,* ° *ληϊάδεω Ἀχιλῆ* °—we have the form of the elegiac pentameter. Or take the English distich which Coleridge translated from Schiller, but unluckily forgot to mention Schiller's name in connection with it: "In the hexameter rises the fountain's silvery column, In the pentameter aye falling in melody back." Here fill out in words the pauses of the second line, "In the pentameter aye it is falling in melody downwards," and you have a hexameter line, like the one before it. Hephæstion had the grace to see this: he has given a correct description of the so-called pentameter, which recognizes its true relation to the hexameter. But there were writers who gave it a different description, who made it consist of five feet, whence the false name of pentameter—five feet, of which the first two were either dactyls or spondees, the third always a spondee, and the fourth and fifth anapæsts. Such a description answers certainly to the succession of long and short syllables in this verse; but it utterly fails to give an intelligible conception of its rhythm.

But beside the ancient writers on metric, there were others who treated of rhythmic, according to the distinction before drawn between these terms. Unfortunately the works on rhythmic seem to have been much less numerous than those on metric, and the remains of them which have come down to us are exceedingly scanty. In these, nearly everything of any value has come directly or indirectly from a single author, from Aristoxenus of Tarentum. This eminent philosopher was a pupil of Aristotle, and after the death of the master aspired to lead the school of his followers, but Theophrastus of Lesbos was preferred before him for this station. He wrote on many subjects, but especially on music and the arts connected with it. Among his works of this class was one entitled *'Ρυθμικὰ στοιχεῖα*, 'Rhythmic Elements,' in which he drew out for the first time in scientific form the principles of rhythm which were embodied in the music and poetry of his countrymen. If this work were preserved in its entireness, we should doubtless have a systematic and tolerably adequate conception of the ancient rhythms. But we have in fact only fragments—one large fragment and a number of small ones. The large fragment was found in a Vatican manuscript containing works or parts of works on musical subjects. It was first published by Morelli at Venice in 1785, and recently by Westphal in his *Fragmente und Lehrsätze der Griechischen Rhythmiker* (Leipzig, 1861). As printed by the latter, it amounts to about 270 lines: it formed the beginning of the second book in the work of Aristoxenus. Of the smaller fragments, several come from a little tract, *προλαμβανόμενα εἰς τὴν ῥυθμικὴν ἐπιστήμην*, by Michael Psellus, a Byzantine writer of the tenth century; and others from an anonymous manuscript in the Royal Library at Paris. Next in importance to these remains of Aristoxenus, but next at a great interval, is a work of Aristides Quintilianus, who seems to have been a thinker of the revived Pythagorean school, and probably lived in the century before Constantine. His work may be called an Encyclopædia of the Musical Arts. In the first of its three books he treats of Harmonic, Rhythmic, and Metric; in the second he discusses the influence of musical art upon the soul; in the third he sets forth the numeral relations which subsist among the tones of the musical scale —the numbers which express the ratios of the vibrations by which the tones are produced—and then proceeds, after the Pythagorean fashion, to show the cosmical significance of these numbers. The rhythmic, it will be seen, forms only part of one book, though the second book contains an important passage on the different ἦθος or character (pathetic, animating, terrifying, etc.) of different rhythms. But even if we include this passage, the rhythmic of Aristides, as printed in Westphal's collection just referred to, contains less than four hundred lines: it is curt and meagre, and altogether insufficient to give any satisfactory conception of the subject. In parts of this brief sketch, Aristides has relied on Aristoxenus, or perhaps on a writer who drew his materials from Aristoxenus, so that what we find here represents the Aristoxenian theory of rhythm; but in other parts he evidently follows a different, and far inferior, authority. This mixture of different authorities and views adds greatly to the difficulties which attend the interpretation of Aristides. Besides Aristoxenus and Aristides, Westphal's collection contains a few pages of fragments drawn from other sources, mostly anonymous. The student of ancient rhythmic is not oppressed by the extent of his authorities. It would be no extraordinary feat for him to commit to memory every line of the texts which he has to work upon. It is only of late that the importance of studying these texts has come to be recognized. It has been the prevailing impression of scholars that, in order to understand the rhythm of Greek poetry, it was enough for us to examine the extant remains of Greek poetry, being aided in the work by the old writers on metric, and guided at the same time by our own sense of rhythm. But it is coming to be understood that there is great uncertainty and hazard in thus applying our own notions of rhythm to the poetry of the Greeks. The sense of rhythm is indeed common to all men. There are many forms and successions which all men would accept as rhythmical, many others which all would reject as unrhythmical: but there are some which are not so definitely marked, about which different men might differ as to their rhythmical character. And among forms acknowledged to be rhythmical, some men would prefer one, some another; the choice depending very much on fashion and education. Where a particular verse admits of different rhythmic constructions, we cannot assume it as certain that the one which seems preferable to us would have seemed so to the Greeks. There are many particulars in which we can never know the actual rhythmus of Greek verses without an authentic statement from the Greeks themselves. I need not insist further on this point. It will become more apparent as we proceed. The first scholar who pointed out the importance of carefully studying the remains of Greek writers on rhythm was Böckh, in his Essay on the Metres of Pindar. In this study, however, he did not himself proceed to any great extent.

It is only about twelve years since two young scholars in Tübingen, August Rossbach and Rudolf Westphal, set themselves in earnest to the work. A volume, entitled *Griechische Rhythmik*, appeared in 1854, written by Rossbach, but presenting the results of their united study. It was succeeded in 1856 by a volume bearing the names of both scholars, the *Griechische Metrik*, in which the doctrines of rhythmic developed in the former work were applied to the treatment of Greek metres. It appeared, however, that in the interval of two years which separated these works the views of the writers had undergone changes on various points, and some of considerable consequence—a circumstance not to be wondered at, when we consider the newness of the subject and the great difficulties which attend it. These volumes attracted much attention, and were generally regarded as containing new and important truth—though how much, few would undertake to decide. There were not many critics whose studies had fitted them to pass a comprehensive and independent judgment on works of this kind. But it is proper to except one or two articles by H. Weil of Besançon, who is known for an elaborate book on Latin accent, published by him and Benloew. The articles to which I refer appeared in Jahn's *Jahrbücher*, and contain valuable contributions to a knowledge of Greek rhythmic. In 1861, Westphal came out again with a volume entitled *Die Fragmente und die Lehrsätze der Griechischen Rhythmiker*. It professes to be a supplement to the Greek Rhythmic of A. Rossbach. It is dedicated by the author to his former associate Rossbach, who seems to have withdrawn from these studies. The dedication speaks of numerous changes of opinion as having been the result of further research, and apologizes for the appearance which the new book has of being in no small degree a polemic against the old one. The work opens with an Introduction, on the sources from which a knowledge of Greek rhythmic is to be derived, the manuscripts in which we find them, the books in which they have been printed, and the like. Then follow the texts themselves, occupying some fifty loosely-printed pages. But by far the largest part of the book consists of the Commentary on the Doctrines of the ancient Rhythmic Writers. This Commentary follows, not the order of the texts to be elucidated, but the natural arrangement of the subject: beginning with the general idea of rhythm; proceeding thence to arsis and thesis in general, thence to kinds of feet, thence to extent of feet, and so on; giving under each head the dicta of the rhythmic writers, and discussing, comparing, and illustrating their statements. Only a few weeks after Westphal's book was given to the public, there appeared another on the same subject, and on somewhat the same plan, by Julius Cæsar, a scholar of long-established reputation. Its name is *Die Grundzüge der Griechischen Rhythmik, im Anschluss an Aristides Quintilianus, erläutert von Julius Cæsar*. The Introduction to this work contains a very thorough investigation of all that is or can be known concerning Aristides, with a view especially to determine the time when he lived and wrote. Then comes the text of Aristides—that part of it which relates to rhythmic—with careful statements of various readings. And then a long Commentary, in which particular points of rhythmic are taken up, one after another, and the statements of Aristides are discussed in comparison with those of other authorities. In these discussions Cæsar is often led to notice and criticise the views expressed by Rossbach and Westphal in their *Rhythmik und Metrik*; and his criticism, though intended to be respectful and courteous, is somewhat irritating in its tone. He assumes that they have been so biassed by their own preconceived notions of rhythm as to be unfitted for a fair understanding and appreciation of the texts on which they build. This tone is especially marked in the Preface and the Appendix; these were written after the appearance of Westphal's *Fragmente und Lehrsätze*, and the last is taken up with a discussion of the various points in which they differ.

One might suppose from Cæsar's tone that there was a fundamental difference between his views and those of Westphal. But upon looking more closely it would be found that on most of the main points they are agreed, and that the matters about which they disagree are generally of minor consequence. It is not strange perhaps that Westphal should have felt himself somewhat aggrieved by Cæsar's criticisms; but the way in which he shows his resentment is not altogether to be approved. He brought out last year (1863) a long-promised work, a part of the same series with the *Rhythmik und Metrik*, viz. *Harmonik und Melopöie der Griechen*. To this he has prefixed a long preface of fifty pages, much of it taken up with one or two points on which he and Cæsar are at issue. And it is somewhat curious, as a manifestation of feeling, that he everywhere suppresses the name of Cæsar while combating his views, although he is thus obliged to use some rather inconvenient circumlocutions. Just at the end, however, he does bring out the name, as if he had been reserving it to that place for a grand final explosion. To rebut this attack, Susemihl, who seems to have been a pupil of Cæsar's, appears in Jahn's *Jahrbücher* for Dec. 1863, with an open letter to his master, in which he says that Westphal has carried on his polemic in such a way that Cæsar's self-respect will hardly allow him to reply, and he (Susemihl) therefore takes up the cudgels for him. But if he is a partisan, he is a fair-minded one; he concedes so much to his opponent that Cæsar finds it necessary to append a lengthy note, protesting against the admissions of his friend, and fighting against his champion hardly less than against his enemy.

Before taking up the principles of rhythmic, it may be well to notice some objections urged against this study, which Westphal states and answers in the Introduction to his *Fragmente und Lehrsätze*. The first is, that the doctrine of the ancient rhythmists refers not so much to the rhythm of poetry as to that of music. Westphal's reply runs thus: "This error, which has arisen from the relation of our modern poetry to music, appears to have been shared even by Hermann, and to this day many philologians seem not to be wholly free from it. The relation of the poet to the musician in classic Greek was wholly different from what it is with us. It is true that the ancients also had an instrumental music separate from poetry; but while this in modern times has been coming more and more to be the crown of musical art, it was confined in antiquity to the kitharistic and auletic nomes; but the centre of gravity lay in vocal music with instrumental accompaniment, in melodized poetry. Was then, we ask, the rhythm which the ancient poet gave to his compositions different from the rhythm of the song? In our time this is certainly the case. Our dramas are either designed to be declaimed throughout —and this is true of all which make pretensions to any high poetic merit—or the drama takes the form of an opera, in which the music predominates with such unlimited ascendency that the text, with rare exceptions, is insignificant as poetry, and even the metrical form is indifferent, for the composer in general arranges his rhythms (*bars* in music) without reference to the number of verse-feet, and in the religious opera frequently makes use of an unmetrical prose text. Such, too, is the procedure of a musician when he melodizes a lyric poem which he finds ready to his hand, a poem written without reference to musical composition. Very different was the case in classic Greece. Excepting the Epos and a few other species, every poem was expressly intended, in whole or in part, for musical performance. To write a lyric poem for mere reading or declamation was, with few exceptions, an unknown effort of poetic art, and every drama (as Aristotle says) contains the μελῳδία as an essential element, as μέγιστον ἡδυσμάτων. Not only choral songs and monodies, but also parts of the dialogue were sung, and even when the iambic trimeter of tragedy was spoken, it was delivered in a melodramatic way, *i. e.* with instrumental accompaniment. To this we must add that poet and composer were united in one person. In the great lyric and dramatic authors of Greece we are wont to see poets merely, but in antiquity they were no less esteemed as the Coryphæi of music. When Aristoxenus, the great musical art-theorist, protests against the overloading of music with affected ornament, a style which had been introduced by Philoxenus and Timotheus, and which threatened a general corruption of taste, he refers to the representatives of the good classical style as models for imitation, naming as such Pindar and Pratinas: 'Whoever' (he says) 'has in his youth earnestly and zealously studied the *μέλη* and *κρούματα*, the melodies and instrumentations of these masters, will remain ever after secure from many aberrations, even if he should apply himself to the complex and ornate *ποικίλη μουσική* of Philoxenus' (Plut. Mus. 31). If Aristoxenus would show that the noble simplicity of classical music was conscious and intentional, and by no means founded in a defective knowledge of the resources of art (*οὐ δι' ἄγνοιαν ἀλλὰ δια προαίρεσιν*), he refers to the compositions of Æschylus and Phrynichus, who were well acquainted with the chromatic treatment of the keys, but never applied it in their tragedies (Plut. Mus. 20). So, too, Sophocles was a composer: Aristoxenus calls him the first Athenian who introduced the Lydian mode in *ἴδια ᾄσματα, i. e.* in monodies and threnes, after the fashion of the dithyrambic poets (Vit. Sophocl. fin.): and of later tragic poets we know that they were active as musical artists—as of Agathon, who took up the chromatic keys, which his predecessors had declined to use. The lyric and dramatic poets of the classical time were therefore the composers of their own *μέλη*. Why now do these poets apply to the metrical form of their choral songs and dramatic monodies a degree of care so extraordinarily great? Why do they constantly appear in this field as original artists, never once repeating a strophic form, whether used by themselves or by any of their predecessors? For reading or declamation their *μέλη* were not intended, but for musical performance. Why then—we repeat the question—have they taken so much pains with the metrical form of the λέξις? The answer can be none but this: the rhythm given by the metres of the words was the same which appeared in the musical delivery, the same which the audience were to hear in the performance of the poem.

"It is true then that the writers on rhythm have especially in view the rhythm of the song, but this is identical with the rhythm of the metre, as manifested by the words. In a time like ours, when poetry and music are two independent arts, it may happen that a composer like Beethoven, in melodizing three similar verses of five feet, should make three bars out of the first, two out of the second, and again three out of the third (we refer to the song *Einsam wandelt dein Freund im Frühlingsgarten*). Beethoven takes a song which a poet before him had composed in a traditional metre, simply for reading or recitation, without any reference to melodizing, and in the treatment of this metre he proceeds with perfect freedom. Only in this respect does the composer attach himself to the poet, that the strong part in every musical bar coincides with an accented syllable in the poem, though it is not true conversely that every accented syllable of the poem appears in the melody as the strong part of a bar; in reference to the weak part of his bars the composer pays no attention to the poet. So stands the case with modern rhythmic. But in classical antiquity, where the poet himself was always composer, where he worked out his artfully constructed metres only with a view to musical performance, every metrical arsis is also an arsis in the melody, every metrical thesis a thesis in the melody, and as many feet as belong to the verse, so many bars belong to the musical period. We repeat, then: The tradition of the writers on rhythm relates indeed to the rhythm of the melody, but the rhythm of the melody is identical with the rhythm of the text. Hence it is that the feet and kinds of feet of which these writers speak take their names from the feet of the metre (*γένος δακτυλικόν, ἰαμβικόν, παιωνικόν, τροχαῖος ἄλογος*, etc.); and moreover, when the rhythmic writers wish to illustrate the form of a rhythm or a rhythmic series, they always take their examples from metric. Never does it appear that any rhythmic form of which they speak finds no application to poetry: even the *pæon epibatus*, which had its principal application in mere instrumental music, seems, in the earlier time at least, to have been used also as a foot in poetry."

I have made this long quotation from Westphal, because the views contained in it, if not altogether novel, are very justly and forcibly expressed, and are important to be recognized and understood. A second objection brought against this study is that the system of the ancient rhythmists had a theoretical rather than a practical character, that it consisted more of speculations than of facts, that it was not so much a description of actual usage as a series of ideal principles and categories. "If this were so, the rhythm which Aristoxenus talks about might not be identical with that of the ancient poets: Aristoxenus would stand on much the same level with Hermann and Apel." In reply to this objection, Westphal traces the procedure of Aristoxenus from point to point, and shows that it is purely empirical; "he states facts, one after another, and states them simply as facts; he seeks appropriate definitions for current expressions of musical art; and beyond this he aims only to bring the facts designated by those expressions into an intelligible order, and to show that they are justified by some principle or analogy."

But there remains a third objection; that the writers on rhythm lived and wrote when art was in its decline, and may therefore be supposed to represent, not the true classic usage, but that of degenerate times and inferior artists. In regard to this, I quote again at some length from Westphal: "Aristoxenus stands on the border of the classic period: his father might have seen Socrates, Epaminondas, and other men of classic Greece; but he himself belongs to a later generation. He resided in Corinth at the time when the younger Dionysius lived there as an exile; of professed musical artists he was particularly acquainted only with Telestes, the dithyrambic composer, whom he met in his wanderings through Italy. Afterwards he came into connection with Aristotle, and after his death aspired to be his successor in the Lyceum. This in truth was no longer the time of classic life: it was a period when the creative spirit in rhythmic had died out, when men like Chæremon and Theodectes held the first rank in tragedy. But amid this corruption of ancient art, Aristoxenus took a very peculiar place. Trained in the conservative school of the Pythagoreans, he had early imbibed a predilection for the norms of ancient art, and this partiality for the old showed itself through his whole life, in an opposition to the tendencies of contemporary art. He appears in his works as an admirer of the art-style represented by Pratinas, Pindar, Simonides, Phrynichus, and Æschylus; in this style he recognizes the proper ἦθος (art-character)

(Plut. Mus. 31 and 20); even Euripides and Sophocles are not named by him; while against the dithyrambic composers Timotheus and Telestes, and their modern style, he commences an exasperated strife. The good old time—that was for him the time when art reached its greatest height, when choral melody was in its bloom, when musical art had its genuine ἦθος and truly served for παιδεία: but *now* was the time of σκηνικὴ μουσική, of exaggerated and affected stage-airs and concert-solos. *Then* the ποικιλία ῥυθμική had a meaning, the artists were φιλόρρυθμοι: but *now* all ἦθος was lost in the rhythms of the κεκλασμένα μέλη. His stand-point is most clearly exhibited in the work called σύμμικτα συμποτικά (Ath. 14. 632). In these colloquies, which he held with friends and pupils on matters of musical art and afterwards gave to the public, he begins by referring to the people of Posidonia in Italy, who among Tyrrhenian and Latin neighbors had gradually become barbarians, forgetting their Hellenic customs and language, and even their very name; but on one day of every year they held a feast in commemoration of the old Greek time, now passed and gone, and broke up their assembly with tears and lamentations. 'So will we also do,' says Aristoxenus: 'while the theatre is sinking more and more into barbarism, and musical art is suing only for the favor of the multitude and hastening on to its ruin, in our own little circle we will remember the ancient μουσική.' And so he conversed with his scholars on the θηλυνομένη μουσική of the contemporary theatre (Themist. Or. 33, p. 364), and to the tasteless compositions of Philoxenus and Timotheus opposed the norms of classic art as represented by Pindar and Pratinas. . . . From this oppositional stand-point, which Aristoxenus holds toward the musical art of his own time, like the battle waged by Aristophanes against the monodies of Euripides and the new dithyramb-writers of Athens, it follows, of course, that the rhythmical doctrines of Aristoxenus are drawn from the norms which are fundamental to the classical rhythmic of Pindar, Simonides, Æschylus; they are derived by abstraction from the compositions of those great masters. In a word, the rhythmical doctrines which Aristoxenus presents to us are the same that were followed by the classical poets of Greece. Yet, on the other hand, it would not be correct to assume that the doctrines of Aristoxenus apply only to the times of Æschylus and Pindar, and are inapplicable to the rhythmic of later times, as that of Euripides. Widely as the rhythmopœia of Æschylus differs from that of Euripides, and the rhythmopœia of Pindar from that of Philoxenus, in particular forms and combinations, the fundamental principles of rhythmic—as regards kind of feet, extent of feet, division of feet, composition of feet, change of feet, etc.—are the same for both periods of musical art; they remained without change from the time of Alcman and Stesichorus to that of the Romans. Now it is just these fundamental principles which we learn from the rhythmic writers; into the detailed description of art-forms in rhythmopœia (rhythmic composition) they have not entered. And thus no well-informed scholar would think of constructing a complete metric from the doctrines of the rhythmists: for this purpose we must have recourse to the old writers on metric, and above all to the old poets themselves; but no system of metric can have a sure foundation unless it bases itself on those fundamental doctrines of the rhythmists. Unhappily, of these fundamental doctrines we are far from knowing all, for only a very scanty portion of the rhythmical literature of the ancients has been preserved to us; but what we have received is absolutely invaluable, and sheds clear light upon the darkest points."

We proceed now to consider some elementary facts and principles of rhythmic as set forth in these remains of ancient rhythmic. And we begin with arsis and thesis. As rhythm consists in a regular succession of proportional times, it is necessary that the successive times should be so marked off and distinguished that their proportionality and regularity shall be made clearly perceptible. This is accomplished by a greater intensity of action falling upon particular moments, and distinguishing them from the intermediate moments of weaker action. It is by alternate intension and remission of effort that rhythm is made obvious to our senses. The portion of time thus marked off by an intension and a remission of effort is a rhythmic foot. It divides itself, of course, into two parts, one of them being the time of intension, the other that of remission. To these two parts of the foot were given the names of arsis and thesis. The names, as we have already seen, connect themselves with the dance: the θέσις was the setting down of the foot, and the ἄρσις was the raising of it up. They are appropriate also to the practice of beating time, whether with the foot or with the hand: the θέσις corresponded to the downward beat, the ἄρσις to the upward. But the downward movement was stronger than the upward, the force of gravity being an addition to the former, and a subtraction from the latter. Hence, when these times were applied to musical and metrical feet, the name thesis was used for the stronger part of the foot, that which was distinguished by the intension of voice or instrument, and the name arsis for the weaker part, that which showed a remission of voice or instrument. In dancing to the sound of music, there was a θέσις of the dancer's foot on the accented part, and an ἄρσις on the unaccented part, of the musical foot or bar. In beating time to poetry, when sung or recited, there was a θέσις, or downward beat, on the accented part, an ἄρσις, or upward beat, on the unaccented part, of the metrical foot. This is unquestionably the proper use of the terms arsis and thesis: it is the only use among the extant Greek writers on rhythmic and metric, down to a very late period. But it is remarkable that the Latin writers on metric show a very different use. They employ arsis, or *elatio*, for the first part of a foot, and thesis, or *positio*, for the last part, without reference to the rhythmic accent. In an iambic foot the short syllable is arsis, the long thesis; in a trochaic foot, the long syllable is arsis, the short thesis. The terms thus used are mere designations of place, and have no rhythmical significance. The singular accordance of the Latin writers in this misuse makes it probable that they have derived it from a common source, which would have to be placed as early as the second century after Christ. This source would seem to have been some Greek author on metric: I say some Greek author, for we find the same usage in late Byzantine writers, who would hardly have taken it from a Latin source. Wherever and whenever it arose, it was the result of ignorance and misapprehension. A writer who had heard or read that in the common dramatic trimeter the first part of each foot was called arsis and the last part thesis, may have inferred that this was the case in all kinds of verse. Or he may have been misled by the circumstance that the writers on rhythmic, where they had occasion to speak of arsis and thesis together, always coupled them in this order—arsis and thesis. But whatever the explanation, the mistake was a most unfortunate one. For the consequence is that the statements which we find in Latin sources as to arsis and thesis are almost wholly uninstructive; they do not show us where the rhythmic accent fell. And even when they speak of the ictus or beat, the case is no better; for these Latin metricians—who, it must be remembered, were not practical musicians—seem in their scanning of poetry to have beat time in the same way, raising the hand on the first part of the foot and lowering it on the second—thus, in *arma virumque*, raising the hand for *ar-* and lowering it for *-ma vi-*. But the confusion in regard to arsis and thesis has become still greater in modern times. As the Latin metricians misunderstood the use of these terms in Greek metric, so Bentley, the first modern scholar who really applied himself to metrical studies, misunderstood the use of the Latin metricians: he took arsis for the accented part of the foot and thesis for the unaccented, thus exactly reversing the original and proper use. In this he has been followed by all scholars from his time to ours. Even Rossbach, Westphal, and Cæsar, while protesting against the prevalent use of these terms, have felt themselves obliged to conform to it. But Westphal, in his *Fragmente und Lehrsätze*, has ventured to break loose from the bonds of custom, and return to primitive usage. In this, it seems to me, he has done well, and the example will doubtless be followed by other writers. But as our scholars are familiar with the Bentleian use, of arsis for the accented part of the foot and thesis for the unaccented, so that statements in accordance with this use would be most readily understood, I shall adhere to it in the sequel of these remarks.

The foot, then, consists of the arsis or accented part, and the thesis or unaccented part. The arsis, however, does not always precede the thesis, as in the bars of our modern music.

It would have been simpler and better, perhaps, if the foot had been constituted like the bar, so as always to commence with an accent: an unaccented syllable at the beginning of a verse could then have been treated as an anacrusis, introductory to the proper rhythm. But the ancients regarded the proper rhythm, the verse foot, as commencing with the commencement of the verse, and hence constituted feet of thesis followed by arsis, as in iambic and anapæstic verses, not less than feet of arsis followed by thesis, as in trochaic and dactylic verses. The two components of the foot, the arsis and thesis, may have different ratios to each other. Thus, they may have a ratio of equality, as in the dactyl, the anapæst, the spondee, in which arsis and thesis divide the foot into equal halves; or they may have a ratio of two to one—a *diplasic* ratio, as the ancients called it—as in the trochee and the iambics, where the long arsis has twice the length of the short thesis. It is obvious that these two ratios correspond to the two varieties of time in modern music: the equal ratio answers to our common time, and the diplasic ratio answers to our triple time. But ancient rhythm has another ratio, which is not recognized in the theory and the notation of modern music. Though much less frequent than either of the others, it is still by no means rare. I refer to the *hemiolic* ratio, as the ancients call it, in which arsis and thesis are as $1\frac{1}{2}$ to 1, or as 3 to 2. Thus, in the cretic foot, an arsis consisting of a long and short syllable is followed by a thesis consisting of a long; in the first pæon, an equivalent of the cretic, an arsis consisting of a long and short is followed by a thesis consisting of two shorts. The hemiolic ratio appears in cretic and pæonic, as the equal ratio does in dactyl, anapæst, and spondee, and the diplasic ratio in iambus and trochee. Westphal asserts that in modern music the bar is sometimes divided into five equal parts, as in the hemiolic ratio; and he gives as example of this rhythm the German popular song of Prince Eugene, the music of which he writes with the fractional prefix $\frac{5}{4}$. Beside these three ratios of arsis and thesis—the equal, diplasic, and hemiolic—Aristoxenus mentions two others: the *triplasic*, in which the two parts of the foot are as 3 to 1, and the *epitritic*, in which they are as 3 to 4. He intimates, however, that they differ widely from the preceding, not being used continuously in rhythmic composition. Their real character has been ingeniously divined and convincingly explained by Rossbach. I shall pass by the explanation for the present, and return to it further on. All other ratios between arsis and thesis, aside from those which have been mentioned, Aristoxenus sets aside as unrhythmical: they are too complex to be appreciated by our senses and enjoyed by our feelings.

We proceed now to describe the rhythmic feet, according to the definitions of Aristoxenus. The shortest which he admits consists of three short times. The pyrrhic, of two short times, is unsuited for rhythmical purposes; the arses and theses would succeed each other with too much rapidity for distinct impression and agreeable effect. This reason would apply to a verse made up of pyrrhics in immediate succession. Whether Aristoxenus would disallow the occasional use of a single pyrrhic—as the Æolian poets appear to use it in the opening of a logaœdic verse—is a point on which we have no express testimony. Laying this out of account, we have:

First. The foot of 3 short times, trochee, iambus, or tribrach. The ratio is diplasic, an arsis of 2 times, a thesis of 1 time. It corresponds to our $\frac{3}{8}$ time: thus, $\frac{3}{8}$.

Second. The foot of 4 short times, dactyl, anapæst, spondee, proceleusmatic. The ratio is equal, an arsis of 2 times, a thesis of 2. It corresponds to our $\frac{2}{4}$ time: thus, $\frac{2}{4}$.

Third. The foot of 5 short times, cretic, first pæon, fourth pæon. The ratio is hemiolic, an arsis of 3 times, a thesis of 2. It may be represented by $\frac{5}{8}$ time: thus, $\frac{5}{8}$.

Fourth. The foot of 6 short times, ionic *a majore*, ionic *a minore*, etc. The ratio is diplasic, an arsis of 4 times, a thesis of 2. It corresponds to our $\frac{3}{4}$ time: thus, $\frac{3}{4}$.

But 6 short times admit of another rhythmic arrangement, corresponding to our $\frac{6}{8}$ time: thus, $\frac{6}{8}$. To this $\frac{6}{8}$ we give the name of compound time, as it is made up of two

$\frac{3}{8}$, one of which has a stronger accent than the other. This stronger accent dominates the whole bar, and makes it a unit, though a compound unit. In like manner the corresponding Greek foot is called by Aristoxenus a compound foot; it is made up of two trochees, iambi, or tribrachs: *i. e.* it is a trochaic or iambic dipody. The ratio is equal, with one trochee or iambus for arsis, and one for thesis. Observe that the ratio of the whole compound foot is equal, though each of the two feet from which it is compounded has a diplasic ratio.

A foot of 7 short times would be unrhythmical, or at least unfitted for continuous composition. Dividing the 7 times between arsis and thesis, we should have 6 to 1, or 5 to 2, or 4 to 3, none of them ratios which Aristoxenus recognizes as fitted for continuous rhythmic composition. We come, then,

Fifth. To the foot of 8 short times. This corresponds to our $\frac{4}{4}$ time, a variety of compound time made up of two $\frac{2}{4}$: thus, $\frac{4}{4}$. Here, then, we have another compound foot, a dactylic or anapæstic dipody. The ratio is equal, with one dactyl or anapæst as arsis, and one as thesis; and here the simple feet themselves have the same ratio.

Sixth. The foot of 9 short times. This corresponds to our $\frac{9}{8}$ time, a variety of compound time made up of three $\frac{3}{8}$ thus, $\frac{9}{8}$. It is a compound foot, a trochaic or iambic tripody; the ratio is diplasic, with two trochees or iambi for arsis and one for thesis. And the single feet themselves of which the compound foot is made up have a similar diplasic ratio.

Seventh. The foot of 10 short times. It may be represented with our notation as $\frac{10}{8}$ time: thus, $\frac{10}{8}$. It is a compound foot, a cretic or pæonic dipody; the ratio is equal, with one pæon as arsis and one as thesis; while the single feet themselves have the hemiolic ratio.

A foot of 11 times would be unrhythmical, for the same reason as one of 7 times. You cannot divide the times between arsis and thesis so as to have a ratio that is rhythmical.

Eighth. The foot of 12 short times. This may be represented with our notation by $\frac{12}{8}$: thus,  This is the trochaic or iambic dimeter, a compound foot with equal ratio, one trochaic or iambic dipody for thesis, and one for arsis. But the 12 shorts may also take a form which we should write as $\frac{6}{4}$: thus, . This is an ionic dipody, with equal ratio, one ionic foot for arsis and one for thesis. But yet again, the foot might be written thus : . This is a dactylic or anapæstic tripody, with diplasic ratio, two dactyls or anapæsts for arsis, and one for thesis.

A foot of 13 short times is inadmissible, as not allowing any rhythmical ratio between arsis and thesis. One of 14 short times might be divided in an equal ratio, as a compound foot with 7 times for arsis and 7 for thesis; but the simple feet of 7 times each would themselves be unrhythmical, and the compound foot must therefore be unrhythmical also. We have, then,

Ninth. The foot of 15 short times. This may be written thus : . It is a cretic or pæonic tripody, a compound foot with diplasic ratio, two cretics or pæons for arsis, and one for thesis. But again we may write . This is a trochaic or iambic pentapody with hemiolic ratio, three trochees or iambi for arsis and two for thesis.

Tenth. The foot of 16 short times. This may be written . It is a dactylic or anapæstic tetrapody, with equal ratio, having a dactylic or anapæstic dipody for arsis and another for thesis. According to Aristoxenus, it is the longest foot with equal ratio, the longest foot in which arsis and thesis are equal to each other.

A foot of 17 or of 19 times would allow no rhythmical ratio between arsis and thesis. But we have

Eleventh. The foot of 18 short times. We may write it

$\frac{18}{8}$  . It is a trochaic or iambic trimeter, with diplasic ratio, having two trochaic or iambic dipodies for arsis, and one for thesis. We cannot divide it in equal ratio, making it consist of two tripodies, one for arsis and one for thesis. For this would be contrary to the rule of Aristoxenus just mentioned. There is, however, another combination possible, which we may write after this fashion: $\frac{9}{4}$  . It is an ionic tripody, with diplasic ratio, two ionic feet for arsis and one for thesis. According to Aristoxenus, the foot of 18 times is the longest foot with diplasic ratio, the longest in which arsis and thesis are as 2 to 1. But the hemiolic ratio may extend, according to his express assertion, to the length of 25 short times. This gives us two additional feet, viz.:

Twelfth. The foot of 20 short times. We may write it $\frac{10}{4}$  . It is a dactylic or anapæstic pentapody, in hemiolic ratio, with three dactyls or anapæsts for arsis, and two for thesis.

Thirteenth. The foot of 25 short times. We may write it $\frac{25}{8}$  . It is a cretic or pæonic pentapody, in hemiolic ratio, with three cretics or pæons for arsis, and two for thesis.

Of the feet just described, by far the greater part are compound. The foot of 3 times is simple, so that of 4 times, that of 5 times, and the first of 6 times. But the second of 6 times and all that follow it are compound, and are made up of two or more simple feet, each having its proper accent, though all under the power of one dominant and unifying accent. These compound feet are precisely analogous in rhythm to the varieties of compound time in our music, to $\frac{4}{4}$, $\frac{6}{4}$, $\frac{6}{8}$, $\frac{9}{8}$ and $\frac{12}{8}$. The only differences are, 1. that the ancients allowed ratios such as $\frac{5}{8}$, $\frac{10}{8}$, $\frac{15}{8}$, etc., which are not definitely recognized in modern theory, and are not found, at least with such notation, in our written music; and, 2. that the ancients gave to these compound feet a much greater extension than they have in modern praxis—an extension reaching in the equal ratio to $\frac{8}{4}$, in the diplasic to $\frac{18}{8}$, and in the hemiolic to the seemingly enormous extent of $\frac{25}{8}$. This great extent, however strange it might seem to us, in the musical bar, has evidently nothing impossible; there would be nothing impossible in a bar of 16, 18, 20, or even 25 quavers under the dominion of one principal accent. And we are assured by the express testimony of Aristoxenus, a most competent witness, that ancient rhythm made use of feet in which 16, 18, 20, 25 short times were thus united under the dominion of one principal accent.

I ought to say that the foot of 8 short times was not always a compound foot. It was sometimes a spondee—the *σπονδεῖος μείζων*, or greater spondee, which I have already referred to—in which each long was equivalent to four shorts. In like manner there was a foot of three long syllables, in which each long had this same dimension of four shorts: this foot, when it had trochaic rhythm, was called *trochæus semantus*, when it had iambic rhythm, it was called *orthius*. The *trochæus semantus* and the *orthius* were feet of 12 short times, but still they were regarded as simple feet. In this connection we must notice also the *pæon epibatus*, or pæon of five long syllables, with hemiolic ratio, three longs for arsis and two for thesis. The *pæon epibatus* was a foot of 10 short times, but it was a simple foot.

As regards the beating of the compound feet, we are told that, if the ratio was equal, the compound foot received two beats, one of which was doubtless given to the arsis and one to the thesis. If the ratio was diplasic, the compound foot received three beats, two of which were doubtless given to the arsis and one to the thesis. If the ratio was hemiolic, we should expect five beats for the compound foot, three for arsis and two for thesis; but, singularly enough, we have it on express and undeniable testimony that these hemiolic feet received four beats instead of five. Simple feet of six short times or less received only two beats, whatever the ratio, whether equal, diplasic, or hemiolic; the single trochee, dactyl, or cretic had two beats, one for the arsis and one for the thesis.

The doctrine of the extended or compound feet is the most valuable piece of instruction which we gain from the remnants of the old Greek rhythmic. Let us look at some of the conclusions which either flow from it directly, or may be inferred from it when combined with other statements and notices. We learn that the common iambic trimeter of the dramatic dialogue was a single foot, that it had one accent which was sensibly stronger than any other in it and made it a rhythmic unity. This is a fact which could never have been guessed at from the descriptions of the writers on metric. They represent the verse as consisting of three dipodies, but they say nothing which would suggest the idea that these three dipodies are of unequal weight, or connected as principal and subordinate. But now we learn that one was stronger than either of the others. It is probable that the first dipody had the strongest accent, the second a weaker accent, and the third the weakest of all. But it is a question what part of the dipody received the accent, whether it fell upon the first or second iambus of the dipody. It was assumed by Bentley, without any attempt at proof, that it was the first iambus which was distinguished by the accent; and the assumption has been tacitly accepted by all succeeding writers. But Westphal denies the correctness of the assumption. He maintains, not only that it is unproved, but that it is in conflict with the express teaching of the ancient authorities. He concludes with undoubting confidence that the accent fell on the second iambus of the dipody: thus, *ὦ τέκνα Κάδμου τοῦ πάλαι νέα τροφή*. But Weil, reviewing his argument, shows that it rests on statements of Latin metricians, and that the misuse of these writers in reference to arsis and thesis (which we have before spoken of) deprives their statements of all authority. At the same time, he points out an expression of Aristides which implies pretty clearly (though nobody had noticed it before) that the iambic dipody was accented on the first foot. We are allowed, therefore, to go back to the rendering of the trimeter which since Bentley has been the usual one, and which is certainly far more consonant with our modern notions of rhythm, and to read *ὦ τέκνα Κάδμου τοῦ πάλαι νέα τροφή*.

But if the six feet of the dramatic trimeter form but one compound foot, the same cannot be true as to the six feet of the epic hexameter. For the six dactyls or spondees mak

24 short times—which would have to be divided either in equal ratio, as 12 and 12, or in diplasic, as 16 and 8. But the longest foot with equal ratio has only 16 short times; the longest with diplasic ratio only 18. The epic hexameter, then, is not under the dominion of one superior accent: it must consist of at least two parts, the principal accents of which are equal to each other. It appears certain, in fact, that it was made up of two compound feet, of 12 short times each, with diplasic ratio, having two dactyls for arsis and one for thesis. Which of the three dactyls in each division of the verse had the principal accent it is not so easy to determine. Westphal finds reason to believe that it was the third: he would give the opening line of the Æneid thus: *Ȁrma virùmque canȍ̀ Trojæ̏ qui prìmus ab ȍ̀ris.* But the conclusion seems to be far from certain.

The dactylic tetrameter is doubtless a single foot of 16 short times, the longest which the equal ratio admits of; and the dactylic octameter consists of two such feet. So too the anapæstic dimeter is a single foot of 16 times, and the anapæstic tetrameter consists of two such feet. In like manner the iambic and trochaic tetrameters consist of two feet of 12 times each, with equal ratio. But what shall we say of the trochaic tetrameter catalectic, of such a verse as πολλὰ μὲν γὰρ ἐκ θαλάσσης, πολλὰ δ' ἐκ χέρσου κακά? If the first half of the line has its 12 short times, the second or catalectic part would seem to have but 11: but Aristoxenus, as we have seen, rejects the foot of 11 shorts as being unrhythmical.

The true answer doubtless is that the pause at the end of the line makes up for the deficient syllable, and supplies the one time which is wanting. The iambic tetrameter is also often catalectic, as in ὦ δεξιώτατον κρέας σοφῶς γε προυνοήσω or ὦ πᾶσιν ἀνθρώποις φανεὶς μέγιστον ὠφέλημα. Here the second compound foot, μέγιστον ὠφέλημα, or σοφῶς γε προυνοήσω, appears to consist of 11 times, instead of 12. Shall we adopt here the same explanation as before, and assume that the deficiency was made up by a pause at the end of the verse? The more probable explanation for this case is, that the last iambus has lost, not its second syllable, but its first; that the short syllable of the last iambus is suppressed, and its time made up by prolonging the long sylla ble of the preceding iambus. In the line just quoted, the η of νοη would be equal to three short times, and νοησω, having six short times, would be equivalent to an iambic dipody. We can now understand, in connection with this example, what Aristoxenus means when he speaks of a foot with triplasic ratio—*i. e.* a foot in which arsis and thesis are as 3 to 1: such feet, he says, are used occasionally, though not in continuous composition. The foot νοη, just before the close of the catalectic verse, answers perfectly to this description. Its thesis is of one short time, its arsis of three. Its peculiar ratio arises from a special cause, its arsis being prolonged so as to occupy the time of a short thesis suppressed in the next foot. It has therefore an occasional character, differing in this respect from the ordinary iambus with diplasic ratio.

It is well known that in the iambic trimeter, and in other iambic and trochaic verses, feet of 4 short times, spondees, dactyls, anapæsts, are to some extent intermixed with the proper three-timed feet of these rhythms. How does the ancient rhythmic regard these apparently unrhythmical intermixtures? It partly acknowledges their unrhythmical character. Aristoxenus says there are three varieties of times—the ἔρρυθμοι or rhythmical, which have distinct and obvious ratios to each other; the ἄρρυθμοι, or unrhythmical, which have no intelligible or appreciable ratios; and an intermediate class, the ῥυθμοειδεῖς, or rhythm-like, the ratios of which are not indeed unintelligible, like the last, but are also not distinct and obvious, like the first. There is no doubt that by the last term, the ῥυθμοειδεῖς, he meant to designate such times as belong to spondees in iambic or trochaic verse. A term more frequently applied to them is ἄλογοι, 'irrational, without ratios,' *i. e.* without integral ratios. The ordinary long syllable is equal in time to two shorts: the ratio here is 2. A moment ago, we saw in the penult of a catalectic tetrameter a syllable which contained three short times: the ratio here is 3. We have seen that there were certain spondees in which each long syllable was equivalent to 4 shorts: the ratio here is 4. These longs of two, three, or four times are all rational: their ratios to the short syllable taken as the unit of measurement are all expressed by integers. But if we should find that, in a particular foot, a certain long syllable had the time of 1½ shorts, such a long syllable would be irrational; the number which expresses its ratio to the unit of measurement is not an integer, but a fraction. Now this is the case, according to explicit testimony, with one long syllable in the spondees of iambic and trochaic verses. The long arsis of those spondees has the usual length, that of two shorts, but the long thesis, we are told, was intermediate between one and two shorts; in other words, it bore to the unit of measurement the fractional ratio of 1½ to 1. It was an irrational long; and the foot to which it belonged was irrational also, the whole length of the foot being expressed by a fractional designation, viz. 3½ short times. The arsis and thesis of this irrational foot bear to each other the ratio of 4 to 3. And there can be no question that Aristoxenus refers to this foot, when he speaks of the epitritic ratio (4 to 3) in the same terms that he uses of the triplasic, as a ratio that does indeed occur, but not in foot after foot through a continuous rhythmic series. These irrational feet of the iambic and trochaic verses form one of the most remarkable features of ancient rhythmic. It is something which, to the same extent at least, does not occur in modern art. It is analogous to a *ritardando* movement, by which certain bars—or rather, certain parts of certain bars—receive a length greater than the ruling *tempo* of the passage to which they belong. But the definiteness in the amount of retardation and in the places of its occurrence, and particularly the great frequency of its use, often three times in one trimeter verse, are circumstances which have no parallel in our music.

In regard to the feet of which we have been speaking, their irrational character rests upon positive testimony. That there were other cases of irrationality is probable enough in itself, but they can only be determined by processes of inference which are more or less uncertain. In the dactylo-epitritic verses of Pindar, where dactyls are followed by epitrites, each epitrite consisting of a trochee and spondee, Westphal considers the trochees as equal in time to the dactyls and spondees with which they are associated. In that case, they would contain irrational times; the long of the trochee would be $\frac{8}{3}$ and its short $\frac{4}{3}$ of the short time which serves as the unit of measurement; while together they would make $\frac{12}{3}$ or 4 short times, which is the normal length of the dactyls and spondees. But on the other hand, in logaœdic verses, which show dactyls mixed with trochees, Westphal regards the trochees as having rational times, and the dactyls irrational. To the long of the logaœdic dactyl he gives the length of $\frac{4}{3}$, to its first short $\frac{2}{3}$, to its last short the rational length 1: the dactyl consists then of $\frac{4}{3}$, $\frac{2}{3}$, 1, making in all 3 times, which is the normal length of the trochees. To this measurement of the logaœdic dactyl Cæsar strenuously objects: he makes the logaœdic dactyl equal to a trochee, but divides it into $1\frac{1}{2}$, $\frac{3}{4}$, $\frac{3}{4}$—the long syllable $1\frac{1}{2}$ instead of two, and each short $\frac{3}{4}$ instead of 1. This difference of opinion has been the theme of some pretty acrimonious discussion; but I cannot enter here into the merits of the quarrel.

I have already pointed out a long syllable of three times as occurring in the penult of catalectic trimeters. I may now say that the ancient rhythmic recognizes also a long syllable of four times (this, too, we have had occasion to notice); and even a long syllable of five times, equal to a whole cretic or pæonic foot. It is often matter of doubt whether we are to recognize such a lengthened long, or whether we are to assume a pause of one, two, three, or four times. Such vacant times, *κενοὶ χρόνοι*, are fully recognized in the theory of ancient rhythmic. Thus, in the so-called elegiac pentameter, *αἰσχύνη δὲ φίλοις ἡμετέροις ἐγένου,* where the one syllable *λοις* takes the place of a dactyl, we might question whether *λοις* was actually prolonged to a length of 4 times, or whether it had its usual length, but was followed by a pause of two short times. In this case we have ancient testimony showing that the syllable was not prolonged, but that a pause was made after it. But if times are wanting in the middle of a word, as often happens, we may safely assume that they were made up, not by a pause, which could hardly be tolerated in such a place, but by the prolongation of a long syllable to three, four, or five times. The recognition of deficient times, which were made up in one way or the other, by a pause or by the prolongation of a long syllable, has put a new face on ancient metres. It is perhaps the most important peculiarity in the work of Rossbach and Westphal on Greek metric. In the little metric at the end of my Greek grammar I have adopted it from them, with the name of *syncope*, which they had given it. Its effect in giving simplicity and unity to many things which before appeared unconnected and unmeaning may be shown by a brief illustration. In looking over the index of metres to President Woolsey's Electra, I find five different names given to what I should regard as syncopated forms of the iambic trimeter: 1. Antispast and iambic penthemimeris; 2. Two iambic penthemimeres; 3. Iambic penthemimeris and iambic tripody; 4. Iambic dimeter hypercatalectic; 5. Iambic dipody and ithyphallic. By looking over the indexes to other plays, I have no doubt that I could have increased this number. It is evident that these names, beside their number, fail most of them to suggest any clear idea of a rhythmical unity. But if in all these various and strange-looking lines we can truly recognize various forms of the iambic trimeter, we have certainly made a great and most satisfactory advance in our understanding of their rhythmus.

VI.

ON THE NATURE AND THEORY OF THE GREEK ACCENT.

1869.

EVERY Greek word of two or more syllables had one syllable which was sounded on a higher key than the rest of the word: thus, *λυ* in *λελύκοιμι*, *κε* in *λελυκέναι*, *κος* in *λελυκός*. For a long time, the Greeks in writing their language made no attempt to distinguish the syllable which was thus sounded on a higher key: they aimed to represent the substance of their sounds, the different articulations, but not their relative pitch. It was not until the development of grammatical study, in the Alexandrian period, that the grammarian Aristophanes of Byzantium, about 200 years before our era, invented a sign for this purpose. Over the vowel which was sounded on a higher key he placed a wedge-like mark, sloping downward to the left, which was called *ἡ ὀξεῖα προσῳδία*, 'sharp accent,' 'acute accent.' But it often happened, in the utterance of a long vowel or diphthong, that the higher key with which the word began was not maintained to the end; that, after pronouncing the first part on a higher key, the voice dropped down to a lower, and on this pronounced the last part of the long sound. For such cases Aristophanes introduced a compound sign; representing the higher key as before, he added, to represent the lower key, a similar mark, but sloping downward to the right. The roof formed by the joining of the two marks was rounded off in writing, and the whole sign was called *ἡ περισπωμένη προσῳδία*, 'twisted accent,' 'circumflex accent.' The ordinary lower key was not generally represented by any distinctive mark: if the vowel of a syllable had no mark of higher pitch written above it, this was a sufficient indication of its lower pitch. And, indeed, there was nothing in this lower pitch that called for designation. The essential fact to be recognized and made evident in the writing was not that some syllables were lower than the rest: it was that some were higher than the rest; or rather, that one syllable in each word was made conspicuous and important above all others by the higher key on which it was sounded. Yet there were two cases in which the lower pitch was represented in writing. One of these has just been noticed—when the lower pitch followed the higher in the same syllable, in the same long vowel-sound. The circumflex accent used for such a syllable consisted of two marks, a first representing the higher, and a second representing the lower pitch. The other case relates to oxytone words, where the higher pitch comes at the end of the word and belongs to the last syllable: ἀγαθός, στρατηγός. If such a word is followed by other words in immediate grammatical connection, the higher pitch of its last syllable changes to a lower one, as in ἀγαθὸς στρατηγὸς ἐγένετο. Here now, on the last syllable of an oxytone word, when in the connection of discourse its higher pitch changes to a lower, the lower pitch is represented in writing, and represented in the same way as in the latter part of the circumflex accent: that is, by a mark sloping downward to the right, and called ἡ βαρεῖα προσῳδία, 'heavy accent,' 'grave accent.' Aside, then, from these two cases, the ordinary lower pitch is always left without designation.

In this description of the Greek accent, it has been taken for granted that there was an actual regular difference of pitch between different syllables of a word, and that the proper use of the written accent was to represent that difference. The correctness of this assumption is implied in the very names of the accents. The words ὀξύς, 'sharp,' and βαρύς, 'heavy,' are the ordinary words used in Greek music for what we in our music call 'high' and 'low.' They are not used to denote difference in stress, or strength of utterance. We might find it natural that ὀξύς, 'sharp,' should be applied to a syllable which was pronounced with marked stress; but it would be strange if βαρύς, 'heavy,' was used of syllables pronounced without stress, the weaker or lighter syllables of a word. The term προσῳδία itself, as well as the Latin *accentus*, which is used to translate it, comes from a root which means 'to sing;' and in explaining the name, the ancient grammarians, both Greek and Latin, tell us that it is a singing of the syllable. There is a remarkable passage in a work of Dionysius of Halicarnassus (*de Comp. Verb.*, 11), in which he compares the melody of speech with that of song. The melody of spoken language, he tells us, is measured by a single interval, the so-called fifth, or, as he explains it immediately after, the interval of three tones and a semitone. He says that when the voice rises to the acute, it does not go higher than this interval; and when it falls off again to the grave, it does not sink lower than this interval. He adds that the two intonations, the acute and the grave, may be combined in the same syllable, and that such syllables are said to be circumflexed. It is perfectly evident that he is here speaking of the accent, that he describes it as a difference of pitch, and that he makes this difference about the same as the musical interval of a fifth, that is (as he himself says), three tones and a semitone. All this is pretty clear; but it is made still clearer by the contrasted description of music, which comes directly after it. Music, whether vocal or instrumental, uses a number of intervals, and does not confine itself to the fifth alone (these are his own words); but employs, for purposes of melody, first the octave (this being first named, as the most important interval), and the fifth, and the fourth, and the full tone, and the semitone, and, as some think, even the quarter-tone (the chromatic diesis), so as to be distinctly perceived. Further, he says, music claims the right to subordinate the words to the tune, instead of having the tune subordinate to the words; by which he means that it is the right of the musician to sing the words to any tune he pleases, without reference to the natural tune (if we may call it so) which by the accent they have in spoken utterance. That this is his meaning becomes abundantly evident from a subjoined illustration. He quotes two or three lines from a chorus of Euripides, and points out at some length how the natural tune or accent of the words was wholly disregarded in the music to which they were sung. Thus, the first word, *σῖγα*, is sung upon a monotone, both syllables on the same pitch, though the spoken word had two tones, the acute and the grave, and indeed both of them combined in the circumflex accent of its first syllable. In another word, ἀρβύλης, which had the acute on the second syllable, the music gave both second and third syllables the same pitch, though in a spoken word the higher pitch of the acute accent was never maintained through two successive syllables. In τίθετε, the natural tune of the word, a high sound followed by two low ones, was completely reversed by the music, the first syllable being sung to a lower note and the last two syllables to a higher note. In κτυπεῖτε, the circumflex of the second syllable, with its combination of acute and grave, was lost in the music, that syllable being sung upon a single note. And in ἀποπρόβᾰτε, a word of five syllables with acute accent on the middle one, the higher intonation, which belonged to the προ, was in the music transferred to the βᾰ. These are the illustrations and explanations given by Dionysius himself, whose authority on such a subject must be very high from his intelligence and learning, as also from his date, in the first century before our era. This passage alone, if there were nothing else to confirm it, would leave no doubt as to the melodic character of the Greek accent.

But is it not possible that this elevation of pitch, which characterized the accented syllable, was accompanied by an increased effort of the vocal organs, by a greater stress of pronunciation, such as marks the accented syllable in our own language and in other languages of modern Europe? It is possible, certainly; but there is scarcely any evidence to prove it true. In all that the ancient grammarians and other ancient writers have left us on the Greek accent—and the aggregate is far from inconsiderable—there seems to be no statement or expression which implies that the accented syllable was pronounced with more force than the rest of the word. No such implication can be found in the remarkable passage just referred to, where Dionysius speaks of the melody of spoken language. We might perhaps expect to find it rather in a following section, where his subject is the rhythm of spoken language. But nothing of the kind appears there. In speaking of rhythm, he refers to quantity of syllables, to the succession of longs and shorts; and he remarks that common speech, the utterance of prose, does no violence to these,

8

but keeps the syllables long and short according to their received or natural quantity. But music, which disregards the natural tune of words, disregards likewise their natural rhythm; it changes (so he says) the length of the syllables, increasing or diminishing their quantity, and occasionally even reversing the natural proportions; for (he adds), instead of making its own musical times subordinate to the natural quantity of the syllables, it makes the quantity of the syllables subordinate to the times of the music. In all this, there is no hint that any one syllable of a word was regularly distinguished from the others by its more forcible enunciation. Göttling, who believes that the accented syllable was actually pronounced with greater stress, can only refer in support of his belief to the modern Phavorinus. The silence of the ancient authorities may not prove that there was absolutely no difference in stress between accented and unaccented syllables; but it certainly warrants the conclusion that the difference, if there was any, cannot have been great or striking: it must have been far slighter than in English or in modern Greek. The grand fact about the accented syllable, to the mind of the ancients, was its higher pitch; its greater stress, if it had any, was either not noticed by them, or was felt to be comparatively unimportant.

The same conclusion—that the stress of voice on the accented syllable was little, if at all, greater than on other syllables—may be supported by probabilities resting on other grounds. It is the natural effect of a decided stress-accent to weaken the following syllables of the word, and especially the one which immediately follows the accent, so that the vowel of that syllable is apt to be shortened or to be omitted altogether. In our own language, this tendency may be seen in the short *e* of *mystery* as compared with the long sound in *mysterious*, and in the suppressed *e* of *every*, *wond(e)rous*. In Greek such changes are confined to a few words, as τίπτε in Homer for τί ποτε, ἦλθον for earlier ἤλυθον. They are perhaps hardly more numerous than the cases where an accented vowel has disappeared: cases like θύγατρες in Homer for θυγατέρες, βῆν for ἔβην, etc. So far from being disposed to shorten the vowel which follows the accented syllable, the

Greek shows rather a predilection for such forms as *ἄνθρωπος*, *τίθημι*, *λυθήσοισθον*. Latin proper names like *Dentatus*, *Modestus*, *Salernum*, the Greeks were perfectly able to pronounce with their Latin accent; there was nothing in their own system which forbade it: yet we often find such words accented on the first syllable, *Δέντατος*, *Μόδεστος*, *Σάλερνον*—showing that an accented antepenult followed by a long penult was a combination agreeable to the Greek ear and regarded with a kind of preference.

Another consideration which goes to show that the Greek accent was not accompanied by any very decided stress of voice is found in the structure of Greek verse. In this, the word-accent is wholly disregarded, the ictus of the verse being quite as likely to fall on an unaccented as on an accented syllable. In the heroic hexameter, for example, we know that there was an ictus, or verse-accent, that is, a special stress of voice, on the first syllable of each dactyl or spondee. But if we look at the first seven lines of the Iliad, out of the forty-two cases of ictus which they present, only sixteen are found on syllables which have the written accent. Now it would seem to us unnatural in our own language to take the words, "regarded with admiration and uncommon esteem," and read them as a hexameter, "régardéd with admíratíon and úncommon ésteem;" or to take the line, "'tis as moonlight unto sunlight or as water unto wine," and read it as an iambic tetrameter catalectic, "'tis ás moonlíght untó sunlíght or ás watér untó wine." But we must suppose that the Greeks did something very much like this, if we assume that with them, as with us, there was a decided stress of voice laid on the accented syllable. It is true that there is something hazardous in such reasoning. The Greeks, in the construction of their verse, may have treated their language with more freedom than we allow in the treatment of ours. Different languages, or, rather, the people who use them, differ widely in this respect. Thus the German poet has greater liberty than the French in departing from the established forms and idioms of prose speech. We have seen that in Greek music the natural tune of the word, the differences of pitch depending on the accent, were not observed, but were freely superseded by other combinations of tones at the pleasure of the composer. If, then, the Greeks in their music were willing to substitute other tones for those given by the accent of the spoken language, it is conceivable that in their verse also they may have been willing to substitute other stresses for those of ordinary speech, to lay the emphasis on other syllables, according to the rhythmical arrangement of the poet. Yet we cannot but regard it as highly improbable that a stress-accent, if it were as decided as ours, should be wholly neglected and superseded in the composition of verse. And in this view we are confirmed by the modern Greek, which, having a decided stress-accent, makes it, as we do, the basis or determining element of its verse-system.

Taking all these considerations together, we hold it all but certain that the Greeks did not lay any marked or forcible stress on the accented syllable. It is even doubtful whether they laid any stress upon it, more than on other syllables of the word. It is certain, however, that in the history of their language they have either adopted a stress-accent, or have given strength to a weak one existing from the first. In the modern accent, the leading element is stress, and difference of pitch, if it is not wanting, has at any rate ceased to be prominent and uniform. The distinction between acute and circumflex has been wholly obliterated. The forms δηλῶσαι, 'to make manifest,' and δηλώσαι, 'might make manifest,' are undistinguishable in the modern pronunciation. With this change in the character of the accent was connected, as we just saw, the adoption of accent as the basis of versification. When verses began to be constructed on this basis, they were called στίχοι πολιτικοί, 'political' or 'popular verses,' in contrast with the old quantitative verses, which continued to be written, as a kind of literary exercise, long after the pronunciation on which they were founded had ceased to be heard. Now these political verses were composed as far back as the eleventh century, and probably much earlier. Whenever they began to be made, we may be sure that the Greek accent had already changed its character, and had come to exhibit a decided stress. But the change, we may presume, was very slow, and may have been going on for centuries before the stress element was strong enough to express itself in verse composition. It is quite supposable, therefore, that a weak stress may have been heard on the accented syllable, as regular accompaniment, even in the time of Herodian, the principal authority on accent, if not yet earlier in the time of Aristophanes of Byzantium, the inventor of the accentual signs. If this were so, we might find in it an explanation of the fact already noticed, that the last syllable of an oxytone word has an accent written upon it, even when its tone changes from high to low. In *βασιλεὺς ἐγένετο*, the grave accent on *λευς* shows (so we are told) that it was pronounced on a low tone. But why then should it have any mark over it, more than the other syllables of the same word *βασιλεὺς*? Or why should *βασιλεὺς*, which in this case has no high tone, which is all pronounced on a low tone, have any mark of accent over it, more than an enclitic word, more than *ἐστίν* (for instance) in *χαλεπόν ἐστιν*, where the verb appears without accent? To such questions it might be replied, not wholly without plausibility, that though *βασιλεὺς* in the case supposed had no elevated pitch, no accent properly so called, its last syllable was yet distinguished from the rest by a slightly superior stress, and was therefore allowed to have a distinctive mark over it; while the enclitic *ἐστιν* was written without any such mark, because it had neither elevated pitch nor superior stress on either of its two syllables. This, I say, would be a possible solution of the difficulty. But there is another solution, of which I am now to speak, and which brings up a question of much interest for the theory of the Greek accent.

Did the Greek accent distinguish only two tones, a high and a low? Or was there some middle tone, having a regular place in the system, some intermediate between the two extremes? It must be confessed that the evidence given on this point by the ancient writers is not so distinct as could be wished. In general, they speak only of two tones, high and low, or (as they term them) acute and grave. Still, they do not explicitly assert that all grave tones were equally low. It may be that they thought it important only to distinguish the high tone, as dominating the whole word, and that differences between the lower tones seemed to them of too little practical consequence to require mention. Yet we do find in ancient writings indications of a middle tone. Thus Aristotle (Rhet., iii. 1. 4) speaks of three "tones, acute, grave, and middle;" though it is possible that by "middle" here he intends the circumflex, which, combining as it does both acute and grave, might be regarded as having an intermediate character. But the Greek grammarian Tyrannio of Amisus, as quoted by Varro, enumerates four accents, grave, middle, acute, and circumflex. Tyrannio, indeed, may have been speaking of the Latin accent; but Varro refers to other writers as recognizing a middle accent, Glaucus of Samos, Hermocrates of Iasos, and the Peripatetics Theophrastus and Athenodorus, some, if not all, of whom must have referred to the Greek. And the grammarian Servius says: "It must be understood that this doctrine of a middle accent is no invention of recent times, but belongs to all who before the time of Varro and Tyrannio have left anything on accent; since the majority of these, and the most distinguished writers, have made mention of this middle accent, all of whom Varro refers to as his authorities." This language of Servius, doubtless, overstates the case. The number of writers who expressly recognized a middle accent cannot have been so great as here represented. But a reason may be found for this in a remark of Servius himself, that "the middle accent, which is a sort of border between the two others, resembles the grave more than it does the acute, and is therefore reckoned with the lower rather than with the higher tone."

The evidence of a middle tone which has come to us from ancient writers, deficient as it is in definiteness and consistency, seems on the whole sufficient to warrant the inquiry, whether the phenomena themselves of the Greek accent furnish any indications of such a tone. G. Hermann, in his essay *De emendanda ratione Grammaticæ Græcæ* (p. 66), suggested that the grave accent, where it was written for the acute on the last syllable of an oxytone word, was the sign of a middle tone, intermediate between the acute and the unmarked grave. On this point Buttmann also, in his *Ausführliche Grammatik*, takes substantially the same ground. More recently, G. Curtius, reviewing Bopp's *Accentuationssystem* in Jahn's *Jahrbücher* (1855, vol. 71), expresses the opinion that the grave accent, where it forms the second part of the circumflex, represents not the ordinary low tone of the word, but an intermediate tone. This view seems to have been suggested to his mind by the Sanskrit system of accentuation: here, the *udâtta* (or elevated tone), corresponding to the Greek acute, is regularly followed in the next syllable by the *svarita*, which certainly differed from the *anudâtta* (unelevated, depressed tone) of the other syllables. The Indian grammarians describe the *svarita* as a combination of the *udâtta* and *anudâtta*, similar to the Greek circumflex; and this must clearly have been its character when used as an independent accent. But where it is the mere follower of an *udâtta*, and especially where it belongs to a short syllable, the statement that it was a compound accent, a circumflex, seems far from probable; we could much more easily believe it to have been an intermediate tone. Curtius intimates that he would not confine his recognition of a middle tone in Greek to the last part of the circumflex accent; yet he has not actually given further development to the theory. But a recent writer, Franz Misteli, in an able article contributed to the 17th volume of Kuhn's Zeitschrift, has taken it up and carried it to a much greater extent. He holds that the acute accent in Greek, as in Sanskrit (?), was regularly followed by a middle tone, this middle tone being either written as the last part of a circumflex, or being merely understood on the syllable which comes after the acute. If the acute stands on the last syllable of a word, where there is no room for a middle tone after it, the acute itself loses its high pitch and becomes a middle tone, represented by the so-called grave accent. Only at the end of a sentence, or before an enclitic, does the acute under such circumstances retain its high pitch, and the word appear as an oxytone. This theory of a middle tone Misteli applies with much ingenuity to account for the general laws of Greek accentuation. In showing how it may be made to answer this purpose, I shall not confine myself to his statements, but shall take the liberty to depart from them in various particulars, and shall introduce some views (especially those on Latin accent) which do not appear in his exhibition of the subject.

The general laws here referred to are the four following: 1. The acute cannot stand on any syllable *before* the antepenult. 2. The antepenult, if accented at all, must have the acute; but it cannot be accented at all, if the ultima is long: thus ἄνθρωπος, but ἀνθρώπου. 3. The penult, if accented, must have the acute, when the ultima is long (has a long vowel-sound): thus ἀνθρώπου, τοιαύτη. 4. A long penult (one which has a long vowel sound), if accented at all, must have the circumflex when the ultima is short: thus τοιοῦτος.

The Greek accent is confined to the last three syllables of a word. But in Sanskrit there is no such restriction. The accent may go back to any syllable, however far removed from the end of the word. In *ábubodhishâmahi*, 'we wished to know,' it stands at the beginning of a seven-syllable word. The same freedom, we may presume, belonged to the primitive Indo-European language. There must have been some time, therefore, in the history of the Greek language, whether before or after it became distinctively Greek, when a change took place in this respect—some time when all accents standing before an antepenult were carried forward and thrown upon one of the last three syllables. If we ask for the cause of such a change, none could be imagined more natural or probable than a fondness for some particular succession of tones at the end of a word. If the earlier accentuation had a threefold distinction of tones, a high tone, middle tone, and low tone, we can easily conceive that this succession, these three tones in the order of their height, should have been found an agreeable cadence for the close of a word. It is a cadence which appears in Sanskrit in very many words; it may have been common in the Indo-European language prior to the separation of its branches. What we should have to suppose in regard to the ancestors of the Greeks would be that at some time a special taste or fondness for this cadence developed itself among them, with a dislike for any cadence in which the high and middle tones were followed by more than one low tone, so that, in order to secure what they liked and avoid what they did not like, they came at length to change the accent of words, to shift it from an earlier to a later syllable. Changes in an opposite direction, from a later syllable to an earlier, were not made, even to secure this favorite cadence ; or, if such a change took place in particular cases, it did not become the general law. One thing further we must suppose, to account for the Greek accent: that in this cadence the Greeks preferred that the final low tone of the word should be a short one: they did not like to have it maintained through a long syllable. Our hypothesis, then, may be stated in a single sentence—that the early Greeks changed the older accent of words so as to secure this cadence—high tone, middle tone, short low tone—wherever it could be secured without throwing back the accent. This single hypothesis will be found sufficient to account for the four general laws already given. Thus :—

1. "The accent cannot stand on any syllable before the antepenult." In ἐλείπετο, 'was left,' the accent (it can hardly be doubted) was originally placed on the augment, as it regularly is in Sanskrit: it fell, therefore, on the syllable before the antepenult. The middle tone would then fall on the antepenult λει, and the remaining two syllables πε and το would have the low tone. But the preferred cadence allowed only one syllable, and that a short one, for the low tone at the end of the word. It was necessary, therefore, to place the high tone or accent on the antepenult λει, leaving πε for the middle tone and το for the low tone.

2. "The antepenult, if accented at all, must have the acute." Of course, if accented at all, it must have either the acute or the circumflex. Suppose, then, that in the word ἐλείπετο the circumflex accent was placed on the antepenult λει: that syllable, from the nature of the circumflex, would have the high tone on the first part and the middle tone on the last; and thus again as before there would be two syllables, πε and το, for the low tone. The circumflex on the antepenult would, therefore, be incompatible with the cadence required. But the rule asserts also "that the antepenult cannot have any accent, even the acute, if the ultima is long." For suppose that the first person ἐλειπόμην could have the acute, the high tone, on the antepenult λει: the middle tone

would fall on πο, and the low tone on μην, a long syllable. But the cadence required was "high tone, middle tone, *short* low tone." Hence the high tone or acute must be placed on the penult πο, and the final long syllable μην must be divided between the other two tones, its first half being sounded with the middle tone, and its last half (which, of course, has the quantity of a short syllable) being sounded with the low tone.

3. "The penult, if accented, must have the acute when the ultima has a long vowel." For in the feminine τοιαύτη, 'such,' suppose that the circumflex could stand on the penult αυ. This syllable, then, by the nature of the circumflex, would have both high tone and middle tone, and the low tone would fall on τη, a long syllable, which is inconsistent with the required cadence. To secure this, the high tone, or acute accent, must be placed on the penult αυ, and the final long τη must be divided between the other two tones, the first short time contained in it being sounded with the middle tone, and the last short time with the low.

4. "A penult with long vowel-sound, if accented at all, must have the circumflex when the ultima has a short vowel." For suppose that the masculine τοιοῦτος, 'such,' had the acute or high tone on the penult ου; the middle tone would then fall on the last syllable τος, and the final low tone would be excluded. In many words, as in λόγος, 'speech,' this was something unavoidable: the high tone falling on λο, the short penult, must fill that syllable, the middle tone must fill the last short syllable γος, and there is no room left for the closing low tone. But with a penult long by nature, as in τοιοῦτος, there was no such necessity. It was enough to divide the long ου between the high tone and middle tone—in other words, to sound it with the circumflex accent: the ultima τος was then left for the short low tone, and the desired cadence was thus obtained.

We see, then, that these four general rules of Greek accent, which have the appearance of being unconnected, arbitrary, and capricious, are all of them direct corollaries from a single hypothesis, all of them necessary results from the extension of a single cadence—high tone, middle tone, short low tone—at the end of words. But what shall we say of polysyllables like χαλεπός, 'harsh,' with acute on the last syllable, or like χαλεπῶς, 'harshly,' with circumflex on the last syllable, or like λελυμένος, 'having been loosed,' with acute on the penult before a short ultima? In these words there is room for the favorite cadence, but they do not have it: they close either with the high tone itself (as in χαλεπός), or with the high tone followed by the middle (as in χαλεπῶς, λελυμένος). How can this be accounted for? By the last clause in our hypothesis: "The Greeks changed the older accent of their words, so as to secure the favorite cadence, *wherever this could be secured without throwing back the accent.*" We hold it to be true, as a general fact, that words like those just given were thus accented in the primitive period—*i.e.* either on the last syllable, or on the penult with short ultima following—and that they did not assume the threefold cadence, because the tendency to this was not strong enough to produce a retraction of the accent from a later to an earlier syllable. By this we do not mean that such a retraction never occurred. It may have taken place in numerous instances, but it never became the general law. And thus the Greek has many oxytones, which of course end with a high tone; many perispomena, which end with a middle tone; and not a few paroxytones with short ultima, which likewise end with a middle tone: and these, not in short words only, when the full cadence was impossible, but in very many longer words, where there was room enough and to spare for the succession of 'high tone, middle tone, and short low tone.'

But there was one branch of the Greek people—the Æolians of Asia Minor—which went farther than the rest in the fondness for this cadence. The Æolians did not hesitate to retract the accent for the purpose of securing it. Thus λελυμένος was changed by them to λελύμενος, χαλεπός to χάλεπος, χαλεπῶς to χαλέπως—χάλεπως they could not say, for that would make a long low tone. If there was not room for the complete succession of three tones, they secured as much of it as they could, saying (for instance) σόφος with high tone and middle tone, instead of the common Greek σοφός, 'wise,' an oxytone word. Hence in the Æolic dialect the only oxytones were monosyllables, and even these were oxytone only when the vowel was short, as the articles τόν, τό, τᾰ́. If the vowel was long, there was room for a middle tone after the high tone: the monosyllable was then pronounced with circumflex accent, as τῆν, τοῦς, instead of the common Greek τήν, τούς. It was only in prepositions and conjunctions that the Æolic, in agreement with the other Greek dialects, admitted oxytone words of greater extent than one short syllable.

We observe now that a similar hypothesis may be used to explain the peculiarities of Latin accentuation. The Latin, beside the acute accent, or high tone, has a circumflex, which it uses just where the Æolic dialect would use the circumflex—that is, on all monosyllables with long vowel (except only *ne* with the imperative), and on all penults with long vowel followed by short ultima. On all other accented syllables the acute was used: viz., on antepenults followed by short penult, on long penults followed by long ultima, on all penults long only by position, on short penults of dissyllables, and on all monosyllables with short vowel, enclitics of course excepted. It is evident that in changing the primitive accent the Latin has not confined itself to one direction, from earlier to later syllables: like the Æolic Greek, it has freely moved the accent backward, from later syllables to earlier, in order to secure the desired cadence. But the cadence required to account for the Latin accent is in one respect different from that which served to explain the Greek. The Greek would not allow the middle tone to be followed by a long low tone: the Latin would not allow the low tone to be preceded by a long middle tone, a middle tone extending over the whole of a long syllable, whether long by nature or by position. Hence for the Latin the cadence becomes "high tone, short middle tone, low tone." For example, in *legere*, *legeres*, *legeret*, the low tone fell on the last syllable, *re*, *res*, *ret*, without reference to its quantity, whether long or short; the middle tone on the short penult *ge*, and the high tone on the antepenult *le*. This example is enough to show that, by the necessity of such a cadence, the accent could never go farther back than the antepenult; that the antepenult, if accented at all, must take the acute; and that the antepenult could only be accented when the penult was short. In such forms as *gaudere* or *gau-*

deret, the acute must stand on the long penult *de;* but if the desired cadence is to be obtained, it must admit the middle tone to the latter half of the long vowel, for the short ultima has only room enough for the low tone: the word, therefore, could only have the circumflex (the combination of high and middle tone) on the penult. But in forms like *gauderes*, where both penult and ultima have long vowels, the Latin preferred to divide the long ultima *res* between the middle and low tones, leaving only the high tone for the penult *de:* the word, then, has the acute on the penult. So too have forms like *legendus*, where the penult has a short vowel, and is only long by position. Here the circumflex is impossible: the short vowel in *gen* cannot be divided between two tones, the high and middle; *gen* must have the high tone, *dus* the middle, and the low tone is excluded by the necessity of the case. In *legendi*, the cadence could be made complete by dividing the long *di* between the middle and low tones; but in *legendus* it is necessarily incomplete, as much as in *legit* or *legunt*, where both vowels are short, or in the Greek λόγος, having only the high and middle tones.

It is not necessary to go further into details to show that all features of the Latin accentuation may be accounted for by the assumed tendency to close all words with the succession of "high tone, middle tone, low tone," or so much of it as possible, consistently with the one restriction that the low tone must never have before it a middle tone which occupied the whole of a long syllable. But if we compare the Greek accentuation with the Latin, and both with that freer system of primitive Indo-European speech which is best represented to us by the Sanskrit, we may naturally conclude that the first step in the series of changes which gave the accentual systems of the Greeks and Romans their peculiar character was caused by a simple distaste for a succession of low-toned syllables at the end of a word. I repeat, the beginning of a special Greek and Roman accentuation would seem to have sprung from the mere unwillingness to hear more than one low-tone syllable at the end of a word. This unwillingness, carried into practical effect, would confine the accent (that is, the high tone) to the last three syllables of the word. But it would not cause any retraction of the accent; it would allow such forms as χαλεπός, χαλεπῶς, λελυμένος; for these have not even one low tone, still less have they a succession of low tones at the end. And further, this simple distaste or unwillingness, as it implies no restriction on the long or short quantity of the single tones, would allow such forms as ἐλείπομην, ἄνθρωπου, in Greek, and such forms as *gaúderet*, *légendus*, in Latin. This first step we may naturally suppose to have been made in the Græco-Latin or Græco-Italican period—that is, while the common ancestors of these peoples spoke a language, differing indeed from the original Indo-European, but not yet divided into branches having a distinct character as Greek, and Italican or Latin. But the next step must have been taken after this division, as it is different in the two branches. In the Greek, it springs from a distaste for a long low tone, a low tone stretching through a whole long syllable, following the high and middle tones at the close of a word. This would require ἐλειπόμην instead of ἐλείπομην, ἀνθρώπου instead of ἄνθρωπου. The corresponding step in the Latin springs from a distaste for a long middle tone, a middle tone stretching through a whole long syllable, between the high and low tones at the close of a word. This would require *gaudéres* instead of *gaúderes*, *legéndus* instead of *légendus*. In Greek the effect of this second step was to make the cadence, "high tone, middle tone, short low tone," the prevailing one for words which were long enough to admit of it; though there still remained a large number of words, represented by χαλεπός, χαλεπῶς, λελυμένος, which did not have it. Now one section of the Greek race, the Æolic of Asia, went further than this: they took a third step, probably much later than the second; they threw back the accent of these words, so as to make the already prevailing cadence universal, so far at least as the length of the word would allow. Whether the whole Italican race, in all its branches, Umbrian, Oscan, Sabine, etc., took a similar third step, we are unable to say. It is certain that one branch did so, the Latins; they threw back the accent, so that the cadence already prevailing should be made universal, as far as the length of the word would allow.

Perhaps I should leave a false impression, if I were to close without calling attention in one word to the hypothetical character of what has been said here about a middle tone. The existence of a middle tone in Greek and Latin has a good deal of positive ancient testimony in its favor. But that a high tone, when it did not come at the end of a word, was regularly followed by a middle tone, is a proposition which, however supported by Sanskrit analogies, has no direct evidence in the statements of the ancient writers. And of course, if there were no doubt of its truth, still the use here made of it to account for the ante-historic changes and the earliest historical appearances of Greek and Latin accentuation, would be purely hypothetical. At the same time, it may be said with justice, that the hypothesis is so natural in itself, it is so readily suggested by known facts, and it offers so simple and perfect an explanation for a variety of seemingly unconnected and capricious phenomena, that one can hardly help believing that it has a foundation in truth.

To some persons it may seem hard to believe that the ordinary utterance of discourse and conversation should have had so much of musical intonation : that this threefold distinction of tone should have found place in it as a recognized and constant element. But in the Chinese, and the languages cognate to it, as spoken at the present day, we find the musical element playing a much larger and more important part. In some of the popular dialects of China, a large proportion of the syllables which make up the language are pronounced with seven or eight intonations : thus, as a short abrupt monotone (compare the English preposition *to* in its ordinary short pronunciation) ; or as a prolonged monotone (compare the English numeral *two*) ; or with mixed falling tone (like the Greek circumflexed τοῦ) ; or with mixed rising tone (like the English *two* at the end of a question : "*two?*") ; or with similar intonations duplicated on a lower key. Thus the same syllable may be pronounced in seven or eight different ways, having each their special and widely diverse meanings. Compared with such complexity of musical intonation, that which we have hypothetically ascribed to the early speakers of Latin, Greek, and Sanskrit, and the yet earlier speakers of the undivided Indo-European speech, is a very simple and easy matter.

VII.

ON THE BYZANTINE GREEK PRONUNCIATION OF THE TENTH CENTURY, AS ILLUSTRATED BY A MANUSCRIPT IN THE BODLEIAN LIBRARY.

1870.

IN the second part of Mr. Alexander J. Ellis's work on "Early English Pronunciation," mention is made (pp. 516–527) of a document which seems to me of considerable interest in reference to the history of Greek pronunciation. It consists of a few manuscript leaves, written apparently by an Anglo-Saxon hand, not far from a thousand years ago. On these leaves are given passages from the Greek text of the Septuagint, written not in Greek, but in Anglo-Saxon characters. They are Anglo-Saxon transliterations of the Greek Septuagint, in which it seems to have been the object of the transliterator to represent, at least approximately, in Anglo-Saxon letters the current pronunciation of the Greek words. These transliterations were noticed as long ago as 1705, by the famous Anglo-Saxon scholar Hickes, in the preface to his *Linguarum Veterum Septentrionalium Thesaurus* (pp. xi–xiii). The codex in which they are found is of a composite and fragmentary character. There is a brief account of it in the second volume of Hickes' Thesaurus, with a description of its contents, given by Humphrey Wanley. Mr. Ellis describes it more at length, on the authority of Mr. G. Waring of Oxford. He speaks of it as a small quarto volume, containing several unconnected pieces of great age and value. Thus, in folios 1–8, we have part of the treatise entitled *De Conjugationibus distinguendis*, by the grammarian Eutychius; in folios 10–18, an Anglo-Saxon homily on the finding of the cross by St. Helena, the mother of the Emperor Constantine; in folios 20–22, a Lunar and Paschal Calendar for the years 817–832; in folio 23, *Pauca de Mensuris et Ponderibus*, 'a few statements on weights and measures ;' and in folios 37 to the end of the volume, the first book of Ovid's *Ars Amatoria*. It is a curious fact that three of these pieces—the Eutychius, the *Pauca de Mensuris*, and the Ovid's *Ars Amatoria*—have a number of Welsh glosses, renderings of Latin words and phrases into the Welsh of that time. Zeuss, who makes much use of these in his *Grammatica Celtica*, refers them to the latter part of the eighth or the earlier part of the ninth century. He pronounces them the oldest monuments of the Welsh language ; and regrets that they are too scanty to show us the system of the language as it then was. From similar material, but more abundant, he has been able to reconstruct the Irish of the ninth century ; for the Welsh, there is no sufficient material before the twelfth. This, however, is aside from our present subject. The only parts of the manuscript which concern us now are folio 19 and folios 24–36. These contain extracts from the Septuagint, with the corresponding passages from the Itala (or old Italian, ante-Vulgate, version). And, of these, we may leave out of consideration folios 24–28, where the Greek text is given in Greek characters, with many inaccuracies, which show that the copyist had but little acquaintance with the Greek language. There remain then folio 19 and folios 28 to 36, in which the Greek text is given in Anglo-Saxon characters. Unfortunately this transliterated text has never been published as a whole. But Hickes in his preface before referred to has given specimens of it, which belong to the 1st and 22d chapters of Genesis, the 42d Psalm, and the 4th, 5th, and 55th chapters of Isaiah : a few verses from each, in all 25 verses. These same specimens are reprinted by Ellis, in a corrected form, having been carefully collated with the manuscript by Mr. Waring. In our remarks on Greek pronunciation as indicated by the manuscript, we are confined of necessity to these 25 verses ; but the evidence they give is probably as distinct on most points as we should be able to draw from an examination of the whole text.

But, before taking up particular points of Greek pronunciation, it may be well to notice one or two questions which naturally suggest themselves. What is the age of this manuscript? On this point I do not find that Hickes expresses any judgment. Mr. Waring thinks that it was written in the last half of the tenth century. His opinion does not seem to be founded on the forms of the letters, though these would probably give ground for a near guess to one expert in Anglo-Saxon diplomacy, but on external or historical reasons. It is not likely that an Anglo-Saxon, even of the better educated clergy, would have known or cared much about the Greek pronunciation of his time, unless his interest had been awakened and his information extended by living communication with Greek persons. Now Mr. Waring observes that Eadgith, an Anglo-Saxon princess, married Otho I. of Germany in 930, and her son Otho II. married Theophania, a Greek princess, in 972. He supposes that "at the court of Otho a constant connection was kept up with the Anglo-Saxons and the Greeks, and thus a means was opened for the priests of the former to receive some tincture of Hellenic letters. We shall therefore hardly be wrong," he says, "in referring such transcriptions to the latter part of the tenth century. Want of opportunity is against an earlier date, and the confusion and ruin occasioned by the Danish invasion in the early part of the eleventh century, the close connection of Canute with Rome, and the subsequent Norman influence through Edward the Confessor, render a later date almost impossible." To these historical reasonings, which do not seem to me very decisive, he adds "the agreement of the Saxon homily in the same book with the language of the tenth century;" and we may the more readily accept his conclusion, as most of the extant Anglo-Saxon manuscripts belong to that century.

Is it certain that the scribe intended his transliteration to be a phonetic one, that he aimed to represent the sounds rather than the letters of the Greek text? On this point there seems to be no reasonable question. The single fact that he represents *οι* uniformly by the letter *y* may be considered decisive; no reason can be imagined for this except a desire to indicate the pronunciation. Neither the Greek letters themselves, nor the *œ* diphthong which the Romans used for them, could suggest a *y* as the symbol. It must be admitted, indeed, that our writer is not uninfluenced by the Roman mode of writing Greek words. Occasional variations from his normal method can be traced to this influence. Thus, in general, he takes no notice of the rough breathing, which undoubtedly was no longer pronounced in his time; we may presume, therefore, that in the very few cases (six only out of seventy-nine in the verses before us) where he writes it by *h*, he was affected by the ordinary Roman transcription. For αι he usually writes a simple *e* (pronounced nearly as our *e* in *they*); in a few instances (eleven only out of eighty-eight), he writes *æ*, as in the ordinary Roman transcription. In this case the variation was the more excusable, because the writer was probably accustomed in Latin texts to sound *æ* exactly as he did *e*. So as to the consonant φ, which he generally represents by *f*; if in two instances out of fifteen he represents it as the Romans did, by *ph*, he certainly did not think of *ph* as having any sound different from *f*. Other variations and inconsistencies might be pointed out; but with one remarkable exception, of which we shall speak further on, the cases of deviation from the rule bear only a very small proportion to those of conformity with it. We are thus able to make out in all points what may be called the system of the writer, his normal method. We see clearly what letters he thought best fitted to represent the several vowels, diphthongs, and consonants of the Greek.

We proceed now to examine in detail this system of notation, and to point out some conclusions which may be drawn from it as to the current pronunciation of Greek in the time of the writer. The vowel α he represents, as we should expect, by *a*; ε, by *e*; ι, by *i*; ο and ω, by *o*. There is no reason to suppose that the Greek pronunciation of these vowels has altered since the earliest times, except that the distinction of long and short quantity has ceased to be observed. Whether the distinction was still observed in the time of our writer can hardly be determined. It is true that the Anglo-Saxon scribes often mark the long sounds of their own vowels by an accentual stroke; but in this practice they were so far from uniform that we can lay no stress on the general omission of the stroke in this manuscript. Only four instances of it occur in the 25 verses given. In three of these it stands over *ο*, in one over *η*; in all the four it coincides with a Greek accent. That the Anglo-Saxon vowels *a, e, i, o* had the same sounds with the *α, ε, ι, ο* in ancient and modern Greek is sufficiently proved by other evidence, though the confirmation which we find here is not unwelcome. The Greek *υ* our writer represents by *y*. He invariably distinguishes it from *ι*: he never uses *y* for *ι*, and he never uses *i* for *υ*. This is unquestionable evidence that the two vowels differed in pronunciation. Had *ι* and *υ* sounded alike, as they do in modern Greek utterance, our scribe would have confounded them in writing, as he confounds *ε* and *αι*, as he confounds *υ* and *οι*. Now, without reference to this manuscript, there is strong reason to believe that the Anglo-Saxon *y* had the sound of French *u* or German *ü*. And the general opinion of scholars has recognized this as the prevailing ancient pronunciation of the Greek *υ*. But here comes independent testimony that Greek *υ* and Anglo-Saxon *y* were sounded like each other, and both differently from the Greek *ι*. In what other sound different from *ι* can they have agreed, but in that which is most probable on separate grounds for each of them, the sound of French *u* or German *ü*?

The only simple vowel yet to be mentioned is *η*. And in reference to this we find a strange vacillation on the part of the writer, a vacillation which has no parallel in his treatment of other letters. He sometimes uses *e* and sometimes *i*, both with nearly equal frequency. In some of the fragments *e* prevails, in others *i*; but when all the instances are counted, there is little difference in the sum. In πάσης τῆς γῆς, Gen. i. 26, the *η* of the first word is given as *e*, that of the second and third as *i*. In ἐδίψησεν ἡ ψυχή, Ps. xlii. 2, the case is exactly reversed; the *η* of the first word is given as *i*, that of the second and third as *e*. Mr. Ellis's statement, here, has not his usual accuracy. "For *η*," he says, "we have most generally *i*, but in about 50 instances *e*." If he had counted, he would have found 55 instances of *i*, but 62 of *e*. The *e*'s have a majority, though only a small one, over the *i*'s. Mr. Ellis suggests that there was some confusion in the mind of the scribe, "perhaps arising from the Latin transcriptions of *η*, with which he was necessarily more familiar." But this is contrary to the analogy of the manuscript. The scribe was familiar with *œ* as a Latin transcription of *οι*, but in these verses he scarcely uses it all. He was familiar with *æ* as a Latin transcription of *αι*, but the instances in which he uses it are only one-eighth of the whole number. In the other seven-eighths he uses *e*, though he doubtless regarded *æ* as expressing the same sound. If *η* had sounded to his ear like Anglo-Saxon *i*, he would have represented it in general by that letter, and only by an occasional slip have fallen into the *e*, which for him expressed a different sound. On the other hand, if *η* had sounded to him like *e*, he would have represented it in general by that letter, and only by an occasional slip have fallen into the *i*. That he vacillates as he does between the two is a sufficient proof that both were unsatisfactory; the Greek *η* did not seem to him like either his *e* or his *i*. Now the ancient Greek *η* was a longer *ε*, an open sound which must have been essentially the same as that of Anglo-Saxon *e*. And the modern Greek *η* is not different in sound from *ι*, and of course not different from Anglo-Saxon *i*. It appears, then, that in this manuscript we have caught the letter in a state of transition; it was on its way from the ancient to the modern sound; it had become closer than the first, but was not yet so close as the second. It cannot have differed very widely from the final sound of English *they*, *pray*, *convey*, etc., which is certainly closer than Anglo-Saxon *e*, and has in fact a vanishing sound like Anglo-Saxon *i*. The difficulty which puzzled our writer may be illustrated by taking the three English words *ell*, *ail*, *eel*. The Anglo-Saxon *e* was like the vowel sound of *ell*; the Anglo-Saxon *i* like the vowel sound of *eel*. For the vowel sound of *ail* he had no equivalent in his language: how was he to represent it? If he writes an *e*, the word will sound *ell*, not *ail*; if he writes an *i*, it will sound *eel*, not *ail*. No wonder that he vacillates between the two, unsatisfied with either. I suspect the *η*, as he formed it, was a little closer than our *a* in *ail*; if not, I think he would more generally have used his *e*. But that the *η* was then less close than our *e* in *eel*—that is, than Modern Greek *η*—seems to me proved beyond a doubt.

If now we pass on to the diphthongs, we shall find, as we might expect, that a large part of them have lost the diphthongal character. Beside those written with iota subscript, which are represented here in the same way as simple *α*, *η*, *ω*, we have *ου* represented by *u*, *αι* represented by *e*, and *ει* represented by *i*. In all these cases, the change from the compound diphthongal utterance to the simple sound had begun to prevail either before, or not long after the Christian era. Another very interesting change of this kind appears in *οι*, which our scribe, as already stated, uniformly represents by *y*. He does not distinguish it from *υ*, and doubtless heard it pronounced with the same sound, that of French *u* or German *ü*. The fact that *οι* was for a long time sounded like *υ*, while as yet they were both distinguished from *ι*, has already attracted the notice of scholars. On this subject I may quote some statements made by G. Curtius in the *Erläuterungen* to his Grammar (p. 21). He tells us that Liscovius, in a work on the pronunciation of Greek, published in 1825, cited from old grammarians a number of orthographic rules which imply this identity of *οι* and *υ*. Thus in the *Erotemata* of Basil, written in the fourth century after Christ, it is said: πᾶσα λέξις ἀπὸ τῆς κυ συλλαβῆς ἀρχομένη διὰ τοῦ ῡ ψιλοῦ γράφεται πλὴν τοῦ κοῖλον. It is strange that the rule should omit to mention κοιμάω, κοινός, and several others with initial κοι; but it says, plainly enough, that the first syllable of κοῖλον has the sound of κυ. Similar rules are found in the *Epimerismi* ascribed to Herodian, and in the Greek Etymologica. Thus in the *Etymologicum Magnum* (p. 289, 11): τὰ εἰς υξ ἅπαντα διὰ τοῦ υ ψιλοῦ γράφεται πλὴν τοῦ προῖξ. The word προῖξ, then, must have sounded as if written πρυξ. If the modern pronunciation had prevailed at that time, the writer should have added words in ιξ, as θρίξ, κύλιξ, μάστιξ, πέρδιξ, τέττιξ, φοίνιξ, χοίνιξ, and a multitude of others; also words in ηξ, as βήξ, σφήξ, ἀλώπηξ, μύρμηξ, νάρθηξ, πήληξ, and many more; for the modern Greek pronounces all these as he would if they were spelled with υξ in the last syllable. Other facts of this kind are given by R. F. A. Schmidt in his *Beiträge zur Geschichte der Grammatik* (p. 73 ff.); and he derives from them a new and beyond all doubt a correct explanation of the name ὖ ψιλόν as well as ἔ ψιλόν. The old name of the letter was ὖ, *i.e.* the long sound of the vowel with circumflex accent. But when οι came to be sounded in the same way, the adjective ψιλόν, 'bare, simple,' was often added: thus ὖ ψιλόν, 'simple υ,' written with one letter, in distinction from ῡ δίφθογγον, written with two letters, that is, οι. As to ε, it was first named εἶ, just like the Greek word for 'if,' only given with circumflex accent; afterward it was named ἔ, the short vowel-sound itself serving as a name for the letter. But when αι was sounded in the same way, the word ψιλόν was often added: ἒ ψιλόν, 'the simple, one-letter ε,' in distinction from ε̄ δίφθογγον, 'the two-letter ε'—that is, αι.

How οι should get the sound of υ it is not difficult to understand. First, the close ι may have caused the ο before it to assume the closer sound of *u*. This would give the diphthong *ui*, which might naturally pass into the intermediate υ. If, instead of sounding the *u* and *i* each in its own position, the vocal organs take the position for *u* and in that position try to utter *i*, the result will be a simple υ. It is a curious fact that this pronunciation of οι appeared among the Bœotians several centuries before the Christian era, as in τῦς ἄλλυς for τοῖς ἄλλοις, Ϝυκία for οἰκία. What adds to the wonder is, that the changes in αι and ει should have been likewise anticipated among the Bœotians: as in γράφεσθη, Bœotic for γράφεσθαι; ἶμι, Bœotic for εἶμι. The Bœotians, backward as their Athenian neighbors thought them, were certainly, as regards pronunciation, in advance of their age.

We have yet to speak of the diphthongs αυ and ευ. Our scribe represents them by *au* and *eu*. In modern Greek they are sounded as *af* and *ef* before surds (*i. e.* smooth and rough mutes, also σ, ξ, ψ), but *av* and *ev* before sonants (*i. e.* all other consonants and all vowels). It seems clear that this writer did not hear them as *af* and *ef* before surds; for in that case he would have used *f* in writing them. To suppose that he would uniformly give up a phonetic representation for the sake of conforming to ordinary Latin transcription is contrary to the analogy of his procedure in other cases. Nor is it probable that he heard them as *av* and *ev* before sonants. The *u* with which he writes them is the same letter that he uses for *ου*; it is most likely that he meant it to express the same sound. This, however, is not entirely certain. The Anglo-Saxons, while they had a *w* (or what we write as such), had no *v*; the Anglo-Saxon *u* is always a vowel. But, in writing Latin, they used the same letter *u* both for *u* and for *v*. We cannot, therefore, be quite sure that our scribe would not have written *au* and *eu* for *av* and *ev*, as he was wont to do in writing Latin words like *gravis* and *levis*. But if he did so, if his *au* and *eu* were meant for *av* and *ev*, we may be sure that the Greek *β* did not sound to him as *v*, which is its present pronunciation. The modern Greek confounds *αυ* before sonants with *αβ*; but this writer distinguishes them, giving the former as *av*, the latter as *ab*; he cannot have sounded both of them as *av*.

As to the rough breathing, we have already said that our writer leaves it unrepresented in all but a very few cases, where we may presume that he was influenced by the ordinary Latin transcription. Undoubtedly it had ceased to be heard in pronunciation: and the Roman *h*, we know, has suffered the same fate in the modern descendants of the Latin.

The consonants will furnish little subject for remark. We have already observed that *φ* is pretty constantly represented by *f*. It is remarkable that for a long time the Romans never represented *φ* by *f*. At first they used *p* for this purpose, as in *Poino-s* for Φοῖνιξ, *purpura* for πορφύρα, etc. But afterward they begin to express the Greek aspirates; and thenceforward—that is, from about the time of Cicero—they used *ph* for *φ*. It is not until late in the period of the empire that we begin to find *f* for *φ*. This fact shows that the classical pronunciation of *φ* must have been more than slightly different from that of *f*: it must have been broadly distinguished from the *f*, and nearer to Latin *p*. It was, in fact, what the ancients describe it as being, a *p* followed by an *h* distinctly audible. But from this, its true aspirate sound, it passed into the spirant *f*; and that change had probably become fixed some centuries before the date of our Anglo-Saxon writer. The other aspirates must have undergone a similar change at about the same time. They are represented here by *th* for θ, and *ch* for χ. It is surprising that we nowhere find the simple character which is used in Anglo-Saxon writing for the *th* sound of *think, throw;* but there can be no real question as to the sound represented.

It is worth noticing that, wherever two rough mutes succeed each other, the first is always represented here as becoming smooth. Thus the word ἰχθύων occurs twice, and both times is spelt with *cth*, not *chth;* the participle λειφθέν occurs three times, and in each instance is spelt with *pth*, not *fth*. Can it be that the long current pronunciation of the word *diphthong* as *dipthong* was founded on the usage of the Greeks who served as teachers of their language at the revival of learning?

In modern Greek pronunciation a smooth mute (π, τ, κ), when it follows a nasal, is vocalized and becomes sonant, through the influence of the sonant before it. Hence μπ is sounded as *mb*, ντ as *nd*, γκ as *ng*. No such change is indicated in our scribe's transliterations: he writes *ampelon* (not *ambelon*) for ἀμπελών, *panton* (not *pandon*) for πάντων, *prosenencon* (not *prosenengon*) for προσένεγκον.

The modern Greek pronunciation has no middle mutes except after a nasal. Everywhere else the β, γ, δ have ceased to be mutes and have passed into spirants, with sonant utterance. From being the sonants of π, κ, τ, they have become the sonants of φ, χ, θ, in their present pronunciation. The writing of our scribe, who represents them by *b*, *g*, and *d* respectively, affords no clear indication of these spirant sounds. It is true that the Anglo-Saxon *g* must often have had a weak sound, not very different from our consonant *y;* but there is no reason to suppose that *b* and *d* had any other than their present English sounds. But for the spirant sound of δ—the sonant *th* in *other*—the Anglo-Saxon had a simple character, which we should expect to find here, if that was really heard by the writer. Still, as he has not used the corresponding character for the surd *th*, we can hardly lay very much stress upon this fact.

In all that has been said thus far, I have spoken of the scribe who wrote this transliterated text as being of Anglo-

Saxon race. But this cannot be regarded as certain. The codex which contains it is composed of half a dozen pieces; and we have seen that three of them contain Welsh glosses. Though there is one piece of Anglo-Saxon in the book, it is evident that a Welsh hand or hands have had a large share in its making up; and it is altogether possible that this transliteration may have been made by such a hand. This possibility derives some support from the fact that not one of the special characters used by the Anglo-Saxons—the *w*, the two signs for *th* surd and sonant, the compound *æ*—is found in this text. And none of them occurs in the Welsh glosses of this volume, as printed by Zeuss at the end of his *Grammatica Celtica* (with perhaps one exception, on p. 1087). It must be said, however, on the other side, that the *y*, which occurs so often in the transliteration, is not to be found in these glosses. If it was a Welshman who made the transliteration, we must suppose that, having in his own language no sound that corresponded to the Greek *υ*, he fell back upon the familiar Latin equivalent *y*, which he used also for *οι*, because that had the same sound as *υ*. But it would still be true that, if *υ* and *οι* had a common sound, different from *ι*, that common sound could hardly have varied much from German *ü*, which appears on independent grounds to have been the ancient power of the *υ*. And it might be shown in detail, if there were time for it, that the other conclusions which we have drawn from the manuscript would require little modification, if we suppose it to have been written by a Welshman rather than a Saxon.

The object of Mr. Ellis in giving a specimen of this transliterated text, and commenting at some length upon it, is mainly to throw light on the current pronunciation of the Anglo-Saxon in the tenth century. The light thus obtained, if it does not discover anything absolutely new, gives a welcome confirmation to views which were already probable on other grounds. But Mr. Ellis is led to say something on the pronunciation of Greek in ancient times. Without entering into any discussion of the subject, he gives utterance to a general conclusion, in the following terms: "We may never be able to recover the pronunciation, or appreciate the quantitative rhythm, of the Athenian tragedians or of the Homeric rhapsodists, but we can read as Plutarch and as Lucian, and we should be satisfied with that privilege, remembering that if we pronounced these later authors otherwise than as the modern Greeks, we should certainly pronounce wrongly. It would indeed be just about as absurd to read Lucian with the pronunciation of Aristophanes, as to read Tennyson with the pronunciation of Chaucer." This is a kind of *obiter dictum* in Mr. Ellis's book, for which, perhaps, he should not be held to a very strict account. But we must be allowed to express our surprise at hearing it from a scholar of so much candor and judgment. He is right, indeed, in assuming that Greek pronunciation changed in the five centuries between Aristophanes and Lucian. No one would deny this except those who, like Professor Ross of Halle, maintain the antediluvian antiquity of the modern Greek sounds. But can we suppose that Greek pronunciation has undergone no changes in the seventeen centuries between Lucian and our own day? Have not the external and political conditions been at least as unfavorable to continued uniformity of pronunciation in the seventeen centuries since Plutarch and Lucian as they were in the five centuries before them? But Mr. Ellis asserts that "if we pronounced Plutarch and Lucian otherwise than as the modern Greeks, we should certainly pronounce wrongly." How any man can say this who looks at the manuscript we have been discussing, and who believes in it, is beyond my comprehension. Mr. Ellis recognizes in the manuscript an attempt to represent the current Byzantine pronunciation of the tenth century. But, so regarded, it shows unequivocally that in the tenth century, seven or eight hundred years after Plutarch and Lucian, the current pronunciation was still in many important points essentially different from that of the present day. Unquestionably the most characteristic feature of the present pronunciation is its *iotacism.* Like ι are sounded the two vowels η and υ, and the four diphthongs, ει, ῃ, οι, υι: that is, there are six written forms beside ι which have the same sound with it. Now how does it appear in this manuscript? Here only one of these six forms—the diphthong ει—is as yet fully identified with ι.

Three others, the vowel *υ* and the diphthongs *οι* and *υι*, are uniformly distinguished from it, while the remaining two, *η* and *ῃ*, though clearly on the way toward an *ι*-sound, have not yet reached that goal. But the manuscript gives similar testimony in regard to other prominent features of the modern Greek pronunciation: so as to the sounds of *af* and *ef*, for the diphthongs *αυ*, *ευ* when followed by surds; and probably also the sounds *av* and *ev* for the same diphthongs when followed by sonants. So, too, as to the medial sounds for the smooth mutes *π*, *κ*, *τ*, where they follow a nasal. I say nothing as to the spirant sounds of the middle mutes, for in regard to these the testimony of the manuscript can hardly be regarded as decisive. But leaving these out of the account, the differences indicated between the pronunciation of the tenth century and that of the nineteenth are extensive and important. How then can it be said (as Mr. Ellis in effect says) that there is no material difference between the pronunciation of the second century and that of the nineteenth?

VIII.

ROSS ON ITALICANS AND GREEKS.

1858.

I PROPOSE to call the attention of the Society* for a short time to a pamphlet of some ninety pages, recently published by Professor Ross, of Halle, and entitled "*Italiker und Gräken.—Sprachen die Römer Sanskrit oder Griechisch?*" 'Greeks and Italicans.—Did the Romans talk Sanskrit or Greek?—In letters to a friend, by Ludwig Ross, Halle, 1858.' This rather quaint title is followed by an equally quaint dedication, "to the Greeks, as being, in race and language, parents of the Romans." The theory here indicated as to the relation between Greeks and Romans is more distinctly stated in the Preface—a lengthy but lively document, addressed to Professor Keil, of Pforte. The Preface, however, does more than announce the author's views of this subject; it explains the reasons which have led him to the present publication of his views. The immediate occasion for preparing the essay came, as we learn, from the recent appearance of Mommsen's History of Rome. The general merit of that extraordinary work is fully and even warmly recognized by Professor Ross. But he objects strongly to the opening chapters, complaining in severe terms of the "rash, confident, and overbearing manner" in which Mommsen dogmatizes "on the ante-historical period and the primitive history of Rome, on the sources of our knowledge concerning them, on the ethnographic relations of the Latins and other populations of middle and southern Italy, on the early importance of the Etruscans, and all other matters connected with these"—a manner which (as he goes on to say) "makes it evident enough that he has not thought it worth while to give these subjects any serious investigation." The most important of

* That is, of the American Oriental Society, at its meeting in November, 1858.

Mommsen's errors, and the one specially combated in this work, is found in a passage quoted by our author, asserting that "philological researches teach us to distinguish three primitive Italian stocks, the Japygian, the Etruscan, and the Italican, as we may call it, the last of which divides itself into two main branches, the Latin idiom, and that to which belong the dialects of the Umbrians, Marsians, Volscians, and Samnites." Professor Ross, on the other hand, maintains (we give his own words) that "in all middle and southern Italy, up to Etruria and Umbria, so far as our knowledge extends, but one great stock of languages—the Greek—prevailed, in different dialects; so that Latins and Volscians, Sabines and Oscans, Messapians and Japygians, spoke nothing but corrupt Greek, and that admixtures of Greek are found even in the Etruscan." And again, he asserts, in another place, that "the Latin, Sabine, Oscan, and, in general, all the idioms of lower Italy, the Japygian and Messapian included, are nothing but Greek, corrupted in speaking, and at last written with differently formed alphabets; and that all these idioms, and all forms of words developed in them, ran together at last into the Latin as sole heir to all of them." So certain and obvious does this character of the Italican idioms appear to Professor Ross, that from the failure of Bopp and his followers to recognize it he does not hesitate to infer the worthlessness of their methods. The passage in which Indo-European philology is weighed in a balance and found wanting is sufficiently curious to deserve extraction:

"You will ask, indeed," he says to his friend, Professor Keil, "in what relation I stand to the Sanskrit, as I have placed upon the title of these letters the question whether the Latin was Greek or Sanskrit, while in the following pages the Sanskrit is hardly mentioned. My answer is perfectly simple, 'I do not understand a word of Sanskrit.' But I comfort myself with the reflection that Mommsen and Curtius, whose statements have called out this tract, understand hardly any more of it, and have themselves been led by others into the path of error. The thorough learning of a language requires far too much time for a classical philologist to get it up in his spare hours: and with the mere skeleton of a language there is very little gained. How Sanskrit sounded in actual living utterance is probably pretty much unknown to our students of Sanskrit; and without the living sound a language is a stiff corpse, which you may recognize, dissect, and understand, but can hardly set in motion or action. Of Sanskrit studies in general I have a pretty low opinion, for I do not see that, since they have come to flourish in Germany, and are represented in almost all our universities, they have produced any important result, least of all any of a positive historical character, unless it be the word 'Indo-Germanic'—a designation hardly sustained even yet by sufficient grounds—with which so much speculation of all sorts (*Wesen und Unwesen*, 'business and bother') has been carried on, and which after all says nothing more than that the European nations and their languages have their furthest roots in Asia—a fact known ever since the famous tower-building at Babel, only expressed in a different way. As all comparative philology, in the many volumes it has sent into the world, has never yet, to my knowledge, demonstrated *in extenso*, as I have done in these pages, that the Latin is only a mixture of different Greek dialects, written in other letters, and afterwards raised into a literary language—I am fully justified in thinking of it thus disrespectfully. I do not mean to deny that now and then a Greek or Latin form or inflexion may properly be associated and compared with the Sanskrit, but the same thing can be done with other languages."

By other languages which, according to Professor Ross, throw as much light as Sanskrit on the forms of Greek and Latin, he refers, as it appears, especially to the Egyptian and the Phœnician. He suggests an attempt to point out the Egyptian and Phœnician words in Greek and Latin, as a desirable antidote to the Sanskrit. And to this end he makes a beginning himself with a long list of words, in which, among others, ναῦς *navis*, and πούς *pes* are traced to the Egyptian. That the same words are found in Sanskrit (*nâu*, *pad*), and in Anglo-Saxon (*naca*, *fot*), he would probably explain, if his dislike of Indo-European philology would permit him to take notice of the fact, by referring to the conquests of Sesostris. These he regards as the historical basis for the Greek mythus of Dionysus conquering India (a mythus, by the way, of which we find no trace before the time of Alexander), and in both—the Dionysiac myth and the supposed history of Sesostris—finds reason to believe that the language and religion of India may have been largely influenced by those of Egypt; so that "the multiform and grotesque divinities of the Indians" (as he is pleased to term them, with an evident unconsciousness of the immense difference between the earlier and later mythologies of India), "instead of being older than the Egyptian, are perhaps after all only a disfigured copy of the latter." How this may be, we will not stop to inquire; we will rather imitate the judicious forbearance of Professor Ross, who only throws out the suggestion, without entering on the proof.

But we must be allowed to point out some misconceptions which appear in the passage just extracted. In the first place, he misconceives the significance of the term Indo-Germanic or Indo-European (which Bopp with good reason prefers to use)—so strangely misconceives it as to furnish ground for a suspicion that his frank and manly confession in reference to his knowledge of Sanskrit should be construed as extending to Indo-European philology. The term, he assures us, signifies nothing more than that "the nations and languages of Europe have their furthest roots in Asia." Now this in one view is saying too little: in another, too much. Too much: for it scatters the roots of Greek and Latin through the continent of Asia; so that, in following the indications of this statement, we might look for them quite as much in Chinese and Manchu as in Zend and Sanskrit: indeed, Professor Ross, as we have seen, finds them still more in Phœnician and Egyptian. But this is not only not the meaning of the term Indo-European: it renders the term absolutely unmeaning and absurd. Again, it says too little: for it fails to express the fact that certain languages of Asia have, not only the same ultimate roots as the Greek and Latin, but also, what is vastly more important as proving identity of origin, the same grammar to a great extent, the same systems of formation and inflexion. We cannot help regretting that Professor Ross should have resolved to learn no Sanskrit, because his other pursuits would not allow him to learn all. He says, indeed, that "with the mere skeleton of a language very little is gained." But the present case, we think, furnishes clear proof to the contrary. If Professor Ross would get some friend, who knows the Sanskrit alphabet, to interline the paradigms of Bopp's Sanskrit Grammar with European equivalents for the oriental characters, it would be easy for him to read them all over in less than two hours. Among the nouns he would find such forms as Fem. *vâk*, 'speech,' in which he could not help recognizing the Latin *vox;* Gen. *vâcas*, Lat. *vocis;* Dat. *vâce*, Lat. *voci;* Acc.

vâcam, Lat. *vocem;* Nom. Pl. *vâcas*, Lat. *voces*, etc. Among the verbs he would find such forms as Aorist *adixam*, Greek ἔδειξα (originally εδειξαν); 2d person *adixas*, Gr. ἔδειξες; 3d person *adixat*, Gr. ἔδειξε (originally εδειξετ): Dual, 2d person *adixatam*, Gr. ἐδείξατον; 3d person *adixatâm*, Gr. ἐδειξάτην: Plural, 1st person *adixâma*, Gr. ἐδείξαμεν; 2d person *adixata*, Gr. ἐδείξατε; 3d person *adixan*, Gr. ἔδειξαν. We are greatly mistaken, if, after seeing such phenomena as these, which even the most cursory view of the Sanskrit paradigms would force upon his notice, he could regard them as adequately represented by saying that "the languages and nations of Europe have their furthest roots in Asia." And if he could be persuaded further to spend two hours or two days or two months on the languages of Egypt and Palestine, with a view to find in their grammars any fair offset or antidote to these Sanskrit parallels, we are greatly mistaken if after such an attempt he could still assert that the same comparison of Greek and Latin forms can be made with these languages as with the Sanskrit. We believe that a few hours of grammatical study applied in this way to the Sanskrit and other oriental languages, though he might only become acquainted with their skeletons, would effect a great change in his views of comparative philology, and that thus very much would be gained, if not for the cause of science, at least for the enlightenment and reputation of Professor Ross.

But again, he misconceives the views of Indo-European philologists as to the relation between Greek and Latin on the one hand, and Sanskrit on the other. He evidently regards them as deriving the Greek and Latin from the Sanskrit—as making this the parent language, and those its descendants. This is implied in the interrogatory of his title-page, "Did the Romans talk Greek or Sanskrit?" According to him they talked Greek—that is, a language formed from the Greek: and of course he assumes that according to his opponents they talked Sanskrit—a language formed from the Sanskrit. But no philologist of reputation maintains, so far as we know, that the languages of Europe are derived from the Sanskrit. The Indo-European languages have many things in common —things which it would be absurd to attribute to accidental coincidence; things which can only be explained as inherited from a common parent. But it is agreed on all hands, that neither the Sanskrit nor any other extant language can claim to be that common parent. The oldest of the Indo-European dialects are only descendants of the primitive mother. All of them have departed more or less widely from the original type, modifying, omitting, and adding each in its own way. The common language from which all have sprung is to be reproduced, if at all, only by comparing all its descendants. And if in such a comparison we derive especial advantage from the Sanskrit—more than from any sister dialect, more than from the Greek, which in this respect yields only to the Sanskrit—the reason is, partly, that the early language of India is preserved to us in monuments which are at once very ancient and very copious; and partly, that the Aryan people of India, having wandered less widely from the early home of their race, and being perhaps endowed by nature with less mobility of character and habit, seem to have preserved the primitive roots and forms of their language with more tenacity than their kinsmen of the West. The original Indo-European language must have had an extraordinary abundance of undiscriminated synonyms, both in roots and in formative syllables. Among such synonyms, the languages of the West, as a general thing, take their choice, retaining each of them one root or form, and suffering the rest to drop. Or, if they retain more than one, it is usually by establishing some distinction of sense between them, so that they are no longer completely synonymous. The Sanskrit, on the other hand, certainly stands nearer in this respect to the primitive condition. It presents—especially as found in the Vedas—a similar copiousness of synonymous words and forms: a characteristic which of course renders it peculiarly valuable for the purposes of linguistic comparison.

But let us proceed now from the preface to the sequel of Professor Ross's pamphlet. It will be observed that he thinks of Latin as holding to Greek much the same relation that French does to Latin. As French, though containing some non-Latin elements, is yet substantially Latin, only altered by time and corrupted by popular use: so Latin itself is in the same sense substantially Greek, only subjected to similar modifying and degrading influences. This he endeavors to prove by an extended lexical comparison of the two languages, Greek and Latin, embracing a large number of words, and conducted with an openly avowed and evidently sincere contempt for exact philological criticism. Of grammatical comparison, between the systems of inflexion and formation in the two languages, we find but little, though in a passing remark he acknowledges its importance. His strength is in numbers—the number of words which can be pointed out and put together as really or apparently identical in Greek and Latin. "A twentieth," he says, "at the utmost, a tenth, of my comparisons, I am willing to surrender as still uncertain. Even then, if you take into account formations from radical words, derivatives and compounds, more than half the entire stock of words in Latin is shown to be Greek, and a key furnished for deciphering the rest. *Quod erat demonstrandum*," he concludes with triumphant emphasis. Now if Professor Ross had not been so averse to a little knowledge of Sanskrit, a cursory examination of Bopp's *Glossarium Sanscritum* would have shown him that the Latin words cited in that work, as more or less probably connected with words found in Sanskrit, make a list little less numerous than that of his index—a list which Bopp could easily have doubled, if his philological principles had been of the same easy and accommodating character as our author's. And yet, were it even quadrupled, Bopp would not have drawn the inference, which according to Professor Ross would be inevitable, that the Latin language was derived from the Sanskrit. He would only have seen in it additional proof of a fact, too clearly proved before to need confirmation, that the Latin and the Sanskrit are both descendants of a common parent. Professor Ross must of course be aware that two languages may have a close and pervading lexical resemblance, without either of them being derived from the other. For French words we have to a great extent similar words in Latin: and the French language is in fact derived from the Latin. But again, for French words we have to a great extent similar words in Spanish: yet the French language is not derived from the Spanish. The Scottish *bane* is not of necessity derived from the English *bone:* in fact, there is no reasonable doubt that both have arisen independently from the Anglo-Saxon *bân*. The Latin *genu* is not of necessity derived from the Greek *γόνυ*: it is at least equally supposable that both may have arisen independently from a third form—say *ganu*—which we find, though with a degradation of the initial guttural, in Sanskrit *janu*. If numerous resemblances exist between the Greek and Latin, there are three possible suppositions to account for the fact. We may suppose, 1. that Latin is derived from Greek; 2. that Greek is derived from Latin; or, 3. that Greek and Latin are separately derived from a common source. Professor Ross adopts the first of these suppositions as the true one: to prove it true, he was bound to show, not only that the resemblances are numerous—for so they are between French and Spanish—but that they are of such a kind as to require the first supposition rather than the other two. It is a little surprising that he should have overlooked this obvious and capital necessity of his argument. He has contented himself with showing that Greek and Latin words are related in form, assuming in general, without attempt at proof, that the Latin form was made out of the Greek by some euphonic alteration or corruption. Yet in many of these cases it is improbable, to say the least, that the Latin form should have had such an origin; and in not a few, it is clear enough that the Latin stands nearer than the Greek to what must have been the primitive form. We will give one example from the multitude which offer themselves to our hand. Professor Ross says in express terms, "The usual origin of the Latin *j* is directly (*geradezu*) from the Greek *ζ*." As one instance he gives us *jugum*, 'yoke' (pronounced *yugum*), from the Greek *ζυγόν*; and at the same time refers, apparently with approbation, to a passage in Plato's Cratylus, in which *ζυγόν* is derived from *δύο* and *ἀγωγή*, as that which binds 'two' animals for 'drawing.' Probably, however, he would lay but little stress on this etymology, which is evidently conjectural, and is far from being supported by analogy. But what shall we say as to the main point: has *jugum* arisen out of *ζυγόν*? The thing, it must be owned, has very much the appearance of a phonetic miracle. How a *za*-sound should transform itself to *ya*, it is not easy to imagine. We assume here that the Greek ζ had the ordinary sound of English *z*, for the real sound cannot have been far remote from this, and Professor Ross is fully satisfied that this and nothing else was the real sound. The opposite change from *ya* to *za* would not be difficult to understand; for the *ya*-sound is closely connected with the palatals *cha*, *ja*, which contain a sibilant element and readily pass into sibilants. It is moreover attested by indisputable cases: thus the Latin *jugum*, which preserves its initial sound in Spanish *yugo*, becomes *giogo* in Italian, with a palatal, and *joug* in French, with a sibilant at the beginning. Can any cases equally indisputable be adduced for the change of *za* to *ya?* for if it can be shown to have taken place, we must believe it possible, even though we cannot understand the *rationale*. Our author presents no such cases, beyond two or three similar parallels between Greek and Latin words. Of these we need not notice Latin *jungo* referred to Greek ζεύγνυμι, Latin *jugo* to Greek ζυγόω, Latin *conjux* to Greek σύζυξ, which present the same root as *jugum* ζυγόν, and of course only repeat the same question. The connection of Latin *jus*, *juris*, 'broth,' with Greek ζωμός, 'broth,' ζωρόν, 'pure wine,' is made pretty doubtful by the difference of form in one case (ζωμός), and the difference of meaning in the other (ζωρόν): if admitted, we must still ask which was the primitive sound, *j* or *z*. The comparison of Latin *jejunus*, 'fasting,' with Greek εὔζωνος, 'well-girded'—*scilicet*, because a fasting man can more easily clasp his girdle—if made by an opponent of Professor Ross, would have seemed a broad burlesque of his view. Latin *major* is compared with Greek μείζων: but here it is evident that *j* has not arisen from ζ, nor *vice versa*, but both *j* and ζ from a combination γι, *gi*, or *gj*: μείζων is for μεγιων (compare ἐχθρός, ἐχθίων), and *major* is for *magior*, *magjor* (compare the adverb *magis*, which retains the guttural). There remains *Jupiter*, Greek Ζεὺς πατήρ. But here it is plain that *j* and ζ are not derived one from the other; but both from a common δι, *dj*, which appear in the Greek Genitive Διός, ΔιϜος, and in the Italican *Diuvei*=*Jovi*, to say nothing of the

Sanskrit *dyaus*, Gen. *divas*, 'heaven,' which corresponds with wonderful exactness to the Greek **Ζεύς**, *Δι(ϝ)ός*. It thus appears that the Greek and Latin parallels by no means require us to assume, notwithstanding the phonetic difficulty, a change from ζ to *j*. If other languages gave no testimony on the subject, or if, with Professor Ross, we closed our ears to their testimony, it would still be probable that the initial ζ in ζυγόν is of later origin than the *j* of *jugum*. But the moment we turn to look at other languages, it becomes impossible to doubt. Even our author would probably shrink from maintaining that the Sanskrit *yuga*, the Gothic *juk*(*a*), the Lithuanian *junga-s*, and the Slavonic *igo*, all show in their initial sound a corruption of the Greek ζ.

A remarkable error which Professor Ross has made in this connection illustrates the danger of indulging too far in an ignorant contempt for Indo-European philology. Though he regards the *j* of *Jupiter* as a corruption of the ζ in **Ζεύς**, he justly recognizes the *j* of *Jovis* as having arisen from *dj*; and in like manner identifies, no doubt with correctness, the divine names *Διώνη* in Greek and *Juno* in Latin. But unhappily it occurs to him to go a step further in the same direction, and identify the Latin *juvenis*, 'youth,' with the Greek διογενής, 'akin to Zeus,' which occurs so often in Homer as an epithet of princes. Now here is at once a difference of form and a difference of meaning, either one of which might have deterred a less adventurous and uncompromising philologist. Apart from the initial sounds, there is a variation of ending—the Greek stem being διογενες, not διογεν, while the Latin stem is *juven* (seen in Gen. Plur. *juven-um*), or, by a frequent assumption of *i*, *juveni* (hence Nom. Sing. *juveni-s*). Professor Ross, however, regards it as weak-minded to attach importance to such variations of ending or inflexion. Then the change of γ to υ might occasion some uneasiness to weaker consciences. True, we ourselves have *guard* and *ward*, *guile* and *wile*, *guaranty* and *warranty*. But in these, *w* was the original sound, which first strengthened itself by a prefixed guttural, but afterwards fell away: thus *ward*, *gward*, *g*(*u*)*ard*. A change in the opposite direction is not so lightly to be assumed. Yet if it were altogether common, we should feel some surprise at finding it just here. For the Latin has the root *gen* in *gigno*, *genus;* and developes it, not less widely than the Greek, in a long series of derivatives and compounds; it might be expected, therefore, in this word as well as in others, to preserve the well-known root in its pervading and familiar form. And, again, the connection of meaning between 'one of Jove's kin' on the one hand, and a 'young man' on the other, is hardly close enough to tempt an ordinary philologist to encounter the difficulties of form just enumerated. Indeed, it would seem as if Professor Ross himself were not entirely at ease about it. For he adds, in a tone of confidence which sounds a little hollow, "For *juvenis*, I think I have given the correct explanation." Now here again the cognate languages supply us with testimony, which of course Professor Ross rules out of court, but which, if admitted, must carry overwhelming and decisive weight. The Latin *juvenis* reappears with the same meaning and with little difference of form in nearly all the Indo-European languages. The Sanskrit stem *yuvan* may be pronounced identical with *juven* in the Gen. Plur. *juven-um:* for the short *ĕ* and *ŏ* of other languages are represented in Sanskrit by short *ă*, that language having but three short vowels, *ă*, *ĭ*, *ŭ*. The Sanskrit stem has moreover in part of its inflexion the contract form *yûn*, which is completely identical with the root of the Latin comparative *junior*, as also with the Slavonic *jûn*, 'youth.' The Lithuanian has *jauna-s;* the Gothic, *juggs* (=*jung-s*); and even the Welsh presents us *ieuanc*, 'youth,' *iau*, 'younger.' We have here a word which must have belonged to the primitive Indo-European language, since we find it in unmistakable identity from the banks of the Ganges to those of the Severn. The Greek only has suffered it to drop, supplying its place by another word not less early in its origin and not less extended in its diffusion, the adjective *νέος*, or rather *νεϝος*, 'new.' A somewhat similar case of omission is presented by the Latin in the words for 'son' and 'daughter.' The prevailing Indo-European designation for 'son' comes from a root *su*, 'to beget,' found in Sanskrit. Hence Sanskrit *sûnu* and *suta*, 'son,' Greek *υἱός* for *συ-ιος*, Gothic *sunu-s*, Lithuanian *sûnú-s*, Slavonic *syn*. That for 'daughter' comes, it should seem, from the root *duh*, 'to milk.' Hence Sanskrit *duhitar*, Greek *θυγάτηρ*, Gothic *dauhtar*, Lithuanian *dukte(r)*, Gen. *duktere(s)*, Russian *docj*, Irish *dear*. These, now, the Latin has discarded, substituting for them *filius* and *filia*, which have been generally regarded as derivatives from the root seen in Greek *φίλος*, 'dear.' This derivation, it must be confessed, is by no means certain; though it seems to be more probable than the one proposed by Professor Ross, who takes *filius* and *filia* from the Greek *φυλή*, as if for *φύλιος φυλία*, with the meaning 'one of the family,' male or female. But Professor Ross goes further, and derives the Greek *υἱός* itself from the same *φύλιος*. In this instance he departs from his usual practice: for he has to admit here that the Latin *filius* is far nearer to the supposed original form, shows vastly less corruption, than the cognate Greek *υἱός*. Probably the admission seems to him harmless, so long as the original form is seen to be genuine and unquestionable Greek. But the manner in which he makes *υἱός* out of *φύλιος* is too characteristic to be omitted. First, the aspirate *φ* passed into the *spiritus asper*—into *h*. For this change he adduces no parallel instance from the Greek, but finds it in the Latin *herba* for Greek *φορβή*, 'feed,' a comparison already made by others, but of doubtful correctness. He finds it also, and no doubt correctly, in the Spanish *hablar* from *fabulari*, *hierro* from *ferrum*, *hijo* from *filius*. "Thus," he says, "the Greek made *ὕλιος* from *φύλιος*: then *λ* was elided, and the *ι* which arose in its place was absorbed by the preceding *υ*. Hence [*υἷος* or] with change of accent, *υἱός*, to distinguish the word from *ὕειος* ['belonging to swine']. The Italian," he continues, "retained the old full form *filius* = *φύλιος*; but, as if to leave no doubt as to the identity of the word, the elided Greek form returns again letter for letter in the Spanish *hijo* = *υἱός*. Can all this," he concludes with natural exultation, "be made out and explained from the Sanskrit?" Alas, no—we are forced to confess, at the risk of degrading the Sanskrit still further in his eyes—no, it cannot. But just as little can it be made out from Greek and Latin. It rests mainly on the Spanish. For the change of *φ* to *h* no Greek example is given; for the disappearance of *λ* between two vowels, no Greek or Latin example. But the first occurs in Latin, and both are frequent in Spanish; and, therefore, we need not hesitate to recognize them, both at once, in a single Greek word.

We have said that it is the general practice of Professor Ross, in his comparisons of words, to give priority to the Greek form, and to represent the Latin as made from that by additions, retrenchments, and other alterations. It would even seem as if he regarded such words as *sex*, *sedes*, *somnus*, etc., as made from ἕξ, ἕδος, ὕπνος, by prefixing an *s*; and words like *vinum*, *volvo*, etc., as made from οἶνος, εἰλύω, by prefixing a *v*. For though in his lists of these words he puts the Latin form first, and thus appears to give it the priority, yet he tells us further on, that "the Italican idioms sometimes, though not often, prefix to the Greek vowels other consonants than *s* or *v*," which would seem to imply that, after all, the *s* and *v* were really nothing but prefixes added to the corresponding Greek words. We are willing, however, to regard his expression in this case as an unobserved inaccuracy of language. For an opinion so perverse ought not to be fixed on any scholar without the clearest evidence. But there are cases beside that of υἱός from φύλιος, in which he distinctly acknowledges corruptions in the Greek form which do not appear in the Latin. Thus he admits that the Greek has dropped an *n* in the common verb ἐάω, 'to permit,' and the Homeric adjective ἐΰς, 'good' (whence the adverb εὖ, 'well'). These words he identifies with Latin *sino* and *bonus*. Whether he considers the *s* and *b* as added by the Latin or dropped by the Greek, does not distinctly appear. Nor in regard to the *n* do we clearly understand why he speaks of it more than once as having been restored to these words by the Latin. Can he suppose that the Latin received the words in the forms *seao* and *beüs*, or *sio* and *bous*, and reinserted the *n* which had before fallen out? How came they to put in the precise letter which had been lost, rather than some other one? Or is this only a further instance of inaccuracy in expression, similar to that which charity compelled us to assume a moment since? As to the identity of ἐάω and *sino*, of ἐΰς and *bonus*, we will allow it to rest on Professor

Ross's authority. We can more confidently indorse his comparison in another case where he admits the corruption of the Greek form: we refer to the genitives γένεος in Greek and *generis* in Latin, from the nominatives γένος, *genus*. Yet even here he does not escape from his besetting inaccuracy of expression: for he describes this as one of the cases in which "the Latin inserts a liquid, *l*, *n*, or *r*, between two vowels—which liquid," he continues, "must therefore have existed originally in the Greek form." Why, if it existed in the original Greek form, the Latin should have been compelled to insert it, does not appear. But perhaps our author only means that the Latin has it there and the Greek has not—though at an earlier period, as he thinks, the Greek also had it. But in this point again we cannot fully concur with him. For we think it certain that the Greek γένεος never at any time had an *r* in it: that it has arisen, not from γενερος, but from γενεσος. In proof of this we shall not appeal to Sanskrit neuters in *-as*, Gen. *-asas*, which correspond to Greek nouns in -ος, -εος: as *manas*, Gen. *manasas*=Greek μένος, Gen. μένεος (for μενεσος). Professor Ross is proof against proof of this kind, however convincing to others. But there is no need of it here. We have only to mention three facts which our author himself would not think of disputing: 1. The Greek Nom. γένος has *s*, which is most naturally explained as belonging to the stem, since neuters of the third declension have no case-sign in the Nom. Sing.; 2. The Greek, while it retains ρ between two vowels, has in a multitude of cases dropped σ standing in that position: as τίθεαι, τίθῃ, for τίθεσαι; 3. The Latin, though it does not drop *s* between two vowels, has in a multitude of cases changed it to *r*: as in *Lares*, earlier *Lases* (*Carmen Fratrum Arvalium*); *erant*, Greek ἦσαν (τ).

Our author's eagerness to derive every Latin form directly from a Greek one, coupled with his fixed resolution to know nothing of Sanskrit, has betrayed him into many palpable errors. Even where the words which he compares are really connected, he often misconceives the relation between them. Thus he brings the Latin *bibo* directly from the Greek πίνω, assuming that both π and ν are changed to *b*. A change of π to *b* involves no particular difficulty: but the change of ν to *b* is not so easily admitted, and even our author calls it *vereinzelt*, 'isolated.' He seems not to have observed that *bibo* has the appearance of a reduplicated form, analogous to *sisto*. In the latter verb, *sta*, the stem-syllable, by reduplication becomes *sista*, which then allows its final *a* to be treated as a mere connecting vowel, and thus conforms to the third conjugation. The stem of πίνω, πο (as we find it in πέπωκα, ποτός), if treated in the same manner, would give πιπω or *bibo*. This derivation of *bibo*, which would appear, even without reference to the Sanskrit, a plausible hypothesis, is converted into absolute certainty when we turn to that language: for we find there that the root *pâ*, 'to drink,' follows the third or reduplicated conjugation, though instead of the regular *pipâmi*, it makes Present *pivâmi*, and in the Vedic dialect *pibâmi*, thus approaching very closely to the Latin form.

Again, our author in many cases overlooks a certain or probable connection between the two languages, substituting for it a superficial and illusory comparison. Thus the Latin *cerebrum* is set down as a corruption of the Greek ἐγκέφαλον, 'brain;' though we must say, in justice to Professor Ross, that he adds an expression of doubt. But surely, if he had not been so intent on making every Latin word to be an actual Greek word, only more or less corrupt, he would have connected *cerebrum* with κάρα, 'head,' even if he did not explain it with Bopp as a compound of *cere*, κάρα, Sanskrit *çiras*, with *fero*, φέρω, Sanskrit *bhri*, meaning 'head-borne, carried in the head'—equivalent to ἐγκέφαλον, though wholly distinct in etymology.

The Latin *luna*, 'moon,' is repeatedly identified with the Greek σελήνη. Now we have already noticed the relation of Latin *sex* and Greek ἕξ, *serpo* and ἕρπω, *salio* and ἅλλομαι, to which fifty more might be added of the same kind. We see how tenaciously the Latin preserves the initial *s*, and how readily the Greek sacrifices it, unless connected with another consonant, as in σκάπτω, στέλλω, etc. If σ is retained in σύν and its compounds, the reason is obvious in the earlier form ξύν, where we find it connected with κ. That σελήνη itself has preserved the initial σ, is owing probably to a consonant ϝ, which must originally have followed it; for it coincides in root with Sanskrit *svar*, another form of *sur*, 'to shine.' Yet along with σελήνη, we have the personal, or rather the divine name Ἑλένη (moon-goddess), which is probably the same word, but with the ordinary Greek mutation of initial σ to *h*. If, therefore, *luna* had been the Greek form, and σελήνη the Latin, the connection of the two might have appeared more plausible; as it is, we must regard it as in a high degree improbable. But, if unconnected with each other, neither of the two is without connections in the other language. *Luna* is for *luc-na* (compare *lumen* for *luc-men*), connected with *lux* and *luceo* in Latin, and with λευκός, λεύσσω in Greek. And σελήνη, on the other hand, is connected with σέλας, 'brightness,' which is clearly akin to the Latin *sol*. These obvious relations our author has overlooked, in consequence of his determination to connect every Latin word directly with a Greek word of the same meaning.

The Latin *opus* is represented as identical with the Greek ἔπος, "word,' the exact correspondence of form and inflexion being regarded as decisive proof of identity, notwithstanding a pretty wide difference of meaning. Why our author should lay so much stress here on coincidence of form is not quite easy to understand: for with the almost unlimited range which he allows to mutations of form, such coincidences might easily arise by accident in words originally different. And in fact he himself says elsewhere, in opposing some etymologies of Mommsen, that "like-sounding is not necessarily of like sort" (*gleichlautendes nicht nothwendig gleichartig ist*): and proceeds to illustrate the maxim by giving three different explanations to the *sul* in *consul*, *exsul*, and *præsul*: *præsul*=*præ-siliens*, 'leading in the dance;' *ex sul*=*ex solo*, 'driven out from his native soil;' while *consul* is only a corruption of the Greek—σύμβουλος! Σύν and *con* are one preposition, and βουλος, by a simple change of β to *s*, comes very near to *sul*. But in speaking of *opus* and ἔπος, he says that "where letters and inflexion both coincide, we cannot refuse to acknowledge the identity;" and he mentions Latin *sidus*, 'constellation,' and Greek εἶδος, 'form, figure,' as another instance of the same kind. Unluckily the supposed coincidence does not exist in either case. *Εἶδος* is not for σειδος, but for ϝειδος: the original ϝ is abundantly proved by the appearances of the Homeric verse, and by the close relation to εἶδον, 'I saw,' where Professor Ross justly recognizes it, comparing Latin *video*. So, too, ἔπος is really ϝεπος: no word in Homer presents more unquestionable traces of the initial ϝ, to say nothing of inscriptions which show us the letter itself. But ϝεπος cannot properly be said to coincide in form with *opus*, unless we are willing to say that λέπος, 'peel,' or νάπος, 'glen,' coincides with *opus*: and even in meaning these are not much further away than ἔπος. We will venture here to offer a suggestion. A Sanskrit root like *âp*, Professor Ross, we fear, would reject with scorn. After deriving *mas*, 'male,' from Greek μάχλος, 'wanton,' by omission of χ and change of λ to *r* (though, by the way, *masculus* shows the Latin stem to be, not *mar*, but *mas*), he says to his correspondent, "if that won't do, make me another *mas*: but, mind you, he must be Greek (*aber wohlgemerkt, griechisch muss er sein*)." Now we wonder that he did not find his Greek *opus* in κόπος, which has the meaning 'toil, fatigue.' The decapitation of the word (if I may so term the suppression of initial κ) he could defend by Latin *aper*, which he identifies with Greek κάπρος. And the neuter ending *us* (3d decl.) instead of masculine ος (2d decl.), if it gave him any trouble, could be supported by Latin *corpus, corporis*, 'body,' which he derives from Greek κορμός, κορμοῦ, 'a block cut from a tree.' And yet it is almost a pity to say anything against the ἔπος-*opus* etymology: for thereby hangs an interesting piece of literary history, which we give as we find it. "According to these analogies, *opus* is nothing but ἔπος, and we gain the conclusion, certainly not unimportant for Greek literary history and the question as to the antiquity of Greek literature, that, in the earliest period, ἔπος had passed from the meaning 'word' to the meaning 'work of poetry,' and hence 'work' in general: for only thus could it come to the Italican *opus*. As, therefore, in the last centuries *opera*, 'work,' has passed into the *opera* of music and poetry, so in *opus* the opposite change must have taken place from three to four thousand years ago." But we must add that ἔπος, though unconnected with *opus*, has its kindred in Latin. The same root ϝεπ appears in the aorist εἶπον, Homer εϝειπον for εϝεϝεπον; and, with a regular variation of vowel, in the noun ὄψ, that is, ϝοπ-ς, 'voice.' But no one who observes how often the Greek has substituted a labial sound for a primitive guttural can hesitate to identify ϝοπ-ς with Latin *vox*, *voc-is*, whence the verb *voco*, *vocare*. This unquestionable connection is overlooked by our author, who derives *voco* from Greek βοάω, 'to cry.' He must certainly have forgotten the Latin *boò*, *boare*, which corresponds exactly in form and in meaning to Greek βοάω. Both these have a common derivation, either directly from βοῦς, *bos*; or, more probably, from a root βυ=Sanskrit *gu*, 'to sound,' from which βοῦς *bos* are also derivatives: in any case they are radically distinct from *voco* and εἶπον.

We will mention further an interesting, not to say amusing, derivation of *populus*. Professor Ross considers it as a diminutive of πόπος, a word which occurs only in the Homeric exclamation ὦ πόποι. This has been regarded generally by recent grammarians as a mere interjection; but our author contends, not without force, from its connection with ὦ, and its appearance only at the commencement of addresses, that it must have been a real vocative. But he discards the explanation of ancient grammarians, who make it mean δαίμονες, 'divinities,' and adopts out of his own head the meaning 'men, people.' It thus serves him a double purpose, not only accounting for *populus*, but also for *pupus*, *pupa*, *pupulus*, 'a boy or girl, a mannikin or doll.' At the same time, he does not altogether discredit the statement of Plutarch that the Dryopes used πόποι for δαίμονες, 'divinities;' and that of a grammarian in Bekker's Anecdota, that the Scythians used it for ἀγάλματα, 'images.' He suggests in explanation that, as the oldest idols of the Dryopes were certainly pretty rude and inartificial, people may have given them the name of *mannikins;* and that the Greeks may have ridiculed the Scythian images by the same disparaging epithet. And if Zeus in Homer commences a speech to the divine assembly on Olympus with ὦ πόποι, our author looks upon the address, 'O folks' (*oh leutchen*) as a flattering expression of familiar confidence (*vertraulich und schmeichelnd*). He fails to observe that ὢ πόποι is used by Homer even in addresses to a single individual, showing that it must already have lost its meaning, if it ever had any, as a plural substantive, and sunk down into a mere exclamation. Nor does it strike us as very probable that the Dryopes would call their sacred images *puppets*, or that the Italicans would designate the collective nationality as a *little man*. Considering these improbabilities, as well as the total absence of direct proof for the meaning 'men' given to πόποι, we shall adhere for the present to the etymology which makes *populus* a reduplicated form of the stem which appears in πλέως, 'full,' πλῆθος, 'multitude,' and perhaps in πόλις, 'city.'

It must be evident already that Professor Ross is one of those resolute philologists who are not easily turned aside from their purpose by vowels and consonants. He laughs good-naturedly at his weaker brethren, who trouble themselves about *anlaut*, *inlaut*, *ablaut*, *umlaut*, and all the other *lauts*. For himself, he has no idea of paying too much respect to letters and syllables; he has in fact the lowest possible opinion of their steadiness. This is a result of his extensive and valuable travels in lands and islands where Greek is spoken. The endless variations of the local dialects have impressed him deeply with the extreme mutability of spoken sounds, and have thus given him what he regards as a peculiar qualification for his present undertaking. He commences his Preface with a long list of corrupt forms, brought together out of the various and widely separated *patois* of the modern Greek: and he has no difficulty in admitting such corruptions, any or all, as means for effecting the proposed transmutation of Greek into Latin. In particular the modern Greek καραφλός, 'bald,' for the ancient φαλακρός, has convinced him that the order in which the letters of a word may stand is pretty much a matter of indifference, and that so long as you have all of them in one aggregate, or most of them, or others more or less resembling most of them, you need not concern yourself about the particular succession. The transposition of vowels and liquids—*metathesis*—is an ordinary and familiar phenomenon of language. But our author's transpositions take a far wider range. Thus *verto* is derived from τρέπω by spelling the root backwards, τρεπ—*pert*, and by change of *p* to *v*, *vert*. The Latin word is thus made to illustrate its own meaning by a complete turn-about: and if the Sanskrit has the same form *vart*, Present *vartâmi*, it may perhaps be ascribed to a certain original perversity in that mischief-making language. The adjective ταχύς, 'swift,' by a similar process is converted into χατυς, which readily furnishes *citus*: though the Latin word, if we could suppose it endowed with consciousness, might feel some surprise at this sudden disruption from *cio*, 'to move, stir,' with which it has been so long and so comfortably connected, and the total revolution which it is compelled to undergo. The Latin *famulus* is derived by transposition of μ and λ, and by interchange of rough mutes, from Greek θάλαμος, 'chamber.' That a *valet-de-chambre* should be called simply and shortly *chamber*, is perhaps not incredible; yet we must confess a preference, on the score both of form and meaning, for the derivation from *facio*—*fămulus* for *fac-mulus*, with the same ending and the same omission of a guttural as in *stĭmulus* for *stig-mulus*, which Professor Ross refers, probably with good reason, to the root of Greek στίζω, 'to stick.' In some cases we should be much at a loss if our author were not kind enough to explain his processes. In διψάω, 'to thirst,' he assures us (we quote his words) that "the π falls out, the σ and δ are transposed and thus we get σιδάω, Latin *sitio*." In αἰσθάνομαι, 'to perceive,' the Future αἰσθήσομαι gives evidence of a Present αισθεω, which is supposed to be for ανσθεω: and this, by transferring σ from the middle to the beginning of the word, gives σανθεω, from which any one can easily find his way to Latin *sentio*. In other cases the explanation itself requires to be explained. For the Greek ἰχθύς, 'fish,' he assumes a change of χθ to ψ, giving ιψυς (which has remained, he thinks, in the common word ὄψον, 'fish, or flesh eaten with bread'), and then he adds: "From ἰψύς the Italicans by transposition formed their *piscis*." We have tried to spell the word ιψυς in every possible order of the letters: but we have not yet succeeded in making out the form *piscis*. Manage as we will, there is always a κ = *c* wanting. May it not be that the Italican secured his *piscis* by an ingenious combination of the real ἰχθύς with the supposed ιψυς, getting his *p* from one and his *c* from the other? And were the Goths then obliged to go through with the same process, which certainly is a little complex, to form their *fisk(a)s*, which corresponds exactly to the Latin *piscis?*

We will only add two or three cases to illustrate further the startling originality and the bold defiance of difficulties which characterize Professor Ross as an etymologist. The Latin *amnis*, 'river,' he derives from Greek ἄελλα, 'blast' ('stream of air,' and hence 'stream of water'); and in like manner *omnis*, 'all,' from Greek ἀολλής, 'collected together;' in both he assumes, without other examples, the rather remarkable euphonic change of λλ into *mn*. *Amo*, 'to love,' he derives from Greek ἀγαπῶ, through a supposed intermediate form αγπω, which most philologists would regard as still inconveniently and discouragingly remote from *amo*. *Amicio*, 'to clothe,' he derives not from *am* and *jacio*, 'to throw around,' but from Greek ἀμφιέννυμι. The prefix *am* is doubtless connected with ἀμφί: but few philologists would venture to derive *icio* from ἕννυμι (or ϝεσ-νυμι); even our author only states the fact, without adding an explanation. Of course he could give one, if called upon: did he think it too easy and obvious to require insertion? He does better for us, when he derives *duco*, 'to lead,' from Greek ἡγέομαι: for he gives us the Etruscan *lucumo*, derived from Greek ἡγεμών, as a key to unlock the enigma. The *l*, he tells us, takes the place of a *spiritus asper:* but *l* and *d* are often interchanged (as *lacrima* =δάκρυμα); and the vowel-change is supported by *luna* from σελήνη: and thus—all is clear.

It must not be supposed from what we have said that Professor Ross recognizes no such thing as fixity or permanence in language. Whatever else may change, one thing has remained constant from the beginning, secure "amid the wreck of letters and the crush of words;" and that is the modern Greek pronunciation of vowels, consonants, and diphthongs. "I consider it," he says, "as being from the time of Inachus, or whatever else may be more ancient than Inachus, the only correct pronunciation." All honor to courageous faith! It is something, as the world goes, to believe in the historic reality of Inachus, a millennium earlier than the earliest known monuments of the Greek language. But it is much more to believe that the Greeks, when they first adopted the Phœnician alphabet, added a *υ* only to express a sound already expressed by *ι*; and that, having afterwards applied the *η* to express the long quantity of this same sound, they were not yet satisfied, but took up *ει*, *ηι*, *οι*, *υι*, as four additional representatives of a sound which had three representatives already: and then that the old Greek grammarians should have made the enormous blunder of describing this sound, when represented by *η*, as a prolongation of *ε*: with much more of the same kind, which is inseparable from a belief in the primitive antiquity of the modern Greek pronunciation. It is not surprising, perhaps, that early prepossession and patriotic enthusiasm should lead the modern Greek to credit such marvels: though in a distinguished member of our own Society, who has written on the ancient pronunciation of his language, we see that such influences are not always proof against investigation and reason. But we should hardly have expected that Professor Ross's travels in Greece, extensive and useful as they have been, would so far transform him into a native Greek.

We have seen that our author, though always disposed to regard the Latin word as the corruption of an extant Greek word, is yet obliged to acknowledge that in some cases the extant Greek word is the corruption of a form more faithfully preserved in Latin. Nor is there any good reason why he should not have done this much more frequently. For he holds that the separation of the Greek and Italican races occurred at a very remote period, ages before the time at which the Greek language first becomes known to us. He supposes that the Greek colonization of Italy may have commenced some two thousand years before the Christian era, and perhaps far earlier. And though he regards it as having been in progress for several centuries, he intimates that nearly all the words which passed from Greece to Italy must have been carried over before the Greek itself was reduced to writing. And the Greeks, he tells us, had the art of writing, and used it, for fifteen centuries before Christ. Professor Ross, it appears, believes in Cadmus as well as Inachus, and perhaps in tradition generally: he thinks it very hard that Dædalus, for instance, should be stripped of his individual historic personality, and made to be only what his name means, a 'cunning artificer,' merely because he was unfortunate enough to live a few centuries earlier than some other men. Possibly a respect for tradition may have led him to assign a date so early for the Italican migrations. For he might naturally think that a body of tradition, which he accepts as reliable, would have included these migrations, if they had not been in great part anterior to its beginning. Let us then take the year 2000 B.C. as a convenient middle term between the extremes of time suggested by his language: his theory would be, that two thousand years before Christ, be the same more or less, the Greek language was carried into Italy. But what, we may ask, was the Greek language of the year 2000 B.C.? It might be hard to tell; but it would be easy to see that it was something widely different from the language of Homer. For if we carry Homer back to the year 900, and he cannot with probability be carried further, he is still separated from 2000 B.C. by a broad gulf of eleven centuries. What was English eleven centuries ago? Something quite as hard for us to understand and learn as modern German. Who from the English of the present day, or the French or German of the present day, could without other helps form any tolerable conception of those languages as they were eleven centuries ago? Our author, it is true, appears to regard the Greek of 2000 B.C. as not very different, either lexically or grammatically, from the literary language. The division of dialects he conceives of as already established at that early period. But what assurance can he give that even the grand distinctions which separate Ionic and Doric—the η for long ᾰ among vowels, and the σ for a primitive τ among consonants—were developed eleven centuries before the time of Homer? Yet he goes so far as to point out Laconian forms in the Italican idioms, and asserts that the Sabines were mainly Laconians. The philological reason for this statement, which has no support in tradition, must be that some Sabine words are thought to resemble the peculiar forms of the Laconian dialect more closely than they do the other dialects of Greek. But many Latin words have a closer resemblance to the Sanskrit forms than to those of any Greek dialect: as *septem*, Sanskrit *saptan*, Greek ἑπτά; *jugum*, Sanskrit *yugam*, Greek ζυγόν; *jecur*, Sanskrit *yakrit*, Greek ἧπαρ; *corvus*, Sanskrit *kâravas*, Greek κόραξ; and a hundred others. Shall we say then that the Latins were mainly Hindus?

But the comparative philologist can prove conclusively that the Greek of 2000 B.C., assuming that the Latin was derived from it, must have differed immensely from any known Greek dialect of the historic time. For in cases where the Latin agrees with the prevailing type of the Indo-European languages and the Greek departs from it, this departure, it is plain, could not have belonged to that supposed Greek language which was imported into Latium. To assert that the original type was first abandoned in Greece and afterwards restored in Italy (as our author appears to do in one or two places, if his language is to be strictly construed) is a gratuitous assumption, and an improbable one. We can only bring forward here a few prominent facts to illustrate the mode of reasoning just indicated, and for convenience we will give the name "Græco-Italican" to that primitive Greek (if Greek it was) from which the Italican idioms are supposed to have sprung, and which our author imagines to have been the spoken language of Greece about 2000 B.C. We say then that this Græco-Italican must have preserved the initial *s* before a vowel, which all the Greek dialects have changed into *h*: thus it must have had *sex* not ἕξ, *serpo* not ἕρπω, *sistâmi* not ἵστημι, and many others. So too it must have preserved the medial *s* between vowels, in many forms where all the Greek dialects omitted it, and where the Latin has changed it to *r*: thus *nusos*, 'daughter in law,' not νυός, Latin *nurus*; *visos*, 'poison,' not ἰός, Latin *virus*; *genesos*, 'of birth,' not γένεος, γένους, Latin *generis*. It must have preserved the final *m*, which all the Greek dialects have changed to ν, or (after *a*) have dropped altogether: thus *ŏvom*, 'egg,' not ᾠόν, Latin *ovum*; *pateram*, 'father,' not πατέρα, Latin *patrem; esiêm*, 'I might be,' not εἴην, Old Lat. *siem; êsam*, 'I was,' not ἦα or ἦν, Latin *eram* for *esam*. It must have preserved the final *t*, which all the Greek dialects have rejected, but which the Latin retains either as *t* or *d*: thus *esiêt*, 'he might be,' not εἴη, Old Lat. *siet; êsant*, 'they were,' not ἦσαν, Latin *erant* for *esant; alyot*, 'other,' not ἄλλο, Latin *aliud*. It must have preserved the consonant *y*, which, after producing a multitude of euphonic changes, vanished from all the dialects of Greek, but which the Latin retains or changes to *i*; thus *yugom*, 'yoke,' not ζυγόν, Latin *jugum; jêpar*, or rather *jêkar*, 'liver,' not ηπαρ, Latin *jecur; salyomai*, 'to leap,' not ἅλλομαι, Latin *salio*. In the inflexion of nouns, the Græco-Italican must have had a case which in all the Greek dialects has vanished from case-inflexion, the ablative in *t*, Latin *d*: thus *dolôt*, 'from art,' Oscan *dolud*, Old Latin *dolod=dolo; nuctot* 'from night,' Latin *nocte*, earlier *nocted*. In the comparative degree of adjectives, it must have had the form *ions*, Gen. *ionsos*, or *iyons*, Gen. *iyonsos*, like Sanskrit *îyans*, Gen. *îyasas*. From this ending the Greek in all its dialects omitted the *s*, leaving ιον (Nom. ιων, ιον), Gen. ιονος; while the Latin omitted the *n*, leaving *ios*, *iosis*, which afterwards became *ior*, *ioris*. Thus to Sanskrit *mahîyânsas*, 'greater' (Nom. Plur.), corresponded a Græco-Italican *magi(y)onses*, Greek μείζονες, Latin *ma(g)joses*, which is expressly handed down as the earlier form of *majores*. In the verb it must have preserved the old infinitive in *tum*, *tu*, which remains in Latin as in Sanskrit, but which in all the Greek dialects appears only as a verbal noun, without the proper character of an infinitive. It must have preserved likewise the old perfect participle passive in *tos*, which remains in Latin as in Sanskrit, but which in all the Greek dialects appears only as an adjective, without the proper character of a participle.

This enumeration of a few leading points may suffice to show that the supposed Græco-Italican must have differed very widely, not only from the known dialects of Greek, but also from the common or unitary Greek language, out of which these dialects sprang, and to which we may ascribe such features as belong alike to all of them. Now we cannot, with any approach to certainty, assign the period at which this unitary Greek began to undergo the changes which resulted in the formation of its various dialects. But one thing we can say with entire certainty, in view of such evidence as that just presented. We can say that the period here referred to, however remote it may have been, was long subsequent to another—to the period when the assumed Græco-Italican began to undergo the changes which terminated at last in the formation of the Greek with its dialects on the one hand, and on the other in the formation of the Italican idioms, Latin, Oscan, Umbrian, and the rest. Our Græco-Italican is thus driven far back into the darkness of an ante-historic past. When our author asserts that it was spoken in Greece and carried over by sea from Greece to Italy, he asserts that which may be true, though he is very far from having proved it so. But when he puts it later than the formation of the Greek dialects, and makes it in fact a mixture of those dialects, he maintains that which is certainly and demonstrably untrue. The real question for philological study at the present time is, whether there was any such Græco-Italican, distinct from the primitive Indo-European language; in other words, whether there was any special relation between Greek and Latin, more than between either of them and the Armenian, for instance, or the Gothic. It has been, and still is, the prevailing opinion that there is a special relation between Greek and Latin; that both have sprung from a common Græco-Italican, distinct from, and of course posterior to, the primitive Indo-European. This view is set forth in the works both of Mommsen and of Curtius. But there are respectable philologists who maintain the opposite opinion.

Before concluding, we ought, perhaps, to offer a word of apology. We have, perhaps, fallen below the dignity of this occasion, in giving an extended notice of a work so slight and unimportant—a work proceeding, it is true, from an accomplished classical scholar, and a justly esteemed traveller in classic lands, but unworthy alike of his position and his reputation. Possibly some little mixture of the light or the amusing may be found to season not disagreeably the ordinary gravity of our assemblies. We will not confess here—

we are ashamed to own it even to ourselves—a certain secret satisfaction in finding that Germany—before which we hide our diminished heads, acknowledging her to be first without second in philological studies—can send out from the high places of her universities specimens of fantastic absurdity scarcely equalled on this side of the Atlantic. A more legitimate pleasure may be derived from a book which allows us to see the immense difference between the present and the past—between the Indo-European philology, with all the deficiencies and uncertainties that cleave to it, and the unscientific and unsatisfactory etymologizing that preceded it. If at times we grow weary of the twilight in which we still move, and sigh with despairing hope for the perfect day, it may be well that a Professor Ross should come, and open for us a glimpse into the darkness visible, the realm of chaos and old night, which we have left behind us, as we trust, finally and forever.

IX.

ON INDO-EUROPEAN ASPIRATE MUTES.

1862.

IN order to understand fully the relations of the Indo-European languages, we need to know the forms of that primitive speech from which they have all set out on their divergent progress. Hence it must be the object of comparative philology to reconstruct the original Indo-European language as it was spoken by the common ancestors of Hindu and Persian, Greek and Goth and Gael. That this is an object not to be easily or soon attained, is obvious enough : it is rather an ideal to be aimed at than a result which we can expect to see realized. In any such attempt at reconstruction, the first point must be to determine the phonetic system of the primitive language ; what elements of sound were heard and uttered by our forefathers in that early time when as yet Sanskrit and Greek, German and Celtic, had no separate existence. It may seem at first view almost chimerical to think of recalling the fugitive sounds of a period so remote from our own ; but it must be remembered that their echoes have been sounding in Asia and Europe down to the present day. By comparing the phonetic systems of the different Indo-European languages, we may ascertain in many cases with a high degree of probability the phonetic elements which belonged to their common mother. I propose to give a specimen of such inquiries, by discussing the aspirate mutes of the original Indo-European language. Did that language possess aspirate mutes ; and if so, what were they, and how were they sounded ? First, then, let us see what letters of this class we find in the various languages, especially the ancient languages, of our family.

The Sanskrit has the greatest abundance of aspirate mutes. In this language and in its modern descendants, every unaspirate mute, whether surd or sonant, has its corresponding aspirate, made by pronouncing after it the sound of *h;* at least, such is the modern pronunciation. Thus, of surd mutes, along with *k*, we have *kh;* with *t*, *th;* with *p*, *ph*. And in like manner of sonants; along with *g*, *gh;* with *d*, *dh;* with *b*, *bh*. We have also aspirates for the so-called "cerebrals," lingual sounds peculiar to India, and borrowed probably by the Sanskrit-speaking people from languages which they found in that peninsula—sounds produced by turning the tip of the tongue far back into the mouth: thus, without aspiration, *ṭ*, *ḍ;* with aspiration, *ṭh*, *ḍh*. Even the palatals *c*, *j* (as in our *church*, *judge*), which are not exclusively mutes, but contain a fricative element, have their corresponding aspirates, *ch*, *jh*. These aspirates, as sounded in the living languages of India and in the traditional Indian pronunciation of the Sanskrit, have a compound character; they are made up of the unaspirate mute with an *h*-sound distinctly audible after it. It is conceivable, however, that these letters may have changed their sound in the course of ages, and that the living pronunciation of the old Sanskrit may have been something quite different. This, then, is a question which requires to be considered: whether there is reason for believing that the ancient pronunciation of these letters was materially different from the modern. Now if they were not originally compound aspirates of the kind just described, they must in all probability have been simple spirants, like our *f* and *v* and our two sounds of *th* (surd in *thin*, sonant in *this*). In that case, the aspirate corresponding to *k* would have sounded as German *ch* (in *machen*) or as modern Greek χ; the aspirate of *g*, as γ in modern Greek λόγος; the aspirates of *t* and *d*, as the two sounds just described of English *th;* the aspirates of *p* and *b*, as *f* and *v* respectively. It might be urged in favor of these sounds that, in the Sanskrit alphabet, the aspirate mutes are represented by single letters—a procedure which is perfectly natural if they were in reality simple sounds, like *f*, *v*, and the rest, but is somewhat surprising if they were compounds containing a distinctly audible *h*. But this argument is much more than balanced by others on the opposite side. Thus, it would be difficult to find simple spirants which should answer to the cerebrals, *ṭ*, *ḍ*; to pronounce anything like our *th* with the tip of the tongue bent back to the roof of the mouth seems almost a physical impossibility. It would be perhaps even more difficult to imagine any spirants which should answer to the palatals *c*, *j*. Besides, if the letter which is now pronounced *ph* was anciently pronounced *f*, we must recognize a change of sound from *f* to *ph*. But this seems a very improbable change, and cannot be supported, so far as I know, by any certain example. And if it is hard to suppose that such a change should have occurred in one case, how much harder to assume it for the whole series of mutes, surd and sonant; to admit that *v* has passed into *bh*, and *th* (as in *this*) into *dh* (*d-h*), and so throughout. We should have to suppose, too, that the change took place over the whole extent of northern India, in Bengali, Hindui, Marathi, and other languages, varying widely from each other, but none of them preserving any of the supposed original spirant mutes. But there is another circumstance which strongly supports the traditional pronunciation, by making it probable that these letters contained an audible *h*-sound; and this is that even in the Sanskrit we find them occasionally changing into *h*. This is true particularly of those which, as we shall see further on, are the most important of the whole series, the aspirates of *b*, *d*, and *g*. Thus the common root *han*, 'to kill,' shows in many of its derivative forms that it was originally *ghan*. The word *hansa*, 'goose,' is proved by the Greek χήν and the German *gans* to have been originally *ghansa*. The original ending *dhi* of the imperative, 2d sing., which corresponds to Greek θι in στῆθι, ἴσθι, is preserved in many Sanskrit verbs, but in many others it becomes *hi*. The pronoun *mahyam*, 'to me,' is proved by the analogy of *tubhyam*, and also by the analogy of those case-endings which contain the *bh*-sound, to have been originally *mabhyam*; though in this instance the change to *h* might seem to have been much more ancient, and to have preceded the separation of the languages, since we find it also in the Latin *mihi* as compared with *tibi*. These changes of the aspirate mutes to *h* have been carried to a much greater extent in the Prakrit dialects, which supplanted the old Sanskrit in the mouths of the people some centuries before the Christian era. In these the surd aspirates, as *kh* and *th*, have also been reduced in many cases to a mere *h*. Now it is true that in some languages a spirant sound—*f*, for instance, or *ch*—has passed into *h*; but a movement of that kind so general as we have seen it in the languages of India is a thing unexampled and almost incredible. But if the Indian aspirates were what tradition shows them, compounds of mutes with a distinctly audible *h*, then the change we have described is a perfectly intelligible and natural phenomenon. It is merely slurring and sinking one element in the phonetic compound. The *h* was perhaps uttered with a degree of force which threw into the shade, and at length totally eclipsed, the mute sound that preceded it. We are brought to the conclusion, then, that the letters in question could not have been simple spirants, but must have sounded in ancient, very much as they do in modern India, like the unaspirate mutes followed by a clearly pronounced *h*.

The argument here drawn from the change of aspirate mutes to *h* seems unfavorable to certain views which have been recently expressed by Lepsius in a valuable memoir on the sounds of the Arabic language and the mode of representing them in occidental characters. Speaking of the Sanskrit aspirates, he recognizes their compound character, as differing from the unaspirate mutes only by an added breathing: but this added breathing he holds to be nothing more than belongs regularly to the *p*, *t*, *k* of the English and the German. He declares, indeed, that English, French, and German have no tenues, but only aspirates and mediæ; their *p*, *t*, *k* are not tenues, but aspirates. And he says that he cannnot see how *t*, for instance, can be more fully aspirated than it is in the German *tau*, 'cable,' or *thau*, 'dew.' On the other hand, he tells us that the Hungarians have true tenues, but no aspirates. The Greek and Sanskrit had both tenues and aspirates: they had one *p*, for instance, pronounced in the Hungarian manner, and another *p* in the English. Now it is true that in forcible enunciation we speak our *p*, *t*, *k* with a sharp explosive utterance which approaches perhaps to the character of an aspiration. At the same time, it seems almost absurd to suppose that an *h* could arise from these letters, pronounced as we pronounce them. If the slight trace of aspiration which we sometimes give to these letters should become constant, and then should be intensified so as to bear a measurable proportion to the proper mute sound, the latter might in time fall away and leave only the *h*. But the substitution of this sound for the original mute could only come about by some such process. It may be considered certain that, before the Sanskrit aspirates passed into *h*, they had assumed sounds in which the aspirate element, the *h*, was vastly more prominent than anybody can reasonably suppose it to be in our English *p*, *t*, *k*. But if they had such sounds when the change to *h* took place, it would be difficult to say when they did not have them. For some changes of this sort are to be found even in the earliest Sanskrit; and in *mahyam* for *mabhyam* (Lat. *mihi* for *mibi*) we have a case which perhaps goes back beyond the formation of the Sanskrit itself.

If now we turn to the ancient Bactrian, the language of the Zend-Avesta, we find aspirates, both surd and sonant, as in the Sanskrit. Their use, however, seems to depend in a great degree on euphonic conditions, so that in kindred roots they do not correspond with regularity to the aspirates of the Sanskrit, the Zend often showing an aspirate mute where the Sanskrit has the unaspirate, and *vice versâ*. Whether they were pronounced with a distinct *h* sound is a point which it might be hard to determine in reference to an ancient language which has left no direct descendants, and which is so imperfectly represented by documents.

Coming next to the Greek, we find the three aspirate mutes φ, θ, χ. In the present pronunciation of the language these are spirant letters, with the sounds of *f*, English *th* surd, and German *ch*. There is reason to believe that this pronunciation goes back at least to the time of the later Roman Emperors. In many inscriptions of that period, the Greek φ is represented by a Roman *f*; which never was the case in earlier times. The Latin grammarian Priscian, about 500 A.D., tells us that the sound then expressed by *f* was originally signified by *p* with an aspiration (that is, by *ph*). This original *ph*, he adds, was retained in the Latin writing of

Greek words, as *Orpheus*, but changed to *f* in the writing of Latin words, as *fama*. He thus implies clearly that he regarded the *ph* of *Orpheus* and the *f* of *fama* as substantially identical. In fact, he says in another place that the lips are more firmly fixed in pronouncing *ph* than in pronouncing *f*, and this is the only difference between *f* and *ph*. Here the expression "this is the only difference" seems naturally to imply that he regards the difference as not considerable. Now the Latin *f* was unquestionably a spirant; and if the Greek φ in Priscian's time was likewise a spirant, we can hardly doubt that at that period the θ and the χ had the same character, though we have not the advantage of being able to compare them with any similar sounds in the Latin.

But there is a variety of considerations which go to show that these letters were not originally sounded as spirants, but like the Sanskrit surd aspirates, as compounds of *p*, *t*, *k* with a distinctly audible *h*. In the first place, I may mention the fact that they are never doubled, but that πφ is used for φφ, τθ for θθ, κχ for χχ. The spirant sounds are easily doubled. Thus *Saf-fo* offers perhaps less difficulty in pronunciation than *Sap-fo*. But if φ was sounded as *p-h*, then it must obviously have been almost impossible to double the aspiration. The organs closing on the first *p*-sound would open with the second, which would then be followed by its aspiration (*Sap-p-ho*); and this would give the sound of πφ, not of φφ. In the second place, these letters have actually arisen in many cases from the combination of a smooth mute with a rough breathing. Thus ἀφ' οὗ, 'from which,' has arisen out of ἀπ' οὗ; ἔφοδος, 'approach,' has arisen out of ἔπόδος. There can be no doubt whatever that these were once sounded *ap hou*, *ep-hodos*: the only question would be one of time—when did they change from *ap hou* to *af ou*, from *ep-hodos* to *efodos?* In the third place, two of these letters were originally written as compounds of a smooth mute with a following *h*—thus, φ as *ΠH*, and χ as *KH*—a mode of writing abundantly attested by extant inscriptions. When letters are first used to write a language, they are used according to phonetic principles: the presumption certainly is that the *Π* and *K* and *H* had the same sound in these combinations that they had elsewhere.

As to θ, the grammarians tell us that this also was once expressed, like the other aspirates, by ***TH***. But this statement is not borne out by the evidence of inscriptions, and is not probable in itself. The truth appears to be that, as the primitive Semitic alphabet had two signs for *t*, one for the ordinary lingual and the other for an intensive variety of it, the Greeks from their first adoption of Phœnician characters employed the second to express their own aspirate *t*. And it was probably the fact of their having already a simple character for this aspirate that led them afterwards to invent simple characters for the other two. Should any one wish to infer from this adoption of simple characters that the sounds represented were likewise simple, we need only point to the double consonants ξ and ψ to show the hazardousness of such an inference. In the fourth place, we must attach some weight to the well-attested difference between the Greek ϕ and the Latin *f*. Thus Cicero, it is said, in pleading for Fundanius, ridiculed a Greek witness on the other side, because he could not even pronounce the name (Fundanius) of the accused party. This perhaps might not necessarily imply that there was anything more than a slight difference between the Latin letter and the Greek. But it is a more significant circumstance, that for centuries the Greek ϕ is never represented by a Latin *f;* if the difference between the two sounds was a slight one, it is strange that, with the constant occasion to express Greek words in Roman writing, the familiar *f* should not occasionally be used for a sound approaching nearly to it. And in the fifth place, the preceding argument is confirmed by a similar fact in relation to the Coptic. The alphabet of this language, like the Roman, has what is believed to be a spirant *f:* but this letter is never used in transcribing the Greek proper names Philippos, Philotera, and the like. The Greek ϕ itself is borrowed by the Coptic for this purpose.

These arguments in their collective weight seem to be decisive, and to make it certain that the Greek aspirates were once sounded as the surd aspirates of the Sanskrit. It is true that this conclusion involves one pretty serious difficulty—a difficulty presented by the familiar combinations $\phi\theta$ and $\chi\theta$. It is well known that, before θ, the Greek not only allows ϕ

and χ to stand unchanged (ἐγράφθην, ἐτύχθην), but even changes π and β to φ, κ and γ to χ (ἐπέμφθην, ἐλέχθην). These combinations, φθ, χθ, with the spirant pronunciation, are natural and easy; but to pronounce *p-h-t-h*, giving each of the four letters its proper sound, appears well-nigh impossible. It would seem that euphony must require us in such cases to give up the first aspiration, to say πθ (*p-t-h*) instead of φθ, and κθ (*k-t-h*) instead of χθ. This, in fact, is the prescription of Sanskrit euphony. I must confess my inability to offer any satisfactory solution for this difficulty. We might suppose that the earliest Greek had πθ, κθ, and that these were changed by assimilation into φθ, χθ, after the aspirates had assumed their present spirant sounds: but this would carry the spirant sounds so far back that they would precede the time of transcription into Coptic and Latin, and we should be unable to account for the peculiarities just noticed in that transcription. However this may be, it can scarcely be doubted that there was a time when the Greek aspirates differed from the smooth mutes only by the addition of an *h*-sound. They were thus, as before remarked, identical in sound with the surd aspirates of the Sanskrit. But it is a curious and important fact that, in roots and words common to both languages, it is almost always the sonant aspirates of the Sanskrit, rarely the surd, that correspond to the Greek φ, θ, χ. Thus Greek φύω answers to Sanskrit root *bhû;* Greek φέρω to Skt. root *bhar;* Greek τίθημι, root θε, to Skt. root *dhâ;* Greek οὖθαρ to Skt. *ûdhar*, our *udder;* Greek ἐλαχύς, 'small,' to Skt. *laghus*, 'light;' Greek ἔχις, 'serpent,' Skt. *ahis* for *aghis*. The Sanskrit roots and stems which have surd aspirates, if they reappear in Greek, appear there almost always with tenues instead of aspirates: thus Skt. *sthâ*, Greek στα in ἵστημι, not σθα; Skt. *prithus*, Greek πλατύς, 'broad,' not πλαθυς; Skt. root *sphur*, 'to tremble,' Greek σπαίρω, ἀσπαίρω, not σφαιρω. It should be said also that, among the Sanskrit roots and stems which have these letters, there is a very large proportion which have not been satisfactorily identified either in the Greek or in other languages of the Indo-European family.

Passing on now to the Latin, we seem to lose sight almost

completely of the class of letters under discussion. The only Latin mute of this species is the labial *f*. It appears to be certain that, from the time of our earliest notices, this letter was no compound of a smooth mute and rough breathing, but a simple spirant, not differing essentially from our English *f*. It is true that, from the expressions of Quintilian and Priscian in relation to it, Corssen has inferred, with some appearance of probability, that it was pronounced with a very loose and imperfect contact between the upper teeth and lower lip, so as to have a particularly rough or aspirate sound. But this belongs to the special coloring of the sound, not to its general nature, and is unimportant in relation to our present inquiry. It concerns us more to observe how it corresponds to the Greek and Sanskrit aspirates in words which belong to the Latin in common with those languages. At the beginning of words, the Greek φ, Sanskrit *bh*, appears in Latin as *f:* thus Skt. root *bhar*, Gr. φέρω, Lat. *fero;* Skt. *bhrâtar*, Gr. φρατήρ, Lat. *frater*. But a Latin initial *f* corresponds also in a number of cases to Gr. θ, Skt. *dh:* thus Gr. θύρα, Skt. *dvâram* for *dhvâram*, Lat. *fores;* Gr. θήρ, Lat. *fera*. But the Greek initial χ, Skt. *gh* or *h*, is usually represented by Latin *h:* thus Gr. χειμών, 'winter,' Skt. *himas*, 'snow,' Lat. *hiems*. In the middle of a word, on the other hand, the aspirates of the Greek and Sanskrit usually appear in Latin as unaspirated sonants; that is, as *b*, *d*, *g*. Thus Gr. ἄμφω, 'both,' Skt. *ubhâu*, Lat. *ambo;* Gr. ὀρθός, 'straight, steep,' Skt. *ûrdhvas*, Lat. *arduus;* Gr. λείχω, 'to lick,' Skt. root *lih* for *ligh*, Lat. *lingo*. It is instructive to look at the words for 'red' in these languages. The Greek has ἐρυθρός, the Sanskrit *rudhiras*, showing a primitive *rudh* or ρυθ. In Latin, the lingual aspirate passed into a labial, which appears either as an unaspirated sonant, in *ruber*, or as an aspirate surd, in *rufus*.

If in Latin we find the aspirate mutes reduced to a minimum in the single spirant *f*, we are met by a still more complete deficiency when we turn to the languages of North-eastern Europe, to those of the Letto-Slavic class. The *f* itself is wanting in the Lithuanian and in the Old Slavonic, and in both, the aspirates of the Greek and Sanskrit appear regularly as unaspirated sonants, as *b, d, g*. Thus Gr. φύω, Lat. *fui*, Skt. root *bhû*, Lith. inf. *bûti*, 'to be,' O. S. *byti;* Gr. φρατήρ, Lat. *frater*, Skt. *bhrâtar*, O. S. *bratrŭ*, Lith. *brolis, broterelis;* Gr. ἐρυθρός, 'red,' Skt. *rudhiras*, Lith. *raudónas*, 'red,' O. S. *rŭdyeti*, 'to redden;' Gr. ὀμίχλη, 'mist, cloud,' Skt. *megha*, O. S. *migla*, Lith. *miglà*.

In the Celtic languages, we are struck at first view with the great abundance of aspirate mutes. For each of the three tenues, *p, t, k*, and for each of the three medials, *b, d, g*, we have corresponding aspirates, which in the Irish are written *ph, th, ch, bh*, etc. These are sounded, not as compound aspirates, but as simple spirants. The proper spirant sounds of the *th* and *dh*, though corrupted and lost in the modern Irish, are preserved in the Welsh. We find, however, on a little examination, that the use of these aspirates depends on euphonic conditions and principles peculiar to the Celtic languages, and that they do not correspond, save rarely and exceptionally, to the aspirates of the Greek and Sanskrit. These latter, indeed, are represented in the Celtic languages precisely as they are in the Letto-Slavic, by *b, d, g*. Thus, for Gr. φύω, Skt. root *bhû*, we have Ir. *bi;* for Greek φρατήρ, Skt. *bhrâtar*, O. Ir. *bráthir*, 'brother;' for Gr. ἐρυθρός, Skt. *rudhiras*, O.W. *rhud*, 'red;' for Gr. χειμών, Skt. *himas*, O. Ir. *gaim*, O.W. *gauam*, 'winter.'

Turning now in the last place to the Germanic languages, we find much the same state of things as in the Celtic. The Mœso-Gothic, the oldest specimen of this class, has spirant mutes, but those only surd. Thus it has the labial *f;* it has the lingual *th* surd (as in *thin*), represented by a single character. For the palatal spirant *ch*, it shows the simple breathing *h*. In the further development of the Germanic languages, we find added to these their corresponding sonants, the sounds of *v*, *th* in *this*, and *gh*. But even the aspirates of the Mœso-Gothic, like those of the Celtic, are of secondary origin; they do not connect themselves with those of the Greek and Sanskrit. The Germanic languages stand here on the same footing with the Celtic and the Letto-Slavic. They show unaspirated sonants, *b, d, g*, in place of the Greek and Sanskrit aspirates. Thus in our *be* and *brother*, compared with φύω and φρατήρ; in *red*, compared with ἐρυθρός; and in *goose*, Germ. *gans*, compared with χήν, χηνός (apparently for χηνσός).

After looking thus at the different branches of our family, we are prepared to take up the question whether there were aspirates in the primitive Indo-European language. If they were found only in the Sanskrit and the Zend, we might suppose that they had sprung up in the Aryan or Indo-Persian branch after the separation of the other branches. But the fact that they appear in Greek, and that the same roots and words which have them in Greek have them also in Sanskrit, compels us to carry them back to a more ancient period, to times when the mother-tongue of Greek and Sanskrit was yet undivided. Possibly, however, it might be imagined that the languages of Northern and Western Europe, the Letto-Slavic, the Germanic, and the Celtic, which present only medials in place of the Greek aspirates, were separated from the common stock at a yet earlier period, while the ancestors of the Greeks and Hindus continued to live and speak together; and that it was then, after the separation of those former branches, that this class of letters began to develop itself. But even this hypothesis will be found untenable. For our Germanic languages, while they have lost the primitive aspirates, afford yet very curious indications of their primitive existence. If we take the Greek words θύρα, δύο, and τρεῖς, and look for their English equivalents, for θύρα we have *door*, for δύο, *two*, for τρεῖς, *three*. If, prior to the separation of the Germanic languages, the word *door* began with *d*, we ought in English to have *toor* (as for primitive δύο we have *two*); if in the same period it began with *t*, we ought in English to have *thoor* (as for primitive τρεῖς we have *three*). So with the series Gr. χήν, Eng. *goose*, Gr. γένος, Eng. *kin*, Gr. κύων, Eng. *hound*: if the ante-Germanic *goose* began with *g*, we should have *koose* in Eng. (like *kin*); if it began with *k*, we should have *hoose* (like *hound*). But these series are only examples of a general law of consonant relations (Grimm's *Lautverschiebung*). We see then that the Germanic languages represent the aspirate mutes of the Greek in a different manner from its tenues and mediæ; from which it follows that the aspirate mutes were already distinct from the tenues and mediæ before the Germanic branch came to be separate from the parent-stock. And this is equivalent to saying that there existed in the Indo-European language, prior to the separation of its branches, a class of mutes distinguished from the unaspirated surds and sonants, a class represented in later times by the surd aspirates of the Greek and the sonant aspirates of the Sanskrit.

It now remains for us to ask how this peculiar class of mutes was pronounced in that primitive language. Had they simple spirant sounds, like our *f* and *v* and our two *th*'s, or were they, like the Greek and Sanskrit aspirates, compounds of tenues and mediæ with an audible *h*-sound? That they must have had one or other of these two characters can hardly be doubted, when we see what sounds have proceeded from them in the linguistic history of our family. Nor can there be much doubt that they had the character last-mentioned, that they were in reality compound aspirates. If the spirant sounds were the earliest, it would be strange that we should not find them either in the Greek or in the Sanskrit, which present to us the most ancient specimens of Indo-European speech. And besides, if the spirant sounds were the earliest, we should have to suppose both in Greek and Sanskrit such changes as that from *f* to *p-h*, from *v* to *b-h*, etc.—a supposition which has been already characterized as forced and improbable.

But there is still another question to be considered. We have seen that the Greek aspirates were surd, made up of a smooth mute and rough breathing. Yet we have seen that in corresponding words and forms they answer to the sonant aspirates of the Sanskrit, made up of a middle mute and rough breathing. Which now was the original pronunciation? Did the primitive Indo-European give to the root of our verb *to bear* the sound of *phar* as in Greek φέρω, or of *bhar* as in Skt. *bharâmi?* Now the foregoing survey has shown us that in nearly all the great branches of our family the primitive aspirates are represented by sonant letters. Thus the labial aspirate of the original language appears in Sanskrit as *bh*, in Zend as *bh* or *b*, in Letto-Slavic, Germanic,

Celtic, and partly in Latin, as *b*: only in Greek, and partly also in Latin, does it appear as a surd, *ph* or *f*. Here, then, we find strong reason for believing that the Indo-European aspirates were originally sonant, *bh*, *dh*, *gh*. And accordingly this opinion has been generally adopted by the most eminent philologists: by Curtius in vol. ii. of Kuhn's Zeitschrift (1853), by Bopp in the second edition of his Comparative Grammar (1856), and by Schleicher in his recently published Compendium of Comparative Grammar (1861).

Only one voice, so far as I know, has been raised on the other side. Kuhn, in a late number of his Zeitschrift (vol. xi., 1862, p. 302 ff.) reviewing Schleicher's work, expresses his dissent from the commonly-received view, and his belief that the primitive aspirates were surd, as in Greek. In Sanskrit, he thinks, they have been generally weakened into sonants, while the surd aspirates of that language are mostly of later origin: though in some cases he holds these to be remnants of primitive usage. His reasons he only indicates in a brief sketch, promising to exhibit them more fully at some future time. They are in part directed against a view which I suspect that no one entertains: namely, that the Sanskrit surd aspirates were not only produced after the sonant, but were actually developed out of them in the same words and forms. This may, not improbably, have occurred in some exceptional and anomalous cases; but it is quite certain that the mass of surd aspirates did not originate in this way. Let us look then at his other reasons, which may be reduced to three. *First*, if the primitive aspirates were sonant, then in Greek they must have changed to surd. But this is a change from weaker to stronger sounds, and is therefore unnatural and improbable. There is doubtless force in this argument. The change from sonant to surd is certainly less probable than a change in the opposite direction. And yet there are abundant and striking examples of the less probable mutation. It is enough to mention that in the Germanic languages, by the first *Lautverschiebung*, all medials have passed into tenues (*two* for *δύο*, etc.); and that the modern Armenian pronounces all the medials of the ancient language as tenues, making up for this by pronouncing all the old tenues as medials (thus the ancient

Tigranes is the modern *Dikran*). *Second,* whenever new, unoriginal aspirates have arisen in the Indo-European languages, they have always been surd aspirates, never sonant, though sonant aspirates and mediæ have often been developed from them in the progress of time. The remark has reference especially to the Germanic and the Celtic languages. Of the first I believe it to be strictly true; but not altogether so of the second. The sonant aspirates of the Irish and Welsh have not been developed out of surd aspirates, but out of mediæ. It is not even quite certain, in case of the Irish, that they are of later development; for though the earliest monuments have only *ph, th, ch,* the aspirates of *p, t, c,* yet there are not wanting indications that the *b, d, g* had already undergone a change analogous to the aspiration of the *p, t, c.* Still, I think it more probable that in the Celtic, as in the Germanic, aspiration began with tenues, and that medial aspirates were of later growth. And the presumption thence arising of a similar progress in early Indo-European times is not without its force. *Third,* he says that if the surd aspirates have arisen from the sonant, it is very strange that in a number of cases the Sanskrit *ph, th, kh* correspond to Greek φ, θ, χ, and this partly in forms which, like verb-endings, go back to the beginnings of linguistic formation. Of Greek and Sanskrit words thus related, the number yet pointed out is not large, and in part of them there may be no real etymological connection. In some, we may suppose that, by an exceptional and anomalous change, the Sanskrit *bh,* etc., has passed into *ph,* etc. In others, it may be that both languages have independently changed the tenuis into a surd aspirate, *p* into *ph,* etc.: for it could easily be proved that such changes have been frequent in both languages. As regards the verb-endings referred to by Kuhn, it is curious to compare the Greek and Sanskrit forms. The Sanskrit has the sonant *dh* in several endings: in the 2d person sing. imper. active, *dhi* corresponding to Greek θι; in the first person plural of the middle, *mahe, mahi* (originally *madhe, madhi*), corresponding to Greek μεθα; and in the 2d person plural middle, *dhve, dhvam,* corresponding to Greek σθε. Here the relation of the aspirates is regular and constant.

But it is not so where the Sanskrit has the surd *th*. To be sure, *thâm* in the 2d person dual of the middle answers to *σθον* in the Greek, though for *σθον*, *σθην*, of the 3d person dual the Sanskrit has *tâm*. So *tha* in the second person singular perfect active may correspond to Gr. *θα* in *οἶσθα, ἦσθα, ἔφησθα, κλαίοισθα*. But for *thâs* in the 2d person singular of the middle there is no corresponding aspirate form in Greek, and as little for *thas* in the 2d person dual of the active, and for *tha* in the 2d person plural of the active. So that in verb-endings the surd aspirates of the Sanskrit do not appear to stand in any definite and satisfactory relation to those of the Greek.

But to my own mind these arguments, giving them all the weight which they can possibly claim, seem insufficient to balance that general consent of the Indo-European languages, by which, in all except the Greek and partly the Latin, the original aspirates are represented by sonant consonants. The only way, as it seems to me, to weaken the overwhelming weight of this fact, would be to show that the sonancy may perhaps have arisen from the aspiration; that there is a tendency in such an aspiration to change a preceding tenuis into a medial, so that we might expect an original *ph* to produce a *b* rather than a *p*, an original *th* to produce a *d* rather than a *t*. Now there are some facts which might lend a color to this view. In the Irish language there are certain influences which change an original *p*, *t*, *c* into *ph*, *th*, *ch*: aspirating influences, we may therefore call them. But in the kindred Welsh, *p*, *t*, *c*, under the same conditions, pass into *b*, *d*, *g*; the aspirating influences have here changed the surds into sonants. That the influences in question tend to aspiration even in the Welsh is evident from the fact that they change an original Welsh *b* into *v* (=*bh*), an original *d* into *dd* (=*dh*), an original *g* into a spirant *gh* sound, which has disappeared from the language. A very curious parallel to these phenomena of Celtic euphony is presented on Romanic soil, among the descendants of the Latin, in the dialect of Central Sardinia. Here, too, we find that the same euphonic conditions which aspirate an initial *b*, *d*, *g* change an initial *p*, *t*, *c* into the sonant *b*, *d*, *g*. Thus *boe*, 'ox,' preceded by the indef. art. *unu*, gives *unu oe*, 'an ox,' the aspirated *b* disappearing in pronunciation; but *póveru*, 'pauper,' with the same article, *unu bóveru*, 'a pauper.' If these analogies would authorize us to assume that there is a phonetic tendency in an aspirated *p*, *t*, *k* to pass into *b*, *d*, *g*, we might suppose with plausibility that the original aspirates, which have produced *b*, *d*, *g* in so many classes of languages, were not *bh*, *dh*, *gh*, but *ph*, *th*, *kh*, as Kuhn supposes.

I confess, however, that these analogies do not seem to me as yet definite and extensive enough to be fully relied on. In the present state of the question, I regard it as probable that the primitive sounds under discussion were sonant rather than surd.

X.

ON THE FORMATION OF INDO-EUROPEAN FUTURES.

1859.

I PROPOSE to occupy a short time in describing the different methods used in different languages of the Indo-European family for making a future tense. The contrivances resorted to for this purpose are for the most part intelligible to us; and in their variety we may find a striking illustration of that abundance of resources which the makers of language (and that is only another term for the users of language) have always had at their disposal. The facts which I shall have to present are generally known; but it may not be uninteresting or unsuggestive to see them brought together and exhibited in one view. I shall not, of course, undertake in this paper to give all the expressions which are used in any one of the languages mentioned to convey the idea of futurity. Such an attempt would be almost without limit. We shall consider merely those modifications of the verb by inflection, composition, or use of auxiliaries, which are most constantly and regularly employed to refer the action expressed by the root of the verb to a time posterior to the present of the speaker.

Let us, at starting, cast a glance outside of our own class of languages, at those of the Semitic family. Here, at first view, a remarkable prominence appears to be given by the grammatical organism to the idea of future time. For, while the system of verb-inflection embraces only two tenses, one of these, and the one most extensively used, goes by the name of "future." But this first appearance is hardly borne out by a closer scrutiny, directed to the actual use of the tense-forms; for this so-called future does service also as a present, and even, under particular conditions, as a past tense. And, in fact, Ewald in his Hebrew and Arabic grammars denies it the name of a future. According to him, the proper office of the two Semitic tenses is to express, not past and future, but finished and unfinished action. Thus an action thought of as finished, at whatever time, past, present, or future, is expressed by the Semitic perfect: and, in like manner, an action thought of as unfinished, or thought of without any idea of completion, is expressed by the Semitic future, to whatever time it may belong, whether future, present, or past. This theory, which goes far to account for the seemingly irregular and capricious use of the tenses in the Hebrew and its sister-languages, has found many adherents: it appears even in the recent editions of Gesenius's Grammar, published by Rödiger. In the Hebrew Grammar of Dr. Nordheimer, we find a view essentially the same as this, but with an ingenious and interesting modification of form, which in a measure reconciles it with the old established view. In this, the Semitic perfect and future are made to represent, not strictly past and future time, but prior and posterior action—action prior and posterior to some assumed stand-point or dividing position—this assumed stand-point, or dividing position between prior and posterior, being often coincident with the immediate present time, or instant of speaking, but very often also some different epoch suggested in the context. The main peculiarities in the Semitic tense-system, according to his view of it, would be: first, the freedom with which this dividing-point is allowed to shift its place, and to take up any required position; and, second, the fact that every action is thought of as preceding or following, never as contemporaneous with, the moment of time thus fixed upon. It is not my purpose, however, to enter upon any discussion with reference to these points of Semitic grammar, but only to draw attention to the fact—which is equally true, whatever theory we may adopt in accounting for it—that the present and future of our Indo-European languages are to a great extent confounded, that is, represented without distinction of form, in Semitic expression. And I do it with the purpose of adding that the same confusion, the same want of formal distinction between present and future, is to be found also within the domain of Indo-European speech; and that, too, at a point very near home to every one of us. If we look at our own mother-tongue, or, more properly, the mother of our mother-tongue, the Anglo-Saxon, we shall find a corresponding deficiency. As in Hebrew, so in Anglo-Saxon, the same form of the verb is regularly and ordinarily employed both as a present and as a future. The words which appear in the Anglo-Saxon New Testament as a version of John xvi. 2, might be rendered into modern English, either "They will put you out of the synagogues, and the time will come, that whosoever shall slay you, will think that he doeth God service," or, if we look only at the forms of expression, without reference to the actual circumstances of the case, "They put you out of the synagogues, and the time cometh, that whosoever slayeth you, thinketh that he doeth God service." Nor is the Mœso-Gothic, the most ancient and most perfect representative of the Germanic class of languages, better off in this particular than the Anglo-Saxon. If we turn to the translation of the Bible made by Bishop Ulfilas in the fourth century for his Mœso-Gothic countrymen, we shall find that the inflected forms of the verb which are used for the present, and which are shown by a comparison of other Indo-European languages to belong properly to that tense, are also in constant use for the expression of the future. The same thing is true likewise of the old Norse; and it appears, indeed, that this want of a special form for the future in distinction from the present belongs to the Germanic languages generally, in all the earliest forms with which we are acquainted. Perhaps it was even characteristic of primitive Germanism. By this I do not mean that the common Indo-European stock had not developed a distinct form for the future at the time when the progenitors of the Germanic people began to have a separate subsistence and dwelling-place. I mean, rather, that a distinct form for this tense—supposing it to have been, as I believe it was, already in existence—may perhaps have been lost by the primitive Germans at a very remote period, and thus the confusion of present and future may have been among the earliest of those deviations from the common type which at length impressed a peculiar character on the Germanic idioms. The modern languages of this class have endeavored to supply the want of a future by the use of auxiliaries: of these attempts we shall speak further on. We observe now, that a similar deficiency exists in one of the Celtic languages, the Welsh; and not only so in the older forms of that language, as the laws of Hywel Dda (Howel the Good), which belong to the ninth century, but also in the current idiom of the present day. In one verb only do we find a distinction made between the present and the future—in the verb 'to be.' *Sum, es, est*, etc., are expressed by *wyv, wyt, yw*, or *ydwyv, ydwyt, ydyw*: but *ero, eris, erit* are expressed by *byddaf, byddit, bydd*, etc. The root *bydd*, employed for the future, is only a modified form of *bu*, which is also found in Welsh, and, like our English *be*, is identical in origin with Sanskrit *bhû*, Greek φύ-ω, and Latin *fu-i*. The added aspirate of *bydd* is perhaps to be compared with the Greek θ in forms such as πελάθ-ω= πελά-ω, 'to draw near,' μινύθ-ω=Lat. *minu-o*, 'to diminish,' and many others. This formative θ is now generally identified with the root *dhâ*, Gr. θε in τίθημι, Eng. *do*, Germ. *thun*. If the dental in *bydd* is to be explained in this way, we should have for the primary meaning of *byddaf* 'I do be,' 'I do or make the being,' a present form of expression, which, however, as it implies that the being is not already done, that the existence of something is not already brought to pass, may naturally enough be employed as a future. The Welsh forms of the verb 'to be' are much used in periphrastic expressions for continued action, which are even more prominent in Welsh than in English; and in these, of course, it is able to discriminate the future from the present: 'he will be loving' is expressed by *bydd yn caru*, 'he is loving' by *yw yn caru*: though 'he loves' and 'he will love' are both expressed by one and the same form, *câr*. We cannot, however, suppose in this case—what we saw to be at least not improbable for the Germanic idioms—that the want of a special future form was an original and distinctive feature in the class of languages, the Celtic, of which the Welsh is a member. For in the Irish, the Gaelic of Ireland, which in many respects has preserved the primitive characteristics of Celtic speech better than the Welsh, we find a regular formation for the future, one which goes back evidently to the earliest periods of the language, and bears a remarkable analogy to the Latin future in *bo*. Thus from the root *mol* (infinitive *molain*, 'to praise') come the present, *molaim*, *molais*, *molaidh*, '*laudo*, *laudas*, *laudat*;' and the future, *molfad* (with *f*), *molfair*, *molfaidh*, '*laudabo*, *laudabis*, *laudabit*:' while the Welsh has *molaf*, *molit*, *mawl*, for both tenses. And yet the Welsh has a single remnant which shows that it anciently participated in the Irish formation of the future. Forms like *moliff* (with final *f*) are occasionally met with, in the third person singular only, and always in a future sense.

But while the Germanic idioms, as a class, with one branch of the Celtic, resemble the Semitic tongues in confounding future and present, the great body of the Indo-European languages have distinct forms for the expression of the future. In examining these forms, which present considerable variety, we notice first the fact that some of them have been derived from a subjunctive or potential. The future is uncertain; it is dependent on conditions, either now existing or to arise hereafter. We need not be surprised, therefore, to see it expressed under the form of contingency—expressed as that which 'may or might be.' A rudiment of this practice is seen in the Greek language, where the subjunctive, especially the aorist subjunctive, with or without the contingent particle ἄν or κέν, is sometimes found in cases where we should expect a future indicative. Thus in the first book of the Iliad, Nestor, speaking of the heroes of an earlier time, says: οὐ γαρ πω τοίους ἴδον ἀνέρας οὐδὲ ἴδωμαι, 'for never yet saw I such men, nor (may I see, am I likely to see, *i.e.*) shall I see hereafter.' This usage, however, is nearly confined to the Epic poetry. But that which we see in Greek occurring in this occasional and irregular way is matter of regular formation in Latin. It is a fact now generally recognized, that the future indicative of the third and fourth conjugations, and, of course, the future indicative of nearly all primitive verbs, was originally a subjunctive—that it corresponds to the potential in Sanskrit and the optative in Greek. The characteristic of this mode in Sanskrit is *yâ* or *i*: in Greek it is ιη or ι (δοίην, δοῖμεν). In Latin it was the same as in Greek, *ie* or *i*. These two forms are seen in the Old Latin *siem*, and its later equivalent *sim*. The vowel *i*, used as mode-sign of the subjunctive, is seen also in *velim*, *nolim*, *malim*, *duim* =*dem*, and perhaps one or two other old forms. It is implied likewise in the present subjunctive of the first conjugation, as *amemus*, *laudemus*, if these forms are really, what they are generally regarded as being, contracts made from *amaimus*, *laudaimus*. This is the contraction which has occurred in the future indicative of the third and fourth conjugations, and has made *legemus*, *luemus*, out of *legaimus* and *luaimus*—forms which correspond perfectly to the Greek optatives λέγοιμεν, λύοιμεν (or more closely to the Doric forms, λέγοιμες, λύοιμες). It is probable, too, that in the future of the verb *sum*, in *eris*, *erit*, *erimus*, the *i* is in fact this same sign of the contingent mode, attached to the syllable *er*, originally *es*, the stem of the verb. Now it is a curious fact that the Armenian language, which belongs to the Iranian branch of the Indo-European family, and is therefore quite remote from the Latin, forms its future tense in a manner closely analogous to that just described. The Armenian future has for its characteristic a letter which is pronounced as *ts*: thus, from the stem *da*, 'to give,' comes *dats*, 'I shall give,' *datses*, 'thou wilt give,' *datse*, 'he will give,' etc. At first view, we should think of this Armenian *ts* as connected with the Greek σ of the future, and should compare *dats*, *datses*, *datse* with δώσω, δώσεις, δώσει. But Bopp, in the second edition of his Comparative Grammar, has shown that the *ts* which plays an important part in the Armenian system of inflection has arisen everywhere from an original Indo-European *y* consonant, by a phonetic change, an assibilation, analogous to that which appears in English *joke* from Latin *jocus*, English *June* from Latin *Junius*. Thus *dats*, *datses*, *datse* correspond, not to δώσω, δώσεις, δώσει, but to δοίην, δοίης, δοίη, Sanskrit *deyâsam*, *deyâs*, *deyât*: that is, they are potential or optative forms, employed for the expression of the future.

We have just alluded to the common Greek future in σ, as seen in δώσω, δώσεις, δώσει. Identical with this is the ordinary future of the Sanskrit: thus, from the stem *dâ*, 'to give,' we have in the future *dâsyâmi*, *dâsyasi*, *dâsyati*. In these forms, comparative philology has long recognized the character of compound words, made by attaching to the stem *dâ* a future of the verb 'to be.' It is true that, in Sanskrit, the root *as* of the substantive verb (Greek and Latin ες, Germanic *is*) has no future existing as a separate form. It has a potential *syâm*, *syâs*, *syât*, for *asyâm*, etc., made by annexing the potential characteristic *yâ* to the radical *as*, which then loses its initial *a*, as in the corresponding Old Latin *siem*. Now in the ordinary Sanskrit future, we find the stem of the verb, whatever it may be, followed by the forms *syâmi*, *syasi*, *syati*, which very closely resemble the potential forms just given, differing from them scarcely at all, except in having the full personal endings *mi*, *si*, *ti*, instead of the shortened *m*, *s*, *t*. It is therefore natural to suppose that this *syâmi*, etc., was in its origin identical with *syâm*; that it once existed as a separate word, having at the outset a potential meaning ('may be, might be'), but afterwards employed as a future ('shall be, will be'), by a transition the same as that just pointed out in Latin futures of the third conjugation; and that in this use it was compounded with other verb-stems to give them a future meaning, and was thus retained in composition long after it had ceased to exist in a separate state. The compound future made in this way is seen not only in the Zend and the Greek, but also in the Lithuanian, where we find, for example, *dusu*, 'I shall give,' *dusi*, 'thou wilt give,' *dus*, 'he will give.' It will be observed that the proper future element in this formation is not the letter *s*, but the potential *ya* which follows it, and is very distinctly preserved in the Sanskrit *syâmi*, etc., while in the common Greek σω, σεις, σει it is nearly obliterated. But in the Doric Greek, the endings of the future are σιω or σεω, σεεις, σεει, which correspond well, according to the phonetic relations of the two languages, to the Sanskrit endings. The Greek, on the other hand, has this superiority, that it has retained the future of the stem *as* or ες in a separate form ἔσομαι, Epic ἐσσοῦμαι, from εσσεομαι or εσσιομαι, though with middle endings, instead of active. The Sanskrit sometimes appends its future terminations directly to the stem, but more generally inserts a short *i* as a connecting vowel. In Greek this relation is reversed: occasionally we find the connective, as in μαχέσομαι, from μάχομαι, 'to fight,' but in general the ending is applied immediately to the stem. In one case, however, the Greek almost invariably employs a connecting ε—in the case of liquid verbs; though here the σ, standing between two vowels, has fallen away, as it does so often in the Greek language. Thus from μένω, 'to remain,' we have future μενεσω instead of μενσω—from which comes μενέω, contracted μενῶ, the usual form.

If now we return to the Latin, we shall find that the formation just described, by which the future of the root *as* or *es* appears as the final element in a compound verb-form, is by no means unknown to that language. It does not appear, indeed, in the first future; but in the future perfect it is the established method of formation. *Legero*, *dixero*, *docuero*, are nothing but the future of *sum* annexed to the stem of the perfect active: they mean 'I shall be in the state of having read, having said, having taught.' Thus *legero* in the active corresponds closely to *lectus ero* in the passive, the difference being that *legero* is a true and proper compound, while in *lectus ero* the elements retain their separate form and construction.

We have not yet spoken of the Latin future in *bo*, which appears regularly in the first and second conjugations, and sometimes in the fourth—*amabo*, *docebo*, *audibo*. This ending, too, like the one which we have been considering, contains the verb 'to be.' It is not, however, derived like that from the root *as*, but from another root no less widely diffused through the Indo-European languages—Sanskrit *bhû*, Greek φυ (φύω), Latin *fu* (*fui*, *fore*), Germanic and Celtic *bi*, *be*. It is true that the future ending *bo* shows the medial *b*, while the separate *fui*, *fore*, etc. in Latin have the aspirate *f*: but this circumstance involves no real difficulty. The primitive sound was a medial aspirate, *bh*, as we find it in the Sanskrit. In Latin, this *bh* either gives up its *h* and is reduced to the medial *b*, or it fuses *b* and *h* in the homogeneous aspirate *f*: in general, *f* is used for *bh* when it stands at the beginning of a word, and *b* when it stands in the middle. Thus the root *bhar*, 'to bear,' gives *fero* as a separate verb, but appears also in the ending *-brum* of *candelabrum*, 'candle-bearer,' *cerebrum*, 'brain,' lit. 'borne in the head'—a case which is entirely parallel to the one in hand. It is matter of doubt whether *bo, bis, bit* ought to be regarded as present forms of the root *bhu* used in the sense of futures, like what we have seen before in the Welsh *molaf*, etc., or whether they are futures in form as well as in meaning—that is, whether they are not, like the Sanskrit *syâmi*, etc., potential forms applied to designate futurity. In the latter case, *bo, bis, bit* might be looked upon as contractions of *bio, biis, biit*, and this appears to be the most probable explanation.

Closely analogous to this Latin future in *bo*, and resting upon the same root, is the regular future formation of the Irish, which we have had occasion to notice already. Here we find the endings *fad, fair, faidh, famaoid, faidh, faid;* in which the derivation from the root *bhû* may be regarded as unquestionable. The endings in the ancient Irish, as given by Zeuss (Gramm. Celt.), are still more evidently connected with the Latin forms; thus *ub* (from *bu*), Lat. *bo; fe* (from *fi*), Lat. *bis; bid, fid*, Lat. *bit; bem, fam, fem*, Lat. *bimus; bid, fid*, Lat. *bitis; fet* (for *fent*), Lat. *bunt*. That this formation was not peculiar to the Irish, but belonged originally to all the Celtic idioms, is proved by the fact likewise noticed before, that a remnant of the same formation in the third person singular is still found occurring occasionally in the Welsh.

These Latin and Celtic futures have been further illustrated by Bopp from the Slavonic languages. In these the ordinary future is made by combining a participle of the verb with the future of the root *bu*, 'to be.' Here, however, the two elements remain distinct, and do not coalesce into a single compound word, as in the Irish and Latin. Thus in the Carniolan we find *bom igral, igrala, igralo*, 'I will be playing, he, she, or it that plays.' The future of the root 'to be,' which occurs in these combinations, has a singular resemblance to the Welsh future *bydd*, which we have considered already. In the Old Slavonic it is *budu*, which contains, if Bopp is right, the radical of German *thun* and English *do*, so that it would signify 'I do be,' 'I do or make the being.' The Servian language stands distinguished from all its sister idioms of the Slavonic class by the fact that it does not confine this method to the substantive verb, but employs it as a general mode for the formation of a future: thus, in the Servian, *igra-dyu* ('I make a playing') means 'I will play.'

The compound forms which we have thus far described contain a future made from some root signifying 'to be,' which future is combined in one way or another with the different verbs of the language. We might represent them all loosely by such English expressions as 'he will be praising, he will be giving,' etc. But there is another method of proceeding, in which the present of the substantive verb is used, and which may be represented therefore by the English 'I am about to praise, I am about to give,' etc. Such are the Latin *daturus sum, laudaturus sum.* And such is a form of the future which appears in Sanskrit, though much less frequently than the one already analyzed. Thus the stem *dâ,* 'to give,' makes two futures: one *dâsyâmi, dâsyasi, dâsyati,* etc., corresponding, as we have seen, to the Greek δώσω, δώσεις, δώσει; the other *dâtâsmi, dâtâsi, dâtâ,* which answers to the Latin *daturus sum, es, est.* What is remarkable in these Sanskrit forms is that *dâtâ,* except in this formation, has nothing future in its meaning; it is a common *nomen agentis,* and corresponds both in form and sense to the Latin *dator,* 'giver.' Indeed, it can scarcely be doubted that the Latin *daturus* is in its origin only another form of *dator,* and that the idea of futurity was attached to it by a sort of convention, as to the Sanskrit *dâtâ.* In the third person, singular, dual, and plural, of this Sanskrit future, the verb substantive is omitted, and we have only the singular, dual, and plural of this *nomen agentis,* so that in the dual, for instance, we have only the expression 'two givers' to signify 'they two will give.' It is also curious to observe that, although *dâtâ* varies thus in the third person of the different numbers, where it stands by itself, yet in the first and second persons, where it is followed by the auxiliary, the form *dâtâ,* which is the nominative singular, is used also for the other numbers. It is as though in Latin we should say, not *daturi sumus,* but *daturus sumus.* This shows that the Sanskrit expression is not to be regarded, like the Latin, as a mere collocation of the substantive verb and the future participle; but that there is a real fusion, a quasi-composition in the case.

Thus far it is the verb 'to be' which has figured in all the futures, whether made by composition or by the use of separate auxiliaries, that have come under our notice. But other verbs may be laid hold of by the language-making spirit, and compelled to perform a similar service. Among these is the verb 'to have.' The old Slavonic translation of the Evangelists frequently uses the present of *imam*, 'to have,' in connection with an infinitive, to form a future tense: thus, *priiti imaty syn* = '*veniet filius*' (lit. 'the son has to come'). The idiom of our own language makes it easy for us to feel the force of this periphrasis, which, as we use it, always looks forward to the future, though combining with the proper idea of tense the modal notion of obligation or necessity. A similar periphrasis is occasionally found even in the Mœso-Gothic of Ulfilas. But it is in the Romance languages that this mode of "futurizing" (if we may so call it) has shown itself on the largest scale and with the greatest constancy. The Italian, French, and Spanish future is nothing but a combination of the infinitive with the present forms of the verb *habere*, 'to have.' Thus *louerai*, *loueras*, *louera*, *loueront*, are nothing but *louer* (=*laudare*) + *ai*, *as*, *a*, *ont*, the present forms of the verb *avoir*. The origin of these forms, if any doubt could be entertained in regard to it, is clearly demonstrated by the usage of the Provençal, in which there is often a *tmesis*, or separation of the two elements, as in *dar vos n'ai* ('*je vous en donnerai*'), *dir vos ai* ('*dicere vobis habeo*,' 'I have to say to you,' '*je vous dirai*'). The universality of this formation in the Romanic languages is a fine illustration of the reality and power of a *sprachgeist*, a mental attitude and tendency common to all the speakers of a language, however remote in place and disconnected in social relations, which leads them to develop simultaneously and independently similar modifications and new creations in their language. No idea can be entertained, in this case, of a fashion springing up in a particular locality, and propagated thence by intercourse and imitation. The Spanish future could not have been borrowed from the Italian, nor the Italian from the Spanish. The phenomenon is a natural, not an artificial one. The Italian, French, and Spanish have alike grown out of a mixture of Germanism with a degenerate Latinism, and it lies in the nature of the ingredients that, when thrown together, they should precipitate among other things a future such as this.

It is a little singular, however, that the Germanic languages themselves, in their separate and independent development, have not shown the same uniformity as to the creation of the future tense which we have just seen in their influence upon the corrupt Latin, which they altered and adopted in the south of Europe. And yet, even here, the uniformity is too great to be the result of accident. In seeking to supply that ancient deficiency of special future forms which we have before described, not one of these languages has adopted a compound inflexional form, like the Greek and Sanskrit future; not one has combined the verb 'to be' with a participle or a periphrastic form, like the future in nearly all the Slavonic languages; not one has connected the verb 'to have' with the infinitive, like the future of the Romance languages. The Germanic languages have taken up the verbs of volition and necessity, and made their futures by the help of these auxiliaries. In low Dutch, it is the verb of necessity alone, the *shall*, which is thus used to form the future. In Danish and Swedish, both verbs are thus employed. And this is the case in our classical English, which uses them not indiscriminately, but according to a somewhat subtle and refined distinction. In the English of Scotland and Ireland, and a large part of the United States, it is the verb of volition alone, the *will*, that discharges this office, the *shall* being never used except with its primitive and proper notion of necessity. It is a curious fact that the modern Greek has adopted a similar formation of the future, ϑέλει νὰ γράφῃ or ϑέλει νὰ γράψῃ, corresponding exactly to the *he will write* of our own language.

There is, however, one of the Germanic idioms which has departed from the general analogy, and adopted a wholly different auxiliary. I refer to the modern German, and its use of the verb *werden*, 'to become,' to express the future. What makes this peculiarity the more striking is the fact that the *Althochdeutsch*, though standing to a great extent in the position of the Mœso-Gothic and the Anglo-Saxon, and using its present as a future, had begun to introduce the verbs of willing and shalling to their auxiliary function, like the other languages of the same class. So that the *Hochdeutsch* language has actually thrown aside the general expedients of its class, after it had, in part at least, adopted them. Bopp congratulates his countrymen on this difference, as having made a more felicitous choice than the rest of their family. *Werden* is certainly not ill-adapted to the expression of the future; though its use as an auxiliary interferes somewhat injuriously with its use as a separate verb. Yet the reason chiefly urged by Bopp is a damaging one for his own argument. "That which is now becoming," he says, "certainly will be in the future." But, in the first place, this is not true; for the present evolution may be arrested. And next, if it were true, the same thing might be said, with even greater force, of the *shall*, the verb of necessity.

It remains only to add a word in reference to the historical question, whether any of these formations can be referred to the primitive period of Indo-European unity—whether in the common language, which afterwards, under different conditions of place, time, and circumstances, became Sanskrit, Greek, German, and the rest, any of these forms were already in use for the expression of the future—or whether we are to pronounce them all, as we must certainly pronounce many of them, to be of later growth, developed in particular sections of the Indo-European family, after these had separated themselves from the common stock. In regard to one of them, the future in *s*, there can be little doubt of its primitive antiquity. It occurs, as we have seen, with evident identity of form and meaning, in Sanskrit, Greek, and Lithuanian. For such an agreement in languages so remote from one another, there can be but one satisfactory explanation. It is impossible to regard it as the result of an accidental coincidence. We are compelled to believe that the common formation was derived by all the three from a common source; and that can only be the one common language of which they are all descendants. This conclusion, if it needed any confirmation, might receive it from an interesting fact, which seems to prove that the same mode of formation once existed also in the Celtic. The Irish language presents us with an isolated *bhus*, meaning 'it will be,' in which it appears safe to recognize with Bopp a future in *s* made from the root *bu*—a form strictly identical with Lithuanian *bus*, Greek φύσει, Zend *bûsyeiti*, Sanskrit *bhavishyati*, and we may add Indo-European *bhusyati*. But this conclusion as to the future in *s* seems to draw after it, if not with necessity, yet with a good degree of probability, a similar conclusion as to that formation of the future which appears in the Latin third conjugation, and is to be traced in the inflection of the Armenian verb. We have seen that Sanskrit *dâsyâmi* (Greek δώσω) compounds the stem *dâ* with *syâmi* or *asyâmi*, an old future of the root *as*; and that this last was made by adding to that root the potential *ya*, and was in fact a potential formation applied to designate the future. If, then, the primitive Indo-European language made a future from the root *as* by applying to it the potential *ya*, it is very likely to have formed other futures from other roots by a similar process. It may have had these two formations of the future existing side by side, and used perhaps even in the same verbs. Thus the root *dik*, 'to show,' may have had the future *dikayâmi*, *dikayasi*, *dikayati*, corresponding nearly to Latin *dicam*, *dices*, *dicet*, and, at the same time, the future *daiksyâmi*, *daiksyasi*, *daiksyati*, corresponding to the Greek δείξω, δείξεις, δειξει.

The only remaining formation which could be regarded as having any plausible claim to a like primitive antiquity is the Latin future in *bo*. Outside of the Latin, we find it only in the Celtic languages; and our opinion as to the period of its development must depend a good deal on the relation which we conceive to exist between the primitive Celtic and the Latin. If these are as widely separated as the Greek and Lithuanian, the fact that a form belonged alike to both of them would go far to prove it an element of the common Indo-European language. This would be a natural conclusion for those who hold, with Ebel and Lottner, that the Celtic languages are connected by special affinities with those of northern Europe, the Germanic and the Letto-Slavic: unless, indeed, they should hold, as Lottner also does, that the

Latin and the other Italic languages are in the same condition, and stand nearer to Celtic, Germanic, and Letto-Slavic than to the Greek. But there is a different view, set forth recently by Schleicher (*Beiträge zur vergleichenden Sprachforschung*, vol. i.), which I am strongly inclined to believe will be sustained by further study—that the Celtic has a special connection with the Græco-Latin languages, but more particularly with the Latin and its sister languages of Italy. And this formation of the future, which belongs both to the Italic and the Celtic, and to these only, supplies him with one of the main pillars for his theory. Another, similar to this, but even stronger, he finds in the passive formed with *r*, which belongs exclusively to these same languages. According to this view, it would be natural to regard the future in *bo* as having arisen on Italo-Celtic ground, rather than as imported from the common home of the Indo-European family.

XI.

ON PASSIVE FORMATIONS.

1867.

I PROPOSE to occupy your time this evening for perhaps an hour with some observations on the formation of the passive voice in different languages. The object will be to show the nature and variety of the methods which have been adopted by the makers of human language—and it must be remembered that all users of language are makers of language—to express the idea of the passive.

If knowledge is to follow the lead of charity, as St. Paul would recommend, then knowledge must begin at home. Before entering the Babel of outlandish languages, we will linger awhile with our own kindly and intelligible English. Yet we must confess that this good old mother-tongue, with all its resources and faculties, has, strictly speaking, no passive verb: I do not say "no passive," but "no passive verb." For such words as *broken*, *struck*, *loved*, *praised*, etc. are not verbs: they are nouns, adjective nouns, attributive words, appropriate to the object of an action, appropriate to that which somebody breaks, strikes, loves, praises. In themselves they are not predicate-words: they become so only when they are connected with a verb. We connect them with the verb *to be*, as *he is praised*, *he was loved;* and thus, if we do not strictly form a passive verb, we at least supply the place of one; we express under a predicate-form the conception or relation of the passive. In this respect we stand on the same footing as the Anglo-Saxon. Our ancestors a thousand years ago were, like ourselves, without a passive verb, and they supplied the deficiency in the same way that we do. In one respect, however, there is a difference. We have but one verb—the verb *to be*, in its various parts—which we employ regularly for this purpose. The Anglo-Saxon uses the same verb very frequently—*ge gehyrdon, thæt gecweden wæs*, 'ye have heard that it was said (was quothed, or quoted),' etc. But frequently it uses another verb, one which has all but disappeared from the present language. Every one will remember the complaint of Fitz-James in Scott's Lady of the Lake: "Woe worth the chase, woe worth the day, That cost thy life, my gallant grey"—that is to say 'Woe *is* the chase,' or rather, 'woe befalls it, woe betides it.' This *worth* is a remnant of the old Anglo-Saxon *weorthan*, 'to become,' which was often used, like *beón*, 'to be,' for expressing the passive. Thus "when his father saw him (the Prodigal Son), he was stirred with mild-heartedness—*he wearth mid mildheortnisse astyrod;*" strictly, 'he became, he came to be excited with compassion.' Now these two verbs, *to be* and *to worth* (if I may give it so), were similarly used in the older forms of the High German, the Low German, and the Dutch, the idioms most closely related to the Anglo-Saxon. But in the modern forms of all these languages, the verb *to be* has lost this use, and only the verb *to worth* is employed for expressing the passive.

Thus, for 'he is loved,' the German says, not *er ist geliebt*, but *er wird geliebt*. If we find in German such an expression as *er ist geliebt*, the participle has sunk into a mere adjective, as though one should say "he is dear," "he is acceptable." These forms are evidently quite different from the real passive, in which we have the idea of an action proceeding from an agent to an object: as, 'he is loved by his friends,' where the German can only say *er wird geliebt von seinen Freunden*. It is certainly a curious circumstance that out of the two auxiliaries which were originally employed both by our own language and by its nearest kindred, the English should have adopted the one which all the rest have discarded—at least, in this use of it. But it is a fact which admits of a plausible explanation. The English language has not been left to an independent and spontaneous development. Brought by the Norman conquest into contact with the French, it shows many traces of the exotic influence. It is not strange if, in a choice between two forms of expression already existing, the result should be determined by the analogy of the intruding language. If the French had used *devenir*, 'to become,' or some word of similar meaning, in the expression of the passive—if in the present passive of *louer*, 'to praise,' they had said *il devient loué* instead of *il est loué*—it is probable that we ourselves should now be saying *he worth praised* (German, *er wird gelobt*) instead of *he is praised.* But the French language, like its sisters of Italy and Spain, makes the passive by using the verb 'to be.' And for this also there is an obvious historical reason. The Latin, from which they are all derived, which stands to them in much the same relation as Anglo-Saxon to English, forms a large part of its passive in the same way. The method which the Latin adopted in its complete tenses—Perf. *amatus sum* or *fui*, Plup. *amatus eram* or *fueram*, etc., etc.—this method is extended in the Romance languages to all the tenses, the incomplete as well as the complete. In this process the Latin participle in *tus* has lost the idea of time which generally belonged to it in Latin; it has changed from a perfect participle passive to a passive participle pure and simple. The Latin *laudatus est* means (commonly, at least) 'he is the object of a past act of praising,' *i.e.* 'he has been praised;' whereas the French *il est loué* means 'he is the object of an act of praising,' *i. e.* 'he is praised.'

If now we pass on to the Latin passive of the incomplete tenses, we come for the first time to a true passive verb, an inflexional form which is in itself a full predicate, and which is made to take for its subject the real object of the action. Its characteristic element is the *r* at or near the end of the form, which appears in all modes and tenses: as *amor*, *amabar*, *amabor*, *amer*, *amarer*, *amari*, etc.; and in all numbers and persons: as *amor*, *amaris* or *-re*, *amatur*, *amamur*, *amantur*. This statement, however, suggests a very notable exception. The second person plural *amamini* (*amabamini*, *amemini*) is in glaring contrast with the analogy of the other forms. It is in fact a very different thing, being simply a participle, the nominative plural masculine of a lost participle. It is identical with the Greek participles in μενος which are so abundant in the middle and passive voices: as, from λύ-ω, 'to loose,' λυόμενος, λελυμένος, λυσάμενος, λυθησόμενος, etc., etc. The Latin has other traces of this participle, as for instance in *femina*, which appears to be the participle of a root *fe*, meaning 'to milk, suckle.' The familiar word *alumnus* is equivalent to *aluminus*, a participle of the verb *alo*, meaning 'one who is nourished or reared up.' Apparently the Romans must once have used *amamini estis* for 'ye are loved;' but when the participle ceased to be employed in other uses, the true character of *amamini* was forgotten, it dropped the verb *estis*, which would then appear unnecessary; and, though masculine in form, was applied to a feminine subject not less readily (perhaps, if the sense of the word is considered, more readily) than to a masculine.

The passive in *r* is one of the most remarkable features of the Latin language. It is not, however, confined to the Latin. It is found in the scanty remains of the Oscan and Umbrian, and there can be no doubt that it was common to that whole class of languages—the Italian class, as it is called—the ancient idioms of Middle Italy. Outside of this class, it is found in the Celtic languages, and in those only. The Welsh and Irish, down even to the present day, have a passive in *r*, and the forms of this passive, as they are found in the oldest written monuments of the Irish language, dating back about a thousand years, have a marvellous resemblance to those of the Latin. In the Celtic, as in the Latin, the formation in *r* does not extend to the perfect tense. In the Celtic, as in the Latin, the formation in *r* is excluded from the second person plural. Both in the perfect tense, and in the second person plural, the Celtic, like the Latin, uses forms which appear to have been originally participles. These surprising coincidences in reference to the passive are the main prop of the hypothesis recently propounded, according to which the Celtic languages and the Italican stand in a special and close relation to each other—a closer relation than that which the Latin, for instance, bears to the Greek, or the Celtic to the German.

The question comes, now—what is the nature of this passive in *r*; what are its origin and its meaning? Before attempting an answer to this question, let us notice some facts which are not without their bearing on that answer.

The Italian language sometimes uses an active verb with the reflexive pronoun *si*, where we should employ the passive. Thus the sentence 'by a good man virtue is not loved on account of utility' may be expressed in Italian, *da un uomo buono non si ama la virtù per l'utile*—*i. e.*, 'virtue does not love itself' (Lat. *non se amat virtus*). The Spanish has a similar idiom: the sentence 'many lies are told' may be rendered by *se dicen muchas mentiras* (Lat. *se dicunt multa mendacia*)—*i. e.* 'many lies tell themselves,' or, 'get themselves told.' Were this the only instance of the kind, one might suppose that the Spanish people wished to relieve themselves from apprehended blame by representing their little deviations from truth as self-produced. But the idiom is familiar to these languages: it is, however, confined in them to the 3d person singular and plural. But there is one daughter of the Latin, a forlorn and neglected child, which is said to use this as its regular form for expressing the passive in all persons and numbers. I refer to the language of the Wallachians in Hungary and Turkey, the descendants of the Romanized Dacians. For 'I am praised,' these people say *jo me lauder*, *i. e.* 'I praise myself' (Lat. *ego me laudo*); for 'thou art praised,' *tu te laudi*, 'thou praisest thyself;' for 'he is praised,' *el se laudà*, 'he praises himself,' etc., etc.

The same phenomenon presents itself again in a language which as regards place lies very near to the Wallachian, though belonging to a different branch of the Indo-European family—the Old Slavonic, as it is called, or the Old Bulgarian, the language of the Bulgarians a thousand years ago. The Old Slavonic passive is made by using with the active verb the word *sen*, which is plainly a reflexive pronoun, like the Latin *se* and the German *sich*. But while the Wallachian, as we said, uses different pronouns for the different persons—*me* for the first, *te* for the second, and *se* only for the third—the Old Slavonic uses *sen* for all persons of both numbers.* *Sen* thus used does not really signify 'myself, thyself, himself,' etc., though we have to translate it by those pronouns: it signifies merely 'self;' it expresses the reflexive relation and nothing further.

* Thus *citun*, 'I honor,' *citun sen*, 'I am honored,' lit. 'I honor myself;' *citesi*, 'thou honorest,' *citesi sen* ('thou honorest thyself'), 'thou art honored;' *citeti*, 'he honors,' *citeti sen* ('he honors himself'), 'he is honored.'

If I am not mistaken, the reflexive passive here described is found in all the modern languages of the Slavonic class, the Russian, Polish, Bohemian, Servian, etc.

Nearly akin to the Slavonic idioms is the Lithuanian, a language of scarcely any literary cultivation, but of much interest and importance to the philologist. The Slavonic *sen* is reduced in the Lithuanian to a mere *s*, which of course does not form a word by itself, but is attached as a final sound to the forms of the active verb.*

Now these forms in *s*, *vezus*, *vezes*, *vezas*, and the rest, are not passive—the Lithuanian makes its passive by connecting the verb 'to be' (*esmi*, 'I am') with a passive participle. They have a reflexive sense, 'I bear myself, thou bearest thyself,' etc.—they constitute a reflexive voice, like the middle voice of the Greek. But I have brought them in here for the sake of showing how the reflexive pronoun, reduced to a single letter, may attach itself as a grammatical ending to the inflected forms of an active verb. The bearing of this will be obvious as we proceed.

The Scandinavian languages—the Old Icelandic or Old Norse, with its modern descendants, the Swedish and the Danish—form one section of that Teutonic family to which belong the German and the English. But as regards the subject now before us, these Scandinavian languages are strikingly distinguished from the other members of that family. The Swedish and Danish have a passive in *s*, a passive made by adding *s* to the forms of the active. Thus, in Swedish, from *trycka*, 'to press,' or 'I press,' comes the passive *tryckas*, 'to be pressed,' or 'I am pressed;' from *prisade*, 'I praised,' the passive *prisades*, 'I was praised,' etc. Instead of this *s*, the Old Icelandic has *st*. Thus *skjota*, 'to shoot, throw,' passive *skjotast*, 'to be thrown, to fall;' Impf. *skaut*, 'he shot, threw,' passive *skaut-st*, 'he was thrown.' But in the oldest manuscripts we find *sk* instead of *st*: *skjotask*, 'to be thrown,' *skautsk*, 'he was thrown.' And it may be regarded as perfectly certain that this *sk* is only a shortened form of

* Thus, from *vezu*, 'I carry' (Lat. *veho*), with added *s*, comes the form *vezu-s*; from *vezi*, 'thou carriest,' comes *veze-s*; from *veza*, 'he carries,' *veza-s*—and so on, through the dual and plural.

the reflexive pronoun *sik*, the same as German *sich*. The formation here described is in the highest degree interesting, because the process goes on, so to speak, under our own eyes. We see the reflexive pronoun *sik* losing its separate character, and, under the shortened form *sk*, attaching itself to the active verb, which it converts into a passive: then, unconscious of its origin, passing for easier pronunciation into *st*; and finally, going into the yet easier *s*, which only a philologist would think of as ever having been a separate word.

After this somewhat lengthy détour, which has taken us the round of Europe, we come back to our Latin passive in *r*. This is regarded now by the students of comparative philology as a formation of precisely the same nature as the one just considered: it is believed to have been formed by adding the reflexive *se*, or at least the *s* of it, to the forms of the active. Thus *laudor* is supposed to be for *laudos*, or *laudo se*, 'I praise self (myself);' *laudaris* for *laudasis*, or *laudas*(*i*)*se*, 'thou praisest self (thyself);' *laudatur* for *laudatus*, or *laudat*(*u*)*se*, 'he praises self (himself),' etc., etc. The change of *s* to *r* is one of the most familiar phenomena of the Latin language. It occurs most frequently between vowels, as in *genus*, *generis*, *generi* (for *genesis*, *genesi*); in *eram*, 'I was' (for *esam*), from the root *es*, which appears in *es-se*, *es-to*, *es-tis*; and a multitude of other cases. Yet it is by no means unknown at the end of a word: we have both *ărbos* and *arbor*, 'tree,' both *honos* and *honor*, 'honor,' where the form in *s* is unquestionably the older of the two. We can therefore easily believe that *laudor* should be the later form for an earlier *laudos*, and the rest in the same way. It must be confessed, indeed, that the case is not quite so clear a one as this statement would seem to make it. For we have to consider not the Latin only, but the other Italican languages, the Oscan, Umbrian, etc., which have the passive in *r*; and not these only, but the Celtic languages, the Welsh, Irish, etc., which have it likewise. Most of these other languages do not show the tendency so common in Latin to exchange *s* for *r*. Nor is there any reason to suppose that the parent language from which the various Italican or Celtic idioms derived their origin had any general tendency to exchange *s* for *r*. It is enough to point out this difficulty: I need not go into the considerations by which its force perhaps may be in some measure abated. It seems impossible to explain the Latin passive in any other way; to explain it in this way, as a reflexive formation, is at once natural in itself and supported by strong analogies from various quarters. Philologists, therefore, notwithstanding the difficulty referred to, have generally adopted this explanation.

I will only add that this way of accounting for the passive throws a welcome light on the deponent verbs. Why, it may be asked, should verbs of purely active meaning—such as *conor*, 'to endeavor,' *reminiscor*, 'to remember,' *utor*, 'to use,' *orior*, 'to rise,' *precor*, 'to pray,' etc., etc.—why should they receive a passive ending? The best answer would be to deny the facts: these verbs have not a purely active meaning, and they have not received a passive ending. They are verbs of reflexive meaning, and they have received, as it is most proper that they should, a reflexive ending. Thus *conor* means 'to exert one's self,' *reminiscor*, 'to remind one's self,' *utor*, 'to serve one's self' (with something, whence it is followed by an instrumental ablative), *orior*, 'to raise one's self,' *precor*, 'to ask for one's self,' etc.

From Latin to Greek is a natural transition. Here the fact which strikes us first is that the Greek passive is to a great extent borrowed from the middle or reflexive voice. If there are any here who were brought up under the old regime in Greek grammar and fed upon imaginary forms of τύπτω, they will perhaps be surprised by this statement. For they have learned that τύπτομαι and ἐτυπτόμην are true passive forms, which the middle, to supply its own deficiencies, is compelled to borrow. But they must know that all this is changed now-a-days. There has been a revolution, in which the passive (fulfilling its own name) has been a sufferer, and the long defrauded middle has come to its just rights. The passive now has but two tenses of its own, its aorist and its future: for all the rest, for present and imperfect, perfect and pluperfect and future-perfect—this last being the "paulo-post future" of the old grammars—for all these it must acknowledge its dependence upon the middle. In other words, it is now acknowledged that such forms as present λούομαι, imperfect ἐλουόμην, perfect λέλουμαι, pluperfect ἐλελούμην, are primarily reflexive forms, and that their passive use is secondary: that in λούομαι, for example, the first meaning was 'I wash myself,' and the second 'I am washed,' precisely as the Latin *lavor*, according to the explanation just given, must have meant 'I wash myself,' before it meant 'I am washed.' Now the peculiarity of the Greek middle as compared with the active—its formal peculiarity—lies in its personal endings; it is the personal-endings which distinguish the middle voice as such. Thus, in the singular of the active, the original endings were μι, σι, τι: we see them in the verb 'to be'—1st person εἰμί (for εσ-μι), 'I am,' 2d ἐσ-σί (Hom.), 'thou art,' 3d ἐσ-τί, 'he is.' It is obvious that μι, σι, τι are pronouns, and express the subject of the verb: thus, ἐσ-μί='is me' or 'I am;' ἐσ-σί='is thee' or 'thou art;' ἐσ-τί='is that' or 'that (one) is, he is.' For μι, σι, τι, the middle has μαι, σαι, ται; as in ἵσταμαι, ἵστασαι, ἵσταται. Why, then, should an active form become middle by simply changing μι, σι, τι to μαι, σαι, ται? On this point there are two views, each of which has its adherents. According to one view, μαι, σαι, ται are merely lengthened or strengthened forms of μι, σι, τι, and by their greater length indicate the greater importance which belongs to the grammatical subject in the reflexive verb. For, in the expression *I wash myself*, the first person, the I, is a very important person, being at once subject and object of the action, its original and end. The importance of this person may be expressed, not unfitly, by strengthening the syllable which represents it. According to the other view, μαι, σαι, ται are modified forms of μα-μι, σα-σι, τα-τι, in each of which the person is expressed twice, first as object, then as subject. Thus λούομαι, for λουο-μα-μι, would mean 'wash-me-I,' *i.e.* 'I wash myself;' λούε(σ)αι, for λουε-σα-σι, 'wash-thee-thou,' *i.e.* 'thou washest thyself;' λούε-ται, for λουε-τα-τι, 'wash-him-he,' *i.e.* 'he washes himself.' I shall not discuss these two views; neither of them can be regarded as anything more than a hypothesis, until it is shown that some similar explanation can be given for the other personal endings.

I remark, however, that a passive formed in the same way

once existed in our own Teutonic family of languages. There is no trace of it, indeed, in the Anglo-Saxon, nor in the Old Icelandic, nor in the Old High German: but if we go back beyond all these to the earliest monument of our family, to the Gothic Bible-translation made by Bishop Ulfilas in the 4th century, we find it there. The Gothic *bairada*, 'he is borne,' corresponds exactly in every respect to the Greek φέρεται; the Gothic *bairanda*, 'they are borne,' corresponds in the same way to the Greek φέρονται. It is apparent that in the time of Ulfilas the Gothic was already beginning to lose this formation. It is only found in the present, indicative and subjunctive: even here the first person singular is gone, its place being supplied by the third, while in the plural both the first and second persons have disappeared, and the third does duty for them. It is not surprising, therefore, that succeeding monuments of the Teutonic languages, the earliest of which are some three centuries later, should show no trace of this formation. If the Bible of Ulfilas, which survives only in scanty fragments, had perished altogether, there would be no evidence that this middle-passive was for ages the common possession of Teutons and Grecians.

I have said that, while the Greek passive borrows most of its tenses from the middle or reflexive voice, it has two—an aorist and future—which are peculiar to itself. But before looking at these we will glance at the ancient language of India. The Sanskrit passive, as compared with the Greek, shows remarkable coincidences along with remarkable differences. In both languages the perfect passive is borrowed from the middle. But in the aorist and future, where the Greek has a distinct form for the passive, the Sanskrit does not generally distinguish it from the middle. And on the other hand, in the present and imperfect, where the Greek passive is always the same as the middle, the Sanskrit has a distinct formation for the passive. This is made by adding to the stem of the verb the syllable *ya*, which always takes the accent. Thus, from *tud*, 'to strike,' a root which appears in the Latin verb *tundo*, the Sanskrit makes *tud-yá-te*, 'he is struck,' *tud-ya-nte*, 'they are struck.' Now the syllable *yâ* occurs in Sanskrit as the root of a separate verb, which means 'to go:' and it is believed that the formative *ya* of the passive is no other than this root *yâ*, 'to go.' If this be so, *tudyate* would mean 'he goes to a striking, he meets or incurs a striking.' A curious parallel as regards the meahing is found in the familiar Latin *veneo*, 'to be sold,' infin. *venire*, undoubtedly for *venum eo*, *venum ire*, 'to go to sale,' and hence 'to be sold.'

This Sanskrit passive reappears in the Armenian, where the syllable *ya* is reduced to the simple vowel *i*. Probably also it reappears in the Greek, where the second aorist passive is formed by adding to the stem an ε or η, which may easily be connected with the Sanskrit *ya*. Thus ἐπλήγην, from πλήσσω, 'to beat,' would mean 'I went to a beating, I was beaten.' As regards the Greek first aorist passive, the aorist in θην, that is still an enigma: solutions have been proposed for it, but none that can be accepted as satisfactory.

We have now reviewed the modes of passive formation which appear in the Indo-European class of languages. And we have seen that one of the most common modes, perhaps the most common of all, is the use of some form which was originally and properly reflexive. For 'he is praised' it has been, and still is, a very common thing to say *he praises himself*. If we inquire into the *rationale* of this expression, we shall easily recognize in it the principle of *qui facit per alium facit per se*. One who makes others praise him praises himself. I praise myself, if I proceed and act in such a way as to get praise from those around me. And this is tantamount to saying that, if I am praised, I praise myself. What I wish to say is, that the reflexive which serves to express the passive is a causal reflexive. The Latin *laudor*, the Swedish *prisas*, the Greek ἐπαινοῦμαι, all mean 'I make men praise me, I let men praise me, I get men to praise me,' or something of that kind. They are causal reflexives. In this view, it is a significant circumstance that the Sanskrit, which has both a causal and a passive, forms them both in very much the same way: it adds *ya* to form the passive, and *aya* to form the causal. But if we go outside the bounds of the Indo-European family, we shall find cases more striking and unequivocal of a connection between causal and passive. The Magyar, or Hun-

14

garian, belongs, as all know, to that class of languages which is variously called Tartaric or Altaic or Turanian; the same class to which belong the Finnish and the Turkish and the Manchu. The Magyar forms both the causal and the passive by adding the same syllable *tat* or *at* (*tet* or *et*) to the root of the verb: thus, from the root *lát*, meaning 'to see,' comes *lát-tat*, which is used both for the causal and for the passive. How, then, are these two uses distinguished from each other? By the endings. The Magyar has endings which are applied only to transitive verbs, such as to love, praise, strike, etc., and other endings which are applied only to intransitive verbs, such as to sleep, dream, walk, fall, etc., verbs in which the action is confined to the sphere of the agent or subject, affecting no other object. If then *láttat*, which is made by adding the formative syllable *tat* to the root *lát*, 'to see,' is to be used as a causal, it takes the transitive endings: *láttat ok*, 'I cause to see,' *i. e.* I cause a seeing of which (not I myself, but) something else is the object. But if *láttat* is to be used as passive, it takes the intransitive endings: *lattat om*, 'I am seen,' *i. e.* I cause a seeing which has no other object than me, I cause a seeing which affects myself only. In like manner the Finnish, the Esthonian, and other languages which stand nearest to the Magyar, show a close connection between causal and passive, though they do not exhibit the nature of that connection with the same beautiful distinctness. But there is a language spoken by Indians of South America, the Arauack language, which seems to be more transparent in this respect than even the Magyar. It forms a reflexive by adding *nua* to the root of the verb: thus, from *assukussun*, 'to wash,' comes *assukussunnua*, 'to wash one's self.' It forms a causal by adding *kuttun* to the stem: thus, from *assukussun*, 'to wash,' comes *assukussukuttun*, 'to cause to wash.' Now the passive is made by combining these two signs, *kuttun* for the causal and *nua* for the reflexive; it adds *kuttunnua* to the stem of the verb: *assukussu-kuttun-nua*, 'to cause to wash one's self,' to cause a washing of which the object is one's self—*i. e.* to be washed.

It sometimes happens that an intransitive verb is used to express the passive. Thus, instead of "he was killed in battle" we often say "he fell in battle." The Greek hardly ever uses the passive aorist of *κτείνω*, 'to kill,' but substitutes for it the aorist active of the intransitive ἀποθνήσκω: ἀπέθανε, 'he died,' instead of ἐκτάθη, 'he was killed.' Most languages, doubtless, would show occasional instances of this kind; but in some languages the idiom assumes a more definite and formal character. This is the case in Gothic, which, as we have seen, had begun to lose the old middle-passive that belonged to it in common with the Greek. It often uses in place of that a peculiar series of intransitives, made by adding *na* to the stem of the active verb. Thus, *veihan*, 'to consecrate,' but *veihnan*, 'to be consecrated;' *aftairan*, 'to tear off,' but *aftaurnan*, 'to be torn off;' *fraliusan* (Germ. *verlieren*), 'to lose,' but *fralusnan*, 'to be lost, to be forlorn.' In the Semitic languages (Hebrew, Arabic, Syriac, etc.), passives are made to a great extent by merely changing the vowels of the active verb: thus Arabic *qatala*, 'he killed,' but *qutila*, 'he was killed.' Passives such as these are properly regarded as intransitives used to express the passive. This view of their nature may perhaps account for the singular fact that, in the Arabic, passives like *qutila* cannot be used when the agent or doer of the action is to be expressed. If I wish to say in Arabic 'the vizier was killed,' I can use the form *qutila: qutila 'l'vazîru;* but if I wish to say 'the vizier was killed by the sultan,' I can no longer use *qutila;* I must take some other form of expression. If *qutila* had the nature of a true and complete passive, it could hardly be subject to a restriction like this.

In English—and the same thing is more or less true of other languages—there are some verbs which may be used without any change of form both actively and passively. Thus, "the water filled the ship," and "the ship filled with water;" "the bad air sickened him," and "he sickened with the bad air;" "the woman washes the calico," and "the calico washes well," etc. In one auxiliary formation, this double use as active or passive belongs to the established idiom of our language. We say "he is building the house," and "the house is building;" "while he was doing these things," and "while these things were doing." It is in order to avoid the ambiguity of this form that men have latterly begun to say "the house is being built," "these things were being done." These forms of the continued passive have had to undergo much severe criticism, and it can hardly be denied that they are somewhat illogical and perhaps yet more unwieldy. Still, they have their convenience: probably there is no man who, if the fear of the grammarians were taken from him, would not occasionally use them. Like other things which are homely and useful, they will be likely to maintain themselves against all opposition, at least in the language of conversation and extemporaneous speaking, and may possibly gain a place at last even in polite literature.

There are languages, however, in which this indifferent use of the same form as active or passive is carried to a yet greater extent. In the Tibetan language, all transitive verbs can be used as passives; and indeed, this is by far the most frequent use of them. It is not strange that in monosyllabic languages, like the Chinese, which are of course destitute of all inflection, the same verb should be employed at pleasure as active or passive. The Chinese, however, does contrive to make a sort of passive, by prefixing to the verb a certain relative particle: thus, for 'it is seen' the Chinese can say 'it is what see;' for 'it is heard,' he can say 'it is what hear,' and the like.

It might be supposed that when we have come to a language which has no special form for the passive, but uses the same form as active or passive indifferently, we have reached the minimum point. But this is not the fact. There lies beyond it an absolute zero. There are languages which not only have no form of expression for the passive, but have not even the idea of the passive. Such is the language of the Osage Indians, in which the words "knock, and it shall be opened to you" have to be translated by, 'knock and they will open to you.' So, too, the language of the Dacotah Indians, in which the words "Jesus came to John and was baptized in Jordan," are rendered 'Jesus came to John and they baptized him in Jordan.' In these idioms, the agent or doer of the action always appears in the nominative, and if the agent is unknown or unthought of, the indefinite third person plural takes the place of it: as 'they will open it,' instead of "it will be opened;" 'they baptized him,' instead of "he was baptized."

On the other hand, there are languages which show a marked predilection for the passive. This is true of the Tibetan, just mentioned, which with transitive verbs regularly employs the passive construction, except in certain limited and comparatively unfrequent cases. Sometimes languages which are nearly related to each other differ widely in this respect. Thus, in Western Africa, the Mpongwe has a decided preference for the passive, while the kindred Bakele as decidedly prefers the active, and the Benga employs both active and passive with equal readiness.

We have noticed that there are passive formations which are never used where the agent or doer of the action is to be mentioned in the same connection. But as a general thing, the agent is or can be introduced in some dependent construction along with the passive. In such cases, the relation of the agent to the action is differently conceived and expressed in different languages. In the largest number, perhaps, the agent is thought of as the source or starting-point from which the action proceeds. Thus in Latin, *discipulus laudatur a magistro*, 'the pupil is praised by the master,' literally 'from the master.' So in the modern descendants of the Latin: Italian *dal maestro*, French *du maître*, etc. So in German, *von dem Meister*, and so in a multitude of other languages. Some languages (as the Tibetan), which have an instrumental case, use it for the agent with a passive verb. In like manner we, in English, use the instrumental preposition *by;* though it must be observed that the instrumental use of this preposition is a secondary one. Primarily it denotes nearness or association: the instrument is that with which, in presence of which, in connection with which, something takes place. "The resolution was read by the chairman," simply represents the chairman as near to the reading, and closely connected with it. In Greek, the preposition ὑπό, 'under,' is placed before the agent: he is thought of, apparently, as standing over his work, supervising it and having it under his control. Not a few languages put the agent in the genitive—a pretty clear sign that the so-called passive is then in reality a verbal noun.

A curious statement is made in regard to certain languages of the Philippine islands. They have three different forms of the passive verb, according as the subject of the passive is the object of the action, or the instrument of the action, or the place of the action. Thus a sentence like "the servant searched for the book with the light in the chamber," can in those languages be expressed passively in three different ways, with three different forms of the passive verb, according as we take the book, the light, or the chamber, for the subject-nominative. In all of them the agent (that is, the servant) will be put in the genitive ; and this shows that the three passive forms are in reality verbal nouns denoting the object, the instrument, or the place of an action. The first is analogous to the Latin *alumnus*, the object of nourishing, the person nourished; the second to the Latin *aratrum*, the plough, the instrument of ploughing ; the third to the Latin *auditorium*, the place of hearing. The three passive sentences, then, in the Philippine language, would be exactly rendered into English as follows : 1st. 'The servant's object of search was the book with the light in the chamber ;' 2d. 'The servant's instrument of search for the book was the light in the chamber ;' 3d. 'The servant's place of search for the book with the light was the chamber.'

XII.

REMARKS ON THE USES OF THE LATIN SUBJUNCTIVE.

1870.

IN all the uses of the subjunctive there is a common negative element. It never expresses the conception of reality. This conception, which is always present with the indicative, is always absent from the subjunctive. But in the uses of the subjunctive there are also positive elements; there are special conceptions which it is fitted to express. The first of these probably in the order of time is that of *wishing*. There is no doubt that *sim, velim, edim, duim* contain the formative *i* or *ya* of the Sanskrit potential, the Greek optative, the Teutonic subjunctive. So also the present subjunctives in *em, es, et,* etc., of the first conjugation, and possibly those in *am, as, at,* etc., of the other conjugations; though the latter are generally supposed to correspond to the Greek subjunctive and the Sanskrit *Lêṭ*-form of the Vedic language. As to the other tenses of the Latin subjunctive, while the imperfect at least is still involved in much obscurity, it can hardly be doubted that they all contain this same *i* or *ya*. And of that element the primitive function was probably optative; it was at first the expression of a wish. On this assumption, apparently, we can most easily and naturally explain the uses of the forms which contain this element through our whole family of languages. At this point, then, we begin with the Latin Subjunctive.

1. The Latin subjunctive is used to express an action as desired or wished for. Thus in exhortation, request, command, deprecation, prohibition, etc. With the idea of wishing is naturally associated that of aim: from desire we proceed to purpose, and then to effort for the attainment of our purpose. Hence—

2. The Latin subjunctive is used to express an action as aimed at or striven for (acted for). Fearing implies wish or aim that something may not take place; and it is therefore expressed by *ne* with the subjunctive: that is, expressed as negative purpose. In the uses hitherto considered, there is a conscious tendency toward an object which is both expected and desired. But the idea of desire may fade out, leaving only that of conscious tendency toward an expected object. Hence—

3. The Latin subjunctive is used to express an action as looked toward and waited for. So in many dependent sentences beginning with 'until' and 'as long as.' This forward looking of the subjunctive is illustrated by the fact that it is commonly used with *antequam* and *priusquam*, while *postquam* regularly takes the indicative. But the tendency expressed by the subjunctive is not necessarily a conscious (or subjective) one, a movement of the mind; it may be an unconscious (or objective) tendency, a movement of circumstances or causes, tending toward some result, that result being conceived of not as real, but only as the object of a tendency. Hence—

4. The Latin subjunctive is used to express an action as a result, as that toward which there is a tendency. The Latin is apt to think of things characteristic or customary in this way, to conceive them as what the circumstances, conditions, or cases tend to produce. *Non is est qui hoc patiatur*—there is no tendency in his case to such endurance, it is not his habit or character to endure this. But the idea of tendency which we have traced through all these uses may itself grow dim and fade out, partially or wholly, leaving that of an expectable or possible event. Hence—

5. The Latin subjunctive may express an action as a possible event. And by "possible" here I do not mean 'feasible, practicable,' that for whose production there exist adequate powers. I mean simply 'liable to occur,' that which has more or less chance for existence. This is the potential subjunctive. It presents the mode in its dimmest, most attenuated state, with the minimum of positive elements over and above that negative one, that mere absence of a concep-

tion of reality, which we noticed at the outset. In many cases, indeed, it might be argued, not without plausibility, that the positive elements were wholly effaced, and that the subjunctive expressed the action simply as divested of all conception of reality. This is Bäumlein's theory of the Greek optative; but I have never been able to satisfy myself that the uses of the optative could be accounted for with that factor only.

We have thus endeavored to find a probable (or, at least, a natural) genetic development for the uses of the Latin subjunctive, starting from what seems to be the historic starting-point, in the idea of wishing. If we look at the actual uses as they lie before us, irrespective of origin or order of development, the prevailing notion which links them together appears to be that of tendency. The subjunctive expresses an action as that toward which there is a tendency, either in the conscious desires, aims, expectations of some person, or in unconscious bearings of circumstances known or unknown to the speaker. We have in English a form of expression in which this idea of tendency is very explicitly and sharply presented; it consists of the substantive verb followed by the infinitive with *to:* as, *they are to go*, that is, *they are toward going*. But this differs in two points at least from the Latin subjunctive: it is confined in use to objective or outward tendencies, and it contains (where the substantive verb is in the indicative mode)—a conception of reality.

It is often difficult to say, in regard to particular uses of the mode, where they belong in this scale of development, to which of these categories we ought to refer them. Thus, the so-called subjunctive of deliberation, or of deliberative questions. We might think of it as a potential subjunctive, and so Professor Harkness gives it in his Grammar. There may be no objection to this, considered as a practical arrangement. But it can hardly be doubted that the subjunctive here is in reality one of wish or aim. The real question in such cases is what the person addressed would like or would counsel: *quid faciamus*, 'what would you have us do, what would you propose or advise that we should do?' A *visne*, or something of that kind, may always be supplied. To *faciatis* used without interrogation, in the sense 'may you do,' 'you are (by my desire) to do,' corresponds the question *quid faciamus*, 'what may we do,' 'what are we (by your desire) to do?' On the other hand, in the dependent question, and in the so-called intermediate clauses of the *oratio obliqua*, the subjunctive must be referred to the last head, as expressing possible event. What in the *oratio recta* is viewed as a reality becomes a possibility in the *obliqua*. By the first speaker it is conceived as a reality; to the second speaker (the quoter), who sees it only as a conception of the first, the character of reality falls away; to him it is a mere possibility. Thus the question "when did they come," directly put, is equivalent to 'they came: tell me when: let me know the time of what I view as a real coming.' But the indirect form, "my friend asked when they came," is equivalent to 'my friend asked the time of their coming—a coming which I have nothing to say about: however real to him, it is only a may-be to me.' Again, the subjunctive of cause is probably to be explained from the idea of result. *Quæ quum ita sint*, 'the case being such that these things are so,' 'as circumstances tend to these results,' it follows, etc. The most difficult use of the mode is that of the imperfect and pluperfect subjunctive with *quum*, 'when:' as in *quum Cæsar veniret in Galliam*. Though this construction is often used where the two facts, expressed by the principal and the dependent sentence, are connected only in time, it may be conjectured that this was not always so, that the subjunctive with *quum* was at first used where the facts had a causal connection, and that the merely temporal use grew out of a gradual and not strictly proper extension of that form. Not that *quum veniret* became absolutely equivalent to *quum venit*: the conception of reality was still wanting to the former; *quum veniret* was nearly equivalent to *tempore veniendi*. But I think that it stands by itself among the uses of the subjunctive; and that it is not to be explained by a natural development of meaning in the mode, but rather by the extension of a form beyond the sense which properly belonged to it—the form which was properly employed for a causal connection was improperly extended to cases where there was only a temporal connection.

I will notice, further, what seems to me a very unfortunate feature in Madvig's treatment of the Latin subjunctive. Not content with the four tenses usually recognized in this mode, he has given it two more, a future and a future perfect. His future subjunctive is a periphrastic form composed of the future participle with the present subjunctive of the verb 'to be:' *amaturus sim.* His futur eperfect is a mere repetition of the perfect; *amaverim* is given twice over, once as perfect, and again as future perfect. These tenses, however, he confines to the active voice: to the subjunctive passive he allows neither perfect nor future perfect. But if *amaverim* is two tenses in one form, why not *amatus sim* also? If *amaverim* has the two uses 'I may now have loved' and 'I may hereafter have loved,' the passive *amatus sim* is susceptible of the two similar uses, 'I may now have been loved' and 'I may hereafter have been loved.' If we recognize *amaverim* as a future perfect in the active voice, there is no reason why we should not recognize *amatus sim* as a future perfect in the passive. That Madvig has not done so, that he has failed to give a future perfect subjunctive in the passive, is probably because he did not see what to do for a future subjunctive in that voice. He could not find anything which would correspond to his future subjunctive active *amaturus sim.* There is no future participle of the passive voice: *amandus sim* would convey an idea of necessity. But if we leave the passive out of view, and look only to the active, the scheme is misleading. It is right in recognizing a double use of *amaverim*, as a present and a future of complete action. But it covers up the fact, which is of great importance in the theory of the mode, that the form *amem* is similarly double in use: it means not only 'I may now love,' but also 'I may hereafter love.' If *amaverim* is repeated for a perfect and a future perfect, *amem* ought equally to be repeated for a present and a future. The student of Madvig's Grammar would naturally think that *amem* had only the present sense, 'I may now love,' and that the corresponding future 'I may love hereafter' must be expressed by *amaturus sim.* But in fact *amaturus sim* has not precisely this meaning. It differs from *amem* used in future sense just as *amaturus sum* differs from the future indicative *amabo.* The truth is that *amaturus sum* is a present indicative of prospective (or contemplated) action; and in like manner, *amaturus eram* is an imperfect indicative, and *amaturus sim*, *amaturus essem* are present and imperfect subjunctive, of prospective action. We have a full series of these tense-forms for prospective action. To take one of them, as Madvig does, and treat it, without reference to the others, as belonging to the same series with *amem*, *amarem*, *amaverim*, etc., can hardly be a justifiable procedure.

XIII.

ON THE ORIGIN OF THE ENGLISH POSSESSIVE CASE.

1866.

A FAVORITE poet declares, in a passage often quoted, that "Error, wounded, writhes with pain, and dies among his worshippers." The saying has its truth, doubtless, when taken in reference to the grand results of world-history; but it gives no hint of the extreme tenacity of life which error often shows, or of its frequent strange revivals after seeming death. The champion of science cannot presume that an error, once crushed, will never raise its head again: too often he is forced to personate the comic hero of whom it was said that "thrice he slew the slain."

These remarks are suggested by a recent essay on the *s* of the English possessive—the *s* seen in *horse's head*, *Mary's book*, *children's dress*, and the like. Its author's object is to infuse new life into the old theory which viewed this *s* as a remnant of the possessive pronoun *his*; so that the examples just given would be forms, abridged and altered in rapid utterance, of what was originally *horse* HIS *head*, *Mary* HIS *book*, *children* HIS *dress*. As the essay referred to appears in a place so respectable as the published Transactions of the Philological Society (London, 1864), as it occupies nearly ninety pages of that journal, and is written with evident labor and considerable appearance of learning, it may be worth while to spend some little time in reviewing its positions and arguments. In one respect, as an instance of authorship in advanced years, it may almost be reckoned among the curiosities of literature. Its author—"James Manning, Q.A.S., Recorder of Oxford"—describes himself as writing in the eighty-third year of his age. It should seem that, after a life of active labor in his profession as a lawyer, he has found a pleasant and honorable recreation for his old age in philological studies. That these studies have excited a keen interest in his mind must be apparent to any reader of this essay. He discusses his theme—perhaps we should rather say, he pleads his cause—with all the warmth and earnestness of an advocate. His materials of argument and illustration could not have been collected without considerable expenditure of time and effort. He has looked into the grammar of the Anglo-Saxon, and even into that of the Mœso-Gothic. To the grammar of the popular dialects of Germany he has given a good deal of attention; and still more to the Semi-Saxon form of our own language, as represented in the two texts of Layamon's Brut, and to the Old English which followed it. It must be confessed, however, that his knowledge is far from sufficient; and that he has fallen into numerous misapprehensions and errors, from which more thorough study would have saved him.

Mr. Manning's thesis may be stated thus: The old inflectional genitive of the Anglo-Saxon was given up in the 13th century; it was almost wholly discarded at that period; and was replaced in most of its uses by the preposition *of*—which preposition, by the way, he strangely designates as "Scandinavian;" forgetting that it is found, not only in the earliest Anglo-Saxon, but also in the Mœso-Gothic *af*, and even in the High German *ab;* that it belongs, therefore, to the whole Teutonic class of languages, and not specially to the Scandinavian branch of it. He maintains (I say) that the Anglo-Saxon genitive, discarded in the 13th century, was replaced in most of its uses by the preposition *of;* but that for the possessive relation there sprung up at the same time a different form of expression, a form in which the name of the possessor was followed by the name of the thing possessed, with the pronoun *his* interposed between them: thus, *horse his head*. This interposed *his* he describes as sex-less and number-less, denoting mere possession, without distinguishing either the gender or the number of the possessors; so as to be used with perfect facility and propriety in such expressions as *Mary his book*, *children his dress*. From this *his* the *h* was naturally dropped in rapid utterance, leaving *'is;* and in time the vowel of *is* was generally suppressed in pronunciation, leaving a mere *s*, which, since the 16th century, is written with the apostrophe.

On the other hand, the prevailing, and (as we think) the correct view of this subject may be stated thus. The old inflectional genitive of the Anglo-Saxon has never been given up; it has never at any period ceased to be in use; it has come down by uninterrupted tradition from the earliest times to the present day. But it has undergone extensive changes in use and function. In the Gothic—and so, doubtless, in the primitive Teutonic—*s* was the universal ending of the genitive singular, in all genders and for every kind of stem. The Anglo-Saxon preserves this *s* in vowel-stems of the masculine and neuter genders, but has lost it in all feminines and in all *n*-stems: in fact, as regards the *s* of the genitive singular, the Anglo-Saxon stands on much the same footing as the modern German. But in the early English, we find the *s* extended again to the feminines and the *n*-stems (these last losing their *n*); so that *s* becomes once more the universal ending of the genitive singular: although in some few words of common occurrence—such as *fader*, *moder*, *brother*, *ladi*, *sawle* ('soul'), etc.—the genitive without *s*, which belonged to them in Anglo-Saxon, maintained itself, at least in occasional use, down to the time of Chaucer, or even later still. The *s* of the genitive, indeed, extended itself still more widely, and passed into the plural, making, for instance, *men's*, *children's*, as genitives of *men*, *children*. At the same time, there is a change in position and in function: the genitive can no longer stand after the word on which it depends, but must always come before it; and it no longer expresses the same variety of relations as before, but is now, in the main, a possessive case. On this latter point we add a few words of explanation. The Anglo-Saxon genitive, like the Greek and Latin, expresses a great variety of relations between one substantive and another—in general, all the relations which are, or may be, expressed by our *of*. The English genitive, on the other hand, is called a possessive, and properly so; for this is its leading use, and "*a potiori nomen fit*." But Mr. Manning is clearly wrong when he contends that our case in *s* always carries a possessive meaning. In the phrase "in consequence of the prisoner's being absent," he holds that the "prisoner" is thought of as a possessor, and the "being absent" as a thing in his possession. This is, evidently, forced and unnatural. The truth is, that the English case in *s* has not only the possessive use of the Anglo-Saxon genitive, but the other uses which stand nearest to this. Thus it is constantly employed to denote connection in family, or state, or society: as in *John's brother, Henry's neighbor, England's queen, the king's enemies*—in old English we find even *the king's traitors.* Mr. Manning might, perhaps, argue that to say *the king's enemies* implies that "the king *has* enemies," and expresses, therefore, a possessive relation. But the verb *have* is a word of very general meaning, which can be used in a multitude of cases where there is no possession, properly so called, and sometimes even where our possessive case would be inadmissible. Thus, every apple *has* a half, but we cannot say "every apple's half." Still further, our case in *s* is used to express the subject of an action or an attribute: as in *coward's fear, God's love, the prisoner's being absent.* But relations which stand at a wider distance from the possessive cannot be expressed in this way. Thus, the objective relation: we do not say *God's fear*, but *the fear of God;* not *the child's guardianship*, but *the guardianship of the child.* We do indeed say *England's ruler, the child's guardian;* but here it is political or social connection that is thought of, and not the object of an action. In like manner, our case in *s* cannot be used as a genitive partitive (not *women's loveliest*, but *loveliest of women*); nor as a genitive of material (not *leather's girdle*, but *girdle of leather*); nor as a genitive of designation (not *Italy's kingdom*, but *kingdom of Italy*).

We have thus described the view commonly taken by grammarians and philologists in reference to the English possessive in *s:* it is, that this case is derived by uninterrupted tradition, though not without important changes in use and function, from the Anglo-Saxon genitive in *s*. Mr. Manning admits that this is the established view: but he considers it to be only a long-received and deeply-rooted error, which must be dislodged from the minds of men in order to make room for the admission of the truth. He therefore assails it with a strenuous polemic, bringing forward a great array of objections, which he numbers from 1 to 11. In these, however, there is some repetition, and we may reduce them all under a few heads.

First, he contends that, if the English possessive were the same with the Anglo-Saxon genitive, it would be confined, as the latter is, to masculines and neuters, and to a part only of these; it would be excluded from all feminines, from all *n*-stems, and from all plurals. But surely, there is nothing more common in the history of language than to find an inflection extended beyond the class of words that originally had it, and applied to other classes that originally excluded it. Thus the plural of nouns in Spanish ends in *s*; originally this *s* belonged only to masculines and feminines: as *libros*, 'books,' Lat. acc. plur. *libros*; *mesas*, 'tables,' Lat. *mensas*; *virtudes*, 'virtues,' Lat. *virtutes*—but it has been extended to neuters also: *pomos*, 'apples,' Lat. *poma*; *reynos*, 'kingdoms,' Lat. *regna*. The Provençal dialect of the Romance has preserved the Latin *s* of the nominative singular—as in *ans*, 'year,' Lat. *annus*—but has extended it to words which were without it in the Latin—as *libres*, 'book,' Lat. *liber*—and even to neuters—as *aurs*, 'gold,' Lat. *aurum*; *cels*, 'sky,' Lat. *cœlum*; *cors*, 'heart,' Lat. *cor*; *flums*, 'river,' Lat. *flumen*. The ancient Greek itself, in many adjectives of the vowel-declension, has extended the masculine form to the feminine: thus, ἥσυχος, 'quiet,' which is properly masculine, is used also as feminine. That this is an innovation of the Greek appears from a comparison of the Sanskrit, Latin, and Gothic, in which — and, doubtless, in the Indo-European before them—the adjective *a*-stems always have a distinct form for the feminine.

Secondly, it is objected that, if the English possessive were the same with the Anglo-Saxon genitive, it would, of necessity, have all the same functions, and would be capable of serving for all uses of the Anglo-Saxon genitive. But again, it is a common thing in the history of language to find an inflectional form undergoing some change of function, giving up a sense which it once had, or taking on a sense which it had not. An extreme instance of this kind is seen in the Greek present infinitive passive (*e. g.* γράφεσθαι, 'to be written'), which, in the modern Greek, according to the Grammar of Professor Sophocles, is used only after the verb θέλω, to form a continued future passive: thus θέλει γράφεσθαι, 'it will be written,' or, more exactly, 'it will be in process of being written.' Here the identity of form with the ancient γράφεσθαι is beyond all question; but to what a minimum has shrunk the widely extended use of the old infinitive! The Latin perfect indicative has two uses, which are often distinguished as definite and indefinite: thus, *posuerunt* may mean either 'they have placed' (equivalent to the Greek perfect), or 'they placed' (equivalent to the Greek aorist). But in the Romance languages, the corresponding form has lost the first of these uses, retaining only the last: in Spanish, for instance, *pusieron*, which represents the Latin *posuerunt*, means only 'they placed;' for 'they have placed,' the Spanish, like the English, uses the verb *have* with a passive participle: thus, *han puesto*. The Indo-European present tense, as we find it in the old Teutonic languages, has taken on an additional use, and serves both as a present and a future: thus the Gothic *gibith* means both 'he gives' and 'he will give.' In the modern Teutonic languages, this additional use is given up, and the tense has become, what it was at first, a present only. And yet the *th* of our *giveth*, or the *s* of our *gives*, is unquestionably the same ending as the *th* of Gothic *gibith*, the *t* of Latin *dat*, and the *ti* of Indo-European *dadâti*.

Closely connected with the objection we are considering is another which has been urged by Professor Goldstücker in a review of Mr. Manning's essay (see "The Reader;" London, Sept. 24, 1864). It is impossible, he maintains, that an inflexional form, like the Anglo-Saxon genitive in *s*, should maintain itself in use alongside of a prepositional expression —viz. *of* with the accusative—which could be used instead of it everywhere with precisely the same meaning. But to this impossibility we may oppose a reality offered by the Latin language. Here the old inflectional locative did maintain itself in certain words, as a designation of the place 'where,' alongside of a prepositional form—viz. *in* with the ablative—which could be used instead of it everywhere with precisely the same meaning. Examples of this old locative are *Romæ*, originally *Romāï*, 'at Rome,' *Corinthi*, originally *Corinthoï*, 'at Corinth,' *ruri*, 'in the country,' *domi*, 'at home,' etc. It has become greatly restricted in use, being nearly confined to names of towns, and among these to words of the first or second declension. Other words used to designate the place 'where' are put in the ablative with *in*, as *in provincia, in situ;* and even names of towns of the first or second declension are susceptible of the same construction. True, it is not idiomatic to say *in Roma;* but when an appositive (as *urbs*) is added, *in urbe Roma* is the regular form. Even in these points our English usage presents a curious analogy. We do not say *this is the house of Jack;* the form is intelligible, but nobody uses it; we say *this is Jack's house:* but with an appositive added, *this is the house of my cousin Jack* is a familiar form of expression.

Thirdly, the ending *s* of the English possessive is used in various connections and constructions where, in Mr. Manning's opinion, it is impossible to explain it as a genitive case-inflection, or indeed in any way except as the pronoun *his*. Thus in *Cæsar's crossing the Rubicon*, he asserts, with much confidence, that no inflected language could use its genitive to translate *Cæsar's;* that, instead of a genitive, it would be necessary to use some expression with instrumental meaning. But surely, there are scholars enough in his own city of Oxford who could have told him that ἡ Καίσαρος διάβασις τοῦ Ῥουβίκωνος is at once idiomatic Greek and an exact rendering of *Cæsar's crossing the Rubicon.* The Καίσαρος and *Cæsar's* in these expressions are not, indeed, true possessives, as he holds in reference to the latter; they are genitives used to denote the subject of an action. Again, he finds a more reasonable cause of difficulty in forms such as *John and Walter's house, husband and wife's children:* the latter, he says, if *wife's* were a real genitive, would be like saying in Latin *vir et uxoris liberi*, which, of course, would give a different meaning, viz. 'the husband and the children of the wife.' But would this be further out of the way than *vir et uxor ejus liberi* ('husband and wife, the children of that one'), the Latin form which would correspond to Mr. Manning's theory? He has himself suggested the true explanation, when he refers to ordinals such as *three and twentieth*, where the formative ending *eth* is applied to the copulative *three and twenty* taken as one complex whole. He does not deny that *three and twentieth* is good English, though *tres et vicesimus* would be very poor Latin. He refers also to similar forms of expression in other languages, as *hülf- und hoffnungslos* in German, literally 'help- and hopeless,' *i. e.* 'helpless and hopeless;' *feliz- y valerosamente* in Spanish, literally 'fortunate- and valorously, *i. e.* 'fortunately and valorously.' Yet again, he finds a difficulty in such expressions as *King of England's crown:* if our possessive were a real genitive, we should have to say (he thinks) *King's crown of England*, or *crown King's of England.* He will not admit that *King of England* can be treated as one complex whole, receiving inflection at the end; though it is hard to see how this would differ in principle from the formation just noticed in *three and twentieth.* Can any one say that in *three and twenty* the two numerals are more closely connected by *and* than the two substantives in *King of England* are connected by *of?* On the contrary, it would be more plausible to regard the preposition as forming the closer connection. It is to be observed that this formation is not readily used except when we are accustomed to hear the combination—the two substantives connected by *of*—as the recognized name of some well-understood object: thus we say *the King of England's crown*, but hardly *a bishop of the church's income*, rather *the income of a bishop of the church;* hardly *the men of property's influence*, rather *the influence of the men of property.* We observe also that examples are not wholly wanting of other endings applied in the same way: thus, from *Church of England* is formed, at least in popular parlance, if not in the language of books, the expression *Church-of-Englandism*, for which assuredly no one would think of substituting *Churchism of England.* There remains still another form of expression—seen in the examples, *he is a servant of my brother's*, *I am going to try that new horse of my neighbor's*—which Mr. Manning regards as irreconcilable with the genitive origin of our possessive. The preposition *of* (he says) requires an objective case, and, according to his explanation, would have it even here; *a servant of my brother's* being equivalent to *a servant of my brother* HIS, in which *brother* is an objective case, and *his* a possessive agreeing with *servant.* It cannot be denied that there is some difficulty in explaining this usage. Lowth treated the genitive here as having a partitive construction, and depending on a word understood: *a servant of my brother's* he viewed as standing for *a servant of* [*i. e. of the number of*] *my brother's servants:* the latter was the full logical form, but the repetition in it of the word *servant* was unnecessary and disagreeable, and was therefore dispensed with. To this explanation of Lowth, Mr. Manning objects that *a servant of my brother's* does not of necessity mean *one of my brother's servants:* if my brother has but one servant, and I am aware of the fact, I may still say with propriety "the person whom you saw was *a servant of my brother's.*" Or, to take a clearer case, a man might say "that wife of my son's is always teasing me," without in the least accusing his son of bigamy (or of *Brigham-y*, if one may coin a Mormon name for a Mormon institution). It is possible, however, to modify Lowth's explanation so as to escape the force of this objection. We may regard the possessive, when thus used, as depending—at least in many cases—not on a particular word repeated from what precedes, but on a general indeterminate conception of 'that which is possessed.' In speaking of one particular thing, I may say "it is my brother's house;" of a second, "it is my brother's servant;" of a third, "it is my brother's heart;" and so on. Of course, there are a great multitude of things which can be put after *my brother's* in such a sentence. Conceive now the aggregate, the collective totality, of these things, and you have the general, indeterminate conception of which we are speaking. It is an element of some importance in the theory of syntax. In the sentence "deal as thou wilt with him and his," the subject of the possessive *his* can only be this general conception: 'his belongings,' 'the sum of all those things of which each one can be called *his*'—such is the sense of the expression. If we say "all mine is thine," it is plain that both possessives have this same indeterminate subject. If, then, we say "all mine is my brother's," it is plain that the possessive case *brother's* must depend on the same indeterminate subject as the possessive pronoun *mine*. Now it is easy and natural to apply the same explanation to such forms as *this soul of mine*, *that wife of my brother's*. There is a greater difficulty in explaining *that friend of hers*, *of ours*, *of yours*, *of theirs*, where we should expect *of her*, *our*, *your*, *their*. It is known, however, that these forms—*hers*, *ours*, etc.—are not very ancient; and it can hardly be doubted that, from being already accustomed to hear and to say *it is John's*, *it is Mary's*, *it is my cousin's*, *it is the Prince's*, and the like, men were led by false analogy to say *it is hers* for the earlier *it is her*, *it is ours* for *it is our*; and in like manner, *a friend of hers* for *a friend of her*, *a friend of ours* for *a friend of our*, etc. There are very few, probably, who will think it more plausible to explain these forms as Mr. Manning does—that is, as abridged for the fuller and earlier forms, *a friend of her his*, *a friend of our his*, and so on.

Such are Mr. Manning's objections to the common view of our possessive case. It need hardly be said that they are not decisive against it. They do not require its falsity. The utmost we can say is that, if another view were strongly supported by positive proof, these objections might be used, with more or less effect, to clear the ground for its reception. Positive proof for his own thesis Mr. Manning seeks to draw from two different sources, the popular dialects of Germany, and the early English writers. What he has collected on the German dialects forms the most interesting part of his essay. He shows, in fact, that a form of expression analogous to *John Smith his book* is widely current in them. Thus we find in popular German *des Vaters sein Buch* ('the father's *his* book'); *des Goldschmieds sein Junge* ('the goldsmith's *his* apprentice'); *dein Aufwand übertrifft den Aufwand des Fürsten seinen* ('thy expenditure exceeds that of the Prince's *his*'); *Jeder hatte ein Pferd mitgebracht* ('each had brought a horse with him'), *aber des einen seins war blind* ('but the one's *his* was blind'), *des andern seins, lahm* ('the other's *his*, lame'). Similar expressions are met with even in respectable literary works. Schmidt, in his *Geschichte der Deutschen*, says *des Alfonsus seine Mächte* ('Alphonso's *his* powers'). Gellert has *dies Beiwort ist noch mahlerischer als Homers seines* ('this epithet is yet more picturesque than Homer's *his*'). It will be observed that in all the instances now given the name of the possessor is put in the genitive. But in Upper Germany the dative is used instead of this genitive: as in *dem Vater sein Buch* ('*to* the father *his* book'); *dem Goethe sein Gedicht* ('*to* Goethe *his* poem'). And in the popular language the name of the possessor can be put in the same case as the thing possessed: as, *fass Kürdchen sein Hütchen* ('take little Conrad *his* little hat'), where *Kürdchen* and *Hütchen* are both in the accusative; *in dem Wolfe seinem Leib* ('in the wolf *his* body'), where *Wolfe* and *Leib* are both in the dative. Mr. Manning speaks of these forms as very old—apparently, because he finds them in the brothers Grimm's *Kinder- und Hausmährchen*. I cannot see that he traces them farther back than the 17th century. He gives us no example of them from the Middle High German. And there is one thing about them which makes strongly against his hypothesis. When the possessor is feminine or plural, *sein* is not used, but *ihr*, 'her,' or *ihr*, 'their,' is used instead. Thus, *der Mutter ihr Kleid* ('the mother's *her* gown'), *der Kinder ihr Spielzeug* ('the children's *their* playthings'), *den Eltern ihre Sorgen* ('*to* the parents *their* cares'), *Frau Wolf ihre Töchter* ('Mrs. Wolf's *her* daughters'). According to the same analogy, we should expect in English, not *mother his gown*, the supposed original of our *mother's gown*, but *mother her gown;* not *children his playthings*, the supposed original of *children's playthings*, but *children their playthings*. Mr. Manning feels the difficulty, and takes great pains to get rid of it. He shows that, in the old German, *sein*, used as a reflexive, could mean 'her' and 'their,' and that it sometimes had this use even when not reflexive. This may be true, but it makes against his cause: for if *sein* was capable of meaning 'her' and 'their,' it is all the more remarkable and significant that people never said *der Mutter sein Kleid, der Kinder sein Spielzeug*, but always used the pronoun *ihr* instead. Mr. Manning goes back to the Mœso-Gothic, where *sein* is always reflexive, and shows that, as such, it can mean 'her' and 'their' as well as 'his.' He shows that the Latin *suus*, which is likewise always reflexive, has the same range of meaning ('his,' 'her,' 'their'). And from all these facts he draws the conclusion that our English *his* could be used with equal range of meaning—that it could be used for 'her' and 'their.' But this does not follow. *Suus* and *sein* are derived from a root *se*, *sve*, *sva*, 'self,' which denotes personality without gender: *suus* and *sein* mean 'belonging to self,' of whatever gender or number that "self" may be. Not so the Anglo-Saxon genitive *his*. It is true that the root *hi*, from which it comes, is found also in the feminine and the plural; but then it always shows a different suffix: 'belonging to a feminine *hi*' is expressed by *hi-re* (Gothic *hi-zôs*); 'belonging to a plural *hi*' is expressed by *hi-ra* (Gothic *hi-zê*, *hi-zô*); *his* can only mean 'belonging to a singular *hi* of the masculine or neuter gender.' Mr. Manning endeavors to show that the forms *he*, *his*, *him* are pretty promiscuously used in early English, for the feminine as well as for the masculine and neuter. This is true as to *he*, and for an obvious reason: the accusative singular feminine of the Anglo-Saxon pronoun was *hi*, and in early English this accusative (written as *hi* or *he*) is sometimes used as a nominative, instead of the regular *heo* (the nominative *she* is of later appearance). But it is decidedly not true as to *his* and *him*. Where these appear to be feminine, it will be found almost always that they refer to such words as *wife*, *maiden*, *child*, and others, which are neuter in Anglo-Saxon and Old English. Mr. Manning has utterly failed to show that *his* was ever freely applied in reference to feminine words. That it was ever freely used for the plural, he has not even attempted to show. And, indeed, he is evidently aware that his theory is open to objection at this point; he sees that, for some at least, it will be hard to believe that *his* was employed with distinct consciousness of its pronoun-character in such expressions as *the mother his gown*, *the children his playthings*. He has no trouble in believing it himself; but for those "of little faith" who cannot do so, he suggests a way of getting over the difficulty. We may suppose (he says) that *his* was first employed in this manner only after nouns of the singular number and of the masculine or neuter gender; that it was confined for a time to such expressions as *the father his book*, *the horse his head, the land his ruler;* that in these it gradually lost its force as a separate pronoun, restricted (like other pronouns) in gender and number, and came to be regarded as a mere sign of the possessive relation; and that in this condition it began at length to be employed after feminines and plurals. The process, thus hypothetically traced, is certainly not inconceivable. Whether it was a historical reality, must be determined by looking at the literary monuments of our language. We are thus referred to the usage of the Semi-Saxon and the Early English writers. In these, if anywhere, we must find the convincing proofs for the theory under consideration.

In this field, Mr. Manning's battle-horse is the later text of Layamon's Brut. That interesting and invaluable relic of the Semi-Saxon period—which recites the mythic history of Britain in a poem of some 32,000 short lines—is preserved in two manuscripts. The earlier manuscript was written about the year 1200. It shows us the genitive case very much as it stood in the Anglo-Saxon, in form, position, and function; with some restrictions in its use, but still to a great extent the same thing. In the later manuscript, written (it is supposed) some fifty or sixty years after the first, we find considerable changes in this, as in many other features of the language. It is true that the ending *-es* of the genitive is not often extended to words that did not have it in the Anglo-Saxon. But in position, the case is no longer free to stand either before or after the word on which it depends: with only rare exceptions it stands first, as in modern English. In function also it is restricted, for the most part, in the same way as in modern English. In the earlier text, Mr. Manning tells us that he has been able to discover only two instances of the possessive pronoun *his* applied as a substitute for the Anglo-Saxon inflected possessive genitive. Unfortunately he has omitted to specify these two instances. Sir Frederic Madden, the learned editor of Layamon, says that the genitive expressed by *his* rarely occurs in the earlier text, but is found in two places, which he names (vol. i., pp. 175, 279). It is probable that these are the two instances spoken of by Mr. Manning. But any one who looks carefully at the two passages will see that in neither of them does *his* refer to the substantive immediately before it; so that they are not real instances of the form we are discussing. But whether this form does or does not occur in the earlier text, there is no doubt that it is frequent in the later. Mr. Manning says even that "nearly all" the Anglo-Saxon inflexional genitives of the earlier manuscript become pronominal possessives (*i.e.* forms written with *his* instead of *-es*) in the later. This, however, is a strange exaggeration—unintentional, doubtless, but not the less extraordinary. I have run over the first 9,000 lines, or more than a quarter of the poem, with reference to this point. From proper names of persons I have noted, in all, forty-nine genitives. In twenty-three of them the genitive is expressed by *his:* these are all masculine, and in about half the name ends in *s*. In twenty-one instances (four of them feminine names) we have the inflected genitive in *s:* in none of these does the name itself end in *s*. But there are five instances of names ending in *s* which are used without change as genitives, the inflexional *s* being apparently fused (as it often is now) in the final *s* of the name.

We see, then, that less than half the genitives from proper names of persons are expressed by *his*. And it does not appear that in the genitives expressed by *his* the possessive idea is at all more distinct or emphatic than it is in the inflectional genitives. We have "Eubrac *his* sones" (sons), but we have also "Argal*es* sones;" "Gorbonia *his* brother," but also "Morgan*es* brother;" "Julius *his* men," but also "Cesar*es* men;" "Cunages *his* hond" (hand), but also "Belyn*es* hond;" "Jaines *his* temple," but also "Appolin*es* temple" (nom. *Appolin*); and so on. In fact, we find "Albanac *his* lond" (land) followed, eight lines after, by "Albanack*es* folk;" and "Belyn*es* forth-fare" (departure, decease) followed, two lines after, by "Belyn *his* deathe." Is it not evident that these are mere capricious variations of orthography, without difference of use, and apparently without difference of pronunciation? From proper names of places or countries I have noted fifteen genitives: two of these—"Wales *his* louerd" (lord), and "Leogris *his* lond"—are made with *his*; while the remaining thirteen are written with inflective *s*, as "Norwey*es* king," "Lombardi*es* lond," and so on. From common nouns I have observed only two instances of the genitive expressed by *his*: viz., "hem *his* mochele mod" (uncle's mickle mood), and "man *his* frouere" (man's savior). On the other hand, we have "hem*es* name" (uncle's name), "mann*es* hond" (man's hand), and so on. Indeed, the genitives of common nouns, written with inflective *s*, which I have noted, are about eighty in number: of these, many are possessive in the strictest sense, and four-fifths—perhaps nine-tenths—are susceptible of being rendered by our English possessive. Again we ask whether it is not evident—at least as regards the first quarter of the poem—that the genitive expressed by *his* is only an occasional orthographic variation of the old inflectional genitive—a variation restricted, in the main, to masculine names of persons, in which it would be most natural for an unlearned scribe to substitute the pronoun *his* for the inflection *-es*, the two forms being equivalent to his mind, and almost or altogether equivalent to his ear.

The conclusion thus drawn is strongly confirmed by the evidence of the Ormulum. This poem, of about 20,000 short lines, is preserved in a single manuscript, which is, not improbably, the autograph of the author, the monk Ormin himself. It belongs apparently to about the same age as the second manuscript of Layamon. In the character of its noun-inflection it has a decidedly later aspect than that manuscript; it approaches altogether more nearly to the modern inflection of the noun. But when all indications of age are taken into the account, it will have to be considered, probably, as pretty closely contemporaneous with the later manuscript of Layaman. The Ormulum is especially valuable from its regular and careful phonetic spelling. It is a standing refutation of the oft-repeated fallacy, that a cast-iron orthography—a system which follows tradition, without regard for present pronunciation—however inconvenient in other respects, is useful or indispensable for philological purposes. Here is a work, wholly without literary merit, valuable chiefly to the philologist, and to him chiefly from the fact that the scribe, departing freely from traditional modes of spelling, undertook to make his spelling represent his pronunciation. In the Ormulum we find the genitive restricted in position and function almost entirely as it is in modern English. It is regularly made with the ending *-ess*, the *s* being doubled merely as an orthographic sign, to show that the *e* is short. Of the form with *his* (or *hiss*) as a substitute for the inflection-ending, not a single instance is found in the Ormulum. Nor can it be claimed with any probability that this genitive-ending *-ess* has come from the pronoun *his* by suppressing the *h;* for the difference between the vowels *e* and *i*, though in ordinary manuscripts no stress could be laid upon it, is decisive here: when so careful a speller writes *his* always with *i*, and the genitive-ending always with *e*, we may be sure that he sounded the vowels differently in the pronoun and the ending. But, indeed, there can be no reasonable question that the possessive of the Ormulum is the descendant and representative of the Anglo-Saxon genitive. Mr. Manning himself, quoting the line "till helless thesternesse" (to hell's darkness), says that "we find here the old Anglo-Saxon genitive." He was aware, probably, when saying this, that the Anglo-Saxon word *hel*, being feminine, makes *helle* (without *s*) in the genitive; yet he could justly describe *helless* as an Anglo-Saxon genitive—in this sense, that it shows an Anglo-Saxon formation, extended in this instance a little beyond the bounds which it had in that language. But if this formation in the Ormulum is, by Mr. Manning's own admission, identical with the Anglo-Saxon genitive, how can it be denied that our English possessive in *s* is identical with the Anglo-Saxon genitive? The *-ess* of the Ormulum has very much the same range of use as our possessive *s*, being already extended to feminines, to words of the *n*-declension, and to plurals; it takes the same uniform position before the word on which it depends, and it is restricted substantially to the same syntactical relations. And if the *-ess* of the Ormulum has a vowel-sound which is generally wanting to our possessive, we find a perfect parallel to this in the ending of the plural, which is *-ess* in the Ormulum, and is now generally reduced to a mere *s*. It is true that in writing the possessive we use a sign—the apostrophe—which we do not use in writing the plural. And it may be true that those who first used the apostrophe did so because they believed the possessive *s* to be only a remnant of the separate word *his*. But such a belief, entertained at the close of the 16th century, has no more weight of authority than when entertained now. It could have rested then on no proofs which are not accessible now; and if the proofs now appear insufficient to support it, they must have been insufficient then. False etymology is confined to no age. It appears in various particulars of our old established orthography—in spelling *island* (for instance) as if it were connected with *isle*; in spelling *sovereign* as if it were connected with *reign*; and so on. If the apostrophized *s* indicates a supposed connection with *his*, it may be only another instance of the same kind.

Mr. Manning cites, from writers of the fourteenth and following centuries, a series of passages showing possessive cases made with *his*. He carries these citations even into the seventeenth century. In the authorized version of the Bible, as first printed, there were (he says) three cases of the kind; one of which—"Holofernes *his* head"—is to be seen, still unchanged, in the Apocrypha. As for the other two—"Asa *his* heart" and "Mordecai *his* matters"—he complains that they have been "altered by some careless or earless printer" into "Asa's heart" and "Mordecai's matters." But are these three cases distinguished by any special *his*-ness from the common run of possessives in the Bible? and, if not, then is it not, probably, mere carelessness, either of the printer or the scribe, which gave them their peculiar form in the first edition? From Ben Jonson several instances are given, like "Sejanus *his* fall," "Horace *his* judgment." But as this is not the ordinary form of the possessive in Jonson's works, and as Jonson, noticing this form in his English Grammar, calls it (to Mr. Manning's great disgust) a "*monstrous* syntax," might it not be more charitable to ascribe those instances to "a careless or earless printer?" Mr. Manning does not disdain even to gather up some few examples from writers of the eighteenth century, Addison, Pope, and Sterne as if he could add anything in this way to the force of his previous citations; as if he were not rather weakening the force of those citations, by showing that men could write as a separate *his* what they undoubtedly pronounced as a mere inflective *s* or *es!*

Mr. Manning has given many examples of a possessive written with *his:* he might easily have given many more. But we cannot see that he has proved, or even seriously attempted to prove, that this was the prevailing form of our possessive at any period of time, or even in any single author. If in a particular book he finds one, two, or three examples of this form, he seems never to raise the question whether these are specimens of a general practice, or exceptions to a general practice; though, plainly enough, the force of his examples must depend largely on the answer to this question. He notes the fact, as if it were important, that one of Chaucer's Canterbury Tales is entitled the "Nonne Prest *his* Tale." But he does not notice that the same tale was just before designated as the "Nonne Prest*es* Tale." In Wright's text of the Canterbury Tales, which is regarded as the best hitherto published, the possessive written with *his* is not only an exception, but a rare exception, to the prevailing form.

My opportunities for studying old English texts have been exceedingly limited, and I cannot therefore speak with positiveness as to their usage in this particular. I have examined, however, with reference to this point, the series of extracts given in Mr. Marsh's Origin and History of the English Language. Those extracts are somewhat extended; they represent the leading productions of English literature from the close of the Anglo-Saxon period to the middle of the sixteenth century; they are taken from the best texts which had been printed when that work appeared. In these extracts there are many examples of the possessive in *s;* but—aside from the later text of Layamon, which has been discussed already—I have not been able to find a single instance of a possessive written with *his.* I say "not a single instance;" for as to the line in the Surtees Psalter—"man his daies ere als hai"—I do not regard it as an instance of the kind. *Man* here was undoubtedly uttered as an independent word, followed by a pause ; exactly like *homo* in the Latin original—*homo sic ut fœnum dies ejus*—and like *man* in the older Wycliffite version—" a man as hey his dayes."

We conclude, then, that the genitive in *s*, which belonged to the earliest Anglo-Saxon, has never dropped out of the language ; that it has never ceased to be in use. It has undergone great changes, both in the range of words that take it, and in the range of uses for which it is employed ; but the result of all these changes, the modern English possessive, is connected by an unbroken historical tradition with the inflectional genitive of the Anglo-Saxon. This is the common belief of scholars, and it is likely to be sustained, rather than shaken, by the new discussion which Mr. Manning has opened in so spirited a manner. On the other hand, the possessive made by *his* appears, with all the new light which he has thrown upon it, to be only an occasional variation of the English possessive. It is (or rather, it was) a variation, not in the form itself, as heard in living utterance, but in the way of representing that form in writing. It arose, apparently, from a mistaken and fanciful etymology, which seemed to furnish a plausible explanation for the possessive sense ; and the degree of currency which it gained is, at least partly, due to the general inexactness and confusion of early English orthography.

XIV.

ELLIS'S EARLY ENGLISH PRONUNCIATION.*

1870.

THE Second Part, which is to complete this learned and valuable work, was expected, according to the author's statement, to have about the same extent as the First, and to be ready for publication before the close of the year 1869. It will investigate the pronunciation of Anglo-Saxon and Old English prior to the fourteenth century, with that of the Teutonic and Scandinavian sources of the English; it will discuss the correspondence of orthography and pronunciation from Anglo-Saxon times to the present day; and it will contain a series of documents and illustrations relating to the pronunciation of our language in the successive periods of its history. Its appearance will be awaited with much interest; yet it will probably be little more than an extended supplement to the part now before us. It is safe to assume that this first part is much the more important of the two, not only exhibiting the author's method, but presenting us with the general views and opinions to which it has led him. We shall be in little danger of doing him injustice if we criticise what we already have, without waiting for that which is yet to come.

It is saying little, to say that Mr. Ellis has surpassed all predecessors in the same field. We believe that he is the first who has really endeavored to collect everything which can throw light on the history of English pronunciation, and to treat the whole subject with scientific precision and

* On Early English Pronunciation, with especial reference to Shakespeare and Chaucer. By Alexander J. Ellis, F.R.S., etc. Part I. On the Pronunciation of the XIVth, XVIth, XVIIth, and XVIIIth Centuries. London: Published for the Philological Society, by Asher & Co., London and Berlin; and for the Early English Text Society, by Trübner & Co., 60 Paternoster Row. 1869. 8vo. pp. viii, 416.

thoroughness. In the collection of his material he has used exemplary diligence, sparing no pains to make it complete and exhaustive; and in the discussion of it he has shown a fairness of mind, a freedom from prejudice, a simple love of truth, not less exemplary. He is always careful to present the evidence on which his conclusions are founded, and to distinguish conclusions which seem to him only probable, in greater or less degree, from those which he regards as certain. He does not fail to recognize the uncertainties which affect much of the evidence—uncertainties arising either from the nature of the subject or from the peculiarities of individual witnesses. Nor does he keep back the evidence which seems unfavorable to what he thinks the best-supported conclusions; but presents the whole case, making it possible for the reader to form an independent judgment.

In the notation of spoken sounds, Mr. Ellis uses a comprehensive system, which he calls by the name *palæotype* (only the *old types* being used in it), and sets it forth in a brief introduction. It is based on the Roman alphabet, and contains no sign that cannot be found in the cases of an ordinary printing-office. To secure the necessary variety, italics, small capitals, and (in some instances) inverted letters are used to denote sounds distinct from, though akin to, those expressed by the corresponding Roman letters. As a further means to the same end, the forms (h, j, *w*) are used, without any consonant power, merely as diacritical signs, modifying the sounds of the letters with which they are connected; while the forms (H, J, w, and q) represent the consonant sounds in *h*ay, *y*ea, *w*ay, wi*ng*. Long vowels are represented by doubling the signs which stand for the corresponding short vowels; diphthongs, by writing their elementary vowels in immediate succession; successive vowels, if they do not form a diphthong, are separated by a comma. Words and sounds written in palæotype, if mixed with ordinary writing, are distinguished by enclosing them in marks of parenthesis: thus, (H*ee*,*i*q) for *haying*. Mr. Ellis is careful to explain that this mode of writing is not designed to supersede the current orthography in popular use; it is intended for scientific purposes, as a means of designating conveniently and exactly the sounds heard in English and in other languages. In his tabular Key to Palæotype he gives more than two hundred and fifty distinct sonnds, with their notation in his system. He also compares these signs of his with the letter-forms devised by Mr. Melville Bell, and described in his "Visible Speech." The number of signs required in treating of English pronunciation past and present is, of course, much less than two hundred and fifty. Among those which occur often in the book we may be allowed to give here the most important, as it will be convenient to use them in the statements and criticisms that we have to offer. The short vowels (a, e, i, o, u) have the Italian sounds; but these are almost all different from the English short vowels in *pat*, *pet*, *pit*, *pot*, *put*, which are represented in palæotype by (æ, e, *i*, ɔ, *u*). The long vowels (aa, ee, ii, oo, uu), with Italian sounds, correspond more nearly to the English long in *par*, *pale*, *peel*, *pole*, *pool*, which are represented in palæotype by (aa, *ee*, ii, *oo*, uu), where (*ee*, *oo*) are closer sounds than (ee, oo). The forms (y, œ) stand for the German *ü*, *ö*. The English short and long *a* in *want*, *war*, are expressed by the small capital (ᴀ, ᴀᴀ); the short *u* in *but*, by the inverted (ə); the diphthongs in *height*, *house*, by (əi, əu); the diphthongal *u* in *pure*, by (iu). As to the consonants, we have already spoken of (ʜ, ᴊ, w, q); and need only add (ɹ) for the weak final *r* in *fair*, and (th, dh, sh, zh, tsh, dzh) for the spirant sounds in *thew*, *thou*, *shoe*, *azure*, *chew*, *Jew*.

Mr. Ellis commences his inquiry with the pronunciation of the sixteenth, seventeenth, and eighteenth centuries. From the known present he goes back first of all to the recent past. For this period he has the aid of a long series of orthoepical writers; and he begins by enumerating these in the order of time, giving full titles of works, and adding brief descriptions and criticisms. The writers to whom he refers most frequently are: John Palsgrave (French Grammar), 1530; W. Salesbury, 1547, 1567; Sir Thomas Smith, 1568; John Hart, 1569; William Bullokar, 1580; Alexander Gill, 1619; Ben Jonson (English Grammar), 1640; John Wallis (English Grammar), 1653; Philip Wilkins (Philosophical Language), 1668; Owen Price, 1668; C. Cooper, 1685; John Jones, 1701;

an anonymous Expert Orthographist, 1704; James Buchanan 1766; Benjamin Franklin (Scheme for a New Alphabet), 1768. He manifests an especial preference for Salesbury and Wallis. The latter, who was Professor of Mathematics at Oxford, wrote a *Grammatica Linguæ Anglicanæ*, with a prefixed *Tractatus grammatico-physicus de Loquela*, in which he gives an elaborate description of the English sounds, with the positions and movements of the vocal organs in producing them. The former, a Welshman, educated at Oxford, prepared an English Dictionary for the use of his countrymen, with an interesting and valuable introduction, written in Welsh, on English pronunciation.

From such materials Mr. Ellis endeavors to reconstruct the prevailing pronunciation of our language during the three centuries which preceded our own. He does not disguise from himself the very great difficulties of the task. There are few things harder than to understand the descriptions of spoken sounds. Even when the writer is intelligent, it is no very easy matter to reproduce the precise position of the vocal organs, the precise utterance, which he meant to describe. But most writers have been ignorant both of the physical mechanism of speech and of the true relations of sounds. The terms which they have used are very often inexact or unmeaning. Who can be sure as to the force of *thick*, *thin*, *full*, *round*, *flat*, *hard*, *soft*, *rough*, *smooth*, *coarse*, *fine*, *sharp*, *dull*, *clear*, *obscure*, and many similar epithets, which are so commonly and so fancifully applied to vowels and consonants? If the writer identifies a particular English sound with one in some foreign language, as the French, a variety of doubts at once suggest themselves. Are we sure that he meant to assert an absolute identity, or only a resemblance, between the sounds compared? Are we sure that the French sound has not varied since the time in question? Are we sure that it was uniform at that time? Are we sure that the writer correctly apprehended the French sound of which he speaks? Misapprehension of foreign sounds is a thing of constant occurrence. Mr. Ellis mentions a remarkable instance in a lecture by Professor Blackie, of Edinburgh, on the pronunciation of Greek; after saying that long *a* in

Greek had the sound of Italian *a* in *amare*, the lecturer added immediately that "long *a* should always be pronounced like English *aw* or *au*, as in *cawl*, *maul*, etc."! Even experts may differ as to the real character of the foreign sound. Speaking of the French vowels before the nasal *n* in *an*, *vin*, *on*, *un*, Mr. Ellis represents them, first as they seem to his own ear, and then as they appear to Dr. Rapp, M. Féline, M. Favarger, and Mr. Melville Bell; and no two of these gentlemen agree entirely with each other. Mr. Ellis further tells us that he differs from Mr. Bell in his pronunciation of several of the key-words which the latter has used to show the exact phonetic value of his symbols.

While fully recognizing these difficulties which beset his inquiry, our author has not allowed himself to be deterred from pursuing it. Taking up in succession the English vowels and consonants, he endeavors to ascertain, from a detailed examination of his authorities, how each was sounded in the sixteenth century, what changes (if any) it has undergone since then, and at what time they occurred. Most readers, we presume, will be surprised at the amount of change which he finds in English pronunciation, and especially in the vowel sounds, since the sixteenth century. Thus, to commence with the short vowels, he holds that only *ĕ* and *ĭ* were pronounced then as they now are—that is, as (e) and (*i*); as to *ă*, *ŏ*, *ŭ*, he believes that they were then pronounced (a, o, *u*), the first two as in Italian, and that the now prevailing sounds for them, viz. (æ, ɔ, ə), as seen in the words *cat*, *cot*, *cut*, came in during the seventeenth century. This may be true as to *ŏ* and *ŭ*; but we cannot help thinking, for reasons which will appear presently, that our current sound of *ă* is older than he makes it—that it belonged to the pronunciation of the sixteenth century.

Next, as to the long vowels. According to Mr. Ellis, the ē, which in Chaucer's time (the fourteenth century) was always (ee), began to take the sound (ii) during the fifteenth. In the sixteenth, a practice arose of representing the latter sound (ii) by doubling the vowel, as *ee*; while the old sound (ee), where it remained, was often distinguished by an added *a*, as *ea*. Thus *been*, *reed*, *greet* were pronounced as (biin, riid, griit); but *bean, read, great,* as (been, reed, greet). At length, however, the new sound (ii) was extended to words which had for a time retained the old one, the change being particularly rapid about the end of the seventeenth century, so that early in the eighteenth *ea* had come to have in most cases the same sound as *ee*. It is curious to compare the lists of words with *ea*, given by orthoepists during the transition period, and to note the progress of the change. We find here, as in many such revolutions, that particular individuals carry out the innovating tendency to an extent which is not finally sanctioned by the prevailing usage; some writers give *break, great, indeavour, deaf,* etc., with the sound of (ii). Mr. Ellis, by the way, speaks of (diif) as a pronunciation which he has never been fortunate enough to hear.

The ō has up to a certain point the same history as the ē. Before the close of the fifteenth century, it had in many words passed from its proper sound of (oo) into the closer (uu). And here also the practice arose in the sixteenth century of representing the new sound (uu) by doubling the letter, as *oo;* while the old sound, where it remained, was often distinguished by an added *a*, as *oa*. Thus *moon, rood* were pronounced as (muun, ruud); but *moan, road,* as (moon, rood). Here, however, the parallel ceases. The movement had already spent its force before the Elizabethan time. While *ea* in most words passed on from (ee) to (ii), *oa* has never passed from (oo) to (uu); with few exceptions—such as *move, prove,* and (with shortened vowel) *love, dove*—the ō has taken on the (uu) sound only in words where that sound was indicated in the sixteenth century by the writing *oo*.

Long ī and *ou*, which in Chaucer's time were simple sounds, the first being pronounced (ii) and the second (uu), had to a great extent become diphthongs in the sixteenth century. In Mr. Ellis's opinion, they were more clearly diphthongal then than now, being sounded as (ei) and (ou), where each vowel must be understood as having its proper force distinctly audible. In the present pronunciation the first element is obscure; the initial position of the organs is not maintained long enough to give a fully characterized utterance; hence, orthoepists differ much as to the first vowel sound in English long *ī* and *ou*. Mr. Ellis regards it as (ə), and writes the diphthongs as now pronounced (əi, əu). This pronunciation, he thinks, came in during the seventeenth century, or perhaps during the latter part of the sixteenth.

For *ei* and *ai* our author's results are particularly interesting. He shows that in the sixteenth century they were true diphthongs, differing little, if at all, in their pronunciation, which must have been much the same with that of our affirmative *aye*. It is observed that in Shakespeare's minor poems there is but one real instance—in the words *mane*, *again*—of a rhyme between *ā* and *ai*. The change by which these combinations came to be sounded as simple vowels—usually as (*ee*), but *ei* in some words as (ii)—is referred, like so many other changes, to the seventeenth century.

As to long *ā*—in *sale*, *came*, *fate*, etc.—Mr. Ellis's conclusions will cause greater surprise, and will perhaps meet with less acceptance. He holds that in the sixteenth century such words were pronounced (saal, kaam, faat), with the Italian sound of *a*; and that, in the seventeeth, the pronunciation changed to (sææl, kææm, fææt), differing only in length of sound from our *Sal*, *Cam*, *fat*. This sound, which he finds first distinctly apparent in the description of Wallis (1653), would seem to have been only transitional, as it gave place at the close of that century to (ee), which has since passed into the closer (*ee*) : thus, (s*ee*l, k*ee*m, f*ee*t). What now is the reason for believing that English long *a* had in Shakespeare's time the Italian sound of *a*? Palsgrave, in 1530, identifies the English letter with the Italian; but Palsgrave's ear, as Mr. Ellis admits, was none of the most delicate. Hart, in 1569, identifies the English letter with the German, Italian, French, Spanish, and Welsh *a*; but this, as Mr. Ellis says, is too wide a comparison, and leaves us in doubt as to the real sound. The witness really relied upon is Salesbury, who says, in 1547, that "*a* in English is the same sound as *a* in Welsh," and represents the pronunciation of *ale*, *pale*, *sale*, etc., by writing them for Welshmen *aal*, *paal*, *sal*, etc. This testimony makes it pretty clear that English *a* had not then the same sound as at present. If it had, Salesbury would almost certainly have compared it with Welsh *e*; and Palsgrave and Hart, with *e* in Italian, French, etc. No one now could for a moment think of giving *a*, rather than *e*, in those languages as the nearest equivalent for English long *a*. But as proof of the sound (aa), this evidence is not equally convincing. It is curious that in the following century Wallis, whose testimony is regarded as clearest for the sound (ææ), still identifies the English and Welsh *a*. It appears that a fraction of the Welsh people now give this sound (æ) to their own *a;* and such possibly may have been the pronunciation of Salesbury. It is, doubtless, more probable that his Welsh *a* was an (a) ; but if so, he had no Welsh letter which would correctly represent an (æ), and he may very naturally have regarded *a* as the nearest Welsh equivalent. But what is most important, we have distinct positive evidence from independent witnesses that the English *a*, at the beginning of the sixteenth century, differed from the French *a*, and approached to the French *e*. In the fragment of a treatise on the pronunciation of French, by an unknown author, but with the date 1528 (two years earlier than Palsgrave's book), is found the following statement as to the French *a* and *e:* "A. ought to be pronounced fro the botom of the stomak, and all openly ; E. a lytell hyer in the throte, there properly where the englysshe man soundeth his a." Similarly, Gilles du Guez, in his account of French pronunciation, which seems to have been printed about 1532, says: "Ye shal pronounce your [French] *a* as wyde open mouthed as ye can ; your [French] *e*, as ye do in latyn , almost as brode as ye pronounce your *a* in englysshe." These passages do not prove indeed that English *a* was identical with French *e;* in fact, the last of them excludes the idea of such an identity. But they prove an approximation of the English *a* to the French *e*, which is scarcely reconcilable with the sound (a) for the former. If we should assume that English *a*, at the opening of the sixteenth century, had, nearly or exactly, the sound of (æ), we should account in the most natural manner for the expressions of these writers. A similar sound, at the end of this century, is indicated by Peter Erondell, in his French Grammar (London, 1605). Distinguishing the French *a* from the English, he represents the sound of English *ale* by the French writing *esl* with silent *s*: that is, he finds the nearest equivalent for English *ā* in the French open *ê*. And Mr. Ellis himself finds the same sound, *ā* = (ææ), clearly set forth in the description of Wallis (1653). Are we not then warranted in concluding that English *a*, as early as the year 1528, had varied from the normal sound of (a, aa), and had assumed this sound of (æ) for *ă*, (ææ) for *ā*? The change may then be referred with much probability to the fifteenth century; and may naturally be regarded as the starting-point in that great revolution which, since the days of Chaucer, has transformed the whole vowel system of our language.

If we find ourselves obliged to dissent from Mr. Ellis on the pronunciation of long *a*, we are equally unable to agree with him on that of long *u*. He regards this vowel as having had, through the sixteenth century and much of the seventeenth, the same sound as the French *u*. The conclusion is not, indeed, as incredible as it may seem at first view. Our English *ū* is nearly confined to words which have come to us either from the French itself or from the Latin after our language had fallen under French influence. The Anglo-Saxon and the oldest English had a long *ū*, but for five centuries it has been represented by *ou* or *ow*. The *ū* in Chaucer's time, and ever since, belongs to the Romance part of the language. The sound of French *u*—(y, yy), as represented in palæotype—is certainly a strange and difficult one for most speakers of English. But Mr. Ellis assures us that it is common in some of the English dialects at the present time. "In East Anglia, in Devonshire, in Cumberland, as well as in Scotland, (yy) and its related sounds are quite at home." We must admit, then, as something quite possible, that this may have been a current and prevailing sound of *ū* in the sixteenth and seventeenth centuries. It is simply a question of evidence. Here again, as for long *a*, we find a number of orthoepists asserting the identity of the English and French sounds. Among these we may reckon Palsgrave (1530), who speaks only of English *ew*, but appears to have meant the same sound as that of *ū*; also, Sir T. Smith (1568), Hart (1569), Bullokar (1580), and lastly, Wallis (1653), whose testimony on this head is perfectly distinct and positive. Yet in this testimony of Wallis we find the clearest proof of the unreliable character of such identifications. For Bishop Wilkins, in 1668, speaking of the French *u*, declares, not only that the English do not use it, but that it is very hard for them to pronounce it. His language is: "As for the *u Gallicum*, or *whistling u*, though it cannot be denied to be a distinct simple vowel, yet it is of so laborious and difficult pronunciation to all those nations amongst whom it is not used (*as to the English*)," etc. Let it be observed that Wallis and Wilkins were contemporaries, that both were natives of Southern England, that both were for some time fellow-collegians in Oxford, that both must have mixed in the same society, and that their books were separated by an interval of only fifteen years. The discrepancy between their statements cannot be accounted for by difference of time, place, education, association, and the like. One or the other must have been in error. But a writer's statement that a foreign sound is strange to his own people, and difficult for them to utter, is not in itself likely to be erroneous; and in this case it is confirmed by other evidence, all going to show that the pronunciation of *u* since Wilkins's time has been what it now is. If then the sound of French *u* was not used, and could hardly be pronounced, by the English in 1668, it cannot possibly have been the current sound of English *u* in 1653. Wallis's identification must have been an error; the native and foreign sounds which he compared were not really identical. And if a writer so intelligent and careful as Wallis could fall into this error, we need not be surprised to find it in Palsgrave, Smith, Hart, etc. Indeed, the last-named writer seems to be at variance with himself, as in an earlier treatise he identifies the vowel *u* with the word *you*. He also describes it as a diphthong, composed of *i* and *u*; it is true, he applies the same description to the French *u*; but that may only show that he misapprehended the foreign sound.

But we have positive evidence that the French and English sounds were not identical. Erondell (1605), to whose French Grammar we have referred before, gives a careful description of the way in which French *u* is to be uttered, and directs the learner to pronounce *musique*, *punir*, *subvenir*, "not after the English pronunciation, not as if written *muesique*, *puenir*, *suevenir*," with the English *ue* of *sue*, *due*, etc. Holyband ("French Littleton," 1609) says: "You must take paine to pronounce our v [*i.e.* French *u*] otherwise then in English; for we do think, when Englishmen do profer v [*i.e.* their own *u*], they say, you." Here Mr. Ellis finds a distinct recognition of our present sound of *ū*. But we should hardly speak of it as "the first distinct recognition." For Salesbury himself (1547) indicates the same sound, when he says: "U vowel answers to the power of the two Welsh letters *u*, *w*, and its usual power is *uw*, as shown in the following words, TRUE *truw* verus, VERTUE *vertuw* probitas." It is true that the Welsh *uw*, as heard in *Duw*, 'God,' is not quite the same with our long *u* (as in *cue*); but it is a pretty near approximation to it, and the nearest which is possible in the Welsh language. The difference is that in the Welsh *uw* the two elements of the diphthong are a little more distinct; we can hear the initial element as an (*i*), very short, but perfectly recognizable, before the closely following (*u*). The English diphthongal *ū* of *cue*, *pure*, *mute*, etc., has the same elements, but not with the same distinctness of utterance; the initial position of the organs is not held long enough to give a clearly characterized sound. In this respect it resembles the English diphthongs *i* and *ou*; and hence, like these, it has often been regarded as a simple sound. Wallis speaks of it as such, in distinction from the Welsh *uw*; and when he identifies it with French *u*, he gives prominence to this fact, that both are simple vowels.

We believe, then, that English *ū* had in Salesbury's time—that is, in the first half of the sixteenth century—substantially the same pronunciation as at present. In the loose identifications with French *u*, made by some writers, we find no sufficient proof of the contrary; the last and most distinct, by Wallis, is refuted by the nearly contemporaneous statements of Wilkins. In tracing back the pronunciation of the letter from the nineteenth century to the sixteenth, there is a presumption in favor of the present sound, unless pretty strong evidence can be found for a different one. We do find in our authorities some evidence of this kind; but it is liable to grave suspicions, and is more than balanced by positive indications of the present sound. Perhaps we have dwelt longer than we ought both on this point and on the sixteenth-century pronunciation of *ā*. But they seemed to be among the most interesting questions raised by our author in his endeavor to determine the actual living utterance of Henry VIII. and Elizabeth; and they are well fitted to illustrate the amount and character of the evidence on which he relies in the discussion of these questions. We have only to add that the testimonies which we have brought forward in opposition to his views have all been derived from his own pages, where they stand fairly presented and candidly considered.

We pass on to the consonants, the treatment of which by our author will furnish much less occasion for remark. Of the weak final *r*, as heard in *car, care,* which he represents by (ɹ), he finds no trace whatever in the sixteenth century. Even Wallis and Wilkins are silent in regard to it. But Ben Jonson (1640) implies its existence, when he speaks of the letter as sounded in two ways, "firme in the beginning of the words, and more *liquid* in the middle and ends." As to its present weakness, the language of Mr. Ellis is very emphatic; he represents it as little more than a vanishing quantity, and indeed, as having vanished to a great extent from English pronunciation. He says: "This second (ɹ) may diphthongize with any preceding vowel. After (a, ᴀ, ɔ), the effect is rather to lengthen the preceding vowel than to produce a distinct diphthong. Thus, *farther* and *lord* scarcely differ from *father, laud:* that is, the diphthongs (aɹ, ɔɹ) are heard almost as the long vowels (aa, ᴀᴀ). That a distinction is made by many, by more perhaps than are aware of it, is certain; but it is also certain that in the mouths of by far the greater number of speakers in the south of England the absorption of the (ɹ) is as complete as the absorption of the (l) in *talk, walk, psalm,* where it has also left its mark on the preceding vowel. When Dickens wrote Count *Smorl Tork,* he meant *Small Talk,* and *no ordinary reader would distinguish between them.*" And again: "The diphthongs (eɹ, əɹ) are very difficult to separate from each other and from (əə). But the slight raising of the point of the tongue will distinguish the diphthongs from the vowel in the mouth of the careful speaker, that is, one who trains his organs to do so. *No doubt the great majority of speakers do not make any difference.*" It is fortunate for this much-abused letter that so large a part of the English-speaking world is found in America, where the first English settlers brought this *r* in a less attenuated state, and where their descendants have been largely reinforced by users of a yet stronger *r* from Ireland and Scotland and the continent of Europe. Instead of losing the final *r*, like our brethren in Southern England, we are more likely to restore it to its ancient equivalency with the initial letter.

As to the combination *wr*—in *write*, *wreck*, *wrath*, etc.—it appears from the testimony of Hart that the *w* was not entirely lost in the sixteenth century. It is Mr. Ellis's opinion that *wr* was sounded, not only then, but from the earliest Anglo-Saxon times, as (rw), or more exactly as (r*w*), a labialized *r*, the product of an effort to pronounce *r* and *w* at one and the same time. The French *roi* he represents by (r*w*a); and he holds that *wrath*, *wreck*, *write* were pronounced (r*w*ath, r*w*ek, r*w*eit). This seems to us improbable for Old-English, and still more for Anglo-Saxon. If *wrath* had been pronounced thus, it would almost certainly have been written *rwath*. To English ears the French *roi* appears to begin with the sound of *r* followed by that of *w*; it is safe to say that not one man in a hundred would think of it as beginning with a *w* followed by an *r*. Even the words *what*, *when*, *white*, etc., were by the Anglo-Saxons originally and generally written with *hw*, not *wh*. Would they not have followed the same analogy by writing *rw* instead of *wr*, if the sound had been what our author supposes? The copyists were accustomed to spell very much according to their own ear and taste; would they not, sometimes at least, have used the order *rw?* If *hw* has been changed to *wh*, it was probably not from any doubt as to the real order of the elements, but from the influence of the combinations *ph*, *ch*, *th*, *rh*, constantly presented in Latin orthography. There could be no such reason for adopting *wr* in preference to the seemingly more natural order *rw*. And if we look at other Teutonic languages, we find everywhere the same succession. Thus *wrath* appears in the Old Icelandic as *vreidhi*, in

Swedish and Danish as *vrede; wrong* in Icelandic is *vrangr*, Danish *vrang*, Swedish *vrång*. For *wring* the Gothic has *vriggan;* for *wreak* it has *vrikan, vrakjan;* for *write* it has *vrits* (Gr. *κεραία*, 'point of a letter'). In view of these considerations, who can doubt that the Anglo-Saxon writing *wr* represents the real order of the sounds, or what would appear such to hearers generally? If so, then (r*w*) cannot have been the Anglo-Saxon pronunciation; nor is there any reason for supposing that the Old-English pronunciation differed in this case from the Anglo-Saxon. The only argument we can see for Mr. Ellis's (r*w*) is the difficulty of making a true English *w* audible before *r* at the beginning of a word. We do not deny the difficulty; nor do we undertake to determine the precise sound of *wr;* but we could easily believe that *w* may have had in this case a somewhat stronger sound than we are wont to give it—a sound perhaps approaching to the South German *w* (a *v* pronounced without pressure of the teeth against the lips), which Mr. Ellis (p. 290) finds on British ground in the Aberdeen pronunciation of *write* as (bhriit).

In this connection we have to confess some feeling of doubt, if not of skepticism, as to our author's whole theory of labialized consonants. He finds in French *loi* (l*w*a) a labialized *l*, which he thinks existed once in English—*talk* being once sounded (tal*w*k)—"but it has died out:" yet why not recognize it in *always?* So he finds a labialized *k* in *quell* (k*w*el), a labialized *t* in *twin*, a labialized *d* in *dwell*, etc. Here the *qu*, *tw*, *dw* are in his view simple consonants, a *k*, *t*, *d*, pronounced in a labial position. To us they still appear as composite sounds. Compare *high dwell the birds* with *hide well the birds:* in continuous utterance are they not perfectly alike? What Mr. Ellis says of *twin* and *dwell*, "that the opening of the lips [from the rounded closure required for a *w*] is really simultaneous with the release of the (t, d) contact," we are unable to reconcile with the testimony of the ear as to our own pronunciation and that which we hear around us.

The wretched weakness of utterance which has changed *know* to *no* (converting science into mere negation) was, according to all the authorities, still un*k*nown, or at least not prevalent, in the sixteenth century; nor did it become universal before the close of the seventeenth. So too it appears that the *gh* in *light*, *weigh*, *bough*, etc., was heard, though probably with only a feeble utterance, in the sixteenth century. As to the precise sound, there is an uncertainty; perhaps, as in Scotland now, it may have had both sounds of the German *ch*. It hardly survived the middle of the seventeenth century. In most words it simply dropped away without any further change; but a preceding short *i* became long, as in *light*, *night*, etc. In some cases, however, it was replaced by another spirant sound, an *f*, as in *laugh*, *cough*, *rough*, and in the vulgarisms *oft*, *thoft*, for *ought*, *thought*. In *sigh*, *height*, *drought*, it was replaced, at least in occasional use, by the spirant *th:* the pronunciations *sith*, *heith*, *drouth* are mentioned by orthoepists at the beginning of the last century; and *drouth* is still heard in our country, and has even been adopted in an American Dictionary of the English language.

The suppression of the *h*, like that of the weak *r*, would perhaps have become an accomplished fact if our language had been wholly dependent on the people of Southern England. On this subject our author remarks:—

"In England the use of the *h* (H) among the illiterate seems to depend upon emphatic utterance. Many persons when speaking quietly will never introduce the (H), but when rendered nervous or excited, or when desiring to speak particularly well, they abound in strong and unusual aspirations. It is also singular how difficult it is for those accustomed to omit the *h*, to recover it, and how provokingly they sacrifice themselves on the most undesired occasions by this social shibboleth. In endeavoring to pronounce the fatal letter, they generally give themselves great trouble, and consequently produce a harshness quite unknown to those who pronounce (H) naturally. An English author, S. Hirst, writing an English Grammar in German, in which fifty quarto pages are devoted to a minute account of the pronunciation of English, actually bestows one hundred and sixty-seven quarto lines of German, measuring about ninety feet, upon attempting to show that formerly *h* was not pronounced in English, and that it was altogether an orthoepistic fancy to pronounce it, saying that almost all non-linguists would admit that *h* was generally mute, or at most scarcely audible, and that linguists who denied this in theory gave into the practice. The division of the people is not exactly into linguists and non-linguists, but it must be owned that very large masses of the people, even of those tolerably educated and dressed in silk and broadcloth, agree with the French, Italians, Spaniards, and Greeks, in not pronouncing the letter H."

The sounds of *sh* in such words as *sure*, *pressure*, *mission*, *special*, *motion*, and *zh* in such as *measure*, *vision*, *excision*, are unrecognized by the orthoepists of the sixteenth century, and are not mentioned before the middle of the seventeenth. Yet traces of these changes are pointed out in Shakespeare and Rowley. Nor can it be doubted that, of the other changes ascribed to the seventeenth century, quite a number were already in progress during the sixteenth. Thus, if Hart had not written, there would have been no evidence that the pronunciation of *ai* as a simple vowel (ee) was known to the sixteenth century: all other orthoepists of that age make it a true diphthong; but Hart in 1569 gives it uniformly the sound of (ee). Mr. Ellis regards the fifteenth and seventeenth centuries as the grand periods of disturbance and revolution in the history of our language; he thinks, with much reason, that they owed this character to the political agitations, the great civil contests, by which they were shaken. The intermediate century, the sixteenth, he looks upon as a period of comparative stability and repose, both in politics and in pronunciation. Perhaps this is the true conception. Yet to our mind the facts reported in this book suggest rather the view that a great revolution in English pronunciation was going forward from the opening of the fifteenth to the close of the seventeenth century, and that it moved on with uninterrupted and almost unremitted progress from the beginning to the end of its course.

In the fourth chapter, which concludes this first part, Mr. Ellis deals with the pronunciation of English during the fourteenth century. Here he finds his principal means of investigation in the poetry, and especially in the rhymes, of Chaucer and Gower. He foresees that his procedure will be objected to, on the ground that imperfect rhymes, which often occur in modern verse, are likely to have been yet more common in that earlier and ruder age. But he denies the force of the objection, contending that the probabilities of the case point the other way. A rhyme which is good to the eye, but not to the ear, may be tolerated by reading men ; to men who do not read—and such to a great extent were the public of Chaucer and Gower—it is no rhyme at all. Appealing mainly to the ear, these poets were actually less likely than later rhymers to satisfy themselves with loose and inexact correspondences of sound. This *à priori* argument he fortifies with remarkable success by an examination of their verses, as represented by the best manuscripts. In Wright's edition of the Canterbury Tales, founded on the Harleian MS. No. 7334, and containing 17,368 lines, he finds less than fifty rhymes in which the spelling indicates a difference of pronunciation. Of these few exceptions most can be removed, either by the readings of other manuscripts, or by conjectural changes of a simple and natural character. The 33,000 verses of Gower's *Confessio Amantis* furnish only nine instances of faulty rhymes, and for these it is shown that the editor, not the author, is really responsible. The nature and force of the evidence derived from the rhymes of these poets is perhaps most strikingly seen in the case of the long *i* or *y*. These letters appear in a multitude of rhymes like the following: *wyse* and *justise*, *write* and *merite*, *vice* and *office*, *wyn* and *famyn*, *side* and *Cupide*, *lyke* and *retorike*, *while* and *Virgile*, *Bible* and *possible*, *fynde* and *Inde*, *I* and *enemy*, *therby* and *mercy*, *sky* and *truely*, *why* and *almighty*, *by* and *lady*, etc. Of the second words in these pairs, the last three, *truely*, *almighty*, and *lady*, come to us from the Anglo-Saxon. They still have in the last syllable the same vowel sound, or nearly the same, as in that language. It is not to be supposed that in the fourteenth century they should have taken up a sound like our diphthongal *i* long, only to lose it again by the sixteenth. Still less can we suppose this in reference to *justise*, *merite*, *office*, *famyn*, *Cupide*, *retorike*, *Virgile*, *possible*, *Inde*, *enemy*, *mercy*, which in Chaucer's time had just come in from the French, retaining still their native French accent, and could scarcely have undergone a change of vowel sound so sudden and extreme. But these violent suppositions are only to be avoided by admitting that the first words in the several rhyming pairs—*wyse*, *write*, *vice*, *wyn*, *side*, *lyke*, *while*, *Bible*, *fynde*, *sky*, *why*, *I*, *by*, and *therby*—still retained in the fourteenth century their primitive sound of *i* as (ii) or (*ii*). By similar evidence—less abundant, indeed, yet sufficiently decisive—it is shown that Chaucer's *ou* or *ow*, in *hous*, *how*, *dowte*, *aboute*, *powre*, *doun*, *broun*, *founde*, etc., had not yet acquired the diphthongal sound which it bore in the sixteenth century, but was generally pronounced as a simple (uu); only where the *ou* or *ow* corresponded to an Anglo-Saxon *ow*, *aw*, did it have a diphthongal pronunciation, as (oou). And in like manner it is proved that *a*, *e*, *o* had the same sounds as are generally given to those vowels in the languages of continental Europe.

But the most important, and at the same time the most difficult point in the language of Chaucer and Gower is the pronunciation of the final unaccented *e*. Mr. Ellis has greatly enriched his work by taking into it, in a condensed form, the masterly researches on this subject by Professor Child of Harvard University, which were published in the Memoirs of the American Academy, Vol. IX. Professor Child has proved that the unaccented final *e* was generally sounded in the poetry of Chaucer and Gower; but also that it was frequently silent. Of these exceptional cases, he is able to refer much the greater part to certain general principles or habits; but others seem to depend on the mere caprice of the author, and serve to indicate a varying usage and a progressive tendency to suppress the letter. The parallel furnished in German poetry by the frequent and capricious omission of the final *e* is noticed by Professor Child; though here the influences of education and literature will doubtless save the letter from total extinction, while the sensible habit of leaving it unwritten where it is unpronounced will save much time and toil to the philologists of the future.

Mr. Ellis proposes a uniform orthography for Chaucer, which he would wish to apply also to other writers of the fourteenth and fifteenth centuries. It is founded on the orthography of the Harleian MS., already referred to; the usual modes of spelling in that MS., the representations usually given by it to the different sounds of the language as it then was, are to be made universal, the occasional exceptions being altered into conformity with the general rule. It is the spelling

17

which the copyist of that MS. would presumably have used if he had been intent on a uniform orthography. A text of the fourteenth or fifteenth century, printed according to this system, could be read without difficulty, and by a little practice even fluently, with a pronunciation not widely different from that of its own time. It seems to us desirable that some such texts should be prepared and printed for school use. If a historical study of the English language and literature is to be made common in our educational institutions, it is important to lessen, in some degree at least, the difficulties arising from the endless and needless variations of Old-English spelling. It would be possible, and perhaps expedient, in such books, to give in the margin the actual spelling of one or two good manuscripts, in the most important cases where it differed from that used in the text. At the same time we think that, if Chaucer is really to be popularized, it can only be done by modernizing his orthography. The words which belong to the modern language must appear in the spelling with which all are familiar. But it is not less necessary that the text should be so given that it can be read rhythmically. An uncertain and halting rhythm, which fails to fulfil its own promises, and is continually leaving the reader in the lurch, is beyond measure disagreeable, and even painful, to a rhythmic ear; plain prose is infinitely better than such a rhythm. To cure this defect, the unaccented *e* must be supplied just as far as is requisite to give each verse a proper rhythmic succession of syllables and accents. We venture to add the opening lines of the Prologue to the Canterbury Tales, as a specimen of the arrangement which we have in mind. Where the accent of a word varies from that now usual, it is marked in the text by an acute over the vowel of the accented syllable. A double dot over an *e* which is now silent shows that it is to be pronounced, and to make a separate syllable, in reading. A small circle over an *e* which is now heard shows that it is to be suppressed, or at least that it does not count as a syllable in the verse. The double dot and the circle may also be used for like purposes over other vowels. Where an *e* which is not written even now has to be supplied in reading, it is represented by a reversed apostrophe, as [‘].

"When that Aprīl' with his shower's sweet
The drought of March hath piercëd to the root,
And bathëd every vein in such liquór,
Of which virtúe engendered is the flower ;—
When Zephĭrus eke with his sweet' breath
Inspirëd hath in every holt and heath
The tender crop's, and the young' sun
Hath in the Ram his half' course y-run,
And small' fowl's makë melody,
That sleep' all the night with opën eye,
So pricketh them natúre in their [a] coráges :—
Then long' folk to go on pilgrimages,
And palmers for to seek' strangë strands
To [b] fernë [c] halwës, [d] kouthe̊ in sundry lands ;
And specially, from every shirë's end
Of Eng'lánd, to Canterburẙ they wend,
The holy blissful martyr for to seek,
That them hath holpen when that they were sick."

[a] hearts. [b] distant. [c] saints. [d] known.

In such a text we should have a genuine Chaucer, the *ipsa verba*, if not the *ipsissima*, of the poet himself. But it would be free from the worst of those stumbling-blocks which now vex and baffle the ordinary reader. The general aspect of the words would be familiar to his eye; the sense would be almost or quite as easy to comprehend as that of Shakespeare; and the lines would yield without pains and puzzling a rhythm fairly satisfactory to the ear. In thus giving to Chaucer a modernized orthography, we should only be treating him as we do Shakespeare; no editor thinks of reproducing the spelling of the old folios. If Shakespeare were accessible only in that antiquated orthography, it is certain that the number of his readers and the extent of his influence would be seriously diminished.

Since the foregoing paragraphs were written, we have received "Part II." of the work under review. This, however, does not finish the book. "On account of the unexpected length" of the author's "investigations, the Societies for which they are published have found it most convenient to divide them into *four* parts, instead of *two*, as previously contemplated." This second part contains a little more than two hundred pages, of which about two thirds are occupied with the pronunciation of English prior to the fourteenth century, as well as that of the Anglo-Saxon, Old Icelandic, and Gothic; while the remainder treats of the correspondence of orthography with pronunciation from Anglo-Saxon times to the present day. A hasty glance has shown us that it is rich in curious and instructive matter; but we cannot yet undertake to criticise, or even to describe, its contents. We will speak of only one point which has chanced to attract our attention while turning over its pages. In representing, as he does by palæotype, the original pronunciation of various specimen-texts of early English, it seems to us that Mr. Ellis has hardly been as careful and exact as could have been desired in reference to vowel quantities. That he has been satisfied with treating this matter somewhat easily may be inferred from the fact that he occasionally varies from himself in the course of one or two pages. Thus *asė*, 'as,' in selections from Dan Michel, is given (aase) on page 412, but (ase) on page 413. In an extract from Richard de Hampole, on page 414, the adverb *here* is given both as (Heer) and (Her). In a paternoster, on page 442, we find in forms of the verb *do* both (don) and (miisdoon), where, too, one is surprised to see a long quantity in the prefix *mis;* compare also (doon) on the next page. In an ave and credo, on page 443, *lauird*, 'lord,' is represented by (laavird), but *lauerd*, a variation of the same word, by (laverd). On the same page, the adjective *ded*, 'dead,' appears both as (ded) and as (deed); and the imperative of the verb *forgive* appears as (forgiiv), but the indicative as (forgiveth). In this last case, if any distinction was to be made, we might have expected (forgiv) and (forgiiveth); authority for this could be produced from the Ormulum. In the proclamation of Henry III. (1258), the ending *-liche*, the modern *-ly*, appears as (-liitshe) on page 501, but as (-litshe) on page 503.

The English language has sometimes been spoken of as having wholly lost the distinctions of vowel quantity which belonged to the Anglo-Saxon; as if it stood related to the mother language in this respect as the French is related to the Latin, or the modern to the ancient Greek. It is true that, in comparing Anglo-Saxon with English, we find extensive changes of vowel quantity. Long vowels, where they follow the accented syllable, have been shortened almost uniformly. Thus the Anglo-Saxon *-lîce*, early English *-lîche* (-liitshe), has become *lў* in adjectives and adverbs of modern English. But in accented syllables, if we mistake not, a careful comparison will show that the vowel quantity of the Anglo-Saxon has been preserved in a majority of the words which have come to us from that source. And most of the changes, whether from long to short or from short to long, can be referred to a small number of euphonic principles or tendencies. The effect of a weak *r* (before a consonant or at the end of a word) to lengthen the vowel before it, as in *far*, *aware*, *horse*, etc., is one of the most important cases. The similar lengthening before *ld* and *nd*, as in *child*, *find*, etc., is as old as the thirteenth century, being the general rule in the Ormulum; and it is a fair question whether *child* and *wild* on page 483, and *hundes*, 'hounds,' on page 479, should not have been given with a long vowel. Still more numerous changes have been occasioned by the tendency to lengthen the short vowel of an accented penult when separated by only one consonant sound from the following unaccented vowel. The long sounds in *water*, *naked*, *evil*, *open*, etc., owe their origin to this tendency; and so do those in *name*, *make*, *law*, *eat*, *hope*, and a multitude of others, which originally ended in an unaccented syllable. Now this tendency also is found in the Ormulum, which carries it to a greater extent even than modern English: thus, *narrow*, *heavy*, *body*, *love*, *give*, *written*, *summer*, etc., are found in the Ormulum with a long vowel in the first of their two syllables. In such cases as these, the modern English agrees with the Anglo-Saxon in using a short vowel; a fact which shows that the long vowel could not have been universal in the thirteenth century, the time of the Ormulum. We think that Mr. Ellis, who writes a long vowel in some of these words—such as *give*, *written*, *summer*—in other works of that century, would have done better to give them short, as in Anglo-Saxon and modern English. Still less can we approve of his writing in

* See the next following article.

cases where it is at variance with the Anglo-Saxon, the Ormulum, and the modern English, together: as in (wen) for *wen* (page 412), A. S. *wên*, Orm. *wenenn*, 'to *ween*;' (leev) for *leve* (page 414), A. S. *lifian*, Orm. *libbenn*, 'to *live*;' (gret) for *grete* (page 479), A. S. *greát*, Orm. *græt*, 'great.' It is not unlikely, however, that some of these cases are mere errors of the press.

We hope that Mr. Ellis, in the parts yet to appear, may regard this matter of vowel quantity as worthy of a closer attention than he seems thus far to have given it; and may thus add to the completeness and exactness of his admirable work.

XV.

ON ENGLISH VOWEL QUANTITY IN THE THIRTEENTH CENTURY AND IN THE NINETEENTH.

1871.

IT is a well-known fact that the Modern Greek has lost the system of vowel quantity which belonged to the ancient language: *κόμη*, 'hair,' and *κώμη*, 'village,' are pronounced alike by the Modern Greek; nor is it otherwise with λῡ́σεις, 'thou wilt loose,' and λῠ́σις, 'a loosing.' In like manner, the Romanic languages have lost the system of vowel quantity which belonged to the ancient Latin. Thus the Italian and Spanish *mano, rosa*, French *main, rose*, are alike in vowel sound with Italian and Spanish *vano, prosa*, French *vain, prose*, though the former come from Latin *mănus, rŏsa*, and the latter from *vānus, prōsa*. It is an interesting question whether our own language has had in this respect the same experience as the Modern Greek and the Romanic tongues; whether we have wholly lost those distinctions of vowel quantity which undoubtedly belonged to the Anglo-Saxon.

It is sometimes said that we have no proper distinction of long and short quantity in English: all our vowels are alike in quantity; they are all equally susceptible of prolongation and abridgment; or rather, any vowel may be so prolonged as to exceed the ordinary quantity of any other: thus, *fill* may be so prolonged in utterance as to take more time than is ordinarily given to *feel* or *file*. But this must have been the case also with Greek and Latin vowels: their absolute time was not fixed, but variable. One speaker must have talked faster or slower than another; the same speaker must have talked faster or slower at one time than at another; even on the same occasion one sentence or clause must have been uttered faster or slower than another: and thus it could hardly fail to happen that a short vowel would sometimes have a longer sound than the ordinary or average quantity of a long vowel. But the average quantity of a short vowel was less than the average for a long one; or, with the same general rapidity of utterance, the quantity of long vowels exceeded the quantity of short. I say simply, the quantity of long vowels exceeded, was greater than, the quantity of short; not that the former was just double the latter. It may be presumed that in ordinary spoken utterance there was not any so exact relation; with the same *tempo*, the long might equal 1½ of the short, or 1⅝ of the short, or 1¾ of the short, as well as just 2; and probably the average actual ratio was rather less than 2 to 1; the average long would occupy rather less than twice the time of the average short. The fixing of 2 to 1 as the precise numerical relation was probably the work of rhythmopœia, or of rhythmopœia and melopœia together. When longs and shorts were combined in rhythmic composition, and especially when a musical accompaniment was added, the longs and shorts must have a definite and fixed ratio to each other; and the ratio of two to one was the most simple, obvious and convenient.

Now as regards our English syllables, it is certain that we have nearly or quite lost the feeling of length by position. By this I mean that we do not recognize a short vowel followed by two consonants as having any distinct relation to a long vowel followed by one consonant. We can perceive, of course, that there is more sound in *fist* than in *fit*, and more sound in *fight* than in *fit*; but we do not recognize any special relation of quantity between *fist* and *fight*. But in reference to vowel sounds, it should seem that our case is not essentially different from that of the ancient Greeks and Romans. There are certain sounds which, with the same *tempo*, the same general rapidity of utterance, we recognize as occupying more time than others; we thus recognize the former as long, the latter as short. It is true, the English short vowels differ somewhat in quality of sound—that is, in position of the speech organs—from the long vowels which most nearly resemble them, the short being a little more open than the corresponding long: there is a more open sound in *fill* than in *feel*, in *full* than in *fool*, in *fell* than in *fail*, etc.

But this does not affect the relation of quantity. It is clear that we have long vowel sounds in *file* and *foul*, in *feel* and *fool*, in *fail* and *foal*, and in *fall;* and that we have short vowel sounds in *fill* and *full*, in *fell*, in *doll*, in *dally*, in *dull*. Pronounce the two series in succession : on the one hand, *file, foul, feel, fool, fail, foal, fall;* on the other, *fill, full, fell, doll, dally, dull*—the difference of quantity is manifest and unmistakable.

If then we have long and short vowels clearly distinguished from each other, it becomes a matter of interest to inquire whether the distinction is recent or ancient; whether, and how far, the vowels now sounded long or sounded short were sounded long or short respectively in early periods of the language. The question here raised is not whether our vowels have kept the same sounds, but whether they have kept the same quantities. It matters not that long *a* has passed from its original sound (of *ah*) to that heard in *fame;* long *e*, from the sound in *prey* to that in *key;* long *i*, from the sound in *pique* to that in *pike;* long *o*, from the sound in *bone* to that in *boon;* long *u*, from the sound in *prude* to that in *proud*. These changes have taken place to a very great extent, but they do not affect the question now before us: the old long vowel remains long still. So if the short vowels ĭ, ŭ, ĕ (in *fill, full, fell*) have become a little more open; if, on the other hand, ă has generally become closer (as in *dally*), approaching the sound of ĕ (in *dell*); if the old ŏ has disappeared altogether, passing into a sound more open than that of *a* in *fall*, and often described as its corresponding short (thus *făll, folly*); if ŭ, and sometimes other short vowels, have sunk into the obscure and undistinguished sound heard in *dull, done*—these changes do not concern us here, as the old short vowel still remains short.

In the inquiry whether, and how far, we can trace back the present long and short quantities of English vowels, we find our best guide and help in a single (and singular) production of early English literature. I refer to the Ormulum, so called from the name of its author, the monk Orm, or Ormin, who wrote in the eastern part of England, some time in the thirteenth century, or fully six hundred years ago. A series of metrical homilies on the successive daily lessons of the church service, its interest is philological much more than literary. In the only manuscript from which it is known to us—not improbably the only manuscript of it that was ever written —we find on the part of the writer a careful and systematic regard to vowel quantity. He has a spelling of his own, to which he adheres with much consistency; and in this spelling the most peculiar and conspicuous feature is the doubling of every consonant which follows a short vowel. There was a tendency to this in the general English orthography even at that early period; what is remarkable in this author is that he consciously carried out this tendency as a uniform and universal rule. Thus he writes *it* with a double *t*, *if* with a double *f*, *hundred* with a double *n* and a double *d*, *lasteth* with a double *s* and a double sign for *th*. So much is he attached to this spelling, in spite of its strange and whimsical appearance, that in a preliminary address (seemingly very little needed) to the future copyist he insists upon a careful conformity to it:—

Annd tatt he loke wel tatt he
An bocstaff write twiȝȝess,
Eȝȝwhær thær itt uppo thiss boc
Iss wrĭtenn o thatt wise.
Loke he well thatt het write swa,
Forr he ne maȝȝ nohht elless
Onn Ennglissh writenn rihht te word
Thatt wite he wel to sothe.

Which may be modernized thus, in the same measure, all but the unaccented ending of the even lines:—

And that he look [full] well that he
A letter write twice [over],
Wherever it upon this book
Is written on that wise.
Look he well that he write it so
For he (ne) may not else
In English write aright the word,
That wit he well to sooth.

Thus then the spelling of the Ormulum enables us to say, in the case of every vowel followed by a consonant in the same word, whether the author pronounced it—or, at least, supposed that he pronounced it—long or short. In order now to arrive at some general conclusions as to the persistence of vowel quantity in English, I have looked through the vocabulary of the Ormulum, as presented with much fulness and clearness in the second volume of White's edition (Oxford, 1852), and have noted the words which survive in the English of to-day, including some few which, though lost out of the common language, are still generally known from their use in literary works of the modern period. I propose to state the general results of this comparison between the quantities of words as indicated in the Ormulum, and the quantities of the same words as heard in modern English. It should be said that the vocabulary of the Ormulum is not large. The work is nearly as long as the Odyssey; but the number of different words used in it is much smaller than in the Greek poem. There is a great sameness, a wearisome sameness, in the contents of the book: the leading facts, principles, and precepts of the Christian system are repeated over and over again with little variety of expression. Still there are words enough to give a fair idea of the relation between the vowel quantities of Saxon English six hundred years ago and those of Saxon English at the present time. I say "Saxon English," because few Latin words (aside from those already taken into the Anglo-Saxon), and fewer French words, are to be found in the Ormulum. Its language is as purely Teutonic as the modern German.

The most general statement suggested by the extended comparison of which I have been speaking is this: that in the great majority of cases the vowels which had a long sound six hundred years ago are long now; those which had a short sound then are short now. And if the exceptions are pretty numerous—if in a good many cases the long sound of the Ormulum corresponds to a modern short, or the short sound of the Ormulum to a modern long—most of these exceptional cases depend on a few obvious conditions, on clearly marked euphonic influences and tendencies, so that cases of capricious variation, of variation without apparent principle, are comparatively few. It will probably be most instructive, if we consider first (and indeed, chiefly) these euphonic conditions and tendencies which have led to differences of quantity between the language of six hundred years ago and that of to-day.

In the first place, then, let us look at the cases where the loss of a consonant sound has occasioned the lengthening of a short vowel before it: as in *alms*, O. *allmess*; *buy*, O. *biggenn*, and the like. Such changes can hardly be considered as violations of the old system of quantities. If there is here an alteration, an increase, of vowel quantity, it only takes the place of a consonant quantity withdrawn. It is simply that the time before occupied by a vowel and consonant is now occupied by the vowel prolonged. This is sometimes described as an absorption of the consonant by the vowel, sometimes as a vocalization of the consonant. Neither of these expressions gives a distinct idea of the nature of the change. Of course, in every instance of the kind there must have been a time of transition, when the consonant was beginning to be omitted, when the very speakers who omitted it were perfectly aware of its existence, and perhaps generally pronounced it, but occasionally let it drop, with a lengthening of the preceding vowel. Now this consciousness of a consonant with a claim to be pronounced is an important element in the phenomenon. The speaker who does not really pronounce it does not feel that he can omit it altogether; he does not feel that he is altogether omitting it. To his own feeling, he gives it a kind of recognition. He perhaps brings the organs of speech into some sort of approach toward the position required for pronouncing the consonant, so that the preceding vowel passes into a sound more or less modified, which does duty for the consonant. If this modification continues to be made, then the resulting long vowel-sound will not be a mere simple prolongation of the preceding short, but something different, perhaps a diphthong. Yet it may very well happen that, in this *quasi*-pronunciation of the consonant, the approach made by the organs to the position for that consonant will grow more and more slight, and the sound produced will differ less and less from a mere continuation of the preceding vowel; until finally—and perhaps very soon—it comes to be just that and nothing else, and the consonant is replaced, as its claim for utterance is felt to be satisfied, by a simple addition of quantity to the preceding vowel. But, whatever may be thought as to the *rationale* of the process, it is one of which we find numerous instances in comparing the Semi-Saxon of the Ormulum with modern English. Thus where *l*, followed by another consonant, has been suppressed in utterance, though still retained in writing, the short vowel before it has become long in—

O. *allmess* (*alms*), A. S. *älmesse*, Lat. *eleemosyna.*
callf (*calf*), A. S. *cealf.*
follc (*folk*, people), A. S. *folc.*
hallf (*half*, *behalf*), A. S. *healf.*
illc (*each*, every, Sc. *ilk*), A. S. *älc*, *elc*, *ylc.*
sallfe (*salve*, ointment), A. S. *sealf.*
sallme (*psalm*), A. S. *sealm*, Lat. *psalmus.*

In *should* (O. *shollde*), *would* (O. *wollde* and *wolde*), we have a short vowel sound; but we may see from the *ou* that the vowel was first lengthened (*shou'd*, *wou'd*, with *ou* as in *youth*); though afterward it became short again, by a new and independent change, similar to that by which *good* and *stood* have received their present short pronunciation. The same change has occurred also in *could*, which never had an *l* actually sounded. The Ormulum, like the Anglo-Saxon, has *cûthe*, in which the *th* became *d*, and the vowel was afterward shortened. As people were accustomed to write a silent *l* in *should*, *would*, and regarded *could* as a word of similar character, they put a silent *l* into that also. There would have been more propriety in the insertion of a silent *n*; for this letter belongs to the root as seen in *can*. It is a feature of the Anglo-Saxon in its earliest known form that it drops *n* before *th* or *s*, and lengthens the preceding vowel: as *gôs* (*goose*) for *gans*, *sôdh* (*sooth*) for *santh* (which means 'being, existing,' and is identical with Lat. *-sens*, in *praesens*, *-sentis*); and so *cûdhe* for *cunthe* (*could*).

Again, where *g* has been suppressed in utterance, the short vowel before it has become long in—

O. *biggenn* (to *buy*), *abiggenn* (to *aby*, pay for), A. S. *bycgan*, *âbycgan.*
leggenn (to *lay*), A. S. *lecgan.*
seggenn (to *say*), A. S. *secgan.*

But in most cases of this kind the *g* appears in the Ormulum softened into the consonant *y*-sound (ȝ), which after the short vowel is written double (ȝȝ): thus—

O. *daȝȝ* (*day*), pl. *daȝhess*, *daȝȝess*, A. S. *däg*, pl. *dagas*.
driȝȝe (*dry*), A. S. *dryge*.
eȝȝlenn (to *ail*), A. S. *eglan*.
eȝȝtherr (*either*), A. S. *ægdher*.
faȝȝerr (*fair*), A. S. *fäger*.
fleȝȝl (*flail*), Germ. *flegel*, Lat. *flagellum*.
geȝȝnenn (to *gain*), *gaȝhenn* (*gain*), O. N. *gagn* (advantage).
geȝȝnlike (aptly, cf. *ungainly*), O. N. *gegn* (apt, clever), A. S. *ungägne* (of no effect).
laȝȝ (*lay*), from *lin* (to *lie*), A. S. *läg*, from *licgan*.
leȝȝ (impv. *lay*), *leȝȝde* (*laid*), from *leggenn*, A. S. *lege*, *lägde*, from *lecgan*.
maȝȝ (he *may*), A. S. *mäg*.
maȝȝ (*may*, maid), A. S. *mæg* (femina, virgo).
maȝȝdenn (*maiden*), A. S. *mägden*.
naȝȝlenn (to *nail*), A. S. *näglian*.
reȝȝn (*rain*), A. S. *regn*.
seȝȝ (impv. *say*), *seȝȝth* (*saith*), *seȝȝde* (*said*), from *seggenn*, A. S. *sege*, *segdh*, *sägde*, from *secgan*.
inn-seȝȝless (*seals*), A. S. *sigel*, *insegel*.
tweȝȝenn (*twain*), A. S. *twegen*.
twiȝȝess (*twice*), also *twiȝess*, A. S. *twiga* (ī ?).
thriȝȝess (*thrice*), also *thriȝess*, A. S. *thriga* (ī ?).
waȝȝn (*waggon*, *wain*), A. S. *wägn*, *wæn*.
weȝȝe (*way*), *aweȝȝ*, *aweȝȝe* (*away*), A. S. *weg*, *âweg*.

In *eȝȝtherr*, *maȝȝ* (maid), and perhaps in *twiȝȝess* and *thriȝȝess*, a long vowel of the Anglo-Saxon is found shortened (in the last two, however, not uniformly) in the Ormulum. This shortening may perhaps be explained as the consequence of an effort to make the feeble ȝ more fully audible. The vowel may have been passed over lightly in order that a greater force of utterance might be brought to bear on the weak consonant following it, so as to give this a distinct enunciation. It would be perfectly natural, too, that the speakers of the language should become at length weary of this effort required for the weak consonant; and that they should then allow the consonant to be replaced by a mere continuance of the preceding vowel, which would thus recover its primitive long quantity.

In the word *master* (O. *maȝȝstre*, A. S. *mägestre*, *mägstre*, Lat. *magister*) we do not lengthen the vowel: here the Scottish *maister* shows the truer (that is, the more analogical) pronunciation. In *saith* and *said*, the lengthened vowel sound which once belonged to them is still indicated by the *ai* with which they are written.

The ȝȝ of the Ormulum is not always to be traced to an original *g*. In some instances it seems to have arisen from the diphthong *ei* in the Old Norse, the language of the so-called Danes who came as invaders and settlers into eastern England: the vocabulary of the Ormulum shows evident marks of a Norse influence. Thus the plural pronouns *theȝȝ* (*they*), *theȝȝre* (*their*), *theȝȝm* (them) are not to be explained from A. S. *thâ*, *thâra*, *thâm*, but from O. N. *their*, *theirra*, *theim*; *reȝȝsenn* (to *raise*), not from A. S. *râsian*, but from O. N. *reisa*; *heȝȝlenn* (to *hail*, salute), not from A. S. *hâl*, but from the corresponding O. N. *heill* (sanus, salvus), which, like E. *hail*, was often used in salutations. So *aȝȝ* (*aye*, always, ever) is perhaps to be explained from O. N. *æi*, *ei*, *ey*, which correspond to A. S. *âwa*; while *naȝȝ* (*nay*) may be a mere compound of *ne* and *aȝȝ*. The genitive *Keȝȝseress*, usually *Kaseress*, from *Kasere* (*Cæsar*, Emperor), might be accounted for in the same way; but for the ȝȝ in *beȝȝsannz* (*bezants*, coined in *Byzantium*), and in the proper name *Eȝȝnoc* (*Enoch*), we have no explanation to offer.

Yet again, where a consonant *h* has been suppressed in utterance, the short vowel before it has become long in many words. I say "a consonant *h*," for the Anglo-Saxon *h*, where it stands at the end of a syllable or is followed by *t* or *th* (*dh*), must be regarded as a true consonant. Thus in—

O. *bohhte* (*bought*), *from biggenn* (to *buy*), A. S. *bohte*, from *bycgan*.
brihht (*bright*), A. S. *beorht*, *byrht*, *bryht*.
brohhte (*brought*), from *bringenn* (to *bring*), A. S. *brohte*, from *bringan*.
cnihhtess (servants, soldiers, cf. *knight*), A. S. *cniht*.
dohhterr (*daughter*), A. S. *dôhtor*.
drohh (*drew*), also *droh*, from *draȝhenn* (to *draw*), A. S. *drôg*, from *dragan*.
druhhthe (*drought*), A. S. *drugadh*.
duhhtiȝ (virtuous, cf. *doughty*), A. S. *dyhtig*.

O. *ehhte* (*eight*), *ehhtennde* (*eighth*), A. S. *eahta*, *eahtodha*, O. N. *áttundi*.
fehh, *fe* (revenue, money, cf. *fee*), A. S. *feoh*, *feó*.
fihhtenn (to *fight*), A. S. *feohtan*.
flihht (*flight*), A. S. *flyht*.
bi-kahht (*caught*), also *bikæchedd* (*catched*) ; of doubtful origin.
lihht (*light*, levis), A. S. *leóht* (*líht*).
lihht (*light*, lux), A. S. *leóht* (*lýht*).
mahht, *mihht* (*might*), *mihhte* (he *might*), A. S. *meaht*, *miht*, *mihte*.
nahht, *nihht* (*night*), A. S. *neaht*, *niht*.
nohht (*nought*, *not*), A. S. *nâht*, *náwiht*, from *ne* and *áwiht*.
ohht (*aught*), A. S. *âht*, contracted from *âwiht*.
plihht (danger, state, cf. *plight*), A. S. *pliht*.
rihht (*right*), A. S. *riht*.
sahh (*saw*), from *seon*, *sen* (to *see*), A. S. *seah*, from *seón* ; but see p. 293.
sihhthe (*sight*, appearance), *innsihht* (*insight*, knowledge), A. S. *gesihdh*.
sohhte (*sought*), from *sekenn* (to *seek*), A. S. *sôhte*, from *sécan*.
tahhte (*taught*), from *tæchenn* (to *teach*), A. S. *tæhte*, from *tæcan*.
thohh (*though*), A. S. *theáh*.
thohhte (he *thought*), from *thennkenn* (to *think*), A. S. *thohte*, from *thencan*.
thuhhte (seemed, cf. *methought*), from *thinnkenn* (to seem), A. S. *thuhte*, from *thyncan*.
wehhte (*weight*), A. S. *wiht*, *gewiht*, from *wegan* (to *weigh*).
wihht (being, person, cf. *wight*), A. S. *wiht*.
wrihhte (maker, worker, cf. *wright*), A. S. *wyrhta*.
wrohhte (*wrought*), from *wirrkenn* (to *work*), A. S. *worhte*, *wrohte*, from *wyrcan*.

In some of these words (*dohhterr*, *drohh*, *lihht*, *lihht*, *nohht*, *ohht*, *sohhte*, *tahhte*, *thohh*) we find a shortening of the Anglo-Saxon long vowel, similar to that just noticed in *eȝȝtherr*, maȝȝ, etc., and explainable in the manner then proposed ; though the combination of consonants (*ht*), which in most of them follows the vowel, may have had something to do with its change of quantity.

Lastly, in a number of words which in the Ormulum have the consonant *w* repeated, showing that the vowel before it was then sounded short, this consonant is lost in English (or, at least, has no consonant power), and the vowel sound is long. Such are—

O. *chewwenn* (to *chew*), A. S. *ceówan*.
clawwess (hoofs, cf. *claw*), A. S. *clâ*, *clawu*, pl. *clawe*.

O. *cnewwe* (*knee*), pl. *cnewwess*, *cnes*, A. S. *cneow*, *cneó*.
dæwwenn (to *bedew*), from *dæw* (*dew*), A. S. *deáwian*, from *deáw*.
fowwerr, *fowwre* (*four*), *fowwerrtiȝ* (*forty*), A. S. *feówer*, *feówertig*.
strawwenn (to *strow*, *straw*), A. S. *streówian*, *streáwian*.
throwwinnge (*thrœ*, suffering), A. S. *thrówuing*.
trewwess (*trees*), also *treos*, *tres*, sing. *treo*, A. S. *treow*, *treó*.
trowwe (*true*), *trowwenn* (to *trow*), *trowwthe* (*truth*), A. S. *treówe*, *treówian*, *treówdh*.

In most of these words we see an Anglo-Saxon long vowel shortened before the weak *w*, as we have already seen it before *h* and ȝ. In *nowwharr* (*nowhere*), the shortening—which may be compared to that of *no* in English *nothing*—really takes place before *h*, the true order of the sounds being that represented in the Anglo-Saxon orthography, *nâhwær*. The words *owwtherr*, *nowwtherr* (A. S. *âwdher*, *nâwdher*), have the sense of *either*, *neither;* but these last connect themselves with A. S. *ægdher*. The form *nowwt* (cattle, Sc. *nowt*) is to be explained from O. N. *naut*, while English *neat* corresponds to A. S. *neát*. In these words, where the *ww* precedes a consonant, its sound can hardly have differed very much from that of the vowel *u*. Indeed the Latin *au* is represented by *aww* in *clawwstremann* (*cloister-man*, monk) from Lat. *claustrum*, and in the proper name *Sannt Awwstin* (*Saint Austin*, *Augustine*), though the Emperor (*Kaserr-king*) Augustus appears as *Augusstuss*.

We have now reviewed all the cases where a consonant, which in the time of the Ormulum was heard after a short vowel, is lost in modern English; and we have seen that in all but a very few (*should*, *would*, *saith*, *said*, *master*, *them*, *not*), the preceding vowel is long in our present pronunciation: even for these few, there is evidence that the most have been pronounced with long vowel sound, though that in more recent times has become short.

The next important point we have to consider is the effect of a weak *r* on the preceding short vowel. By weak *r* I mean to designate that peculiar sound of the letter which it has assumed in our present English, wherever it stands before a consonant or at the end of a word—as in *far*, *farm*, *for*, *form*, *fur*, *firm*. This is evidently weaker than the sound of *r* in *farrow*, *forest*, *borough*, *merit*, *spirit*, etc. According to Mr. Ellis, Ben Jonson, in his English Grammar of 1640, is the earliest writer who gives any sign of having recognized this distinction between a stronger and a weaker *r* in the pronunciation of our language. Perhaps the phenomenon itself, the weakening of *r* where it is final or followed by a consonant, may not be much older than that time. In the dialectic pronunciation of the Irish, which has in many points preserved the older English sounds, it has not yet established itself. This weak *r* is most easily produced after the neutral vowel, so called, which is heard as short in *cub*, *cud*, and as long in *curb*, *curd*. Except after the sounds of *ah* and *au* (as in *far*, *for*), this *u* sound is always heard before a weak *r*: thus it comes in, as a brief yet perceptible element, after the proper vowel in *fire*, *flour*, *fear*, *four*, *fare*. When the preceding vowel was a short *i* or *e*, this has been overpowered by and merged in the following *u* sound. Thus *fir* and *her* are not distinguished in pronunciation from *fur* and *Hur*. The short *u* itself becomes long when this consonant follows it: as we see in comparing *burgh* with *burrow*, where the first has a long sound before weak *r*, the second a short one before common *r*. The point with which we are now concerned is this, that the weak *r*, whether heard at the end of a word or before another consonant, is always preceded by a long vowel sound; if the preceding vowel sound was originally short, it has become long.

It is altogether improbable that in the time of the Ormulum *r* in this position had begun to assume its present weak sound; but it had begun to affect the quantity of a preceding vowel. We find quite a number of words in which a short vowel of the Anglo-Saxon, standing before *r* in this position, had become long in the Ormulum, as in recent English:—

O. *ærd* (place, region, Sc. *airt*), A. S. *eard*.
ærn (*earn*, eagle), A. S. *earn*.
bærn (children, Sc. *bairns*), also *barrness*, A. S. *bearn*.
bærnenn (to *burn*), A. S. *beornan*.
birde (lineage, cf. *birth*), A. S. *gebyrd* (*birth*, lineage).
bord (*board*, table), A. S. *bord*.
cherl (young man, cf. *churl*), A. S. *ceorl*.

O. *corn* (*corn*), A. S. *corn.*
eorless (*earls*), A. S. *eorl.*
eorthe, *erthe* (*earth*), A. S. *eordhe.*
forth (*forth*), also *forrth*, A. S. *fordh.*
kirrke-gærd (*church-yard*), A. S. *geard.*
hird (company, family, cf. *herd*), A. S. *heord.*
hirde (*herd*, shepherd), A. S. *hirde.*
hord (*hoard*), A. S. *hord.*
leornenn, *lernenn* (to *learn*), but *lerrnde* (*learned*), A. S. *leornian.*
skarn (*scorn*), O. Fr. *escorne.*
stirne (*stern*, fierce), A. S. *styrne.*
swerd (*sword*), A. S. *sweord.*
word (*word*), A. S. *word.*
ȝeornenn, *ȝernenn* (to *yearn*), but *ȝerrnde* (*yearned*), A. S. *geornian*, from *georn* (desirous, O. *ȝeorne*, *ȝerne*).

It is not unlikely that some of these words, though lengthened in the Ormulum, may have retained their primitive short quantity in the prevailing English, until by the weakening of the *r* at a much later time they became long. It is certain that in most cases where an original short vowel has been lengthened before *r*, the change is not so old as the Ormulum. Thus in almost every instance where we have the sound of *ah* or *au* before a weak *r*, the word, if found in the Ormulum, shows a short vowel. Here belong—

O. *arrt* (*art*), *arrn* (they *are*), A. S. *eart*, O. N. *eru* (sunt).
arrctoss (north, cf. *arctic*), Gr. and Lat. *arctos* (bear, north).
arrke (*ark*), A. S. *earc*, Lat. *arca.*
arrmess (*arms*, brachia), A. S. *earm.*
barrliȝ (*barley*), A. S. *bere* (Sc. *bear*).
berrme (*barm*, leaven), A. S. *beorma.*
berrne (*barn*), A. S. *bere-ärn*, *berern*, *bern.*
feorr, *ferr* (*far*), A. S. *feor.*
forr (*for*, prep. and conj.), A. S. *for.*
forrme (*former*), A. S. *forma.*
harrd (*hard*), A. S. *heard.*
heorrte, *herrte* (*heart*), A. S. *heorte.*
herrberrȝhe (lodging, cf. *harbor*), A. S. *hereberga.*
herrcnenn (to *hearken*), A. S. *hyrcnian.*
herrfessttid (*harvest*-time), A. S. *härfest.*
horrs (*horse*), A. S. *hors.*
karrte (*cart*, chariot), A. S. *cräť.*
marrch (month of *March*), Lat. and A. S. *Martius.*
marrtirrdom (*martyrdom*), A. S. *martyrdôm*, Lat. *martyr.*
merrke (*mark*), A. S. *mearc.*

O. *norrth* (*north*), A. S. *nordh*.
orr (*or*), from *oththr*, *otherr*, A. S. *ódher*.
patriarrke (*patriarch*), Lat. *patriarcha*.
scorrcnedd (*scorched*), O. Fr. *escorcher* (to excoriate).
sharrp (*sharp*), A. S. *scearp*.
shorrt (*short*), A. S. *sceort*.
sperrd (closed, barred, cf. *spar*), *unnsperrenn* (to unclose), A. S. *sparrian*.
starrc (firm, cf. *stark*), A. S. *stearc*.
steorrne, *sterrne* (*star*), A. S. *steorra*, O. N. *stiarna*.
thorrness (*thorns*), A. S. *thorn*.
thweorrt, *thwerrt* (with *ut*; throughout, cf. *thwart*), A. S. *thweorh*.
warrm (*warm*), A. S. *wearm*.
werre (worse, Sc. *waur*), A. S. *weor* (evil).
werrpenn (to cast, cf. to *warp*), A. S. *weorpan*.
wharrfenn (to turn, cf. *wharf*), A. S. *hweorfan*.
ȝerrde (rod, cf. *yard*), A. S. *geard* (virga).

Somewhat less numerous are the cases in which the short vowel of the Ormulum corresponds to any other vowel sound than those of *ah* and *au* (*far* and *for*) in modern English :—

O. *barrness* (children, Sc. *bairns*), also *bærn*, A. S. *bearn*.
to-bresstenn (to *burst*, Sc. *brust*), A. S. *berstan*.
currsenn (to *curse*), A. S. *cursian*.
darr (*dare*), *durrste* (*durst*), A. S. *dear*, *dorste*.
ferrs (*verse*), A. S. *fers*, Lat. *versus*.
firrst (*first*), A. S. *fyrst*.
firrthrenn (to assist, cf. to *further*), A. S. *fyrdherian*.
forrtherr (*further*), A. S. *furdhor*.
girrdell (*girdle*), A. S. *gyrdel*.
hirrtenn (to *hurt*), Dutch and M. H. Germ. *hurten* (to dash against).
irre (*ire*), A. S. *yrre*.
kirrke (*church*), A. S. *cyrice*, Gr. κυριακή.
kirrtell (*kirtle*), A. S. *cyrtel*.
mirrthrenn (to *murder*), A. S. *myrdhrian*.
myrrha, *myrra*, *myrre* (*myrrh*), Lat. *myrrha*.
serrfenn (to *serve*), O. Fr. *servir*, Lat. *servire*.
skerrenn (to *scare*), O. N. *skirra* (to drive away).
thirrst (*thirst*), A. S. *thurst*.
thridde (*third*), *thrittiȝ* (*thirty*), A. S. *thridda*, *thrittig* or *thrîtig*.
turrnenn (to *turn*), A. S. *tyrnan*.
turrtle (*turtle*-dove), A. S. *turtle*, Lat. *turtur*.
warr (*aware*), A. S. *wär*.
weorrc, *werrc* (*work*), *wirrkenn* (to *work*), A. S. *weorc*, *wyrcan*.
werrse (*worse*), *werrst* (*worst*), *wirrsenn* (*worsening*), A. S. *wyrsa*, *wyrst*, *wyrsian*.
wurrm (*worm*), A. S. *wyrm*, *weorm*.

O. *wurrth* (*worth*, adj.), *wurrthshipe*, *wurrshipe* (*worship*), A. S. *weordh*, *weordhscipe*.
wurrthenn (to become, be, cf. woe *worth* the day), A. S. *weordhan*.

But *r* is not the only consonant which has had this effect of lengthening the vowel before it. We find it produced also by *l*, a liquid and a lingual like the *r*. Before *l* at the end of a word or followed by another consonant, a vowel originally short has often become long. Cases of this kind, in which the Ormulum still retains the short vowel, are the following:—

O. *all* (*all*), *allswa*, *allse* (*also*), *allmasst* (*almost*), A. S. *eal*, *ealswâ*, *ealmæst*.
allderrmann (chief, ruler, cf. *alderman*), A. S. *ealdorman*.
allterr (*altar*), Lat. *altare*.
bulltedd (*bræd*, bread from *bolted* flour), O. Fr. *bulter*, *bluter*, M. H. Germ. *biuteln*.
fallenn (to *fall*, *fallen*), A. S. *feallan*, *feallen*.
fallse (*false*), A. S. *fals*, Lat. *falsus*.
galle (*gall*), A. S. *gealla*.
hallp (*holp*), *hollpenn* (*holpen*), from *hellpenn*, A. S. *healp*, *holpen*, from *helpan*.
hallte (*halt*, lame), A. S. *healt*.
pall (cloth, cf. *pall*), A. S. *päll*, *pell*, Lat. *pallium*.
sallt (*salt*), A. S. *sealt*.
shulldre (*shoulders*), A. S. *sculdre*, pl. of *sculdor*.
stall (*stall*), A. S. *steal*.
walless (*walls*), *grunndwall* (*ground-wall*, foundation), A. S. *weal*.

This lengthening of a vowel before *l* had already commenced in the time of the Ormulum; and indeed, in most of the instances found in the Ormulum, where a vowel originally short is followed by the combination *ld*, the vowel appears as long in the Ormulum itself. Thus in—

O. *ald* (*old*), but *elldre* (*elder*, *older*) and *allderrmann*, A. S. *eald*, *yldre*.
bald (*bold*), *beoldenn*, *beldenn* (to *embolden*), A. S. *beald*, *bealdian*, *byldan*.
child (*child*), but *chilldre* (*children*), A. S. *cild*, *cildru*.
faldess (sheep-*folds*), A. S. *gefeald*.
feld (*field*), A. S. *feld*.
gold (*gold*), *gildene* (*golden*), A. S. *gold*, *gylden*.
haldenn (to *hold*, *holden*), A. S. *healdan*, *healden*.
kald (*cold*), A. S. *ceald*.
milde (*mild*), but *millce* (*mildness*, mercy), A. S. *milde*, *milds* or *milts*.

O. *saldenn* (they *sold*), from *sellenn* (to *sell*), A. S. *sealdon*, from *sellan*.
shildenn (to *shield*), A. S. *scildan*.
talde (he *told*), from *tellenn* (to *tell*), A. S. *tealde*, from *tellan*.
weldenn (to govern, cf. to *wield*), A. S. *wealdan*.
wilde (*wild*), A. S. *wild*.
ȝeldenn (to *yield*), A. S. *gieldan*, *gyldan*.

Indeed, the Ormulum sometimes lengthens a short vowel before *l*, where the modern English has it short. Thus in *wel*, also *welle* (*well*, A. S. *well* and *wella*, fons); and in *wel*, also *well* (*well*, A. S. *wel*, bene). The variation of quantity, which the Ormulum shows in the last of these words, is seen, continued to the present day, in Scottish *weel*, compared with English *well*. Further, before *ld* a short vowel is lengthened in the following:—

O. *cwaldenn* (they *quelled*, *killed*), from *cwellenn*, A. S. *cwealdon*, from *cwellan*.
dwalde (he *dwelt*), from *dwellenn*, A. S. *dwealde*, from *dwellan* (to hinder, delay).
elde (old age, cf. *eld*), A. S. *yldoäld*, *eld*.
oferrgildedd (*gilded over*), A. S. *ofergylded*.
seldenn (*seldom*), A. S. *seldan*.

In *scaldess* (minstrels, *scalds*, from O. N. *skâld-r*, poet), and *heold*, *held* (he *held*, A. S. *heóld*), the Ormulum preserves an original long sound, which has become short in English. But the first of these is variously pronounced, as *scăld*s and as *scaulds*.

Before the liquid *m* followed by the mute *b*, as before the similar combination *ld*, a short vowel is sometimes lengthened in the Ormulum. Thus in five words, three of which have a long vowel in English, while two preserve the earlier short:—

O. *camb* (*comb*), A. S. *camb*.
climbenn (to *climb*), A. S. *climban*.
wambe (*womb*, belly), A. S. *wamb*, *womb*.
dumb (*dumb*), A. S. *dumb*.
lamb (*lamb*), but pl. *lammbre*, A. S. *lamb*, pl. *lambru*.

In like manner, before the liquid *n* followed by the mute *d*, a short vowel has become long in very many words. In *bihinndenn* (*behind*, A. S. *behindan*), and *hinnderrling* (degenerate, retrograde in character, A. S. *hinderling*), connected with E. *hĭnder*, the Ormulum still retains the short sound; as it does before *nt* in *funnt* (*font*, A. S. *font*, cf. E. *fount*), *munnt* (*mount*, A. S. *munt*), *sannt* (*saint*, A. S. *sanct*), where the vowel has become long in English. But the instances are far more numerous in which a vowel before *nd* is already lengthened in the Ormulum. Thus in—

O. *bindenn* (to *bind*), *bundenn* (*bound*), A. S. *bindan*, *bunden*.
blind (*blind*), *blendenn* (to *blind*), A. S. *blind*, *blendan*.
findenn (to *find*), *fundenn* (*found*), A. S. *findan*, *funden*.
grindenn (to *grind*), A. S. *grindan*.
grund (*ground*), but *grunndwall* (foundation), A. S. *grund*, *grund-weal*.
hund (*hound*), A. S. *hund*.
kinde (nature, *kind*, *kindred*), A. S. *gecynd*.
minde (*mind*, memory), but *minndiȝnesse* (*memory*), A. S. *gemynd*.
sund (*sound*, integer), A. S. *sund*.
-*windenn* (to *wind*), in *attwindenn* (to escape), *wundenn* (*wound*), but *winndeclut* and *windeclut* (*winding-clout*, swaddling-cloth); A. S. *windan*, *wunden*.
wunde (*wound*, vulnus), A. S. *wund*.

In the preterit singular, the Ormulum has *band*, *fand*, *wand*, like the Anglo-Saxon, but with short *a* lengthened; these forms, however, are not represented in English, where the vowel of *bound*, *found*, *wound*, comes from the plural forms, *bundenn*, *fundenn*, etc., A. S. *bundon*, *fundon*, etc. The change of vowel quantity before *nd* (as before *ld* and *mb*) is carried further in the Ormulum than in the modern English, being extended to a number of words in which it failed to establish itself, so that the original short vowel is heard in their present pronunciation. Thus in—

O. *band* (*band*), A. S. *bend*.
ende (*end*, vulgar *eend*), A. S. *ende*.
hand (*hand*), oftener *hannd*, but with added -*e* always *hande*, A. S. *hand*.
land (*land*), A. S. *land*.
sand (*sand*), A. S. *sand*.
sendenn (to *send*), but *sennde* (he *sent*), A. S. *sendan*, *sende*.
shendenn (to *shend*, disgrace), A. S. *scendan*.
strande (*strand*, bank), A. S. *strand*.
sunderr-run (private communing, cf. *sunder*, *asunder*), A. S. *sundor*.
wand (rod, *wand*), O. N. *vand-r*, *vönd-r*, Goth. *vandus*.
wendenn (to *wend*, turn, go), but *wennde* (he turned, *went*), A. S. *wendan*, *wende*.

The word *freond, frend* (*friend*, A. S. *freónd*) does not belong to this series; it came with long vowel quantity from the Anglo-Saxon into the Ormulum, and passed thus into the older English, as we see from the spelling with *ie*, which it has in common with the opposite, but strictly analogous, *fiend* (O. *fend*, A. S. *feónd*).

It is a very curious fact that a lengthening of the vowel before *ng*, similar to that before *nd*, is frequent in the Ormulum, although unknown to modern English, in which the vowel before *ng* is always short.* Examples are—

O. *gang* (journey, cf. *gangway*), but *ganngenn* (to go), A. S. *gang, gangan*.
genge (company, cf. *gang*), A. S. *genge*.
king (*king*), A. S. *cyning, cyng*.
lang (*long*), *bilenge* (*belonging* to), A. S. *lang, gelenge:* but *lannge* (*long*, diu), *lenngre* (*longer*), A. S. *lange, lengra, leng*.
langenn (to *long* after), *forrlangedd* (desirous), A. S. *langian*.
mang, amang and *amanng* (*among*), A. S. *ámang, gemang*.
ringenn (to *ring*), A. S. *hringan*.
singenn (to *sing*), *sungenn* (they *sung*), *sang* (*song*), A. S. *singan, sungon, sang*.
springenn (to *spring*), *sprang* (*sprang*), *sprungenn* (*sprung*), *offspring* (*offspring*), A. S. *springan, sprang, sprungen, ofspring*.
stingenn (to *sting*), *stungenn* (*stung*), A. S. *stingan, stungen*.
strang (*strong*), *strengenn* (to *strengthen*), but *strenncthe* (*strength*), A. S. *strang, gestrangian, strengdhu*.
swingenn (to scourge, cf. to *swing, swinge*), A. S. *swingan*.
thing (*thing*), A. S. *thing*.
bithrungenn (oppressed, cf. *throng*, *i. e.* press of people), A. S. *bithrungen*, from *thringan, gethrang;* but O. *threnngdenn* (they *thronged*), A. S. *threngdon*, from *threngan*.
thwang (*thong*), A. S. *thwang*.
tunge (*tongue*), A. S. *tunge*.
wengess (*wings*), O. N. *veng-r*.
wrang (*wrong*), A. S. *wrang*.
ȝung (*young*), rarely *ȝunng*, comp. *ȝunngre* (*younger*), A. S. *geong, gyngra*.

---

* The Norse grammarians recognize in that language a similar lengthening of primitive short vowels (*a, o, u, i*), when followed by *ng* (or *nk;* also of *a, o, u*, when followed by *lf, lg, lk, lm, lp, ls*): thus *lâng-r* (*long*), *sprînga* (to *spring*), *tûnga* (*tongue*), *væng-r* or *veng-r* (*wing*). It seems, however, to be questionable, whether, or how far, this change belonged to the old language. See Heyne, *Kurze Gramm. der altgerm. Dialecte*, 2d ed., p. 82.

In *heng* (hung, A. S. *hêng*; but *henngde* [*hanged*], A. S. *hangode*), the vowel was already long in Anglo-Saxon. Whether this extension to *ng* of the euphonic analogy which obtains for *nd* ever gained much currency in the language, may well be doubted. It seems certain that it cannot have prevailed at the time (probably in the fifteenth century) when the old long sounds of *i* and *u* (as in *pique*, *prude*) began to pass into the diphthongal sounds heard in *pike* and *proud*; for in that case, instead of saying *kĭng*, *thĭng*, *tŏngue*, *sŭng*, as we now do, we should probably be saying *kīng*, *thīng*, *toung*, *soung*, with the same vowel utterance as in *kīnd*, *sound*. It may be observed, however, that in the most recent English there is a noticeable tendency to lengthen somewhat the short sound of *o* before *ng*, so that *long*, *song* are apt to be pronounced with much the same vowel sound as *or*, *nor*, *for*.

If now we have found in combinations such as *ld*, *mb*, *nd*, *ng*, where the first letter is a liquid and the second its cognate sonant mute, a certain tendency to protract the quantity of a preceding short vowel, it must be remarked that the ordinary tendency of a combination of consonants is in the opposite direction—not to the lengthening of a preceding short, but to the shortening of a preceding long. The speaker slights the vowel in order to concentrate his energy of utterance on the following consonants, which thus massed together present some difficulty of enunciation. It is as in the Greek πενέστερος (poorer), for πενηστερος, *i.e.* πενητ-τερος, from πένης, πένετ-ος. Of this change—a long vowel shortened on account of two or more consonants following it—numerous examples are found in the language of the Ormulum, when compared with the Anglo-Saxon. Thus—

O. *asskenn* (to *ask*), A. S. *âscian*.
blosstme (*blossom*), A. S. *blôstma*.
chappmenn (*chapmen*, merchants), A. S. *ceápmen*; cf. O. *chepinng-bothe* (market-booth).
clennlike (*cleanly*), *clennsenn* (to *cleanse*), from *clene* (*clean*), A. S. *clænlice*, *clænsian*, from *clæne*.
dredde (he *dreaded*), *forrdredd* (alarmed), from *drædenn*, *dredenn* (to *dread*), A. S. *drêd*, *dræden*, from *drædan*; in O., as in E., the verb has passed into the weak conj.
errnde (*errand*), A. S. *ærende*.

O. *fedde* (he *fed*), from *fedenn* (to *feed*), A. S. *fêdde*, from *fêdan*.

fifftiȝ (*fifty*), from *fif* (*five*), A. S. *fíftig*, from *fíf*.

fosstrenn (to *foster*), *fossterrfaderr* (*foster-father*), A. S. *fôsterian*, *fôsterfäder*.

goddspell (*gospel*) belongs here, if the A. S. word is *gôdspel* (good tidings,=εὐαγγέλιον) ; but this is now generally believed to be *godspel* (God's word).

hallȝhenn (saints, cf. *Hallow*-een), *hallȝhenn* (to *hallow*), A. S. *hâlige* or *hâlge*, *hâlgian*.

hiddenn (they *hid*), *hidd* (*hid*), from *hidenn* (to *hide*), A. S. *hýddon*, *hýded*, from *hýdan*.

keppte (he *kept*), from *kepenn* (to *keep*), A. S. *cêpte*, from *cêpan*.

lasstenn (to *last*), also *lastenn*, A. S. *læstan*.

ledde (he *led*), *ledd* (*led*), from *ledenn* (*to lead*), A. S. *lædde*, *læded*, from *lædan*.

mosste (might, cf. *must*), A. S. *môste*.

nesst (nearest, *next*), also *nest* (Sc. *niest*), A. S. *nêhst*.

redd (*read*, part.), A. S. *rêded*, from *rêdan*.

shadde (he parted), *shadd* (parted), from *shædenn* (to part, cf. to *shed*), A. S. *sceód*, *sceáden*, from *sceádan* : of weak conj. in O. and E.

siththenn (*sithence*, *since*), A. S. *sídh tham*, *sídhdhan*, perhaps *sidhdhan*.

sleppte (he *slept*), from *slæpenn* (to *sleep*), A. S. *slêp*, from *slæpan* : of weak conj. in O. and E.

soffte (*soft*), A. S. *sôfte*.

spredd (*spread*, part.), A. S. *spræded*, from *sprædan*.

thratte (he rebuked, cf. *threatened*), A. S. *threátede*, from *threátian*.

wepptenn (they *wept*), from *wepenn* (to *weep*), A. S. *weópon*, from *wêpan* : of weak conj. in O. and E.

wimmann (*woman*), also *wifmann*, A. S. *wífman*, *wímman*, perhaps *wimman*.

wissdom (*wisdom*), also *wisdom*, A. S. *wísdôm*.

Probably the short vowel in *wraththe* (*wrath*), as well as in *laththe* (*loathing*, enmity), and *kiththe* seen in *kiththeliȝ* (familiarly, cf. *kith*), may be accounted for in this way, from the addition of a suffix *the* (A. S. *dh*, *dhu*)—the same as in *strenncthe* (*strength*), *trowwthe* (*truth*), from *strang* (*strong*), *trowwe* (*true*)—to the adjectives *wrath* (*wrōth*, A. S. *wrâdh*), *lath* (*loathsome*, hateful, A. S. *lâdh*), and *cuth* (known, *couth*, A. S. *cûdh*) : compare A. S. *lædhdhu* (offence), *cýdhdhu* (home, household). It is possible that in these words, as well as in *dredde*, *fedde*, *hiddenn*, *ledde*, *shadde*, *siththenn*, *wimmann*, the first vowel may have been pronounced long, the following consonant being written double only because it was sounded twice, first in the stem, and again in the suffix.* It is also possible, or even probable, that in some cases the change from long to short, now under consideration, may have taken place already in the Anglo-Saxon ;† but this makes no difference, either in the reality of the change or in the cause from which it arose.

In the list of words just given, the short sound which appears in the Ormulum is maintained in modern English. The case is otherwise with those which follow :—

O. *allmasst* (*almost*), though the simple word is nearly always *mast* (*most*), A. S. *mæst.*

demmd (judged), from *demenn* (to judge, cf. *doom*, *deem*), A. S. *dêmed*, from *dêman.*

derre (*dearer*), from *deore*, *dere* (*dear*), A. S. *deórra*, from *deóre.*

derrlinng (*darling*), A. S. *deórling.*

dunnwarrd (*downward*), from *dun* (*down*), A. S. *ádûnweard*, from *dûn.*

hehhre (*higher*), also *hehre*, from *heh* (*high*), A. S. *heáhra*, *from heáh.*

---

* Such a supposition must, however, be regarded as improbable for these words, on account of the short quantity which they have in English ; and especially improbable for the preterits in *-dde*, on account of the corresponding participles *dredd*, *hidd*, *ledd*, etc., in which a really double pronunciation of the *d* is hardly to be thought of.

What is here recognized as possible—that a vowel before a double consonant may have been long, the consonant being written twice because actually twice sounded—must be admitted also for *lutte* (he *louted*), as well as the comparatives *derre* (*dearer*) and *nerre* (*nearer*), mentioned in the next paragraph ; and, perhaps with still stronger reason, for the words *clænnesse* (*clean-ness*), *fiffald* (*fivefold*), *læffull* (*belief-full*, believing). As we have *skillæs* (*skill-less*, ignorant), *sefennnahht* (*seven-night*, week), *unnned* (*un-need*, without constraint), *sunderrrun* (*sunder-roun*, private communing), *forrraht* (perverted, Germ. *ver-rückt*), it seems not unlikely that the *r*, *n*, and *f* would have been written thrice in *derre*, *nerre*, *clænnesse*, *fiffald*, *læffull*, if their first vowel had been short in sound ; but the spelling of *fullike* (*full-like*, *fully*), *stilliȝ* (*stilly*), *idelleȝȝc*=*idellnesse* (*idleness*), *drunnkennesse* (*drunken-ness*), *unnitt* (useless, Germ. *un-nütz*), *forrswundennesse* (remissness), *orrath* as well as *orrrath* (inops consilii, O. N. *ör-râdh*), warns us not to lay too much stress on this consideration.

† The same possibility is not to be overlooked in other cases where the vowel quantity of the Ormulum differs from what must have been the primitive quantity in Anglo-Saxon. This is particularly true as to that lengthening of vowels in open syllables which is soon to be considered : the change could hardly have gone so far in the language of the Ormulum, if it had not made a beginning in Anglo-Saxon times.

O. *herrde* (he *heard*), *herrd* (*heard*), from *herenn* (to *hear*), A. S. *hy̑rde*, *hy̑red*, from *hy̑ran*.
laffdiȝ (*lady*), A. S. *hlæfdige;* cf. O. *laferrd* (*lord*), A. S. *hlâford*.
liccness (*likeness*), from *lic* (*like*), A. S. *gelîcnes*, from *gelîc*, but O. *onnlicnesse* (*likeness*, image).
lutte (he bowed, *louted*), from *lutenn* (to *lout*), A. S. *leát*, from *lûtan:* of weak conj. in O. and E.
nerre (*nearer*), from *ner* (*nearly*), O. N. *nærri*, from *nær;* cf. O. *ner* (*nearer*), from *neh* (*nigh*), A. S. *neár*, from *neáh*.
oththr, *orr*, from *otherr* (all meaning *or*), A. S. *âdher* = *âwdher* (*either*): *oththr*, perhaps, by a confusion of A. S. *odhdhe* (or) with *âdher*.
Thurrsdaȝȝ (*Thursday*), O. N. *Thôrs-dag-r*, A. S. *Thunres-däg*.
wennde (he *weened*), from *wenenn* (to *ween*, think), A. S. *wênde*, from *wênan*.
wesste (*waste*, desert, adj. and subst.), A. S. *wêste*.

From a continued working out of the same tendency, the English has a short vowel before two or more consonants in some words where the Ormulum shows the original long vowel quantity:—

O. *adle* (disease, cf. *addle*), A. S. *âdl*.
breost, *brest* (*breast*), A. S. *breóst*.
brethre (*brethren*), A. S. *brôdhru*.
buhsumm (pliant, compliant, cf. *buxom*), from A. S. *bûgan* (to bend, *bow*).
to-clæf (he *cleft*, also *clave*, *clove*), A. S. *cleáf*, from *cleófan* (to *cleave*).
dost (*dost*, usual pron. *dŭst*), also *dosst*, from *don* (to *do*), A. S. *dêst*, from *dôn*.
fifte (*fifth*), *fiftende* (*fifteenth*), A. S. *fîfta*, *fîfteódha*, O. N. *fimtândi*.
freond, *frend* (*friend*), A. S. *freónd*.
gom (care, heed, cf. *gumption*), A. S. *geám*.
hæse (command, *hest*), A. S. *hæs*.
heold, *held* (he *held*), from *haldenn* (to *hold*), A. S. *heóld*, from *healdan*.
monethth (*month*), A. S. *mônadh*.
naness, in *forr the naness* (*for the nonce*), from *æness* (*once*, Sc. *aines*), A. S. *æne*.

In the following words also the shortening may be explained on the same principle, since the vowel which is written before their final liquid is little, if at all, represented in their actual pronunciation:—

O. *æfre* (*ever*), *næfre* (*never*), A. S. *æfre*, *næfre*.
becnenn (to *beckon*), A. S. *bêcnan*, *beácnian*.

O. *bosemm* (*bosom*, often pron. with long *oo* sound), A. S. *bôsm*.
brotherr (*brother*), pl. *brethre* (*brethren*), A. S. *brôdhor*, *brôdhru*.
moderr (*mother*), A. S. *môdor*.
otherr (*other*), A. S. *ôdher*.
wæpenn (*weapon*), A. S. *wæpen*.

The cases which we have been considering show an accented long vowel shortened in a close syllable, where it is separated by more than one audible consonant sound from the vowel of the following syllable. We have next to notice a change which is the converse of this, a change which has cut much deeper into the integrity of the old system of quantities : the lengthening of an accented short vowel in an open syllable (generally a penult)—that is, when separated by only one consonant sound from the vowel of the syllable which follows. This change has been carried to a very great extent in the modern German : *geben* (to *give*), *nieder* (down, cf. E. *nether*), *tragen* (to *draw*), *nehmen* (to take), are examples taken up at random out of an immense multitude. According to Schleicher, this change of quantity belongs to, and is a prominent feature in, the transition from Middle to Modern High German, which was made in the fifteenth century. In England the change must have commenced its progress earlier, as we find it carried very far in the language of the Ormulum, which belongs to the thirteenth century. We give first the instances in which the lengthened vowel seen in the Ormulum became so established in English usage as to remain long in the pronunciation of to-day. Thus—

O. -*ale* (*ale*), in *bridale* (*bride*-feast), A. S. *ealu*, *brŷdealu*. In E. *bridal* it has become short again.
aȝhe (*awe*), but also *eȝȝe* (fear), A. S. *ege ;* cf. O. N. *ægja* (to strike with fear or *awe*).
bakenn (to *bake*), A. S. *bacan*.
bede (prayer, cf. *bead*, *bead*-roll, *beads*-man), A. S. *gebed*.
berenn (to *bear*), *borenn* (*born*), A. S. *beran*, *boren*.
bidell (crier, messenger, cf. *beadle*), A. S. *bydel*.
brasene (*brazen*), from *brass* (*brass*), A. S. *bräsen*, from *bräs*.
brekenn (to *break*), A. S. *brecan*.
bridledd (*bridled*), with ī from *bridell* (? not found in O.), A. S. *bridel*.
bule (*bole*, tree-stem), in *bulaxe* (axe, hatchet, cf. *pole-axe*), O. N. *bolöxi*, from *bol-r*.
care (*care*), A. S. *cearu*, *caru*.

O. *chariȝ* (mournful, anxious, cf. *chary*), A. S. *cearig*, from *cearu*.
chosenn (*chosen*), from *chesenn* (to *choose*), A. S. *coren*, from *ceósan*.
clofenn (*cloven*), A. S. *clofen*, from *cleófan* (to *cleave*).
cnapess (boy's, cf. *knave*), A. S. *cnape*, *cnafa* (boy).
cnedenn (to *knead*), A. S. *cnedan*.
dækenn (Levite, *deacon*), A. S. *diacon*, Lat. *diaconus*.
dale (*dale*), A. S. *däl*: original quantity preserved in E. *dell*.
draȝhenn (to *draw*, *drawn*), A. S. *dragan*, *dragen*.
kirrkedure (church-*door*), A. S. *duru* (*door*).
efenn (equal, *even*), but pl. *effne*, vb. *effnenn*, A. S. *efen*, *efenian*.
ele (*oil*), A. S. *ele*, O. Fr. *oile*, *oille*, Lat. *oleum*.
etenn (to *eat*), but impv. *ett* (*eat*), A. S. *etan*, *et*.
faderr (*father*), A. S. *fäder*.
farenn (to go, *fare*), but impv. *farr*, A. S. *faran*, *far*.
biforenn (*before*), also *biforr*, A. S. *beforan*.
bifrorenn (*frozen*), A. S. *froren*, from *freósan* (to *freeze*).
gate (way, cf. *gait*), O. N. *gata* (way), A. S. *geat* (*gate*).
græfess (ditches, cf. *grave*), A. S. *gräf*.
-gume (man), in *bridgume* (*bridegroom*), A. S. *guma*, *brÿdguma*.
hatenn (to *hate*), *hete* (*hate*), A. S. *hatian*, *hete*.
hefênn (to raise, *heave*), *hofenn* (*hove*, *hoven*), A. S. *hebban*, *hofen*.
hire (*her*), A. S. *hire*.
hiȝhenn (to hasten, cf. to *hie*), *higian*.
hope (*hope*), A. S. *hopa*.
ifell (*evil*), A. S. *yfel*.
kechell (*cake*), O. N. *kaka*.
ladenn (to draw out, cf. to *lade* water, also *ladle*), A. S. *hladan*.
late (*late*), but *lattre* (*latter*), *lattst* (*last*), A. S. *lät*, *lätra*, *latost*.
laȝhe (*law*), A. S. *lagu*.
forrlorenn (*lost*, cf. *forlorn*), from *forrlesenn* (to *lose*), A. S. *forloren*, from *forleósan*.
makenn (to *make*, Sc. *mak*), but impv. *macc*, A. S. *macian*, *maca*.
mele (*meal*, flour), A. S. *melu*.
mete (*meat*, food), A. S. *mete*.
efennmete (commensurate), from *mett* (measure, cf. *mete*), A. S. *gemet*: O. *metelike* (*meetly*), A. S. *gemetlíce*.
nakedd (*naked*), A. S. *nacod*.
name (*name*), but *nemmnenn* (to *name*), A. S. *name*, *nemnan*.
binethenn (*beneath*), but *niththrenn* (to lower, cf. *nether*), A. S. *beneodhan*, *nidherian*.
niȝhenn (*nine*), *niȝhennde* (*ninth*), A. S. *nigon*, *nigodha*, O. N. *níundi* (*ninth*).
oferr (*over*), but also *offr*, A. S. *ofer*.
openn (*open*), but *oppnenn* (to *open*), A. S. *open*, *openian*.
reȝhellboc (*rule-book*), A. S. *regol*, Lat. *regula*.
sake (quarrel, cf. *sake*), A. S. *sacu*.

O. *forrsakenn* (to *forsake, forsaken*), A. S. *forsacan, forsacen.*
same (*same*), A. S. *same* (pariter), O. N. *sam-r* (idem).
seȝhenn, sene (*seen*), A. S. *sewen, segen, sên,* from *seón* (to *see*).
shame (*shame*), but *shammfasst* (*shamefaced*), A. S. *sceamu, sceamfäst.*
shapenn (to form, create, cf. to *shape*), A. S. *sceppan.*
skathenn (to harm, to *scăthe*), A. S. *sceadhan.*
slaȝenn (*slain*), from *slan* (to *slay*), A. S. *slagen,* from *sleán.*
smeredd (anointed, cf. *smeared*), A. S. *smyred,* from *smyrian,* cf. *smeoru* (ointment).
spekenn (to *speak*), A. S. *sprecan* and *specan.*
stĕlenn (to *steal*), A. S. *stelan.*
stirenn (tŏ *stir,* move, Sc. *steer*), A. S. *styrian.*
swerenn (to *swear*), A. S. *swerian.*
anndswere (*answer*), A. S. *andswaru.*
takenn (*to take, taken,* Sc. *tak*), but impv. *tacc,* A. S. *tacan, tacen, tac.*
tale (reckoning, number, cf. *tale*), A. S. *talu.*
tholenn (to suffer, Sc. *thole*), A. S. *tholian.*
wakenn (to *wake,* watch), A. S. *wacan.*
waterr (*water*), but *wattrenn* (to *water*), A. S. *wăter, wăterian.*
weorelld, werelld (*world*), but gen. *weorrldess, werrldess,* A. S. *weoruld, woruld, world.*
wrekenn (to *wreak*), *wræche* (*wreak,* revenge), A. S. *wrecan, wracu.*
wuke (*week*), A. S. *wucu.*
ȝate (*gate*), also *gate,* A. S. *geat.*

It is remarkable that this change is carried to a much greater extent in the Semi-Saxon of the Ormulum than it is in modern English. It should seem that there must have been a reaction early established, which set limits to the tendency, and maintained the short vowel in many words where it had begun to be lengthened. Instances of this kind—where an accented short vowel in an open syllable is lengthened in the Ormulum, but the same vowel is found short in English (mostly, indeed, in monosyllables with final consonant sound)—are the following :—

O. *abufenn* (*above*),=*bufenn,* from A. S. *á, be,* and *ufan.*
beodenn, bedenn (*bidden*), A. S. *boden* (commanded), *beden* (entreated. [The A. S. verbs *biddan* (to entreat) and *beódan* (to command) are pretty much confounded in O.]
bisscopess, pl. of *bisscopp* (*bishop*), A. S. *bisceop ; bisscopess* had a secondary accent on the *o.*
bĭte (*bit,* morsel), A. S. *bite.*

O. *bodiȝ* (*body*), A. S. *bodig*.
bule (*bull*), Dutch *bul*, O. N. *boli*.
clepedd (called, cf. *clept*, *yclept*), from *clepenn*, A. S. *cleopod*, from *cleopian*.
cŭde (*cud*), A. S. *cud*.
cumenn (to *come*, also as part.), but impv. *comm*, *cumm*, A. S. *cuman*, *cumen*, *cum*.
cwike, pl. of *cwicc* (living, *quick*), A. S. *cwic*.
dide (*did*), from *don* (to *do*), A. S. *dyde*, from *dôn*.
drake (*dragon*), A. S. *draca*, Lat. *draco*.
drifenn (*driven*), from *drifenn* (to *drive*), A. S. *drifen*, from *drîfan*.
fretenn (to *fret*, trans.), A. S. *fretan* (to eat up).
glade, pl. of *gladd* (*glad*), *gladenn* (to *gladden*), A. S. *gläd*, *gladian*.
godess, gen. of *godd* (*god*), but pl. *goddess*, A. S. *god*.
gresess (*grasses*), sing. in *gresshoppe* (*grasshopper*), A. S. *gräs*, *gärs*, *gärshoppa*.
hafenn, but *habbenn* (to have), *hafesst*, but *haffst* (*hast*), *haffde* (*had*), A. S. *habban*, *häfst*, *häfde*.
hefiȝ (*heavy*), A. S. *hefig*.
heofenn (*heaven*), in comp., but as separate word *heoffne*, *heffne*, A. S. *heofon*.
hiderr (*hither*), A. S. *hider*.
hise, pl. of *hiss* (*his*), A. S. *his*.
huniȝ (*honey*), A. S. *hunig*.
kide (*kid*), O. N. *kid*.
kĭness, *kĭne* (comm. *kinness*, *kinne*), gen. and pl. of *kinn* (*kin*, *kind*), A. S. *cyn*.
lifethth (*liveth*), from *libbenn* (to *live*), A. S. *lifadh*, *libban*.
limess (*limbs*), sing. not in O., A. S. *lim*, pl. *leomu*, *limu*.
litell (*little*), pl. *little*, A. S. *lytel*.
lokenn (shut in, cf. *locked*), A. S. *locen*, from *lûcan*.
lotess, pl. of *lott* (*lot*), A. S. *hlot*, pl. *hlotu*.
lufe (*love*), *lufenn* (to *love*), but *luffsumm* (pleasant), A. S. *lufu*, *lufian*, *lufsum*.
maniȝ, *mani* (*many*), A. S. *manig*.
mikell (great, many, *mickle*, *much*), but pl. *miccle*, A. S. *micel*.
mineteress (money-changers, cf. *minter*, *mint*), A. S. *mynetere*, from *mynet* (*money*), Lat. *moneta*.
muneclif (*monk-life*), A. S. *munec* (*monk*), Lat. *monachus*.
naru (*narrow*), but pl. *narrwe*, A. S. *nearu*.
nile (*nill* he, *i. e. will not*), but *nillt* (*wilt not*), A. S. *nelle*, *nelt*.
ofne (*oven*), dat. of *ofenn* (? not in O.), A. S. *ofen*.
peninng (*penny*), A. S. *pending*, *pening*, *penig*.
rathe (quickly, cf. *rathe*, *rather*), A. S. *hradhe*, *hradhor*, from *hrädh* (quick).
risenn (*risen*), from *risenn* (to *rise*), A. S. *risen*, from *rîsan*.

O. *rotenn* (to *rot*), A. S. *rotian*.
Saterrdaȝȝ (*Saturday*), A. S. *Säterndäg*, Lat. *Saturni dies.*
seofenn, *sefenn* (*seven*), but also *seoffne*, *seffne*; *seofenntiȝ* (*seventy*): A. S. *seofon*, *hundseofontig*.
shetenn (to *shut* up), A. S. *scyttan*.
sikerr (sure, Sc. *sicker*), O. Sax. *sikor*, O. H. Germ. *sihhur*, Lat. *securus*.
sĭne, rare for *sinne* (*sin*), A. S. *syn*.
skathelæs (unharmed, *scăthless*), A. S. *sceadha* (harmer).
stafess, pl. of *staff* (letter, cf. *staff*, old pl. *staves*), A. S. *stäf* (*staff*, letter).
stede (place, cf. *stead*), A. S. *stede*.
stekenn (to confine, cf. to *stick*, remain fast), A. S. *stician*.
stoke (*stock*), dat. of *stocc* (? not in O.), A. S. *stoc*.
sume, pl. of *summ* (*some*), A. S. *sum*.
sumerr (*summer*), A. S. *sumor*.
sune (*son*), A. S. *sunu*.
Sunenndaȝȝ (*Sunday*), from *sunne*, rarely *sŭne* (*sun*), A. S. *sunne*, *Sunnandäg*.
thiderr (*thither*), A. S. *thider*.
fullthrĭfenn (complete, cf. *thriven*), O. N. *thrifinn*, from *thrîfask* (to *thrive*).
thripell (*triple*), from Lat. *triplex*, Fr. *triple*, confused with A. S. *thrî*; cf. prov. Eng. *thribble*.
tredenn (to *tread*, *trodden*), A. S. *tredan*, *treden*.
whiderrwarrd (*whitherward*), A. S. *hwider*.
widewe, comm. *widdwe* (*widow*), A. S. *widwe*, *wydewe*.
wilenn (to *will*), but *willt* (*wilt*), A. S. *willan*, *wilt*.
witenn (to know, cf. to *wit*, O. E. to *weet*), but impv. *witt*, A. S. *witan*, *wit*.
writenn (*written*), from *writenn* (to *write*), A. S. *writen*, from *wrîtan*: cf. O. *writess*, pl. of *writt* (*writ*), A. S. *writ*.
wude (*wood*), A. S. *wudu*.
wunedd (*wont*), from *wunenn* (to accustom), A. S. *wuna*, *gewuna* (custom).
ȝetenn (to *get*), *ȝett* (*gets*), *biȝetenn* (*gotten*), A. S. *begitan*, *begiten*.
ȝifenn (to *give*, *given*), also written with *g*, but impv. *ȝiff*, A. S. *gifan*, *gifen*, *gif*.

That this change—the lengthening of an accented short vowel in an open syllable—was still in progress at the time of the Ormulum, so that the usage in respect to it was then unsettled and fluctuating, is apparent from indications in the book itself. A number of the words given in the last two lists have here and there a mark of short quantity written over the vowel, as if the writer, having first given it as long

19

with only a single consonant after it, was afterwards inclined to recall his judgment, to set it down as short, and therefore, drew a curve line over it, this being an easier way than doubling the consonant by interlineation. What makes this explanation more probable is the fact that, while there are more than forty distinct words which in one place or another have this short mark over them, it occurs in almost every case over an accented vowel in an open syllable. That there was a special vacillation on the part of the writer as to the quantity of such vowels seems a natural, if it is not a necessary, inference from this fact. Thus *berenn* (to *bear*) is once at least written with a mark of short quantity over the accented vowel; and the same is true of *bede* (*bede*), *dale* (*dale*), *hatenn* (to *hate*), *hete* (*hate*), *ladenn* (to *lade*), *late* (*late*), *mele* (*meal*), *mete* (*meat*), *name* (*name*), *stelen* (to *steal*), *takenn* (to *take*), *tale* (*tale*); also *bite* (*bit*), *cude* (*cud*), *kine* (*kin*), *lifethth* (*liveth*), *sine* (*sin*), *stede* (*stead*), *thrifenn* (*thriven*), *wilenn* (to *will*), *witenn* (to *wit*), *writenn* (*written*).

Under the broad euphonic analogies and tendencies which have now been described come all but a comparatively small number of the cases in which the modern English quantity differs from that in the Ormulum. There remain, however, some few changes which are not altogether of an isolated character. A long vowel of the Anglo-Saxon and the Ormulum has in a good many instances been shortened before a final mute. This is especially the case with the old long *o* before a final *k*-sound. The long quantity of that vowel was indicated in early English by doubling the *o*: thus *bôc* was written *book*. The sound afterwards changed to that which we hear in *spoon*, *spool*; and still later was shortened to its present pronunciation. Instances of this kind are—

O. *boc** (*book*), A. S. *bôc*.
croc (hook or *crook*, device), O. N. *krôk-r*.
lokenn (to *look*), A. S. *lôcian*.
forrsoc (*forsook*), from *forrsakenn* (to *forsake*), A. S. *forsôc*, from *forsacan*.
toc (*took*), from *takenn* (to *take*), A. S. *tôc*, from *tacan*.

* In this word, and in several others, where a long vowel has become short before a final consonant, the Scotch retains the earlier long quantity: thus, *buik*, *bruik*, *bluid*, *gude*, etc.

Occasionally other long vowels have become short before a *k*-sound, as in—

O. *brukenn* (to use, enjoy, cf. to *brook*), A. S. *brûcan.*
fic (*fig*), in *fictre* (*fig-tree*), A. S. *fîc*, Lat. *ficus.*
seoc, *sec* (*sick*), A. S. *seóc.*
strac (passed, cf. *struck*, O. E. *strook*), A. S. *strâc*, from *strîcan.*
wic (dwelling, street, cf. Swan*wick*, Green*wich*), A. S. *wîc.*

The same change of quantity has taken place not unfrequently before *d*, seldomer before *t*: thus—

O. *blod* (*blood*), A. S. *blôd.*
flod (*flood*), A, S. *flôd.*
god (*good*), A. S. *gôd.*
stod (*stood*), from *stanndenn* (to *stand*), A. S. *stôd*, from *standan.*
wod (mad, Sc. *wud*), A. S. *wôd.*
bræd (*bread*), A. S. *breád.*
dæd (*dead*), A. S. *deád.*
drædenn, *dredenn* (to *dread*), A. S. *drædan.*
hæfedd (*head*), A. S. *heáfod.*
shædenn (to part, cf. to *shed*), A. S. *sceádan.*
shrædenn (to *shred*, pare, cf. Sc. *screed*), A. S. *screádian.*
but, comm. *butt* (*but*, except), A. S. *bûtan.*
fot (*foot*), A. S. *fôt.*
hat (*hot*), A. S. *hât.*
lætenn and *lĕtenn* (to *let*, allow, also as part. *let*), pf. *let* (he *let*), A. S. *lætan*, *læten*, pf. *lêt.*
swat (*sweat*), A. S. *swât.*
wæte (drink), from *wæt* (not in O., *wet*, Sc. *weet*), A. S. *wæt.*
wat, also *watt* (*wot*), from *witenn* (to know, cf. to *wit*), A. S. *wát*, from *witan.*

In *bedeththth* or *biddeththth* (*biddeth*), *forrbedeththth* (*forbiddeth*), the long form comes from A. S. *beódan* (to command), the short one from A. S. *biddan* (to entreat); in *biddenn* (to command, to entreat) of the Ormulum, the forms of the two verbs are very much confounded.

The few cases in which the difference of quantity between the Ormulum and the modern English is not to be explained from principles already set forth, will be found, so far as I have noted them, in the following list:

O. *amæn* (*amen*), Gr. ἀμήν.
an (*an*, *one*), rarely *ann*; *nan* (*none*); *onnan*, *anan*, also *anann*

O. (*anon*) ; A. S. *ân*, *nân*. Eng. *alone*, *atone*, *only*, and Sc. *ane*, *nane*, preserve the original long quantity.

aniȝ (*any*), A. S. *ænig*.

beon, *ben* (to *be*, *been*), A. S. *beón* (to *be*) : the long sound of *been* is still sometimes heard.

caritcth (*charity*), Fr. *charité*, Prov. *caritat*, Lat. *caritas*.

chele, also *chĕle* (*chill*, subs.), A. S. *céle*.

clath (clothing, cf. *clŏth*, but pl. *clōthes*), A. S. *clâdh*.

cuthe (*could*), A. S. *cûdhe*.

dæf (*deaf*, cf. Sc. *deave*, to deafen), A. S. *deáf*.

dæth (*death*), A. S. *deádh*.

deofell, *defell* (*devil*, Sc. *deevil*), A. S. *deófol*, Lat. *diabolus*.

doth (*doth*, usual pron. *dŭth*), from *don* (to *do*), A. S. *dêdh*, from *dôn*.

flæsh (*flesh*), A. S. *flæsc*.

gluterrnesse (*gluttony*), O. Fr. *gloutonnie* (from *glouton*, Lat. *glūtō*(*n*), from *glūtire*) : in *gluterrnesse* English affixes are attached to the root (*glut*) of the Latin and French words.

gyn (art, device, cf. *gin*), shortened from O. Fr. *engin*, but perhaps confused with a derivative of O. N. *ginna* (to deceive).

inoh (*enough*, also *enow*), A. S. *genóg*, *genôh*.

bikæchedd (*catched*), also *bikahht* (*caught*) ; of uncertain origin.

profete, *prophete* (*prophet*), Lat. *prophēta*.

publicaness (*publicans*), Lat. *pūblicāni*.

rædiȝ (*ready*), also *rædĕlike*, A. S. *ræde*, *rædlîc*.

riche (*rich*), A. S. *rîce*.

sariȝ (*sorry*), but *sare* (*sorely*), A. S. *sârig*, from *sâr* (*sore*).

seliliȝ (happily), A. S. *sælig*, *gesælig* (happy, Sc. *seely*), whence E. *silly*.

shephirde (*shepherd*), from *shep* (*sheep*), A. S. *sceáp*, *sceáphirde*.

shunenn (to *shun*), A. S. *scûnian*.

tene (*ten*), rarely *tenn*, *tende* (*tenth*), A. S. *tŷn*, *tên*, *teódha*, O. N. *tíundi* (*tenth*). The old long quantity is preserved in the compounds *thirteen*, *thirteenth*, etc., and in Sc. *teinds* (*tithes*).

onnȝæness (*against*, *again*), *onnȝæn* (*again*, *against*), A. S. *ongeán* (*against*).

ȝet (*yet*), strangely lengthened in O., A. S. *git*, *get*, *giet*, *gyt*.

drunncnenn (to *drown*, trans.), in form=A. S. *druncnian* (to get one *drunk*), cf. O. N. *drukna* (to be *drowned*).

enngell (*angel*), A. S. *engel*, *ängel*, Lat. *angelus*.

flumm (river, cf. *flume*), O. Fr. *flum*, Lat. *flumen*.

funnt (*font*, cf. *fount*), A. S. *font*, Lat. *fons*, *font-is*.

irrene (of *iron*, ferreus), from *irenn* (*iron*), A. S. *îren* (ferrum and ferreus) : *rr* in *irrene* perhaps an oversight.

munnt (*mount*), A. S. *munt*, Lat. *mons*, *mont-is*.

sannt (*saint*), A. S. *sanct*, Lat. *sanctus*.

O. *sleckenn*,* *slekkenn* (to *slake*), A. S. *sleac* (*slack*), *gesleccan* (to *slacken*), O. N. *slökkva* (to *slake*).
thurrh (*through*), A. S. *thurh*, *thuruh* (*through*, *thorough*).
waccnenn (to *waken*, trans. and intrans.), A. S. *wăcnan*: lengthened in E. under influence of *to wake*, O. *wakenn*, A. S. *wacan*.
whamm (*whom*), from *wha* (*who*), A. S. *hwam*, from *hwa*.
ȝocc (*yoke*), A. S. *geoc*, *gioc*.

In the case of *been*, *could*, *deaf*, *death*, *enough*, *ready*, *again*, *against*, the spelling shows that they came into English with the long quantity which they had in the Ormulum. The preterits *barr* (*bare*, *bore*, A. S. *băr*), *bat* (*bit*, A. S. *bât*), *brace* (*brake*, *broke*, A. S. *brăc*), *comm* (*came*, A. S. *cwam*, *com*), *cwathth* (*quōth*, A. S. *cwădh*), *sahh* (*saw*, A. S. *seah*), *spacc* (*spake*, *spoke*, A. S. *sprăc*), *ȝaff* (*gave*, A. S. *geaf*), have not been placed in the foregoing lists, because the English forms, though used in both numbers, correspond apparently to the plurals of the A. S. (*bæron*, *biton*, *bræcon*, *cwâmon* or *cômon*, *cwædon*, *sâwon* or *sægon*, *spræcon*, *geáfon*) and the O. (*bærenn*, *comenn*, *sæȝhenn*, *spækenn*, *ȝæfenn*): in *et* (he *ate*, A. S. *ăt*) with long *e* like pl. *etenn* (they *ate*, A. S. *æton*), the same extension of the plural quantity to the singular appears even in the Ormulum. The *ou* in the English preterits *bound*, *found*, *wound*—A. S. 1, 3 sing. *band*, *fand*, *wand*, pl. *bundon*, *fundon*, *wundon*; O. sing. *band*, *fand*, *wand*, pl. *bundenn*, *fundenn*—is to be explained in the same way.†

We have not yet attended to the suffixes of inflection and derivation; but for these only a few words will be necessary. The inflectional endings are all short in the Ormulum: there is reason, indeed, to believe that such as were originally long had become short during the Anglo-Saxon period. Thus the Ormulum has

-ess in the gen. sing.: as *flæshess kinde* (*flesh's kindred*, A. S. *flæsces gecynd*).
-ess in the plural: as *læchess* (*leeches*, A. S. *læcas*, earlier *læcâs* or *læciâs*).

---

* The digraph *ck*, in the Ormulum, is equivalent to *cc* or *kk*, and marks the vowel before it as short. At the end of a word, or before a consonant, *cc* is alone used; if a vowel follows in the same word, *ck* or *kk* takes its place.

† For several of these preterits the Scottish dialect has forms—such as *brak*, *cam*, *spak*, *fand*, etc.—which correspond to those here given from the Ormulum.

-err in the compar. *forrtherr* (*further*, A. S. *furdhor*), from *forth* (*forth*, A. S. *fordh*) : in the compar. of adjectives the O. has *-re* (A. S. *-ra*, *-re*), as *fulre* (*fouler*, A. S. *fûlra*). In E., *-er* has become long by change of *r*.

-esst in the superl. : as *deresst* (*dearest*, A. S. *deórost*, *deórest*).

-esst in the 2d person of verbs : as *heresst* (*hearest*, A. S. *hŷrest*).

-ethth in the 3d person of verbs : as *lokethth* (*looketh*, A. S. *lôcadh*).

-enn in the past part. : as *haldenn* (*holden*, A. S. *healden*).

-edd in the past part. : as *wundedd* (*wounded*, A. S. *wundod*).

The *-de* of the weak preterit is usually added directly to the stem, as *dredde* (he *dreaded*). The present participle terminates in *-ennde* (A. S. *-ende*), but is rare in the O., the only instances where it is a proper participle being *bærnennde* (*burning*), *dwallkennde* (misleading), *glowennde* (*glowing*), and *stinnkennde* (*stinking*). The suffix *-inng* is very frequent, but always forms a verbal substantive; while *-ung*, which in Anglo-Saxon is more used for this purpose, is in O. confined to the word *reowwsunng* (*rueing*, repentance) and two or three others. Suffixes of this kind, found both in O. and in E., are—

-ell (A. S. *-el*) : as *girrdell* (*girdle*).

-ene (A. S. *-en*) : as *brasene* (*brazen*).

-ere (A. S. *-ere*) : as *mineteress* (*minters*, money-changers) ; very rare in O. ; another instance perhaps in *forrleȝerrnesse* (fornication).

-inng (A. S. *-ing*, *-ung*) : as *biginninng* (*beginning*), *laferrdinngess* (*lordings*).

-issh (A. S. *-isc*) : as *shepisshe* (sheeplike, *sheepish*).

-iȝ (A. S. *-ig*) : as *modiȝ* (*moody*).

-linng (A. S. *-ling*) : as *derrlinng* (*darling*).

-nesse (A. S. *-nes*) : as *godnesse* (*goodness*), *wittness* (*witness*).

-stere (A. S. *-stre*) : only in *huccsteress* (*huckster's*).

In final *-ene* and *-ere*, the first *e*, short in A. S., is lengthened by the open syllable : the English *-er* is of course long. Final *-iȝ* is long in consequence of the partial vocalization of the *g* (compare the effect of a weak *r*), while the corresponding suffix *-y* of the later language, discarding the semivowel, has returned to the short quantity of A. S. *-ig*. The same changes appear in the numerals *twenntiȝ*, *thrittiȝ*, *fowwerrtiȝ*, etc. (*twenty*, *thirty*, *forty*, etc., A. S. *twentig*, *thrittig*, *feówertig*, etc.) But in the suffix *-liȝ* (our-*ly*) the vowel was originally long, the words which contain it being compounds of the adj. *like* (O. *lic*, A. S. *gelîc*). Suffixes of this kind (really words in composition) are the following, found both in the Ormulum and in English:

-dom (A. S. *-dôm*): as *horedom* (*whoredom*).
-fald (A. S. *-feald*): as *threfald* (*threefold*).
-fasst (A. S. *-fäst*): as *stedefasst* (*steadfast*); in *shammfasst* (*shamefaced*) the form has been changed by mistaken popular etymology.
-full (A. S. *-ful*): as *sinnfull* (*sinful*).
-had (A. S. *-hâd*): as *maȝȝdennhad* (*maidenhood*, *maidenhead*).
-lac (A. S. *-lâc*): only in *weddlac* (*wedlock*).
-læs (A. S. *-leás*): as *childlæs* (*childless*); rarely *-less*, as *endeless* (*endless*).
-lic, *-like* or *-liȝ* (A. S. *-lîc*): as *eorthlic*, *eorthlike*, *eorthliȝ* (*earthly*).
-mann (A. S. *-man*): as *allderrmann* (*alderman*).
-shipe (A. S. *-scipe*): as *wurrthshipe* and *wurrshipe* (*worship*).
-summ (A. S. *-sum*): as *halsumm* (*wholesome*).
-warrd (A. S. *-weard*): as *affterrwarrd* (*afterward*).

In *-fald* and *-shipe*, the Ormulum has lengthened an Anglo-Saxon short vowel, from the influence of *ld* in the first case, and of an open syllable in the second; as to the last, the English agrees with the Anglo-Saxon. The short vowel of *-warrd* has been lengthened in English by the weak *r*; while the long vowel has been shortened in *-dom*, *-had*, *-lac*, *læs*, two of which end with mute sounds. In *læs*, the change had commenced in the thirteenth century. The Ormulum has in many words a suffix *-leȝȝc*—as seen in *godleȝȝc*, =*godnesse* (*goodness*)—which corresponds to *-leik-r* (=A. S. *-lâc*), a frequent suffix in the Old Norse. Peculiar cases are *rihhtwis* (*righteous*, A. S. *rihtwîs*), and *stall wurrthliȝ* (stoutly, cf. *stalwart*, A. S. *stälweordh*).

XVI.

TENNYSON'S PRINCESS.*

1849.

MANY readers have confessed the disappointment which they felt upon their first acquaintance with "The Princess:" and perhaps nothing but the want of equal frankness has kept back many others from the same confession. Though [in 1849] not extensively read in this country, Mr. Tennyson had come to be rated, according to his fame at home, as first among the English poets of the present generation. A large class of readers, who had taken this opinion upon trust, were looking to see it confirmed in his forthcoming poem, which, as the public were assured in sundry notices, was to be the longest and the most elaborate of his productions. Great in many cases was their disappointment, when, instead of a second Paradise Lost, they found what seemed to them only a grotesque extravaganza about "woman's rights." But there were others, old admirers of the poet, familiar with his earlier pieces; who had dwelt delighted on the splendid pomp of his "Morte d'Arthur," the epic breadth of his "Ulysses," the energy and passion of his "Locksley Hall," that miracle of condensation; and who were now expecting to find all the merits of their favorite's youthful genius, united and exalted in this effort of his riper years. But lo! instead of the Gothic cathedral or the Egyptian pyramid on which their hopes were fixed, they see, much to their surprise, only a glittering castle in the air. Chagrined to find the work so different from their preconceptions, they shut their eyes to its indisputable merits. Its grace and gayety, its genial humor, its aptness of expression, its brilliancy of coloring go for little with those whose minds were set on greater things. Qualities which might have

* The Princess: a Medley; by Alfred Tennyson. Boston: William D. Ticknor & Co.

pleased them in a Christmas romance or a fairy tale for children, seem out of place in what they had predestined for the master-piece of a great poet. Still they read on, hopeful of a change; hoping that suddenly, as by some flourish of an enchanter's wand, the fantastic air-castle may settle down into the solidity and solemnity of the Egyptian pyramid. Nor are there wanting here and there tokens of such a metamorphosis: the colors seem to deepen; the forms to take on fixity and definiteness; laughing extravagance to give signs of earnestness and truth. These appearances, however, prove illusory: the edifice, though more imposing than it looked at first, has yet neither substance nor foundation; it is thin air, and not genuine brick and mortar; "the baseless fabric of a vision," without strength or unity or grandeur. And so the disappointed reader shuts his book, doubting his past convictions of its author's genius, and renouncing, for the time at least, his faith in Tennyson.

Not a few, it is believed, will recognize in this description a tolerably accurate rehearsal of their own experience. Even of those whose first impressions were more favorable, few perhaps would say that the work fully satisfied their expectations. On the other hand, fewer still would venture to deny that there is much in it which is excellent and admirable. The severest critic must acknowledge that its faults, however serious, are redeemed by many beauties of detail. A recollection of its beauties has won back the complainer, recovering from the first flurry of his disappointment, to a reperusal of the poem. Reading now as one who having formed his judgment is no longer forced to play the critic, he proceeds in a more cheerful mood, with a mind more open to all sources of enjoyment. Things which at first offended him are grown familiar, so that if they do not please they at least cease to be offensive. At the same time, new felicities and beauties, hitherto unnoticed, rise before him; they gather and grow thick about him as he advances; and when he has a second time attained the goal, he is ready to retract, if he has not quite forgotten them, his former disparaging criticisms.

It is impossible to do justice to the work in any abstract

of its story; and yet we know not how to make the criticisms which we have to offer intelligible without some statement of the plot. We shall follow closely in the author's track, and tell the tale as much as possible in his own words.

The performance opens with an overture which for its airy gracefulness of movement and dexterous announcement of the theme could hardly be surpassed. Here the poet shows himself a true man of the nineteenth century; one not so enamored of the past as to have lost all consciousness and sympathy for the present. He can enjoy the fresh breath of the passing day, and drive gayly on with the living currents of contemporaneous thought and action. His "Prologue" contains a spirited miniature of the age, dashed off in a few characteristic strokes which bring the very form and pressure of the time before us.

The scene opens in the grounds of Sir Walter Vivian:—

"No little lily-handed Baronet he,
A great broad-shoulder'd genial Englishman,
A lord of fat prize-oxen and of sheep,
A raiser of huge melons and of pine,
A patron of some thirty charities,
A pamphleteer on guano and on grain,
A quarter-sessions chairman, abler none;
Fair-hair'd and redder than a windy morn."

This variously accomplished knight, we are informed,—

"all a summer's day
Gave his broad lawns until the set of sun
Up to the people; thither flock'd at noon
His tenants, wife and child, and thither half
The neighboring borough with their Institute,
Of which he was the patron. I was there
From college, visiting the son—the son
A Walter too—with others of our set."

The young Walter takes his friends about the house, showing its curiosities, a heterogeneous collection, and producing an old chronicle of its ancient owners, where they read the exploits of Sir Ralph, a crusading hero of the family, and of—

"a lady, one that arm'd
Her own fair head, and sallying thro' the gate,
Had beat her foes with slaughter from her walls."

The party at length set forth on a visit to the ruins of an Abbey in the Park. On their way they view the multitude scattered in groups over the meadow, and variously occupied; some listening, while "the patient leaders of their Institute taught them with facts," or watching illustrative experiments with mimic fountain, fire-balloon, steam-engine, and electric telegraph, while others are engaged in the less scientific amusements of cricket-playing, fiddling, and dancing. Arrived at the Abbey, our youths fall in with Aunt Elizabeth, an elderly maiden lady of grave deportment, and sister Lilia, "half child, half woman," who had just attired the broken statue of Sir Ralph in scarf and shawl, the gay costume of a modern belle. The sight of this "feudal warrior lady-clad" brings up the old chronicle before mentioned, and with it the heroic lady and her martial daring: and then the question rises, "Where lives such a woman now?"

"Quick answer'd Lilia, 'There are thousands now
Such women, but convention beats them down:
It is but bringing up; no more than that:
You men have done it: how I hate you all!
O were I some great Princess, I would build
Far off from men a college of my own,
And I would teach them all things: you should see.'

And one said smiling, 'Pretty were the sight
If our old halls could change their sex, and flaunt
With prudes for proctors, dowagers for deans,
And sweet girl-graduates in their golden hair.
——————Yet I fear,
If there were many Lilias in the brood,
However deep you might embower the nest,
Some boy would spy it.'
At this upon the sward
She tapt her tiny silken-sandal'd foot:
'That's your light way; but I would make it death
For any male thing but to peep at us.'"

The conversation passes on to college recreations: Christmas tales are mentioned, extemporaneous fictions in which the whole company participate, each one taking up the story where his neighbor left it. A new thought presents itself:—

> "'Why not a summer's as a winter's tale?
> A tale for summer, as befits the time;
> And something it should be to suit the place,
> Grave, moral, solemn, like the mouldering walls
> About us.'"

The hint is followed up; a tale resolved on, and the "first person" in our Prologue named as leader, with the direction, "be, if you will, yourself your hero."

> "'Look then,' added he,
> 'Since Lilia would be princess, that you stoop
> No lower than a prince.'
> To which I said,
> 'Take care then that my tale be followed out
> By all the lieges in my royal vein:
> But one that really suited time and place
> Were such a medley, we should have him back
> Who told the Winter's Tale to do it for us:
> A Gothic ruin and a Grecian house,
> A talk of College and of ladies' rights,
> A feudal knight in silken masquerade,
> And there with shrieks and strange experiments
> For which the good Sir Ralph had burnt them all,
> The nineteenth century gambols on the grass.'"

He then commences, representing himself as a Prince whose father rules with rigid sway over a wide kingdom situated somewhere in high northern latitudes. While yet an infant he had been betrothed to the infant Princess of a neighboring country, equally indefinite in situation, being described only as lying south of the former. But when the time has come to execute the contract, and an embassy is sent with costly gifts to fetch the lady, there appears an unexpected obstacle: the Princess cannot be induced to come: "she has a will—and maiden fancies; loves to live alone among her women: certain will not wed." The northern king, furious at this violation of a solemn compact, "sware that he would send a hundred thousand men and fetch her in a whirlwind." Our hero remonstrates; urges milder courses; offers to go himself and ascertain the truth. Failing to gain permission, he takes the matter into his own hands; steals from court "with Cyril and with Florian, his two friends;" flying southward crosses the frontier, and so journeys on until he—

> "gained the mother-city thick with towers,
> And in the imperial palace found the king.
> His name was Gama; cracked and small his voice:
> A little dry old man, without a star,
> Not like a king."

The Prince speaks of his betrothed, and Gama answers—

> "I would you had her, Prince, with all my heart,
> With my full heart; but there were widows here,
> Two widows, Lady Psyche, Lady Blanche:
> They fed her theories, in and out of place,
> Maintaining that with equal husbandry
> The woman were an equal to the man."

Acting under such influences, she had begged from her father a certain summer-palace on the northern frontier of his dominions, and established there "an University for maidens," from which all men, even her own brothers, were rigorously shut out. Gama is ready to give the Prince letters to his daughter, though he rates his chance with her 'almost at naked nothing.' Our hero takes the letters, and sets out again with his associates: but on coming near the summer-palace, "a thought flash'd thro' him which he cloth'd in act." Having "tweezered out what slender blossom lived on lip or cheek of manhood," the three friends array themselves in female gear, and ask admission to the College. They are brought before the Princess Ida, whose appearance surpasses the expectation, and confirms the passion of her lover. She notices the tallness of the new-comers, but without suspecting their disguise: and at their own request enrols them pupils of the Lady Psyche; a pretty widow, described as "a quick brunette, well-moulded, falcon-eyed, and on the hither side, or so she looked, of twenty summers." This attractive person is "lady of three castles in the land," and withal sister to Florian the Prince's friend. Ushered into her lecture-room, Cyril falls in love at once with the lady and her three castles, his regard being pretty equally distributed between them. After her lecture, a report of which is given, she meets her new pupils, and soon recognizes her brother with his two companions. She tells them of the inscription on the gate, "let no man enter in on pain of death," which, approaching after nightfall, they had failed of reading; but she readily agrees to keep their secret, on condition that they take the earliest opportunity to quit the place. This conversation is accidentally overheard by Melissa, Lady Blanche's lovely daughter, whose charms make an instant impression on the heart of Florian. Melissa promises silence, but her mother, artful and suspicious, divines her secret, and succeeds in worming out a confirmation. Cyril, however, by playing on the tutoress's wounded vanity, and holding out bright hopes to her ambition, bribes her to concealment. Yet our adventurers do not long preserve their incognito. They attend the Princess on an excursion "to take the dip of certain strata to the North:" after which at evening the party is gathered for rest and refreshment in a superb pavilion. Here, after two or three songs,—

> "Did Cyril, with whom the bell-mouth'd flask had wrought,
> Or master'd by the sense of sport, begin
> To troll a careless, careless tavern-catch
> Of Moll and Meg, and strange experiences
> Unmeet for ladies."

Angry at his freedom, the Prince cries, "forbear, Sir," and smites him on the breast. The ladies on the instant take to flight: but coming to a stream which crossed their way, the Princess blind with rage misses the plank, and is swept down by the current towards a cataract not far below. Apprized of her peril by the shrieks of her attendants, our hero, as in duty bound, plunges in, and with some trouble bears her safely to the shore. The Princess returns to her palace, ascertains the treachery of her assistants, and summons them into her presence. Lady Psyche, it appears, has fled away with

Cyril; and Lady Blanche, in spite of a fluent and ingenious vindication of her conduct, is sternly banished from the place. Finally the Prince is brought up for judgment, and though the bloody penalty denounced against all masculine intruders is remitted, he is ignominiously thrust out of doors.

Wandering forth he finds himself presently in his father's camp, where his appearance in female garb—

> "drench'd with ooze, and torn with briers,
> More crumpled than a poppy from the sheath,
> And all one rag, disprinced from head to heel,"

provokes ungovernable laughter. The old king, it seems, learning the situation of his son, and fearing for his life, had crossed the frontier and was now beleaguering the summer-palace. King Gama too, who having just found out his daughter's sanguinary edict, was coming "all in haste to hinder wrong," has fallen into the enemy's hands and is held a hostage for the safety of the Prince. But soon the rumor comes that Gama's sons, Prince Arac and his two stout brothers, are approaching with a powerful army. A consultation is held and peace resolved on: only the Prince's claim to his betrothed shall be decided by a grand tournament between fifty champions on either side. To this arrangement Ida gives consent, and appears on the battlements of the palace a spectator of the conflict. Our hero's party is utterly worsted: he himself and his two friends bear down two of the royal brothers on the opposite side, but are all three vanquished by the prowess of the resistless Arac. The struggle over, Ida comes forth with her ladies to give her wounded champions, "brethren of her blood and cause, the tender ministries of female hands and hospitality." As she passes by the spot where the Prince is lying, his aged father mourning over him as dead, she is struck with sudden sorrow and remorse:—

> "Her iron will was broken in her mind,
> Her noble heart was molten in her breast."

Placing her finger on the Prince's brow, she soon announces that he lives, and offers to tend him with her own wounded brethren. A striking colloquy ensues, which ends in the arrangement that all the wounded, friend and foe without distinction, shall be taken to the palace, and there receive the treatment which their hurts require. Meantime the ordinary college business is suspended, the inmates for the most part returning to their homes.

The result is easily foreseen. Cyril and Florian soon recover from their wounds and prosper in their loves. The fate of the Prince is long doubtful:—

> "And twilight dawn'd; and morn by morn the lark
> Shot up and shrill'd in flickering gyres, but I
> Lay silent in the muffled cage of life;
> And twilight gloom'd; and broader grown the bowers
> Drew the great night into themselves, and Heaven
> Star after star arose and fell, but I
> Lay sunder'd from the moving universe,
> Nor knew what eye was on me nor the hand
> That nursed me, more than infants in their sleep."

All this time Ida is unremitting in her attendance:—

> "And still she fear'd that I should lose my mind;
> And often she believed that I should die:
> Till out of long frustration of her care
> And pensive tendance in the all-weary noons,
> And watches in the dead, the dark, when clocks
> Throbb'd thunder thro' the palace floors, or called
> On flying time from all their silver tongues—
> And out of memories of her kindlier days,
> And sidelong glances at my father's grief,
> And at the happy lovers heart in heart—
> And out of hauntings of my spoken love,
> And lonely listenings to my mutter'd dream,
> And often feeling of the helpless hands,
> And wordless broodings on the wasted cheek—
> From all a closer interest flourished up
> Tenderness touch by touch, and last, to these,
> Love."

The long contest between life and death is at length decided in favor of life. The Prince returns to consciousness; discovers the new-born affection of his mistress; converses eloquently with her on the true position, office, destiny of woman, mixing old-world wisdom with high anticipations of a brighter future: when the curtain drops, and a brief "Epilogue," carrying out the action of the "Prologue," brings the work to a conclusion.

A large part of the critical objections urged against "The Princess" relate to the person of the heroine. Her character is charged with inconsistency: "a virago in the progress of the work, she appears at the close in all the modesty and softness of her sex: the reader is offended at the outset by her severity, by the self-will and obstinacy which she shows; and afterwards, when the metamorphosis occurs, when the lioness becomes the lamb, he feels the *incredulus odi*, he cannot trust the transformation." This criticism is not wholly without foundation: yet we feel that it mistakes the earlier phase of Ida's character. The delineation of the poet shows us a being strong in will, with great energy and great persistency, but not destitute of gentleness or tenderness. A generous feeling forms the very basis of her faults. It is not pride and ambition which urge her to engage in her great enterprise for elevating woman: it is the view of wrong, of the weaker suffering from the injustice of the stronger, of female degradation and oppression—evils which the poet in his reconciling conclusion acknowledges as real: "these were the rough ways of the world till now"—evils which we must all deplore in the past, whatever we may think as to the proper remedy for the future. Personally she is not affected by these evils; her station places her above their reach: but, full of generous sympathy, she dedicates her life to the redress of injuries of which others are the victims. Surely there is nothing very vixenish in this. She has indeed her theory as to the way in which her objects are to be effected: a method of her own, a grand catholicon for social maladies. It is her college, on which she has "toiled and wrought and thought;" with which she has become identified in all her feelings, hopes, and wishes. This scheme of hers she comes to regard with the natural fondness of a projector: and now doubtless pride of opinion, ambitious longings for the triumph of her principles and plans, appear among the motives of her conduct. Still, the noble object which at first attracted her is never absent from her mind: a high enthusiasm flashes through mists of vanity and selfishness, which dim but cannot hide its splendor. If she is severe against all that menaces her darling scheme, it is not alone because the scheme is hers, but because it involves to her view a millennium of happiness. The faults of the Princess illustrate, as they were certainly intended to illustrate, the havoc which devotion to a theory may work in the best nature. The reader is made to feel that they are not essential elements of the character, but excrescences upon it, the noxious growth of a mistaken system. The poet exposes them with conscientious love of truth; but at the same time shows us here and there many traits of natural amiable feeling, which prepare us for his heroine's last development, and make us ready to believe the Prince, when he says—

> "Ere seen I loved, and loved thee seen, and saw
> Thee woman thro' the crust of iron moods
> That mask'd thee from men's reverence up, and forced
> Sweet love on pranks of saucy boyhood."

Thus, for instance, speaking of the Prince, she says—

> "To nurse a blind ideal like a girl,
> Methinks he seems no better than a girl:
> As girls were once, *as we ourselves have been:*
> *We had our dreams; perhaps he mixt with them:*"

and shortly after,—

> "Yet will we say for children, would they grew
> Like field flowers everywhere! we like them well—
> Children—that men may pluck them from our hearts,
> Kill us with pity, break us with ourselves—
> O—children—there is nothing upon earth
> More miserable than she that has a son
> And sees him err."

When the Lady Psyche is forced from college precincts, her infant daughter is retained:—

> "For this lost lamb (she pointed to the child)
> Our mind is changed: we assume it to ourselves."

After the tournament, when urged by friend and foe to restore the child, she thus addresses it:—

> "Pretty bud!
> Lily of the vale! half opened bell of the woods!
> Sole comfort of my dark hour, when a world
> Of traitorous friend and broken system made
> No purple in the distance, mystery,
> Pledge of a love not to be mine, farewell;
> These men are hard upon us as of old;
> We two must part: and yet how fain was I
> To dream thy cause embraced in mine, to think
> I might be something to thee, when I felt
> Thy waxen warmth about my milkless breast
> In the dead prime."

Even in her more heroic strain, the attentive reader will discern a something not altogether natural, a nerving of the heart to heavy toils and painful sacrifices, an inward struggle to stifle softer feelings because their indulgence seems inconsistent with the claims of solemn duty. She is apparently forcing herself on to a hardness alien from her real character, but regarded as essential to her arduous enterprise. Hence when circumstances come to modify her views, and a new passion springs up in her heart, and the fanaticism, noble but mistaken, of a narrow system passes away, the reader is not surprised to witness the full blossoming of a tenderness, the germs of which he had before seen, chilled but not destroyed by the frosts of theory and prejudice. The irrepressible passion of her lover, and the hearty fondness of her stout brother Arac have made him feel from the first that there must be something truly lovable about her. This feeling of his gains confirmation from her generous sacrifices for the good of others, from the honest enthusiasm which animates her most unwomanly words and actions; it is strengthened into certainty by the beautiful and natural expressions which from time to time force their way out against all opposition; and it has its full realization in the final purified and softened development of her character.

Some are displeased with the pedantry, as they call it, of the Princess, and vote her an intolerable blue. It is no wonder, certainly, that one shut out from the ordinary objects of attention and pursuit among her sex should seek to fill their place by science: especially as a severer mental discipline is an important feature in her favorite scheme. That it should figure in her conversation follows from the same conditions. What has she left to talk of but her studies and her plans? Her principal theme, however, is not science, but social regeneration: she is not a pedant, but a reformer. She is eloquent on woman's rights, their violation in the past, their vindication in the future: and if when discoursing on these topics she falls into the style of a lecturer or haranguer, it is only a natural result of her theory, and well illustrates the inherent opposition of that theory to true womanly decorum. Yet here, it must be owned, we find a serious difficulty, belonging to the subject of the poem and inseparable from it, one which the poet himself must have felt most keenly: how to engage his heroine in this Amazonian movement without unsexing her, without making her unfeminine, and so breaking the charm with which she was to be invested. His success in the attempt, if not complete, seems to be as nearly so as the nature of the case admits. It should not be forgotten that the prime mover in the business is the Lady Blanche, an artful, selfish, and ambitious dowager, who receives charge of the girl Princess after her mother's death, and by her talents and acquirements has gained an ascendency over her pupil's mind. With her the college scheme originates, designed of course solely for her own aggrandizement. Working on Ida's lively sympathies and taking advantage of her inexperience, she enlists her in the undertaking, which once undertaken her own force of character and sanguine temper, and withal her natural pride, will not allow her to abandon, will not allow her even to weigh in the balance of an impartial judgment.

The two collaborators of the Princess serve admirably as foils, to show the superiority of their head. Lady Blanche is hollow and heartless, plausible in appearances, false in professions, governed in all by sordid motives. Lady Psyche on the other hand is swayed by personal attachment; it is her affection for the Princess which has led her to embark in the grand enterprise: she has indeed some understanding of its objects and a certain sympathy for them; but there is no basis of principle, no disposition to suffer martyrdom for the cause in which she is engaged, though for the person of her mistress she would willingly endure it. The Princess Ida alone has a genuine enthusiasm founded on a firm conviction; she is sustained through difficulty and danger by an unshaken faith in the goodness of her cause; she believes strongly and therefore acts strongly; she rises before us in the dignity of a superior nature, great in its excellences, great even in its errors.

The poem abounds in trios; the most distinctly drawn, and altogether the most striking, being the lady-trio just described. But we have again the three brothers of the Princess, the invincible Arac and the doughty twins—"*fortisque Gyas fortisque Cloanthus*"—undistinguished in character, and serving only as opposites in tournament to the Prince and his companions. Here in this suitor-trio, on the other hand, we find more marked diversity.

> "That morning in the presence-room I stood
> With Cyril and with Florian, my two friends:
> The first a gentleman of broken means
> (His father's fault), but given to starts and bursts
> Of revel; and the last, my other heart,
> My shadow, my half-self, for still we moved
> Together, kin as horse's ear and eye."

Cyril is a light sketchy character, but drawn with great spirit. His unfailing gayety, his careless humor, the mask of recklessness which he contrives to throw over a nature honest and honorable at bottom, remind us strongly of the dashing heroes of Beaumont and Fletcher. As for Florian, he is a mere double to the Prince, convenient in the conduct of the plot, but without any striking specialty of mind and character.

The Prince himself has failed of satisfying critics. His character has been censured as at once meagre and inconsistent. On the one hand, it is urged that there is nothing distinctive about him, no individual traits, no personal peculiarities: he is a mere stock hero of romance. But we should be careful lest we exact too much. What more can justly be demanded of a young Prince than that he be frank and generous and faithful, brave and gentle, beautiful and loving? Do not these qualities suffice to constitute a noble character? do they not afford fair augury for a good life and glorious actions? "True, but then they are too common: we find them in every novel: in a great poem we have the right to claim and to expect something different." But this wide diffusion of the character only proves that it awakens universal interest, and is therefore well suited to the purposes of romantic fiction. Such a hero, it should seem, forms in general the most convenient centre for the various figures and actions of the piece. Nor is it right to quarrel with the character for its ideal perfection, to claim that for the sake of variety it should be made crafty, irascible, or garrulous; as well might you quarrel with the symmetry of an Apollo Belvedere, and insist on giving it a more marked appearance by the truncation of the nose or the elongation of the chin.

But the Prince, again, equally with his betrothed, stands accused of inconsistency. "He starts, a boy, a mere love-sick boy, who steals disguised and undetected into a female college, who finds no difficulty in passing himself off for a woman: yet anon we see him tilting in the lists, a champion of no mean note: soon, recovering from protracted sickness, he appears mature in mind, a poet-sage, uttering maxims of profoundest wisdom." As regards the question whether it is physically possible for one who could successfully disguise himself in woman's weeds to bear his part with honor in the deadly conflict of the tourney, we shall not presume to decide. We are content with referring to the martial heroines of Tasso and Ariosto, whose exploits seem to prove that, whether true or not in actual life, in the imaginary world of the romancer such a thing is not impossible. And in the same imaginary world, the act of donning such disguise assumed for no base end may be looked upon as little worse than what our Prince himself has called it, "a prank of saucy boyhood." The effervescence of a frolic humor, it does not of necessity imply a want of manly energy or honorable feeling. It is not inconsistent even with that noble peroration; in which, however, let it be observed, the quality most prominent is not hoary-headed wisdom, but truth of natural feeling.

The Prince's ideal of woman is founded on the example of a mother, "who was mild as any saint, and almost canonized by all she knew, so gracious was her tact and tenderness;" and whatever such a model could not furnish would be readily supplied by the instincts and the experience of a loving heart. Thus inspired and guided may our hero, without incurring the charge of wisdom beyond his years, break out into a strain of poetry, which we cannot deny ourselves the pleasure of quoting:—

> "For woman is not undevelopt man,
> But diverse: could we make her as the man,
> Sweet love were slain, whose dearest bond is this,
> Not like to like, but like in difference;
> Yet in the long years liker must they grow:
> The man be more of woman, she of man;
> He gain in sweetness and in moral height,
> Nor lose the wrestling thews that throw the world;
> She mental breadth, nor fail in childward care:
> More as the double-natured poet each:
> Till at the last she set herself to man,
> Like perfect music unto noble words."
> ————————"And this proud watchword rest
> Of equal; seeing either sex alone
> Is half itself, and in true marriage lies
> Nor equal, nor unequal: each fulfils
> Defect in each, and always thought in thought,
> Purpose in purpose, will in will, they grow,
> The single pure and perfect animal,
> The two-cell'd heart, beating with one full stroke
> Life."

But the objections take a wider range. Much is said of the improbability—worse than that, the impossibility and sheer absurdity of the story, which, as no one can suppose it true, or make it real to his mind, is declared unfit to awaken interest and call forth sympathy. We cannot deny our skepticism as to the occurrences narrated in "The Princess:" we do not find them in the history of past or present, nor do we look for them in the developments of the future. And doubtless, were we closely questioned, we should be forced to make a similar admission as to the Orlando Furioso and the Midsummer Night's Dream, poems which are nevertheless acknowledged to possess high poetic excellence. The truth is, that the probability required in such a work is not absolute but relative ; it is a probability founded in the assumptions of the author. Is the work adequately *motived?* does it contain the power necessary for its own propulsion ? do the forces given at the outset, with those afterwards brought in, harmonize in all their operation ? will their united action account sufficiently well for the effects described ? We have a right indeed to claim, as this statement obviously implies, that the forces shall be generally intelligible, such as we can understand and feel the meaning of : they must have a true relation to our common nature ; they must be consistent with the universal principles that govern human conduct. But the particular conditions under which they are to act are left to the fancy or the judgment of the poet. If you would form a critical estimate of "The Princess," assume the external conditions of the work. Do not concern yourself about the situation of the northern and southern kingdoms : take them for granted. Do not be surprised that woman's rights have come to be acknowledged even in princely halls : assume the fact of such a recognition. Do not vex your mind with the manifold obstacles which hinder the organization of a female college : leave them to the Princess Ida, and suppose them happily surmounted. But inquire whether, on the given conditions, the enthusiasm of the Princess, her ardor in the prosecution of a great moral work, her attachment to a system of agencies regarded as the necessary means of its accomplishment—whether these motives operating on a nature such as hers are not sufficient to account for her conduct. Let the same method be extended to all the persons and actions of the poem. We are persuaded that the result of such a criticism would be to weaken very much the charges of improbability, so often loosely brought against our author's plot.

It is said, however, that we cannot thus accept the external conditions of the work, because they are inconsistent in themselves ; presenting an aggregate of incongruities, a cabinet of curiosities filled with ill-assorted specimens from every time and country, a confused mass of forms, principles, ideas such as never have been and never can be united in the actual world. This view of the poem is strongly stated by an able critic in the North British Review for May, 1848 :—

"'The Princess; a Medley,' upon the first reading has a very curious effect. It is so thoroughly 'a medley,' its heterogeneousness is so complete, that we wonder how any mind should have been able to escape the apparently inevitable continuity with which feelings and ideas suggest themselves. Tragedy, comedy, love, satire, the old and the new, modern conventionalisms and outrageous fancies, all contrarieties come together, and at first appear to clash."

And again, after a synopsis of the story :—

"There are numerous other instances and characters, all wonderfully elaborated, which we have not noticed because they have no connection whatever with the main plot: but, had we done so, we should still have fallen far short of giving the reader a notion of the utter want of interest, unity, and purpose in this production, considered merely as a narrative poem; and of its miserable weakness and want of integrity, if regarded, as some regard it, as a satire upon learned women. Now by regarding it as neither the one nor the other, and attributing to it some significance of which the incidents and characters are merely symbolical expressions, we at once do away with an overwhelming amount of difficulty and contradiction, and are enabled to reconcile its composition with the quality of Mr. Tennyson's genius."

If this were so, the work might perhaps pass for a tolerable allegory or enigma; but it would be a wretched poem. It could advance no claim to be regarded as a work of art: for art can never be indifferent to outward form; it requires not merely a unity of idea, but a certain order, proportion, and harmony in the symbols by which ideas are represented. The fantastic painting in the Ars Poetica would still be a miserable picture, though you should give it symbolical significance, and show that the intellectual objects denoted by the human head, the horse's neck, and the various plumage stand in the most natural relation to each other. On the other hand, let men, birds, and horses be grouped together in a painting which has consistency and beauty, and we recognize the merit of the picture without much reference to its spiritual meaning. A certain degree of coherence is essential even to the allegory: we should have been displeased with Bunyan, if his Pilgrim had appeared as a monkey or a mouse, in order to adumbrate some moral transformation.

There is no difficulty in admitting that our author in his present work intended to portray the passing time in many of its aspects. This design is clearly indicated in his Prologue, and it accords well with the views expressed in numerous passages of his earlier poems. He is by no means one of those poets who live wholly in the ideal world. He is alive to all that is living and stirring around him; watches with eager interest the great progress of thought and knowledge and action; and stamps upon his works the fire-new impress of the current day. He not merely appreciates the present, but delights in it, as the grand result of all past ages, rich in the spoils of time, in its own acquisitions, and still more in "the promise that it closes." He does not reclaim in impotent vexation against a progress which he cannot check: but welcomes in every hour "a bringer of new things;" acknowledges that "meet is it changes should control our being, lest we rot in ease;" holds it "better men should perish one by one, than that earth should stand at gaze like Joshua's moon in Ajalon;" and kindling with enthusiasm cries, "Forward, forward let us range: let the nations spin forever down the ringing grooves of change." That the works of such a poet should present manifold reflections of the present age can occasion no surprise. Many passages of "The Princess" are direct expressions of ideas, principles, and feelings peculiar to our own time. In many instances he has made use of representative forms: that is, he has taken some particular phenomenon, and made it stand for a large class of similar phenomena to which it is related. This is especially the case with his "university for maidens," which may be viewed as representing a multitude of rampant radicalisms. All this, however, is very different from that continuous allegory, that perpetual succession of metaphors, embracing every detail of the poem, which our Scottish contemporary assumes, though he candidly admits his inability to interpret the greater part of them:—

"Let us frankly confess that an unusually careful study of this poem has not enabled us to discover any such distinct connection between the greater portion of its details, and what we conceive to be the central thought; upon which, if the poem be a truly artistical work, they must every one of them depend for their primary meaning and value. Very many are the thoughts, allusions, traits of character and incidents, the true meaning of which we seem to perceive fully: very many appear to us to possess only some half-perceived capacity of application to the central thought: but very many more have proved too enigmatical for our patience or our powers."

We hardly know why the critic should have given up these latter points. A writer intent on this sort of interpretation, and gifted with a tolerable share of ingenuity, can have little difficulty in educing meaning out of any text; he can even find for the same text as many meanings as Swedenborgians attribute to the words of Scripture. But the whole attempt strikes us as a profitless expenditure of thought, by which nothing like certainty could ever be attained. It is a wandering through labyrinthine forests with an ignis fatuus for your only guide. The work which cannot be justified except by such a guess-work process may be pronounced, in the language of debating societies, "wholly unjustifiable." *Davus sum, non Œdipus.* We shall wait till the author publishes a key to his own riddle-book, before we meddle with its puzzles; before we concede that it was designed by the author and is to be treated by the critic only as a puzzle.

It cannot be denied that the poem shows in different parts a difference of tone and coloring. The author himself admits the fact in his "Epilogue:"—

"Here closed our compound story, which at first
Perhaps but meant to banter little maids
With mock-heroics and with parody:
But slipt in some strange way, crost with burlesque,
From mock to earnest, even into tones
Of tragic, and with less and less of jest."

This mixing up of grave and gay, serious and mirthful, tragedy and comedy, has given some offence, and in the judgment of the ingenious critic quoted above can only be defended on the ground of allegorical significance. Would he say the same of the Midsummer Night's Dream, or Hamlet Prince of Denmark? The example of our great dramatist has shown that the close association of the tragic and the comic, which so constantly presents itself in real life, is not inadmissible in the creations of art; that they may aid each other as the lights and shadows of a picture; that the lighter portions are useful to relieve the eye, while by contrast they throw the dark into still deeper gloom. And whether it be correct appreciation or misjudging fondness we know not; but in this poem of Tennyson's, it appears to us that the two elements, so far from neutralizing one another, are blended into harmony, and receive each a heightened beauty from their union.

After all that may be said about the absurdity and incoherence of the story, it certainly produces the impression of reality in a degree which, when the nature of the incidents is considered, must be thought truly wonderful. So vividly and clearly does the poet delineate the creatures of his fancy that we cannot help viewing them as actual existences. We find ourselves sympathizing with the Prince, and wishing him success in his arduous suit. We feel the rush of breathless expectation in the hot *mêlée* of the tourney. We wait anxiously the turn of fate beside the sick-bed of the wounded lover. We give him our heartiest congratulations on his eventual recovery and success. It is only when we set ourselves to criticizing that we are struck with the improbability of that which moved us, and become ashamed of our former feelings. In no former production has the author succeeded in giving so much the air of reality to the objects of his imagination; nor has he shown in any one so much delicacy and distinctness in the delineation of character.

The poetry of our day has been almost exclusively lyrical. Moving hotly and hurriedly in the career of politics, or swallowed up in business, or prosecuting science with a zeal and success never before paralleled, we have found no time for lengthened poems. Only now and then could we snatch a moment for a brief utterance of feelings which belong to human nature, and can never be utterly lost even in the maddest vortices of life. As for great constructive poems, vast systems of narrative, meditation, and description, built up in the deeps of an ideal world, they have well-nigh disappeared. In America, where the influences that oppose their construction are the strongest, we have nothing of the kind; our poets have to a singular extent been song-writers; while the occasional attempts which we have seen in epic and dramatic composition have been generally unsuccessful. Yet this has been almost equally the case in England. What long poem of any note has appeared there since the "Excursion?" and what is the Excursion itself but a long lyric?—no narrative of action; no development of character; no plot or story; no complication of incidents; no catastrophe or *dénouement;* no unity, but that of a rosary; a series of lyrical exercises, for the most part didactic, strung loosely on the very slightest thread of story. Byron wrote narrative poems of some length; but his genius was essentially lyrical. The plots of his Corsair, Lara, Giaour, etc., will not stand the lightest touch of criticism; barren and confused, they serve only as openings for fine description or eloquent declamation. Nor does Don Juan in the aimless ramblings of its hero show anything more of constructive power. In Southey's epics, if we may use a name which the poet himself rejected with contempt, we find our best recent specimens of epic art. Yet we know not how the critics who blame "The Princess" for its inconsequences and improbabilities could defend the grotesque wonders of "Thalaba the Destroyer" or the "Curse of Kehama." Is it said that these are to be tolerated as forms of actual belief, importations from Pantheons of mythologies currently received among our fellow-men? But how does that lessen the incredulity with which we look upon such wild and monstrous fictions? Or would the college of the Princess Ida seem to us one whit more probable, could we find some Hottentot or Eskimo who held it for undoubted verity? And again, the inconsistency arising from a mixture of incompatible ideas, which is urged against Tennyson, may be charged with equal justice on the elder poet, who has by no means treated the religions of India and Arabia in the spirit of their devotees, but has allowed the notions and feelings of the Christian to appear among the symbols of the Mohammedan and the Brahman.

It may be thought, however, that in naming his work "a Medley" the poet has given up the whole point; that he has decided the question, and decided it against himself. But the name indicates no more than the widely diverse character of the materials employed in the building of his work; it cannot be justly construed as a confession that no care was used in the selection, and no art in the arrangement. And if a writer modestly apply a slighting name to his own production, we should not press the circumstance against him. It is not to be supposed that an artist such as Mr. Tennyson has shown himself to be, would inflict a mere medley on the public. He would feel it beneath himself to waste the treasures of his fancy and the classic riches of his diction on a heap of unconnected, aimless, and incongruous absurdities. Nor would he consent to forfeit a well-earned reputation by bringing such a work, were he even capable of writing it, before the bar of intelligent criticism. We may rest assured that there is some point of view from which the poem will appear as other than a medley; from which we shall be able, not perhaps to justify the composition in all particulars, for the highest genius must still fall short of absolute perfection; but to comprehend at least how it was possible for a man of genius to be the author of such a composition.

Mr. Tennyson has evidently taken extraordinary pains with the construction of his verse. He seems to have felt that a single measure running through a long poem must of necessity become monotonous and wearisome, unless great care be taken to diversify its rhythm. He may have thought also that a narrative piece, where the poet must rely less upon the thought and more upon the form than in other species of poetical composition, requires peculiarly the aid of metrical resources. Certain it is that, in affluence of means and in variety of effects, the blank verse of "The Princess" surpasses all its author's previous attempts in the same kind of measure; nor would it be easy to find its equal in these respects since the time of Milton. To the versification of the Paradise Lost, the greatest exemplar of versification in the English language, Mr. Tennyson, it is clear, has given no little attention; and from this poem, and from the older English poetry in general, he has adopted many rhythmical and metrical expedients—liberties or licenses, as they are sometimes called—which the too finical taste of later times, and the undue passion for uniformity, have generally discarded. Among these we mention the so-called elision—more truly, the blending of a final vowel with the vowel initial of a following word into a single syllable, or at least what passes for such in the rhythm. Thus we have—

> "That made *the old* warrior from his ivied nook
> Glow like a sunbeam."

> "The violet varies from the *lily as* far
> As oak from elm."

> "O Swallow, *Swallow*, *if* I could *follow*, *and* light
> Upon her lattice."

So, too, where the second word begins with a weak consonant easily elided in pronunciation :—

> "Fly *to her*, and pipe and *woo her*, and make her mine."

> "You must not *slay him :* he risked his life for ours."

The same fusion occurs often in a single word, and not only in such forms as *lovelier*, *sapience*, etc., where all our poets have employed it, but in many instances where the last two centuries have renounced its use. Thus, in the following lines, the words *seeing*, *crying*, *highest* go for monosyllables in the rhythm :—

> "And Cyril *seeing* it, push'd against the Prince."

> "Some *crying* there was an army in the land."

> "And *highest* among the statues, statue-like."

The combinations *in the*, *of the*, etc., are often treated as filling but one rhythmical place :—

> "Better have died, and spilt our bones *in the* flood."

> "Poets, whose thoughts enrich the blood *of the* world."

> "*When the* man wants weight, the woman takes it up."

In many instances a short syllable is neglected—that is, does not count as forming by itself a place in the metre. In the following quotation, the words *enemy*, *general*, *soluble* are treated as dissyllables :—

> "Now she lightens scorn
> At *the enemy* of her plan, but then would hate
> The *general* foe. More *soluble* is the knot."

Especially does this occur where a short final syllable is followed by a word beginning with a vowel :—

> "A *palace* in our own land, where you shall reign."
>
> "A tent of *satin*, elaborately wrought."

We could distinguish other cases, in which a reader unfamiliar with the earlier English rhythms might be offended by supernumerary syllables : but to enter upon long details would perhaps be more tedious than profitable. In none of these instances, if we may judge of Mr. Tennyson's pronunciation from his way of writing, would he omit a syllable in reading : nor does the rhythm of the verse (let metrical doctors, like Mr. Guest, say what they please about it) require of us the use of any such expedient. Yet, as the same word or combination may receive in different places a different metrical arrangement, the reader, unless he proceeds with unusual foresight, will sometimes be obliged to take a new start and try it over again. This difficulty might be obviated by the use of some appropriate notation ; the elisions and apostrophes of the old books are of course objectionable, if nothing is to be elided ; but it is much to be wished that some method might be substituted for them, to make the proper mode of reading obvious at first sight.

The poem presents us with many passages in which the rhythm is very studiously adapted to the sense. In some of these perhaps the thing is overdone ; but in most the effect is admirable. We instance the following fine exhibition of "the pomp and circumstance of glorious war :"—

> "They made a halt ;
> The horses yell'd ; they clashed their arms ; the drums
> Beat ; merrily blowing shrill'd the martial fife ;
> And in the blast and bray of the long horn
> And serpent-throated bugle, undulated
> The banner ; anon to meet us lightly pranced
> Three Captains out."

The overwhelming onset of Prince Arac is described in verses not unfit for the exploits of divine Achilles :—

> "But that large-moulded man
> Made at me thro' the press, and staggering back
> With stroke on stroke the horse and horseman, came
> As comes a pillar of electric cloud,
> Flaying off the roofs and sucking up the drains,
> And shadowing down the champaign till it strikes
> On a wood, and takes, and breaks, and cracks, and splits,
> And twists the grain with such a roar that the earth
> Reels, and the herdsmen cry; for everything
> Gave way before him."

A waterfall is thus represented in words which address themselves at once to mind and sense :—

> "And up we came to where the river sloped
> *To plunge in cataract, shattering on black blocks,*
> A breadth of thunder."

In the following passage, describing the rescue of the Princess, the verse is managed with much art :—

> "There whirled her white robe like a blossom'd branch
> Rapt to the horrible fall: a glance I gave,
> No more; but woman-vested as I was,
> *Plunged; and the flood drew: yet I caught her;* then
> Oaring one arm, and bearing in my left
> The weight of all the hopes of half the world,
> *Strove to buffet to land in vain.*"

The rhythm of the last line (which occurs quite frequently in the Paradise Lost) is admirably adapted to express laborious and unsuccessful effort. Not unlike it is the following :—

> "While now her breast,
> Beaten with some great passion at her heart,
> *Palpitated, her hand shook,* and we heard
> In the dead hush the papers that she held
> Rustle."

We are tempted to assume the same movement in another place :—

> "they to and fro
> *Fluctuated as flowers in storm,* some red, some pale"—

and to suppose that the poet, intentionally or inadvertently, extended the line beyond the regular standard. It can be read indeed as a verse of five accents, but not without taking from the aptness of the rhythm. Breathlessness is thus described :—

> "And on a sudden ran in
> *Among us, all out of breath, as pursued,*
> A woman-post in flying raiment."

In this instance, however, the poet seems to have been more ingenious than successful: the verse breaks down under his ménage ; the line, as naturally read, has but four accents, and it is not without difficulty that the reader comes to understand the metrical intention of the writer.

In his use of language Mr. Tennyson has shown himself in this work uncommonly adventurous ; but he has in general adventured with a happy boldness. He abounds in striking novelties, in words, meanings, and constructions seldom or never found elsewhere ; and thus, it must be owned, produces on the reader's mind a first impression that his style is more or less artificial and affected. On a second reading this impression for the most part disappears. Many phrases which at first seem quaint and odd are soon perceived to have a propriety and a beauty which justify their strangeness. We accept the language as the appropriate vesture of the thought, and feel that no other vesture would become it half so well. One thing certainly is true : the words, be they good, bad, or indifferent, are never the unmeaning substitutes for thought : they are always richly freighted with sense and sentiment. Mr. Tennyson is not one of those copious and fluent writers who can turn off verses by the ream ; he has no patent machine for the manufacture of poetry. His compositions are widely different from the voluminous and flimsy job work of literary artisans ; widely different, too, from the productions of many real artists, who are wont to use the best materials, but weave them hastily in thin and ill-compacted fabrics. Our recent poetry even of the better sort has been too generally written *currente calamo;* in many cases it hardly mounts above the reach of a ready-witted improvisatore. You read it, possibly, with interest and pleasure; but it neither makes a definite impression on the mind, nor gains an abiding home in the memory. You may remember the subject of the work and something of its plot or course of thought; but words and images and sentences are gone; quotation is impossible. Seldom, too seldom, do you meet with expressions singularly felicitous, or lines which realize Coleridge's ideal, where every change conceivable would be a change for the worse; or passages which seem like the spontaneous crystallization of great sentiments and principles; or utterances which might make one think he heard the Muse herself pronouncing oracles for the instruction and delight of every coming age. It is a singular circumstance that Coleridge, who was so much of an improviser in his prose, should have been, almost alone among his contemporaries, so sparing and elaborate in his poetry. In Tennyson we see the same frugality of verse, the same studious care and conscientious toil in execution. He does not spread himself out upon paper, but brings his whole material within the narrowest compass. Far from dispersing the rays of his genius in divergent lines, he gathers them in luminous centres, which shine clear and bright like the stars. To one who writes in this way, each word becomes a matter of importance, a subject for careful thought and nice selection. He cannot take whatever comes first or lies nearest; he must ransack the treasury of language, to find that which will most aptly, tersely, forcibly express his meaning. Sometimes it may be an old-world word, which men have latterly forgotten, but may well bring back to memory; sometimes a word from the living mintage of the poet's own brain, carrying its warrant in its use and justly claiming place among the currency of older dates; sometimes a colloquialism that deserves to be ennobled; sometimes an expressive idiom coming from abroad, and naturalized with full rights of native citizenship. A style thus diligently selected and compacted can hardly fail to have a certain quaintness; and some such quality may have been apparent, even from the first, in the writings of Spenser and Jonson and Milton. The time has been when it was regarded as the very *beau idéal* of style that it should resemble fashionable conversation. Fortunately, the feeling now-a-days is very different. We claim for conversation a freedom greater than it once enjoyed, and for writing a freedom greater than we yield to conversation. We allow the writer to consult his own taste as to the colors and the fashions in which he shall present himself before the public. We do not regard even language itself as a thing inflexible and immutable, which all are to accept and use exactly alike. We acknowledge in the writer, especially in the man of genius, a certain power over language; a right of origination, not to make himself unintelligible, but to make himself more intelligible; a right to share actively in that progress which, spite of all conservative resistance, is the inevitable condition of a living language, and the cessation of which proves a language to be really dead, unfit for the living use of living men.

XVII.

THE NUMBER SEVEN.*

1858.

IT is well known that men of different times and nations have associated with particular numbers the idea of a peculiar significance and value. It is also well known that, of all numbers, there is no one which has exercised in this way a wider influence, no one which has commanded in a higher degree the esteem and reverence of mankind, than the number Seven. The mystic preëminence of this sacred number is as ancient as it is venerable. It belongs to the simple wisdom of a primitive age. It had its native home in the East, near the springs of light and of day. True, we find it also in later times, and upon occidental ground, pervading the mind and literature of modern Europe. But we must remember that an Oriental book, an Asiatic book, the Sacred Scripture of the Hebrew, has leavened—may we not add that it has *sevened*—the mind and literature of modern Europe. But before this influence began, before a new religion coming into Europe from the East brought with it the Oriental feeling for the Seven, the case was widely different. Among the ancient Greeks and Romans, but little prominence upon the whole is given to this number. Let us look at the first great monuments of western literature, the poems of Homer. Here we find a number of sevens. Seven talents are more than once bestowed as a present. Seven tripods, seven women, and seven towns are among the gifts by which Agamemnon seeks to propitiate the enraged Achilles. Then there are seven ships of Philoctetes, seven brothers of Andromache, seven sons of Polyctor, seven gates of the Bœotian Thebes, seven layers of ox-hide in the

---

* Von Hammer-Purgstall, Ueber die Zahl Sieben. (Wiener Jahrbücher der Literatur. 1848. CXXII. 182–225. CXXIII. 1—54. CXXIV. 1—105.)

impenetrable shield of Ajax, seven herds of cattle belonging to the sun-god Helios, seven roods of ground covered by the fallen war-god Ares. Seven years the murderer Ægisthus reigns upon the throne of Agamemnon ; seven years Ulysses is kept a prisoner by the fondness of the nymph Calypso ; seven years in his romancing story to Eumæus he professes to have spent in Egypt. In four instances in the Odyssey, some action is described as continuing for six days and terminating on the seventh in some critical event—a curious circumstance, in which we might almost be tempted to trace either a dawning or a vanishing of the *week*. This is the list of Homeric sevens, nearly complete : it may appear somewhat long ; but there are quite as many tens in Homer, and of twelves almost twice as many. In the Greek mythology—and it is the mythology of a nation that most faithfully reflects its early thinking and feeling—the Seven is quite rare, and is nearly confined to the worship of Apollo ; the Twelve again is greatly more important as a mythological number. From Greek philosophy, however, the Seven has received a more respectful attention. The Pythagoreans, who in general laid much stress upon the mystic properties of number, had a special regard for the seven. Thus Philolaus, the contemporary of Socrates, and the first to set forth, in writing, an extended exposition of Pythagorean doctrine, says concerning God, the author and governor of all things, that "he is without variation, ever like himself and like no other, even as the number seven." But it will be recollected that Pythagoras, according to the general tradition, had travelled in the East, and was supposed to have drawn from thence, to a greater or less extent, the elements of his system. All have heard of the Seven Sages, or Wise Men of Greece ; men who, about six centuries before Christ, were highly distinguished among their contemporaries for wisdom and experience ; of whom the most celebrated were the Milesian Thales and the Athenian Solon. It may have been a philosopher who first conceived the idea of selecting out just seven such men to form the group. It is at any rate a philosopher—Plato, himself also a traveller in the East—who first gives us the seven names, selected out and grouped together. But the

Seven in this case does not seem to have taken very strong hold of the Greek mind, or to have possessed inviolable sanctity; for Dicæarchus substitutes ten sages for the seven, and Hermippus enumerates seventeen. Again, the idea of Seven Wonders of the World, which we find among the Greeks, appears to have originated in the East, with the Egyptian Greeks of Alexandria. One of the seven wonders belongs to Alexandria itself, the light-house in its bay. A second is also Egyptian, the pyramids. Of the remaining five, only one is European, the statue of Zeus at Olympia; while four are Asiatic—the Ephesian temple of Diana, the Mausoleum of Artemisia, the Colossus at Rhodes, and the hanging gardens of Babylon. The conquests of the Macedonians, and after them the Romans in the East, the wide dispersion of the Jews, and, following that, the still wider diffusion of Christianity, all had the effect of acquainting the European mind more and more with Oriental ideas. And hence it comes that, in the centuries after Christ, we find a large number even of heathen writers who render homage to the sacredness and dignity of the Seven. We will not dwell upon them here; but will rather turn to lands where a veneration for the Seven appears unborrowed and original. We will look first to the far East, to the banks of the Indus and the Ganges, to the votaries of the Brahman religion.

According to the conceptions of the Indians, Mount Meru, the sacred mountain of the gods, is surrounded by the seven rocks called Cakravarta, rising in the mystic regions of the atmosphere. Indra, the great lord of the sky, governs by seven vice-kings the seven regions of the heaven. Agni, the god of fire, is thus addressed in one of the sacred books: "Seven are thy fuels, seven thy tongues, seven thy holy sages, seven thy favorite haunts, in seven ways thy worshippers adore thee, seven are thy sources; be graciously content with thy clarified butter!" The sun has his seven rays, which are themselves described as suns, and pour down their sevenfold heat on the torrid land of the Hindu. The earth itself has its seven Dvipas, seven islands encompassed by as many seas—the seas of milk, sugar, honey, salt, salt water, sour water, and butter. Over it blow the winds, Maruts, seven times seven in number. The earth is renewed every seven thousand years, or, as others hold, every seven times seven thousand. There are seven Apsaras or nymphs of Paradise ; seven Saktis, or incarnated attributes of the divinity ; seven Rishis, or holy sages ; seven Munis, or holy hermits. These last are not unknown to Christendom : at least, the name of holy recluses might be given with propriety to our old friends, the seven sleepers of Ephesus. All have heard the story : how, in the great persecution under Decius, seven Christian youths fled for refuge to a mountain near the city of Ephesus, and there hid themselves in a cave. They slept during the night without disturbance, and woke, as they supposed, on the following morning. Venturing out, after some time, to obtain provisions, they attracted notice by their uncouth garb and appearance. Having purchased what they wanted, they offered in payment some strange-looking antique coins. Suspicion was aroused, and they were brought before a magistrate. They then told their story, from which it appeared that the supposed night's sleep had lasted well-nigh two centuries. The bishop Martin was called in, and even the emperor Theodosius II., brought by express from Constantinople ; in whose presence they repeated their narrative, and then, praising God, with the halo of sanctity visibly encircling them, gave up the ghost. The reader is not required to believe the story ; Baronius, the famous church historian, though he swallows a wagon-load of marvels, is squeamish as to this one. It is, indeed, almost as much a Mohammedan as a Christian tradition ; the Koran is all but the earliest authority we can quote for it. Even at this day the Ottoman navy is under the especial guardianship of the Holy Seven Sleepers ; and in sleepiness, if not in holiness, does credit to its sainted patrons. But again, the Brahman system has its seven paradises, and seven hells ; these re-appear in the religion of the Moslim, who, however, adds another paradise, on the ground that God's mercy exceeds his vengeance. Nor are they unknown to Christendom. The celebrated Pico della Mirandola left among his manuscript remains a treatise on the seven heavens and the seven earths, and another on the seven places of hell. In a German poem of the middle ages (*Wolkenstain*), we find the couplet—

> *Das ist die Hell mit irem Slund,*
> *Darin wol siben Kammer greulich sind erzund.*
>
> That is hell with its pit of woe,
> Where in fearful flame seven chambers glow.

It would be easy to extend this enumeration of Indian sevens. But the specimens already given will suffice ; especially as we are not in condition to determine how far they belong to the earlier forms of the Hindu religion, or what proportion they bear to other mythological numbers in the same system. Let us now turn westward to Central Asia, to the countries which formed the heart and strength of the ancient Persian empire. Here in ancient times the prevailing religion was that of Zoroaster, which owns the Zend-Avesta for its Bible, and is professed at the present day only by the scanty remnants of the Parsees. The two great divinities of this religion are Ormuzd (Ahura-mazda), the divinity of light and good, on the one hand ; and, on the other, Ahriman (Angra-mainyus), the divinity of darkness and evil. Ormuzd is surrounded by his attendant spirits, the seven Amshaspands, who may be compared with the seven throne-angels, that, according to the book of Tobit, go in and out before the glory of the Holy One. Ahriman in like manner has his court, composed of seven arch-devs or demons, whom, as regards the number, we might compare with the seven that haunted Mary of Magdala, or with the seven more wicked than himself, whom the evil spirit, after his restless wandering through the desert, took back with him to his former habitation, which he found ready, swept, and garnished—"and the last end of that man was worse than the first."

The modern literature of Persia abounds in sevens. Native dictionaries enumerate above a hundred septenaries, groups of objects designated as the seven so-and-so. We will not undertake to name them. We could not say, what it would be most interesting to know about them, how far they have sprung out of the spontaneous feeling and invention of the Persian, or how far they are due to the Arabian influence, itself saturated with sevens, which entered Persia with the religion of Mohammed in the seventh century of our era.

But let us proceed to ground which has for us the double interest of more familiar acquaintance and more sacred associations. The preëminent importance of the number seven throughout the Bible is seen in the extraordinary frequency of its occurrence. It is found in the Old and New Testaments not less than three hundred and eighty-three times. This count includes the ordinal *seventh*, as well as the compound *sevenfold*; but does not include the higher numbers which contain a seven, such as seventeen, twenty-seven, seventy, seven hundred, and the like. If, now, we count the sixes in the same way, we find them to be one hundred and eighteen. The eights counted in the same way are fifty-eight. The sixes and the eights taken together amount only to one hundred and seventy-six, or less than one-half of the sevens.

The preëminence of the Seven is a fact which meets us at the threshold of the Bible, in the first chapter of Genesis, or in what should be the first chapter. It is well known that an unfortunate blunder in the division has deprived the opening chapter of three verses which justly belong to it. The real break is after the third verse of chapter ii.: for the fourth verse, so far from being connected with those before it, is the commencement of a distinct narrative, composed probably at a different time, and indeed, according to the opinion of many good Biblical scholars, composed by a different writer. Now the first account of the creation, as we find it in the opening chapter with the first three verses of the second, represents to us a sevenfold process, which occupies the first week of world-history, and is made up of six successive acts of creation distributed through six successive days, and terminated like the Hebrew week by a day of rest. It is indeed conceivable that in this account the sevenfold arrangement may belong rather to the form and drapery of the narrative than to its veritable substance: and in fact we find no hint of it in the fourth, fifth, sixth, and seventh verses of the second chapter, which also contain a separate account of the creation. Even thus it would remain true that a sevenfold arrangement was adopted for the more elaborate narrative which was to embody the great truth of an original divine creation; and this circumstance alone would be highly significant; it would demonstrate the preponderant value given by the Hebrew mind to the week and to its number the Seven. Or, again, we may suppose with others that an actual week was spent in this way; that, after an immeasurable past of geological mutations, of trilobites, ichthyosauri, and batrachians, when a new and nobler resident was to be introduced upon our planet, then its existing arrangements were thrown into temporary confusion, and a week was passed in fitting and furnishing it anew for the habitation of man. Such a view might perhaps be regarded as still more honorable to the Seven. Or, yet again, with others, we might swell days till they assume the dimension of ages—seven ages, each with its own separate record, written on the tablet of the earth, in characters which science has been able to decipher, and has found to be identical with the words of the Mosaic description. This view, it is clear, gives the highest exaltation to the Seven. For it makes geology a Seven, and so the mightiest of all sevens. It offers the crowning attestation of science to the secular predominance of this majestic number. It is a view adopted by very eminent scientific men; with whose judgment we could not think of matching our own in a question of this nature. Yet we must not seem to glorify our subject at the expense of honest dealing. The confession must be made, that with the best wishes we have not been able to satisfy ourselves in regard to that view; to be certain that it has a positive basis, that it is more than an ingenious and interesting speculation. If it were otherwise, if we could overcome our doubts on this head, then would we profess ourselves with a more unquestioning faith even than now, votaries of the world-regulating Seven.

But let us proceed with the Old-Testament sevens. The Seven bears an important part in ritual observances. In many sacrifices the sprinkling of the blood was to be repeated seven times; and in many we find seven mentioned as the number of the victims to be offered. But it is still more important in reference to holy times and seasons. Not only is the seventh day of the week honored as a Sabbath with perpetual remembrance, but the seventh week of the year brings its festival, the Pentecost or fiftieth day: for it is separated from the Passover by forty-nine days, a week of weeks, and is therefore sometimes called the feast of weeks. So the seventh month has its festival, the feast of tabernacles, and its solemn fast too upon the tenth day, the great day of atonement. Again, there is a week of years terminating in the seventh or Sabbatical year, when the land was to cease from labor and to lie untilled. And once more, after seven weeks of years, forty-nine years, came the great fiftieth or Year of Jubilee.

Returning to the book of Genesis, we find Noah commanded to receive clean beasts and fowls into the ark by sevens. Seven days after this command the rain begins. Wearied with long imprisonment, Noah sends forth a dove, which returns, having found no rest for the sole of her foot. After seven days he sends her forth again, and she returns with an olive-leaf in her mouth. After seven days more he sends her forth the third time, and she returns to him no more. The patriarch Jacob, in his protracted courtship, after serving seven years for the wife he did not want, was forced to serve another seven for the wife he wanted. In Pharaoh's dream interpreted by Joseph, there are seven fat kine and seven lean, the seven years of plenty and of famine. Seven years occur repeatedly as the duration of a famine. The one in Elisha's time lasts seven years, and among three alternative evils offered to David's option, one is a seven years' famine. The descendants of Jacob return at last to the land of their fathers, from which God had promised to drive out seven nations greater and mightier than they. In the siege of Jericho, the people for seven successive days march round the city, headed by seven priests blowing on seven rams' horns. Only on the seventh day they marched seven times round, and at the seventh time the priests blew, the people shouted, and the wall fell down flat. Samson, when he gave his riddle to the Philistines in Timnath, allowed them the seven days of his wedding feast to make out the solution. When the Philistines were endeavoring through Delilah to discover the secret of his prodigious strength, he first directed that they should bind him with seven green withs, and again that she should weave the seven locks of his head with the web. These methods were tried without success; but when at last the seven locks were quite shaved off, his strength went from him; in the well-known language of the hymn, he "shook his vain limbs with sad surprise, made feeble fight and lost his eyes." But it would be tedious to pursue this enumeration through the whole Bible. Let us pass on to notice a somewhat different class of cases.

In numerous instances the Seven appears to be used, as we say a score or a dozen, for a large indefinite number. The great prominence given to the Seven, and the great respect in which it was held, made it natural that it should be used in this way. Thus in Daniel, the fiery furnace was to be heated for the three recusant Hebrews "one seven times more than it was wont to be heated." In Proverbs we are told that a just man falleth seven times and riseth up again. The Psalmist says, "Seven times a day do I praise thee because of thy righteous judgments." Apparently this was not intended for an exact numerical statement; although being interpreted in that way it is relied upon as authority for the seven canonical hours of devotion; *prima* (or prime), *matutina* (matin), *tertia*, *sexta*, *nona* (noon), *vespera* (vesper), and *completa*. Lamech, who was, like Enoch, seventh from Adam, but in the line of Cain, says to his wives Adah and Zillah, "If Cain shall be avenged sevenfold, truly Lamech seventy and sevenfold." And our Lord, when asked by Peter, "how oft shall my brother sin against me and I forgive him? till seven times?" replies, "I say not unto thee, until seven times, but until seventy times seven."

But of all the inspired books, the last in the series, the Apocalypse, is the one which displays most frequently and prominently the mystic sacredness of the number seven. At the outset John addresses himself to seven churches in Asia, greeting them from the Lord and from the seven spirits which are before his throne. He describes his vision on the isle of Patmos, when he saw one like unto the Son of Man, in the midst of seven golden candlesticks, and holding in his right hand seven stars. The golden candlesticks are explained as being the seven churches, and the seven stars the angels of those churches. In the following visions, a throne is set in heaven, and in the right hand of Him that sat on it is a book sealed with seven seals. Then a lamb with seven horns and seven eyes, which are the seven spirits of God sent forth into all the earth, takes the book and opens the seven seals one after another, the opening in each case being followed by different prodigies. When the seventh seal is opened, seven angels appear with seven trumpets, which they blow one after another, and the blowing is followed in each case by new prodigies. Before the seventh angel sounds, seven thunders utter their voices. Afterwards appears a dragon with seven heads and ten horns and seven crowns upon his heads: and anon a beast rising up out of the sea, also with seven heads and ten horns, but with ten crowns upon his horns. Again another sign in heaven great and marvellous, seven angels having the seven last plagues, who pour out one after another the seven vials of God's wrath upon the earth. Then is seen a woman seated on a scarlet colored beast which has seven heads, these being seven mountains on which the woman sitteth; and it is added, there are seven kings, of whom five are fallen, and one is, and one is yet to come. In the last vision, that of the heavenly Jerusalem, the prevailing number is not seven but twelve, derived evidently from the twelve tribes of Israel. But with this exception seven is everywhere the prevailing number of the book; so that, as Von Hammer-Purgstall observes, there are two sevens in the greeting, seven churches and seven spirits; and in the body of the work there are found besides two sevens of sevens: viz., first, seven candlesticks, stars, seals, horns, eyes, trumpets, thunders; and second, seven angels, heads, crowns, plagues, vials, mountains, kings.

Such being the rank and dignity of the number Seven throughout the Bible, it is not surprising that the nations of Christendom, with whom the Bible is at once the best known and most revered of all books, should have attached special importance to the number. Illustrations of this fact, drawn from the literature of modern Europe, might be multiplied to almost any extent. But I shall confine myself to a single author, one who may be regarded with more propriety than any other as the representative of modern European literature.

The following are specimens of the Shakspearian sevens. In the Merchant of Venice (II. 9), the Prince of Arragon, who comes as a suitor for the hand of Portia, having unfortunately for himself made choice of the silver casket, reads this schedule:—

> The fire seven times tried this;
> Seven times tried that judgment is,
> That did never choose amiss.

In Hamlet (IV. 5), Ophelia appears fantastically drest, and cries:—

> O heat, dry up my brains; tears seven times salt
> Burn out the sense and virtue of mine eye.

Of Coriolanus (II. 1) it is said: "He received in the repulse of Tarquin seven hurts in the body."

In Measure for Measure (II. 1), we find an allusion to the seven mortal sins:—

> Sure, it is no sin,
> Of the deadly seven it is the least.

In Julius Cæsar (III. 1), the servant of Octavius says of his master:—

> He lies to-night within seven leagues of Rome.

So in Midsummer-Night's Dream (I. 1), Lysander says:—

> Hear me, Hermia;
> I have a widow aunt, a dowager,
> Of great revenue, and she hath no child:
> From Athens is her house remote seven leagues.

This may remind us of the famous seven-league boots, so long current in popular tradition, which, having now been vamped up with new art by the author of Peter Schlemihl's Wonderful History, may be expected to travel down to the remotest posterity.

In As You Like It (III. 2), Rosalind, speaking of the progress of time, says, "Marry, he trots hard with a young maid between the contract of her marriage and the day it is solemnized; if the interim be but a sevennight, Time's pace is so hard, that it seems the length of seven years."

The designation "seven years" is very frequently repeated. Thus in Much Ado About Nothing (III. 3), the Watchman says, "I know that Deformed; a' has been a vile thief this seven year."

In Coriolanus (II. 1), Menenius says, "A letter for me? it gives me an estate of seven years' health." And again:—

If I could shake off but one seven years
From these old arms and legs, by the good gods,
I'd with thee every foot.

In Pericles (IV. 6), Boult says, "Go to the wars, would ye, where a man may serve seven years for the loss of a leg, and have not money enough in the end to buy him a wooden one."

In King Lear (III. 4), Edgar sings:—

But mice and rats and such small deer
Have been Tom's meat for seven long year.

In As You Like It (II. 7), is found the celebrated passage:—

All the world's a stage,
And all the men and women merely players;
They have their exits and their entrances,
And one man in his time plays many parts,
His acts being seven ages.

Then follow the seven—infant, school-boy, lover, soldier, justice, old age, and second childhood. Everybody knows the passage; but everybody does not know that this division of human life into seven ages is an idea prevalent long before the time of Shakspeare, as far back even as the Greek physician Hippocrates, more than four centuries before our era.

In the same play, we have the seven degrees of offence in affairs of honor. Touchstone says, "I have had four quarrels, and like to have fought one. *Jaques.* And how was that ta'en up? *Touchstone.* Faith, we met and found the quarrel was upon the seventh cause. *Jaques.* How did you find the quarrel on the seventh cause? *Touchstone.* Upon a lie seven times removed—as thus, Sir: I did dislike the cut of a certain courtier's beard; he sent me word, if I said his beard was not cut well, he was in the mind it was. This is called the Retort courteous. If I sent him word again, it was not well cut, he would send me word, he cut it to please himself. This is called the Quip modest. If again it was not well cut, he disabled my judgment. This is called the Reply churlish. If again it was not well cut, he would answer, I spake not true. This is called the Reproof valiant. If again it was not well cut, he would say, I lie. This is called the Counter-check quarrelsome: and so to the Lie circumstantial, and the Lie direct. *Jaques.* And how oft did you say his beard was not well cut? *Touchstone.* I durst go no further than the Lie circumstantial; nor he durst not give me the Lie direct, and so we measured swords and parted."

Further on in the same colloquy, Touchstone says, "I know when seven justices could not settle a quarrel, but when the parties were met themselves, one of them thought but of an If, as, If you said so, then I said so. And they shook hands and swore brothers. Your If is the only peacemaker: much virtue in If."

A word now in regard to the Mohammedans. The religion of the Koran, like that of the Old and New Testaments, made its first appearance among a Semitic people; the Israelite has, in race and tongue, no nearer kinsman than the Ishmaelite. The Koran, too, like the Old and New Testaments, has carried the ascendency of the number Seven over vast regions of the earth. Its preëminence in the Moslem scriptures, though less marked and conspicuous than in ours, is yet not to be mistaken. The sevens of the Koran counted up greatly outnumber the eights and sixes put together. It is possible that in this point Mohammed may have felt the influence of the Bible, with which, though unable to read it, he had certainly picked up some acquaintance. But it is more likely that he gave expression to a feeling which belonged already to his Arab fellow-countrymen, in common with their kindred of Palestine. The most venerated monument of their ante-

Mohammedan literature, the collection of poems known as the *Moallakat*—poems written in golden letters, and suspended at the Holy Kaaba in Mecca—was the production of seven authors. At all events, it is certain that the Mohammedan Arabs have shown an extraordinary predilection for the Seven, not yielding in this respect either to Jews or Christians. They have discovered or imagined an immense number of septenary groups, in religion, history, art, philosophy, and indeed all branches of human knowledge. We shall not undertake to exhibit even specimens of these. They are collected to a great extent in a remarkable work, the *Sukkerdan*, or Sugar Box, as it is called, in which this confectionery of the Arab mind is sorted and stored in innumerable parcels of seven. It is the composition of an African scholar, Ibn Khojle, who wrote in the year of the Hejra 757 (A. D. 1356), and died in the year of the Hejra 776. We may suspect that in this last date a mistake has been made of one year, and that his life actually passed away in 777.

Ibn Khojle is not the only writer, nor is he by many centuries the earliest, who composed an elaborate work on the number seven. Among the voluminous writings of Philo Judæus — Philo, the learned Jew of Alexandria, a contemporary of our Saviour — we find a special dissertation, *De Septenario*, on the number seven; while in another work, on the Mosaic History of the Creation, he dwells at length on the dignity and sacredness of the same number. Nor has the subject been overlooked by Christian writers. The Fathers have frequent allusions to it, though no one of them, so far as we know, has made it the theme of a separate treatise. But in modern times we find the work of Wurffbain which bears the following title: *De numero septenario variarum lectionum collectionem hanc philologicam elaboravit Leonhartt Wurffbain Noribergensis Doctor, anno salutis* 1630, *ætatis suæ septies septimo. Constat septeno quicquid in orbe fuit. Nirinbergæ*, 1633—'This philological collection of various readings on the number seven hath Leonhartt Wurffbain, of Nuremberg, Doctor, elaborated in the year of salvation the 1630th, of his own age the seven times seventh. Whatsoe'er on earth existeth, in a seven it consisteth. Nuremberg, 1633.' Within the last few years, Wurffbain has found among his own countrymen a more distinguished successor. The *Wiener Jahrbücher* for 1848 contains a series of articles on the number seven, the contribution of a veteran Orientalist, whose lamented death occurred about two years ago—the Baron Von Hammer-Purgstall. We have placed his name at the head of our own remarks, and take pleasure in acknowledging that we are dependent to a great extent upon his learned labors. If any of our readers find their curiosity athirst for further details, we can refer them to his two hundred pages. Only a word of caution. We would advise our friends not to attempt those articles, unless consciously animated by a genuine interest in the subject, profoundly impressed by the mystic predominance of this venerable number; otherwise they may find Von Hammer-Purgstall's ocean-flood of septenary erudition somewhat too overwhelming for them, and may prefer to take up with the small specimen-phial which we have the honor of exhibiting.

It remains to say a word in regard to the cause or causes of the honor so early and so widely paid to the number seven. *Arithmetical* reasons have been assigned for it; we find them drawn out at length by Philo the Jew. If we take the ten primary numbers—that is, the series from 1 to 10 (leaving out of view the 1, which is regarded as the basis of all number, but hardly a number itself)—we shall find that some of them are produced by multiplication: as 4 by multiplying 2 and 2; 6 by 2 and 3; 8 by 2 and 4; 9 by 3 and 3; 10 by 2 and 5. Some again are not themselves produced by multiplication, but by their multiplication produce others of the series: thus 2 helps to produce 4 and 6 and 8 and 10; 3 helps to produce 6 and 9; 4 to produce 8, and 5 to produce 10. Thus we have the products of multiplication 4, 6, 8, 9, 10, and the producers 2, 3, 4, 5. Seven alone belongs to neither class; it neither produces nor is produced; and is thus clearly distinguished from its fellows. Another property: if we start with unity, and go on doubling, we form the geometric series 1, 2, 4, 8, 16, 32, 64. In this series the seventh term 64 is at the same time an exact square number, and an exact cube number, its square root being 8, and its cube root 4. Now let us start again with unity and go on trebling: we form the series 1, 3, 9, 27, 81, 243, 729; and here again the seventh term 729 has the same remarkable property of being an exact square and cube number at the same time; its square root being 27 and its cube root 9. And so if we form our series by quadrupling or quintupling, or with any other ratio, the seventh term will still have the same property; which is easily accounted for by our algebra, the seventh term of such a series being the sixth power of the ratio, which is of course the square of the third power and the cube of the second power. It is evident, however, that these properties of the number seven will not explain the origin of the feeling under consideration: they are very far from being obvious; they would probably have passed without notice, or at all events without special attention, had not the established sacredness of the number set men upon the hunt to find out everything remarkable connected with it.

Others rely upon a *chronological* reason: they derive the veneration for the Seven from the early division of time into periods of seven days—that is, from the week. It is certainly probable that the week, if it did not give origin to the feeling, has contributed to give it strength and perpetuity. Even if we regard the week as at first a merely human division of time, suggested by the changes of the moon, though afterwards taken up with divine sanctions into the Mosaic economy, still it could hardly fail, when once established, to invest its number with peculiar interest and importance: just as the widely recognized distinction of the number twelve may be ascribed to the twelve months (mooneths), revolutions of the moon, which correspond nearly to a single revolution of the sun. Still more might this effect be looked for, if we regard the week as being from the beginning of the world a positive divine institution. But some who take the latter view feel prompted to go further, and to explain *why* this number should have been selected by the Deity as the number of the week, and thereby as the subject of peculiar dignity and reverence. Thus Bähr, in his Symbolism of the Mosaic Ritual, observes that the Seven is formed by the union of two symbolic numbers: namely, *three*, which symbolizes the divine, since the Godhead is a trinity, and *four*, which symbolizes the cosmical, the created universe of space, this being all determined in situation by the four cardinal directions or points of the compass, North, South, East, and West. The Seven, therefore, is in the highest degree symbolic, representing the union of the divine and the cosmical, and especially representing that reunion of the world with God which is the great aim and crowning consummation of all true religion. Kurtz also, another learned and pious theologian of Germany, in the *Studien und Kritiken* for 1844, goes into an elaborate vindication of the same view. In like manner, the twelves of the new Jerusalem, which have been already referred to, are explained as being the symbolic product of the same symbolic numbers. We have spoken before of arithmetical and chronological reasons: we may describe this as a *symbolical* reason. Such views will be very differently received by different persons. The example of Bähr himself shows that minds of a high order can find interest and satisfaction in them. At the same time there will always be others, men of positive and critical minds, who will distrust them as wanting an objective basis, or think of them as thin but highly flavored soups, fitted to tickle or to tease the intellectual palate, but affording next to nothing of substantial nutriment.

Next the *physiological* reasons. It is well known that the importance of the Ten, as the universal numerating number of all languages and peoples—for all men count by tens, and tens of tens, and tens of tens of tens, and so on, not in figures only but in words, and not in words only but in conceptions: thought and language have always been decimal, though figures have not always been so—nobody doubts, we say, that this ascendency of the Ten depends upon a physiological reason, one which makes it natural and handy for all men to reckon thus; that our apprehension of number is more than figurative, it is really a taking hold of it with our ten fingers. The science of number appears to be of all others the least artificial; yet there is no art, not even the potter's, which shows more clearly the impress of man's hands. Now some would find similar reasons for the preeminence of the Seven. Thus we have the seven parts of the human body, the head, chest, and loins, with the four limbs, upper and lower. So, too, we have the seven openings of the head, the three twin pairs of eyes, ears, and nostrils, with the monadic mouth to make the seventh. Further, in many diseases, the seventh, fourteenth, twenty-first days are critical periods, and were so regarded by ancient physicians. To these anatomical and pathological sevens Von Hammer-Purgstall seems inclined to give the foremost place, and to consider them as the most effective agents in creating a reverence for the Seven. To us, we confess, they do not appear very striking. We should ascribe a far earlier and more powerful influence to the *astronomical* sevens.

We need not say, that to the men of primitive times the spectacle of the nocturnal heavens was as impressive as it was constant. But in this spectacle there was no object, the moon alone excepted, so striking to the inhabitants of the north temperate zone—that is, to all the cultivated nations of antiquity—as that group of seven splendid never-setting stars, in which the utilitarian imagination of the Yankee recognizes —a dipper. The ancient Greeks saw in it the great northern bear; the Romans, seven plough-oxen, *septem triones;* among Greeks and Romans both, an entire quarter of earth and sky received its name from this constellation. The stars composing it were called by the Persians *heft ereng*, the 'seven thrones,' seats for the monarchs of the sky. The celestial empire would thus seem to be, like Anglo-Saxon England, a Heptarchy. But while in this unequaled constellation the glory of the Seven is most conspicuously blazoned, there are other notable groups which hold forth the same skyey number: as the lesser bear, inferior in brightness to the other, but distinguished as containing that remarkable star, which amid all motions and revolutions of earth and heaven has kept through the ages the same fixed place, the unvarying guide of benighted mortals. Nor must we forget the sweet influences of the Pleiades, "glittering like a swarm of fire-flies tangled in a silver braid;" nor how "through scudding drifts the rainy Hyades vexed the dim sea." In a passage of the Iliad, Homer, describing the shield of

Achilles, tells us that the divine artisan represented within its central circle—

> the earth, the heaven, the sea;
> The sun that rests not, and the moon full-orbed;
> There also all the stars, that round about
> As with a radiant frontlet bind the sky;
> The Hyads, and the Pleiads, and the might
> Of huge Orion, with him Ursa called,
> Known also by his popular name the Wain.

It is worthy of notice that, among the constellations here specified as most interesting to the Homeric Greeks, three out of the four present the septenary number.

But we have yet to mention the great planetary seven. Most of the heavenly bodies, though revolving daily round the earth, maintain the same position relative to each other. But there are seven which wander without resting through the stationary camp. Among these seven wanderers, or planets, are the two greater lights that rule the day and the night, and the two usher stars that herald the morning and the evening. Enumerated in the order of their distance from the earth, as determined by the ancient astronomy, they are the Moon, Mercury, Venus, the Sun, Mars, Jupiter, and Saturn. From the earliest times they have been an object of wonder, of curiosity, of study, to star-gazing men. Their movements have been watched with the minutest observation, and every possible device adopted to unravel the mystery of their wayward courses. The feeling toward them is well illustrated by the Persian literature, in which a great variety of honorary titles are applied to them, such as the seven pearls, the seven golden corals, seven eyes of heaven, seven tapers or torches, seven peers, seven sultans, seven great ladies, seven green daughters, seven heart-breaking boys, and so on, and so on. Each of these bodies has his own heaven, or sphere in which he moves about the earth. Hence the idea of seven heavens, which, with the correlative seven hells, we have noticed already. For these seven heavens the Persians have an even greater redundancy of titular expressions, such as the seven buildings, the seven temples, the seven roofs, the seven domes, the seven vaults, the seven blue curtains, the seven watered-colored sun-screens, the seven castles of gilded enamel, the seven horse-mills or ass-mills (in which the stars go round and round, as the ass in the mill). But we need not multiply illustrations to show how profound, as well as early, were the impressions made by these seven planets upon the minds of men. It is true that science has been making wild work with this ancient and venerable seven. The peerage of England has been more than once menaced with degradation by a large addition of upstart nobles. Something like this has actually happened to the celestial peerage. But let not these parvenu planets—*Dii minorum gentium*—whether condemned to outer darkness like Uranus and Neptune, or huddled together like Astræa, Flora, and fifty more, as if to make up by collective numbers for individual insignificance—let them not suppose that they can take rank with the ancient nobility of the skies. There are prerogatives of the original seven from which they are forever excluded. They can never preside over the revolving week. They can never be the arbiters and exponents of human destiny. For the *seven* planets are the great objects, not only of astronomy, but of astrology. They are the lords of life; by their endless relations to each other and to the fixed stars they determine the endless varieties of human character and fortune. We profess to disbelieve in astrology; our science is against it. Yet still, if anything particularly fortunate befalls us, we bless our *stars* for it. As Max Piccolomini says in Schiller's play:—

> "Still doth the old instinct call back the old names,
> ——————— and even at this day
> 'Tis Jupiter who brings whate'er is great,
> And Venus who brings everything that's fair."

At all events, the days of the week still retain their old astrological designations, still own in name the mastery of the planetary seven. We have our Saturn-day, our Sun-day, our Moon-day. And if, instead of having a Mars-day, Mercury-day, Jove-day, Venus-day, like the people of France, Italy, and Spain, we speak of Tuis'-day, and Woden's-day, and Thor's-day, and Freya's-day, it is a mere translation—the translation of Roman names by their supposed representatives in northern mythology.

And now, who will not admit that the veneration for the Seven is in literal truth a lesson of celestial teaching? In this respect, as in others, "night unto night showeth knowledge—no speech, no language—their voice is not heard—yet their line is gone out through all the earth, and their words to the end of the world."

DECISIONS OF COLLEGE CLASS DISPUTES.

XVIII.

I. ARE THE WRITINGS OF LORD BYRON IMMORAL IN THEIR TENDENCY?

1847.

BYRON, it seems to me, was a bad man. Doubtless he had his good impulses—who has not? A mind so vigorous must have seen the excellence of virtue; a sensibility so keen must have felt it. But was the will subject to its power? Did the man live with good and noble aims? or did he live with vile and selfish aims; live to gratify pride and passion? The life and writings of Byron are consistent with each other: they both alike show a fierce and haughty nature, spurning all restraint, controlled neither by reason nor religion. He never governs himself. He is swayed like a reed by every gust of passion. It is melancholy to speak thus of a man so highly gifted. But it is the truth. I have read Moore's apology nearly through. It is a book which corrects itself. The writer wishes to convey a favorable impression of Byron. In his descriptions everything is softened, and displayed in the most advantageous light. But unfortunately—unfortunately, I mean, for the subject of the biography; fortunately for the reader, fortunately for the interests of truth—he has not muzzled his charge; his protégé is allowed to speak for himself; and he never speaks without betraying the *atra bilis* that was in him. It is impossible to read that book, as it is impossible to read the writings of Byron, without feeling that the moral nature of the man had become corrupted and diseased. Would you become convinced of this? Take another man, and not the highest style of man, either—Walter Scott—and compare Byron with him. His qualities become more striking when placed side by side with those of a sound and healthy nature. Turn from Walter Scott to Byron, and how great the transition! It is like passing from summer to winter. The one healthy in feeling and expression, with a sunny genial nature, radiant with charity, kindness, honesty, hearty affection, and loving humor; a soul at peace with the world, and submitting without a murmur to the laws that govern it. Such is the one. The other is cold and bitter and satirical. According to Moore, his conversation was always spiced with raillery at absent friends; he had a breast haunted by evil demons, devoured by gloomy passions. He is always kicking against the pricks, dashing himself with impotent spite against the barriers which society, which God himself has placed around him. With all his splendid endowments, was there ever a man so little to be envied?

There may have been writers whose moral qualities did not appear in their writings. Byron was not one of these. He was intensely subjective—to use a fashionable term of modern criticism. The man appears in all his works. His personality is everywhere prominent. He is always describing himself; or, if describing anything else, stamps himself on that which he describes. His poems of course reflect the immorality of his nature. And this is true of all of them—grave or gay, true heroic or mock heroic. Childe Harold is as really immoral as Don Juan. The difference between them is that the one scowls and the other sneers. The one bids a sullen defiance to the laws of moral order; the other seeks to cover them with a load of blasphemous and indecent ridicule. A poem is not of course moral because it contains no foul words, no expressions but such as could be repeated in a drawing-room. Immorality and indelicacy are different things. Rabelais is indelicate to the last degree, but he is not really immoral. Congreve is far less indelicate, but far more immoral. The book which breathes an immoral spirit is an immoral book. The book which expresses the feelings of an immoral man is an immoral book. The spirit of Byron's poems is destructive. Discontent, skepticism, scorn are written on every page. He is at war with all that is established; he refuses, at least in spirit, submission to established authority, divine and human.

It is often said that this impatient temper must be forgiven to a man of his genius. The poet, gifted with a soul larger, deeper, stronger than those of ordinary men, cannot be confined within the same narrow limits as they. He bursts the barriers which shut in others; or, if he cannot burst them, chafes angrily and impatiently against them. Was it so with Shakespeare and Milton? The poet, if he sees farther than common men, more clearly than they, will see the necessity of those restraints which God and man have placed about his path—their necessity to himself; for, if he is a genius, he is yet a man, erring and sinful like all his race—their necessity to others; and, seeing this, he will beware how he shakes others' faith or encourages in them a feeling of discontent and insubordination. And if not, if instead of this he chooses to wage war against the laws of moral order, the grand conditions of human life, individual and social, then his guilt will be proportionate to those endowments of the Almighty which he has perverted to wicked and unworthy ends.

To criticize the literary merit of Byron's poems does not come within the scope of this discussion. I am ready to acknowledge his extraordinary powers—though I think that his moral character has had a very injurious effect upon his literary character; that with the calmness, the clearness, the conscious effort, the lofty purposes of a truly moral nature, he would have soared far higher, and produced works of far greater value even as works of poetic art.

I do not say that Byron should not be read at all. The man who would investigate the morbid anatomy of the human mind will find in Byron's works an admirable study. It may be well on some accounts to know how a haughty and malignant spirit will express itself in good set English.

My own course of reading was subject to very little guidance from without, and was at first confined to a small library, to which many of the British classics had not gained admittance. Under such circumstances I read much the greater part of Byron's works. I now regret, not that I read him at all, but that much of the time which I gave him was not devoted to other and healthier writers—especially to those contemporaries of Byron whom he so much affected to despise, but whom he had so little reason to despise, his equals, his superiors even in many intellectual gifts, greatly his superiors in moral excellence—Robert Southey and William Wordsworth.

---

2. IS ANCIENT ELOQUENCE SUPERIOR TO MODERN?

1849.

THERE are two ways of viewing this subject. We might commence with the circumstances and conditions on which eloquence depends, and, by comparing these in ancient and in modern times, judge by a sort of *à priori* judgment which period should naturally have the higher eloquence. We often see and hear the question discussed in this way. On the other hand, we may consider the actual specimens of ancient and modern eloquence, and by direct comparison determine the superiority of this or that, leaving it for after work to determine, if possible, the causes and conditions of that superiority. The form of our question would lead us rather to the latter mode of treatment. But there is a preliminary point to settle: and that is the standard of excellence. What are we to look at—is it elegance, is it feeling, is it passion, is it argument, is it logic or rhetoric; or all combined? Some have a simple test, and that is persuasiveness; the best oration is the most persuasive, and *vice versâ*, the most persuasive is the best; for it best fulfils the end of eloquence, which is persuasion. But there is still a difficulty here. The eloquence of Mike Walsh has an effect as persuasive on the collective blackguardism of New York as the eloquence of Daniel Webster has on the collective dignity and learning of the Senate or the Supreme Court. Shall we therefore decide that the one is no higher than the other? Now persuasiveness, tendency or adaptation to secure that course of action which the orator desires, is indeed an indispensable element in true eloquence. But there is another element, of great importance, which may vary much in orations equally persuasive: and that is artistic perfection, aptness to satisfy the æsthetic sense, the critical faculty in man. An oration may be regarded as a work of art, and subject more or less to the predicates symmetrical, perfect, beautiful, or the reverse. Indeed, no cultivated mind can help taking this view. He who has taste—that is, the critical faculty which judges of form—must be shocked with what is out of taste, must admire that which good taste recommends and sanctions. Now it is precisely here that I would take my stand. In everything else—in vehemence of passion, in depth of feeling, in cogency of argument, in attractiveness of persuasion—I admit that the moderns have shown themselves not inferior to the ancients. But in finish and perfection, in symmetry and beauty of outward form, I bow to the superiority of the ancient masters. I regard the orations of Demosthenes as not only unsurpassed, but as unrivalled specimens of oratoric art. And now, having pronounced this opinion, if you ask me why, why this was so, why an old Athenian should have borne away from all the world the prize of art in oratory, I cannot say, I cannot satisfy your curiosity. I do not ascribe it to a genial climate, or a productive soil; to successful wars with foreign powers, or noble struggles for national independence; nor to agricultural, mechanical, professional, political activity; nor to democratic institutions, to annual magistracies, to vote by ballot or by bean. I do not deny that these things had their influence, as furnishing field and opportunity and encouragement to intellectual development. But that matchless æsthesis of the Greeks, that unrivalled taste, that wonderful sense of beauty and harmony and proportion—where that came from is more than I can tell; I greatly doubt whether it is in any proper sense the creature of external circumstances. I hold, then, that the same causes which made a Homer the first of epic poets, and a Phidias the first of sculptors, and a Pindar the first of lyric bards, and the builder of the Parthenon the first of architects—the same causes rendered Demosthenes the first of orators. Only let circumstances offer fair occasion, and the nation which has the keenest and truest sense of the beautiful and the perfect will present the highest master-works of art.

It fills me with wonder to see how completely some of those old Greeks were under the dominion of their taste, and how much they must have sacrificed to it. Every oration of Demosthenes is to my mind a heroic exhibition of self-denial. So many graces of style and felicities of expression, so many details sublime, pathetic, brilliant must have occurred to his rich and copious mind, which ever and anon shows when such things are necessary that there was no lack of power to originate them—and yet, in general he rigorously rejects them, and, if he ever employs them, employs them most sparingly. Everywhere he sacrifices the part to the whole, beauty of detail to general effect: and so he holds on in his severe simplicity, rarely allowing any embellishment, just as an architect decorates only the capitals of his columns or the cornice of his roof, trusting to the grand and stately proportions of the completed edifice. How different all this from the general character of modern oratory, and above all of American oratory, I need not say. The introduction to one of Colonel Benton's speeches is longer than the three Olynthiacs put together, and contains, I dare say, more figures of speech and more grandiloquent phrases, and questionless more egotism than all three; and yet the world of cultivated, educated men would hardly consent to barter one Olynthiac oration for all the windy declamations of the Colonel, from the fight with General Jackson to the present time.

---

3. IS A REFORM DESIRABLE IN THE METHOD OF WRITING THE ENGLISH LANGUAGE?

1852.

THE Chinese more than any other people have need of a phonographic revolution. With less than five hundred different syllables in their language, they have an immense number of written characters—forty thousand, it is said, in all, though not more than ten thousand are in general use. These characters are most of them very complicated, and requiring, as they do, to be written with perfect accuracy in order to avoid confusion between such as are of similar form, they make it a most arduous work to master them, and it is literally true that multitudes in China are all their lives long learning to read and write. The case is not so bad with us; there is a general relation between the alphabetic signs we use and the vocal sounds for which we use them. But it is a relation so variable, so irregular, so capricious, so subject to manifold and endless exceptions, as to impose grievous difficulties on a learner. It does not matter so much with us who are brought up under it; line upon line, lesson upon lesson, we get hold of the system, if that name can be given to anything so unsystematic; through much weariness, through many blunders, through some floggings, it may be, the successful boy at length learns to spell—fails now and then on a hard word, such as *phthisic;* has to consult his Dictionary now and then, to find how many *g*'s there are in *waggon*, or whether *sibyl* is spelt *sibyl* or *sybil*—but on the whole is entitled, as things human go, with some degree of unavoidable imperfection, to the dignity of Master of Spelling. That is the successful boy; but all boys are not successful, nor all young men either—as college compositions not unfrequently attest. I know a man of talents and of literary cultivation who cannot learn to spell the words which come from the Latin *cedo*, some of which have *ceed*, and others *cede*—such as *accede* and *exceed*, *precede* and *proceed*, *secede* and *succeed*, etc.; he never can tell which is which. And I have heard several well-educated persons say that there are particular words or classes of words which always puzzle them. But, as I was saying, it is of less consequence to us who are born and bred under this sort of spelling; the years which we spend upon it are of no great value to us; we should not accomplish very much beside—except that one might learn two or three decently-spelled languages while he is learning to spell his own; and, if he did not, how much pleasanter to be playing long ball or ranging through the woods! We get a certain discipline, no doubt, from our drudgery; only would it not be better to get our discipline in mastering some useful thing, when there are so many useful things to be mastered? But with us it is less matter; it is for foreigners that my sympathies are most strongly enlisted, for men who in adult years set themselves to learning English. In itself our language is a very easy one. Its sounds are not difficult, except the two *th's*, which are easy for a modern Greek, but hard to all the other European nations; but in general they are easy, though sometimes rendered difficult by harsh accumulations—as in *hosts*, *asked*. Our system of declension and conjugation is an easy one, as the inflexions are reduced very nearly to a minimum. Nor has the language very much of troublesome idiom, like French and Latin; there is a twist about *will* and *shall* in the future, which proved fatal, it is said, to a drowning Frenchman, whose agonizing cry, "I will be drowned; nobody shall help me," was rather calculated to repel than invite assistance —but this distinction is ill-observed by Scotch and Irish, and by Americans, too, out of New England, and seems to be gradually fading out from the language. I am convinced (without particulars) that, apart from its orthography, the English is easier of acquisition than any other idiom of Europe. But the orthography is a very serious obstacle; every foreigner who has learned English in adult years will speak feelingly of his trouble and occasional despair at its numberless and capricious exceptions and irregularities. Perhaps it would not be going too far to say that a uniform orthography, with notation of the accent, would lighten by half the labor of learning English. And many foreigners are studying English now-a-days; the astonishing development of the English race is carrying their language far and wide in every continent. English is now the language of North America, with its rapidly increasing millions; it will soon be the language of millions in the ancient peninsula of India; it will soon, if it does not now, carry a man farther over the world, bring him into connection with greater multitudes and wider regions, than any other tongue. This commanding and ever-growing importance of the language is making it more and more the object of study among foreigners, who might not have been attracted by the treasures of a literature which I do not hesitate to pronounce the noblest of modern Europe. But when you put all things together, its noble literature, its political importance, its simplicity of structure, you will see that, if its acquisition were facilitated by a uniform orthography, it might almost come to be ere long a universal language.

It cannot be denied that the English language is shockingly spelled. The original difficulty lay in the mixture of different languages, Saxon and Norman French, out of which came English; the confusion of different systems, varying and conflicting analogies, is everywhere to be seen in our orthography.

Besides, the French, which makes one element of English, does itself enjoy, next to the English and perhaps the Gaelic, the honor of being the worst spelt language of Europe Franklin used to say that what we call false spelling of the vulgar was really true spelling. I do not know that I should say that, for vulgar spelling is sometimes most ingeniously absurd. But I certainly feel a good deal of hesitation about saying in regard to any man that he spells badly: I say that he does not spell like most of us; he spells singularly, peculiarly; but I do not see, on the whole, that he spells worse than the spelling-books and newspapers.

It is very unfortunate that Johnson's Dictionary should have come to be such a standard of spelling. For the consequence has been that the processes which were going on before—gradual progressive processes, to root out anomalies and bring in greater regularity, processes which went on naturally and almost without notice—were at once arrested, and the system which had before been somewhat flexible became at once a cast-iron affair. That such processes were going on, to the great advantage of the system, will be plain enough to any one who takes a book printed in the Elizabethan age—say one of the earlier translations of the Bible—and compares it with the books printed in the first part of the last century. That such processes were arrested by the appearance of Johnson's Dictionary is evident from the outcry which is raised against any spelling that departs from the prescription of that autocratic lexicographer. No philologist needs to be reminded that Johnson had little fitness for the work of legislation in orthography. This would be evident enough from his famous dictum that it is absurd to regulate your spelling by your pronunciation, for pronunciation changes all the time, and your standard is therefore variable and fluctuating. He did not see that this is one of the strongest reasons for regulating spelling by pronunciation ; for if pronunciation changes all the time while spelling remains fixed, the two will diverge more and more widely from each other, until they cease to have any relation, and we shall write in hieroglyphics. Most evidently the proper aim and object, the ideal of alphabetic writing, is to furnish an exact reflexion of the spoken language, a faithful representation of what we hear in daily utterance. In its most advanced perfection, every elementary sound will be represented by a special character, and each character will be used in every case to represent the same sound. There is no great objection, however, to a combination of characters used to represent a sound different from either—as, for instance, *ch* in *church*, provided always that it is used with perfect consistency. The reform recently attempted has taken high ground, avoiding such combinations of characters, and representing the same sound always by the same alphabetic sign. Perhaps this is the best course, though I have always felt that the introduction of new letters, which this plan requires, might operate pretty strongly to prevent its adoption.

The objections commonly urged against a new system of phonography have in my view very little weight. It is often said that, if this plan were adopted, all books printed hitherto would be useless. It is certain that people would not read them quite so readily as now ; but only for this reason, that they would spend less time in acquiring the power. It would be really as easy as ever for people to learn the old system : or rather, far easier ; for then it would be necessary only that they should learn to read, to recognize the words when they see them ; and not to learn what is far harder, to spell, to reproduce the words when you do not see them. Another objection, which has considerable influence, is that a new system would obscure the etymology of words, which is now shown in many cases by the spelling. But as regards this, the etymology of words is of little practical value except to scholars, who could always get it out of books of lexicography ; it is not worth while for their benefit to impose a heavy burden upon the world at large. But our common spelling is often an untrustworthy guide to etymology. Take the word *sovereign:* the people who first spelt it so supposed no doubt that it had something to do with *reign;* but it most certainly has not. It comes from Latin *super*, through Italian *sovrano*, etc. But I will go further, and say that the wants of the philologist require a different system. What is important for him is that he should know the condition of a language at any given period of the past, that he may be able to trace it through its successive changes to its latest form. Now in doing this he must depend mainly on the spelling, the writing; if this be maintained invariable from age to age amid all mutations of spoken words, the philologist is deprived of his most serviceable guide. I would give a good deal to get a *Fonetic Nuz* of Chaucer's time, that I might know how far some important phenomena of the modern language—as for instance the change of *ā* to *ē*, of *ē* to *ī*, and of *ī* to *ai*—had established themselves five centuries ago.

There are many points of which I should be glad to speak more at length, but I must stop. You will see from what I have said that I recognize fully the evils of our present orthography (as men sarcastically term it), and that I sympathize in the objects of a phonographic revolution. But in regard to the feasibility of such a revolution I am far from being sanguine; a political revolution, I suspect, would be a much easier undertaking. Yet I have no desire to damp the ardor of those who are more sanguine than myself; on the contrary, I wish them all success in their work, being sure at least of this—that, whatever imperfections may belong to their systems, they cannot be so bad as ordinary good spelling.

---

4. WAS CIVIL LIBERTY IN EUROPE PROMOTED BY THE CAREER OF NAPOLEON?

1852.

THE selfishness of Bonaparte is now as universally admitted as his transcendent abilities. There was an English officer who wrote a book, some years ago, to prove that Bonaparte was a bungler in war, that he violated every rule of generalship, and won all his great battles by mistake. A preposterous attempt—as though the voice of a pettifogging critic could drown the pæan of praise that rises to Napoleon from twenty glorious battlefields; as though Jena and Austerlitz, Borodino and Eylau were not stronger arguments than any possible accumulation of professional technics! Equally preposterous would it be to dispute the selfishness of Bonaparte, to pretend that he cared for anybody but himself, and, most of all, to maintain that he cared a straw for civil liberty. His government was the government of the strong arm. It was of espionage, of repression, of censorship, of anything but civil liberty. If Bonaparte did anything to help the cause of freedom, he must have done it undesignedly, by accident or by mistake. This is possible, certainly. A man may work toward ends which he has no idea of. The old Greeks, when they planted their colonies on all the coasts of the Mediterranean, and under Alexander and his successors established their civilization and their language in wide regions of Europe and Asia, had no thought of Christianity, and the progress by which it would one day supplant the gods of Hellas; yet they were contributing all the time to this great progress of Christianity. In the same unconscious way may Bonaparte have contributed to the advance of civil liberty.

Look then to his own country, to France, the special theatre of an activity which extended over the world. What did he do for civil liberty in France? Did he limit or destroy the absolute authority of the throne? He established a throne as absolute as the most despotic court of the Bourbons. Did he erect the fabric of a free representative government? He would as soon have shattered the throne on which he sat, and blown up the palace in which he held his court. Did he break the bonds of an antiquated and oppressive feudalism? He found them broken by the Revolution, and it would have required a hand stronger even than his to fasten them again. He promulgated a body of law, the famous Code Napoleon. But a code of law is intended to secure the people in person and in property, not to secure them in the rights and privileges of citizens. It is designed to protect social rights, not civil. The Roman Law attained its highest perfection in the time of its emperors, when civil liberty was at an end. Its latest and most finished form appears in the Justinian Code; yet nobody speaks of Justinian as having promoted civil liberty, in Europe or elsewhere. It may be said that a good code, giving as it does personal security, will lead men to aspire further after political privilege. But the experience of the world is rather against this. Men who are personally well off, secure, easy, comfortable in their circumstances, are apt to be content with this, and to submit to the existing government, however absolute it may be. It was physical suffering, hardship, and starvation which made the Revolution in France, not the aspiration after citizenship.

But let us look beyond France. The Germans in general speak very bitterly of Napoleon. But Godfrey Hermann, the famous scholar, used to say that it was a good thing to have a thorough shaking up now and then. This is the great benefit which Bonaparte conferred on Europe: he gave it a thorough shaking up. His actions were too great to be hushed up among princes and diplomatists, to be concealed from the common people; they penetrated every class of society, and roused the popular mind from its slumbers. They set men thinking: and it was not strange that, among other things, they should think on civil liberty; that they should raise a thousand questions as to their actual and their proper condition which had never occurred to them before. Men saw—common men, I mean—they saw that the government placed over them was not an immutable fixity, not an inevitable necessity; when Napoleon appeared, it was neither fixed nor necessary—it was obliged to change and yield according to his direction. Might it not feel the influence of some other force—as (say) the declared will of the people? The same lessons, to be sure, had been taught by the American Revolution. But America was far away beyond the ocean, and there were multitudes in Europe who had scarcely heard the name. The same lessons had been taught by the French Revolution—a very great event, the greatest since the Reformation, and one that could not fail to make a deep impression on the general mind of Europe ; and it is not easy always to distinguish between the agitation which Napoleon effected, and that which would have been produced without him by the Revolution of which he was himself in some sort the creature. But this we may say, that whatever lessons were taught by the French Revolution, it was Napoleon who by his wars and conquests carried them to every door in Europe.

In Germany the influence, the indirect influence, of Napoleon went further than this. The legitimate sovereigns of Germany, defending themselves against the Conqueror, found it convenient to make their appeal to a sentiment of German patriotism. Napoleon had said, there are no Germans ; there are Hessians, Saxons, Bavarians, but there are no Germans. He found in his own experience that there were Germans. They rose against him in their anger and their might, and thrust him out of their land, their own German fatherland. This Germanic unity is a strange sort of thing. The people are one in their language, their physical peculiarities, their general type of character, their traditions, and their feelings. The sentiment of their oneness is very strong among them ; it is a positive enthusiasm ; and they are capable of doing great things under its influence, as witness their heroic resistance to Napoleon in 1813. But when it comes to regular, systematic political action, the oneness vanishes, the old divisions reappear ; and, as Napoleon said, we have only Hessians, etc., no longer any Germans. These things were very plain in the movements of the year 1848 ; there was a great deal of talk about a united Germany ; and there was war with Denmark, in order to wrest from her Holstein, which is German, and attach it to this united Germany ; but though Prussia led the attack, Denmark, little as she is, opposed a stout resistance, and has at last got her own again. But this German unity, though it could produce an aggressive war, could not keep the Frankfort parliament together, or soothe the jealousies of thirty petty states. And the case is much the same with Italy.

But, imperfect and defective as it is, this feeling is very strong in Germany, and must some day work out great results in the history of that country. It received a very great start in the Napoleon times; and whatever it may accomplish in the future will be due in some measure to Napoleon. Small thanks to him for it.

But Germany went further still. The common activity of the people, their efforts, contributions, sacrifices for their country, awoke in them the consciousness of their own manly worth, a consciousness of political capacities and energies which they had never felt before; and they began to feel the honorable yearning after citizenship. They had not the political experience and education necessary for the enlarged and thoroughly successful exercise of civic rights; but they were not sensible of their deficiencies; and, if they had been, might have felt that to supply them, the best way was to begin at once under some system of free institutions. And besides, their demands were not extravagant. They did not propose to overthrow their monarchical governments; they desired only constitutions, with provision for popular representation. This the German princes were ready enough to promise in the hour of their extremity; and ready enough to forget their promise in the hour of their restored security. But they could not make their people forget it: again and again have they been reminded of their promise, until the King of Prussia, reluctant as he was, felt himself at last obliged to yield and establish a system of popular representation. It was greatly qualified, indeed, and restricted; still, it was something; it conceded at least the principle; and it might serve as an entering wedge to open the way by slow and sure degrees to greater things. The spirit which extorted this concession is not dead; it is not confined to Prussia. It must make itself felt more and more in the politics of Germany; and as it gained its first strength in the Napoleon times, so whatever it may do hereafter will be due in some measure to Napoleon. And again, small thanks to him for it.

While I hold, then, that Napoleon did something to promote the advance of civil liberty in Europe, my great surprise would be, that one could hold his place and do so little for it. The truth is that progress in civil liberty is the destiny of Europe; it belongs to the inevitable, irresistible tendency of things; no human power can arrest it; and even its greatest enemies cannot in spite of themselves help doing something for its furtherance.

---

5. IS EUROPE TENDING TO REPUBLICANISM?

1852.

I REGARD this question as one not of mere curiosity, but of real practical importance; important not only to the nations immediately interested, but to us also, who are fellow-actors with them in the great historic drama. No man of intelligence and education ought to hold himself apart—no man of enlarged mental activity and moral earnestness can hold himself aloof—from the great world-movements of his time. He must take his attitude in regard to them; he must have his sympathies; he must be prepared to approve the right and to condemn the wrong, to uphold the beneficent and to oppose the harmful: and in order to this, he must have his reasons, intelligible to himself and statable to others, his theory of things, his conception of the world as it is, its condition, purport, and tendencies. Public opinion is only the general resultant of such individual conceptions; it is the grand sum of such private opinions: and if the great aggregate is an immense force in the world, for good or for evil, it is the duty of every man to look carefully to that particular element of it which he himself contributes. Nobody, certainly, can doubt that our government has and will have an important influence in shaping the world as it is to be: what this influence shall be, is a thing to be determined ultimately by the views and feelings of the individual citizens. And therefore it is that I call this a question of real practical importance to every one of us.

The writings of Thomas Carlyle contain a theory of government—such as it is, undeveloped, unsystematic, yet still a theory of government—which I wish to speak of, because Carlyle exerts a powerful influence on the public mind, and especially on the mind of young men; an influence which I have felt powerfully myself, and see frequent traces of in others; an influence in many respects most valuable, but all the more needing correction where it is wrong. Carlyle holds that the great object in government is that the people should be well governed, good laws passed with good sanctions, good roads and bridges made, good schools established, good connections formed with foreign countries, good measures taken for war and for peace—in short, that things should be well done for the people, that they should be thoroughly and effectually governed. Now this requires that the best man should be made governor; the king, the true king, according to Carlyle's derivation, is the 'canning' or able man, the 'cunning' or knowing man; he it is whom the Saxons called *cyning*, or 'king;' he is *de jure* the king, the sovereign of his people. Gifted with faculty to discern what is best for the people, and with commanding energy to execute what he discerns to be best, it is his right to rule; it is the duty of others to obey; and the more implicit and submissive the obedience, the better. This is the political creed of a man who deifies power, and above all power of will; who does not scruple to say that even in this world might is right in the long run—a principle which has its relation to truth, but is as dangerous as its converse, that right is might in the long run, is always noble and elevating. That Carlyle should deride republicanism, and especially democracy, is a natural consequence of this way of thinking. But in his scheme there are two fatal deficiencies; he provides no answer for these two momentous questions: 1. How we are to ascertain this canning cunning man who is to be our king—if without previous trial, by what criteria; if with trial, by what system that shall afford fair field for all competitors; 2. How we are to shift in the mean time; how we are to get along, if he does not exist, until he does; or, if he does exist unknown to us, how we are to get along until we know him.

But the theory of Carlyle, like all absolutist theories, has another, deeper and more fatal deficiency. It assumes that the good of a government lies only in its ends—its acts, laws, measures and so on,—and that when these are given it matters little by what means they come about; only, the simpler and more effectual the means, the better. You have only to consider the grist; if that is good, the way of grinding is a matter of but little consequence. But government in its ideal perfection is valuable not only for its ends, the acts of government, but for its means also, the system of agencies and operations by which these ends are reached, these acts performed. One great design of government should be to serve as a grand educational establishment for the people, to call out, exercise, and train their mental activities. Of course, the highest earthly end of man's existence is the full harmonious development of all his faculties. For this end he should use every means that earth and man and human society can furnish him. Such means he finds in his own private life, its interests and cares and duties; they are making continual demands upon his energies, and giving them the strength and discipline that come of constant exercise. But the community in which he lives furnishes a wider field; the man who can take in its interests and provide for them, feel its cares, discharge its obligations, has a higher and more valuable cultivation; he becomes a stronger, wiser, better man. Now go as far as you can go in this way—let a man feel that his country with its millions rests in part on him, that he has a substantive influence on its affairs, that he must throw that influence on the right side, that he must gain the information and insight necessary for this purpose—and see how far you have widened his sphere of thought and action, and what a powerful stimulus you have given him to mental exertion. This, now, is an object never to be lost sight of, an object of the highest moment, which is practically disregarded in every absolute government. An absolute government may provide as well as a republic for the material wants and interests of the people; but the absolute government holds them in tutelage, and calls them and keeps them children; the republic holds them in partnership, treats them as men, and makes them men. If I am a democrat, it is on this ground; not because a democracy is the safest, strongest, quickest government, but because it is the manliest—it is a gymnasium for making men, strong-minded, vigorous, active men. This gymnastic training has its dangers, its peculiar difficulties and embarrassments; but the advantages are more than worth the risks. It must be a gradual training, which does not at any time impose upon a people more than they can do, which goes on slowly from point to point, increasing the extent and difficulty of its exercises as the people advance in aptitude and strength.

As popular self-government exercises the mental activities of a people, so these activities, if general and strong, require self-government as an arena for their development and training. They may indeed seek and find for themselves some other vent—as, among the Spaniards of the 16th century, in wandering, adventure, and discovery; or as, among the Germans of the present century, in an unprecedented cultivation of literature and science. Yet even here among the Germans we find this mental activity bursting the bounds within which despotic government would confine it, overflowing into politics, and working slowly and heavily but powerfully toward the republic of the future. You may find thus great mental activity under a despotism; and it may seem peaceable enough for a time; but there is always danger; it is a subterranean fire, which may become too fierce and strong for the vent that is left open, and so open for itself a vent by some great shock of earthquake that shall shatter the political edifice to its foundations. It was the mental activity that illuminated France with wit and science under Louis XV. which shook down the throne of his successor Louis XVI., and buried the monarch in its ruins. It was the mental activity of the Elizabethan age that broke out in the age of Charles into open resistance, and at length into successful rebellion. If we had the early history of Greece, we should probably find that the mental activity which produced the Homeric Epos in an age of monarchy was soon after occupied in overthrowing monarchy and setting up republican governments throughout the country. You may think of the Augustan age at Rome as a case that makes against me. But we have learned to regard the Augustan age as a period of outward show but real decline; its culture was not the result of a genuine popular progress, an original movement of the national mind, but of an imitative fashionable dilettanteism.

If we ask where it is that monarchy has been permanent from age to age, from the beginning until now, a thing undisputed and indisputable—the answer must be, In the East, where human life has a stereotype character, where thought and feeling and action stiffen in their moulds and grow more and more solid and unyielding. That the permanence of monarchy in the East is connected with this want of free spontaneous motion in the Oriental mind seems to me quite certain, though I would not say that this is a full explanation of the fact. There is a mystery about it which has not yet been penetrated—that monarchy should be so universal and indefeasible in the East, while in the West it has been so fluxing and unstable. But in the East monarchy is monarchy, worthy of the name; it is the absolute supremacy of a single will. That will may be subject to a hundred influences, of court or camp, or priests or harem; but such influences are irregular and accidental; they do not belong to the system, they impose no constitutional restriction. The enthronement of a single will as the all-controlling centre of political life and action—that is the one political idea of the Eastern world. This absolutism is in fact essential to monarchy as a permanent system. If a constitutional restriction is interposed, it proves that the king is a king no longer; that a power has arisen stronger than the king, able to limit and restrain him—the power that brought in the restriction. And in the natural course of things this power goes on from more to more till it becomes predominant in the state. In most instances, this first encroaching and restricting power has been an aristocracy. The Homeric king was supplanted by his council of chiefs. The old Roman king was supplanted by the Senate of the Patricians, who reigned more despotically than the kings themselves. It was the nobles of England who extorted their great charter of privileges from the feeble John.

The nobles of France were marching on to the same ascendency when the monarchs learned the art of pitting them against the communes, so as to exhaust them both, and establish that absolutism which rose to its highest glory under Louis XIV. If absolutism is to be overthrown in Russia, it will not be by the people, who are devotedly loyal to the Czar, but by the nobles, who have long been and still are disaffected and turbulent, ever ready to engage in conspiracy and rebellion.

The gradual decline of royal power from steady progressive encroachment is best seen in the political history of England. We cannot here trace its progress; but we must inquire into the result: What is the throne in England? It is a political nullity, it is a mere titular dignity, it is a name, the shadow of a name—*stat nominis umbra*—it possesses no real authority, no substantial strength. It is like an old oak from which the heart has rotted out, which stands a mere shell, with the same form, but not the same strength which it had of old. It stands while the air is calm, but it will go down before the first great storm; and so will the English monarchy. The only sure support of a monarchy is loyalty among its subjects; this is sufficient, and this is essential. But loyalty must itself have a foundation. What foundation has English loyalty? Loyalty may be founded on the personal qualities of the sovereign: on his superiority, real or supposed, in strength or courage or talents or character. Doubtless the English sovereigns at present are worthy and respectable people; but such people are common in England; something more than this is necessary. And even this may not continue; it is little more than twenty years since George IV., a worthless debauchee, vacated the throne. Loyalty may be founded on the possession of power by the sovereign; and this is most commonly its main foundation. The despots of the East have at least this claim on the devotion of their subjects; it is reason enough for being loyal to a man if he can cut your head off when he pleases. But the king of England, or the queen of England, is powerless, and is coming to be more and more recognized as such. You may say that the king is still head of the State, and that this is a sufficient basis for loyal feeling; certainly, if he were really so, and not a mere ornamented figure-head on the ship of state. The real head is the real sovereign; and that is not the king, it is the House of Commons, or the constituency that elect the House. What then are the props of English loyalty? They are tradition and habit. The queen, if not powerful herself, is descended from powerful Tudors and Plantagenets, and the feeling that belonged to them has come down to her, a tradition and a habit. Evidently this is an insecure foundation; less so in England than anywhere else, owing to the peculiar tenacity of the people, their attachment to established forms, their submission to prescription and precedent. Still, it is insecure, as anything must be which is founded on the past and has no root in the present. From the very constitution of our nature, the present must in the end prevail over the past; it is always with us, and cannot be overlooked or forgotten. This English loyalty, resting as it does on tradition, could never be transferred to any new dynasty. If any collision should overthrow the present reigning house, no new one could be established in its stead; the idea of setting up Wellington as king or Cobden as king in England would be simply ridiculous. Nor is such a collision strongly improbable. Suppose that an ambitious prince should arise, who should feel the degradation of his situation, and attempt to change his nominal kingship into a real one. The result would be a revolution, in which the princely aspirant must fall, as fatally perhaps as Charles I., and with no hope of restoration for his family. It would be folly to undertake to say when monarchy shall cease in England; but the result in my view is inevitable, and probably not very far distant. English royalty has come to a minimum, and cannot be reduced without being destroyed. The situation of the country, the distress of the laboring classes, the decline of manufacturing and commercial industry, must sooner or later bring about a crisis. The abolition of royalty, however, will involve no essential change of government, for in substance the government is already republican.

France is less fortunate. When monarchy was swept away there was nothing to replace it; no republican institutions had existed before; and it was not possible and never will be possible to build them up in a day, so to build them up as to make them strong and permanent. This, however, is certain: that loyalty as a pervasive national sentiment is dead; and therefore no substantial monarchy can be set up in France—neither Bourbons, Orleaners, nor Bonapartes can be for any long time sovereigns of France.

Italy is notoriously without loyalty. Every throne in the peninsula rests on a basis of force, and is essentially a tyranny. Spain has more of loyalty; Germany perhaps still more.

Yet any one who should compare this century with the last, this generation with the last, would see an immense and most significant change in Germany—a change which is sufficiently evinced in the general demand of the German states for constitutional governments.

The case is different with Russia: her people, half oriental in their character, have a perfectly oriental devotion to the person of their emperor. The throne in Russia is secure, to all human appearance, for a long time to come; and it is the only secure throne in Europe. I used to think differently in regard to this whole subject. I wrote a disputation when in college to show that the progress of Europe was on the whole anti-republican. But the evidence is too strong for me; I have been forced to acknowledge and recant my errors; I am coming to feel more and more that the present is an age of transition; the old order breaking up, the new one not yet established. You may compare it with the two centuries of Grecian history between established monarchy and established republicanism. Centuries of strife and tumult and revolution and usurpation, the period of tyrants. It would not be strange if this remarkable feature of ancient Greek history should reappear in Modern Europe. France, indeed, has already seen two tyrants, in the Greek sense of the word; men who raised themselves by military force to an unconstitutional sovereignty. In this sense, Napoleon Bonaparte and Louis Napoleon are of the same class with Periander of Corinth and Pisistratus of Athens. Such governments, founded on force and not on law, cannot be permanent; they can last at most only one or two generations, and will at length give place to a well-established republicanism. The same progress may be expected in Italy, and the same also in Germany. The only chance here is that the existing dynasties may make timely concessions, and so keep themselves on the throne until men are prepared for complete republican ism. If so, these countries will have the experience of England and not of France—they will make the transition from absolutism to republicanism through limited monarchies, and not through tyrannies. Many English writers have spoken of limited monarchy as if it were a great permanent form of government, like absolutism, or like republicanism ; and find it unpardonable in the ancients that they did not adopt it. Whereas it is rather, like tyranny, a transition form, assumed in the course of a nation's progress, but wanting the conditions of permanence, and subverted at length by the natural operation of the causes that produced it. We have passed through this stage ; and it was a fortunate circumstance for us, as it saved us from a succession of military tyrannies such as we see in our sister republics of South America, which had known nothing but absolutism up to the time when they began to struggle for their independence. Limited monarchy with us must have grown very feeble ; for the crisis of the Revolution, which in other respects made no great change in our institutions, was sufficient to destroy monarchy among us at once and forever. I believe that any great crisis in England would show that monarchy has but little more tenacity there.

The general tendency of things in Europe appears to me certain and undeniable. How fast that tendency is advancing, how soon it will reach its consummation, I for one will not venture to predict. Providence, says Guizot, is strangely and fearfully slow in its great enterprises.

Neither is it possible to say what is ultimate. Republicanism I believe will prevail over all western Europe ; but whether finally or forever is a different question. There have been causes gravitating in the opposite direction. Rome was a republic ; her conquests in Italy, Greece, Africa, her great conquests were republics. And yet Rome became a monarchy, the greatest that the world has ever seen, and her example has done more to sustain monarchy in modern Europe than all other causes put together.

---

6. SHOULD DAY-DREAMING BE INDULGED IN?

1853.

THE human mind moves in two different worlds—the world of reality, and the world of illusion. The objects of the former are matters of fact, things obvious to the senses or cognizable by logical understanding, susceptible of proof, certified by testimony or other evidence more or less convincing. The objects of the latter are imaginations and fancies, sentiments and presentiments, aspirations and enthusiasms. They are not apprehended by logical understanding, but recognized by intuitive perception; certified, if certified at all, not by processes of reasoning, not by arguments which the understanding can analyze and appreciate; whatever warrant of truth they have lies in their native power of attraction, in the response which they call out from unperverted feeling. They belong thus to what Tennyson calls "The truths that never can be proved."

The objects of the first are substantial, positive, definite in outline, capable of being described by precise and intelligible statements. The objects of the last are vague and shadowy, admitting no exact definition, bright often as rainbow colors, but like these without distinct boundaries, melting into each other by insensible gradations. Passing beyond the sphere of sense, transcending the experience of life, often laying hold of the infinite, they have no finite measures by which their dimensions may be ascertained, and their forms laid down in plot.

I have called these two the worlds of reality and illusion rather in conformity with ordinary views, than as describing their inherent nature. I do not mean to represent the latter as wholly illusory. It may be that our ideas, even those which we regard as least substantial, have a root in verity, and are destined to be realized in some form, in other spheres of existence and under other conditions of being; and on the other hand, it may be doubted whether the reality, what we call such, what presents itself as such to our senses and intelligence, does after all conform so perfectly and exactly as we are apt to suppose to the absolute, interior, underlying reality of things as it appears to the view of God. Do not understand me as assuming the attitude of a Pyrrhonist, a universal skeptic, calling in question the reality of everything which is generally received as reality. Our conceptions of the external world and of the properties which belong to it are necessary conceptions—not only that, they are necessary beliefs: even the Pyrrhonist cannot help believing and acting on the belief that they are true, that they correspond to outward, objective reality. It is the height of folly to reject them, not to act upon them, to think of seeing round and beyond them. And yet we cannot help admitting there may be something beyond them, a deeper reality to which our faculties cannot penetrate.

Not to discuss this point, let us go back to our two worlds as we have endeavored to describe them. They belong, I say, to every mind. Perhaps no man can be found (unless wholly insane) who confines himself exclusively to either: none so absorbed in matter of fact that gleams of imagination and enthusiasm never penetrate the crust that surrounds him; and none so devoted to imagination and enthusiasm as not sometimes to touch the *terra firma* of substantial realities. But if this exclusive attachment to one or the other sphere is never fully carried out, we occasionally find a near approximation to it; and it is important for us to note the effects thus produced on mind and character. Rev. Mr. Hudson—Shakespeare Hudson, as he has sometimes been called, from his lectures on Shakespeare—in an allusion to Dr. Tyng's preaching, described it—rather uncharitably, I fear, and untruly, or with an unwarrantable exaggeration of truth—as "lean, hard, dry, bloodless, and bilious." These words describe pretty well what is likely to become the character of the man who confines himself to the world of reality. The spirit of life evaporates, and the residuum is stale and flat: the finer elements of character give place to the coarser. The graceful, delicate, generous and honorable in feeling and action are connected with ideas and sentiments that lie without the sphere of plain substantial matter of fact. Their springs are in the ideal world; if cut off from these, they dry up and disappear. On the other hand, the man who confines himself to the world of illusion, the world of day-dreams, loses robustness and power of action. Dwelling in the creations of his own mind, without practical objects to call out his powers in vigorous and healthy exercise, he is something like Hudibras's sword, "whose trenchant blade, Toledo trusty, for want of using had grown rusty, and ate into itself, for lack of somebody to hew and hack." He becomes lachrymose, sentimental, querulous, and declamatory. His enthusiasm runs to waste for want of objects. Even imagination suffers by being deprived of food which it finds or ought to find in the objects of the real world.

We see then that both these worlds are essential to the true development of mind and character. The man does best for himself who keeps strongest hold on both ; who combines sharp perception and keen enjoyment of practical realities with the glowing visions and high-soaring aspirations of the day-dreamer ; who walks in the clear light of the common everyday sun that rises and sets for all men, while lighted inwardly by "the light that never set on sea or shore, the imagination, and the poet's dream." But it is necessary to bear in mind constantly the essential distinctness of the two worlds, never allowing the imagination and enthusiasm to invest their objects with the character of reality, always remembering that air-castles have no foundation on *terra firma*, and are not built of solid brick and mortar. This is a besetting evil of day-dreamers, and most fully and elaborately illustrated in the immortal prose poem of Cervantes—Don Quixote, a day-dreamer who confounds the two worlds of illusion and reality.

It is necessary in another way to recognize their proper distinctness, by not mixing the language of one with the business of the other. The fault or weakness to which I refer is perhaps most often exhibited in Germany. It was a saying of Richter's, in the early part of this century (in the times of Napoleon), that to the British belonged the empire of the sea, to the French of the land, to the Germans of the air. Their kingdom is that of the day-dreamer. As a consequence one often finds among them, both in literature and in life, an overflow of enthusiasm. They are apt to mix up the business of common life with expressions of enthusiastic sentiment, raptures and transport, which the English mind cannot help regarding as somewhat ridiculous. The mixture of transports and tea-drinking, roast beef and raptures, appears to it incongruous and absurd. The English perhaps go too far in the opposite direction, excluding the sentimental element from everyday life, and the ordinary intercourse of society. But I must confess, my own sympathies are with them. This day-dreamer life is or ought to be an inner life; its light should not be beacon or bonfire for public gaze, but hearth-fire burning in the penetralia of mind, to light and warm the mental home. Its objects of faith and hope, its Lares and Penates, if you choose to call them so, are too sacred to be brought into rude and familiar connection with the coarseness and trivialities of everyday life. A man should not forget, indeed, in the midst of practical life and business, that he has this inner world of thought and feeling. Its influence thus present with him will preserve him from the unfeeling coarseness of the merely practical man. But there is a great difference between this and an open exhibition or free public display of the inner life; a great difference between showing in speech or action that one has feeling, and talking long or loud about one's feelings. It is the latter, not the former, that violates the instinct, and, as I believe, the true and proper instinct, of the Anglo-Saxon mind.

We see then that day-dreaming is not only not detrimental to intellectual development, but, under right conditions and control, indispensable to the best mental development.

So that I may conclude with the concluding words of Thekla in Schiller's wonderful lyric, which I must translate at great sacrifice of its ethereal beauty :—

> "Every thought of beautiful, trustful seeming
> Stands fulfilled in Heaven's eternal day;
> Shrink not then from erring and from dreaming—
> Lofty sense lies oft in childish play."

---

7. CAN IMMORTALITY BE SHOWN FROM THE LIGHT OF NATURE?

1855.

THE obvious fact about death is, that a certain living organism, the living human body, in connection with which certain processes or functions manifest themselves—such as respiration, nutrition, muscular motion, nervous sensation, perception, volition—this organism becomes disorganized, and all these processes or functions cease to be manifested. Now the claim of immortality may be based on one or the other of two assumptions: either, 1. the same organism will be reproduced hereafter, and the same functions or part of them again manifested in connection with it, and accompanied by consciousness of continued identity; or, 2. the same functions may be exercised and accompanied by consciousness of identity, though not connected with the same organism as before; may, in fact, go on without interruption, without being even suspended by death, though no longer manifested to us. Take an illustration. A mill is an organism—not indeed a living organism; something far less complex and mysterious than that, but still an organism—and its function is grinding corn. The mill may be blown down by a hurricane, and the function of corn-grinding ceases to be manifested. But perhaps the scattered timbers will be put together as before, and the same mill will perform the same corn-grinding function. Or perhaps the same identical corn-grinding which belonged to the demolished mill may be going on elsewhere in connection with another mill, unknown to us, or in connection with some wholly different and unimagined system of apparatus. The assumptions in reference to the mill and the man, it may be conceded, are possible. But the *primâ facie* probability is against them. We cannot entertain them even as probable, until supported by some positive evidence. I know there are some who deny this, who maintain that mortality furnishes no presumption even against immortality, that the certain dissolution of the organism with which all our human functions are connected, and apparent cessation of all the functions connected with it—that this does not constitute even a *primâ facie* probability of their real or permanent cessation. I cannot take the same view of the question. To me, one of the most striking proofs of the inherent elasticity of the human mind, its irrepressible buoyancy, is, that death does not drive it to despair; that, with such fearful indications of approaching annihilation, it dares to hope for immortality. What then are the evidences of immortality which can countervail the opposite presumption furnished by the phenomena of physical death ? I think it must be conceded, as to most of them, that singly they are not very strong, though their collective force may be, and in my judgment is, far greater. Let us pass them in review, or at least those most commonly urged, that we may see how far from decisive they are when separately taken, how plausibly they can be met and answered.

And, in doing this, we shall assume that the light of nature is sufficient to prove, notwithstanding all apparent difficulties, both the wisdom of God and the goodness of God. If the light of nature does not prove them, no light can ; for the strongest proof of Christianity, most decisive of its truth as a divine system of revealed religion, is its conformity to our natural reasonable ideas of God as all-good and all-wise.

Thus it is said, the universal belief in immortality is evidence of its truth. We answer : the universal belief in immortality proves only that the cause from which it springs is universal. But this cause, it is said, can only be the obvious truth of the thing believed in. We answer : that cannot be obvious truth which lies so far remote from human knowledge and experience, and concerning which so many wise men have had their doubts. Then it is said, we must believe it to have come as an original divine communication to the parents of our race. We answer : there is no proof of such communication, and no necessity for assuming it. The universal belief in immortality arises from the universal desire for it. Our faith is often the child of our wishes. When we long to find something true, we shut our eyes to all opposing evidence, we dwell constantly upon the arguments which favor it, till at length our judgment is satisfied, our belief is established.

But, it is said, God would not allow us to have such desires, if they were not to be realized. We answer : God allows us to have many desires which are never realized. Such desires, though not directly satisfied, are still useful, by stimulating to exertion, by developing faculties, or in some other way. And even so in this case. The impulse which makes us desire immortality is not only useful but necessary. For love of immortality is at bottom love of life. We cling to life while we can, and when death plucks it from us, we cling to the hope of recovering it, Alcestis-like, from the grasp of death. Now the love of life, which appears also as the love of immortality, is essential to the well-being of man and of society, essential even to their being at all. If love of life were extinguished, the world would come to an end. Again it is said, the mind of man does not attain its perfect development on earth. We answer: it is not the order of nature that everything should have perfect development. Thus of plants, how many perish in the earlier stages of growth, how many are dwarfed and stunted by unfavorable circumstances, by barren soil, ungenial climate, by ravages of insects, and a thousand other causes: how few probably attain the highest perfection of which they are in their own nature capable! So it is with the physical constitution of man and beast; so it is with the mental faculties of brutes. Not every dog or elephant is allowed to cultivate to the utmost the often wonderful sagacity and intelligence with which he is endowed by the Creator. Would you have an immortality for each and all of these, that they may come to their maximum development? But again it is said, there are in nature analogies for immortality, the germination of seed after its rotting in the ground, the transformation of insects, the phenomena of sleep and fainting. We answer: there are no analogies in nature for life after death; *i. e.* for continuance of the function, after the organism on which it depended has become disorganized. Grind the seed, and it will never germinate; crush the chrysalis, and no butterfly will burst from it. Dr. Beaumont's man digested his food, though he had lost a bit of his stomach; but could digestion have continued if the whole stomach had perished? A man may feel and think with only a part of his brain; but can thought and feeling go on without any brain at all?

This brings us to what is generally thought the strongest argument for a post-mortem existence: viz. the immateriality of the soul. Thought and feeling, it is said, are not attributes of bodily organism, but attributes of something very different, something which uses bodily organism for its various purposes; especially for communicating with other somethings like itself. Of course, when its instrument gives out, it can no longer make such communication to others, but it is not impaired in its own inherent powers and activities. Now I am far from denying the immateriality of the soul, yet I think this harder to prove than its immortality. That which is used as proof of immortality, the premise, is more difficult to be established than the conclusion. The question, observe, is not whether thought and feeling are material; they are attributes, and of course immaterial; but the question is, whether the substance to which the attributes belong is material: *i.e.* whether it is the same substance which possesses the attributes of gravity, impenetrability, and the like. Now it is said, these two sets of attributes are so different—thought and feeling on the one hand and gravity and impenetrability on the other—that we cannot suppose them to inhere in the same substance. This is the great argument, in fact nearly the whole argument, for immateriality. But it is greatly weakened by the fact that in regard to substance we know nothing whatever, can know nothing whatever, except that certain attributes belong to it. What its internal nature and constitution may be we know not; what its capacity for taking on other widely different attributes may be, we know not. The organic life of a plant is something very different from gravity and impenetrability. That subtle and mysterious activity which converts shapeless water and lime and potash, the materials of the dung-hill, into beautiful structures of leaf and flower and fruit, is surely very different from the ordinary properties of matter. Shall we infer, then, that the life of a plant is not an attribute of the matter composing it, that the plant has an immaterial soul? Or, if we shrink from this, where shall we begin to find the immaterial soul? Is it in the sponge, which occupies the debatable border between the animal and vegetable kingdoms; in the polyp, which is stomach only, a membranous bag—you may turn him inside out, and he will live as well as before; in the tape-worm, which you may cut into twenty pieces, and each will live for itself, twenty souls carved out of one; in the bivalve, which lies at the bottom of the sea, allowing water to stream through his pulpy body, making his living by digesting the animalcules it contains? All these have properties very different from the ordinary attributes of matter; properties which pass by insensible gradations, as you ascend the scale of being, to the complex mental phenomena, thought, feeling, and intelligence, of the dog or elephant. Shall we give them all immaterial souls, and wonder whether human arithmetic can enumerate the spiritual units contained in that stratum of mosquitoes, twenty feet thick, which has rested for ages on the banks of the Orinoco? Now I say these things, not as denying the immateriality of the soul, but to show how little it can be depended on as a positive argument for immortality. On the other hand, the materiality of the soul, if admitted, is far from a decisive argument against immortality. For if the material inheres in a body as substance, this body may eventually be reproduced with all the conditions essential to conscious identity. Or, very possibly, the substance in which the material soul inheres may be a mere attendant form of matter, capable of existing independently of the body, though not capable of manifesting itself to us except in connection with an organic body.

I have thus far omitted intentionally what seem to me the two weightiest arguments for immortality—in fact, sufficient in my view to countervail the apparent presumption from the phenomena of death: first, the apparent disciplinary character of human life, which certainly appears like a course of training and preparation for something beyond it, and becomes much more intelligible if regarded in this light; and second, the difficulty of reconciling the moral order of the world with our ideas of the divine justice, natural and reasonable ideas of the divine justice, if human existence is confined to the present life. This difficulty is shown very strikingly in the two books of the Bible, Job and Ecclesiastes. It is an extraordinary fact that the Old Testament Hebrews, though not wholly without the idea of existence after death, had yet no distinct idea of future reward and punishment. An extraordinary fact, I say, considering that the Egyptians and Phœnicians, heathen nations around them, had this idea fully developed, and exciting a powerful influence, especially on the Egyptians. But the Hebrew, in his habitual conceptions as seen in the Old Testament, looked for manifestations of divine justice in this life without reference to another. It is impossible, however, that the reflective should remain permanently insensible to the difficulties of this view. That they did not remain so appears from those two books, which in fact turn upon these very difficulties. Both probably belong to the later books of the Old Testament: Job, written perhaps not very long before the captivity in Babylon; Ecclesiastes, probably some time after the return to Palestine. In both, the great burden is this: the differences of human life and fortunes do not correspond to differences of moral character. How then can we vindicate the justice of God, and the claims of duty? In Job the conclusion is: God is strong and wise; man is weak and ignorant; presume not to question where you cannot understand. In Ecclesiastes the conclusion is: virtue on the whole is the best and happiest for this life; practise it with moderation of desires and cheerful enjoyment—that and only that is true wisdom. That neither of these should have fallen upon the solution furnished by the doctrine of immortality is certainly extraordinary, and may perhaps go to show that the natural evidence of this is not so clear as is frequently supposed. That is my own belief—that the light of nature, when all directed to this question, does furnish a presumption in favor of immortality; but not so strong a presumption as to exclude great and reasonable doubt upon the subject.

---

8. IS AN EXCLUSIVELY VEGETABLE DIET ADVANTAGEOUS?

1856.

A VEGETARIAN (dietarian) book was written by a Dr. Cheyne, one hundred years ago. He was a high liver, and tended to corpulency, till his weight rose to four hundred pounds, so that he could not enter a coach door. He then thought it time to retrench, starved himself to two hundred pounds, was much encouraged by success, and wrote a book on the advantages of starvation. I have never seen it, but can easily believe it useful for gentlemen of four hundred pounds weight, who cannot enter a coach door.

The dietetic movement in this country, so far as I know, commenced with a work published in 1827 by President, then Professor, Hitchcock, of Amherst College, entitled "Dyspepsia Forestalled and Resisted." Dyspepsia was then epidemic, spreading gradually over the country and becoming a fashionable disease. It appeared first in Boston, and travelled eastward. The doctors in Springfield and Hartford were much amused when they first heard of the new disease in Boston; they thought it a new Boston notion. By-and-by it came to Springfield; the Hartford doctors were still incredulous. Then it reached Hartford, and the Middletown doctors thought it a city fashion. But they got it themselves in time, as country people get all city fashions. Dyspepsia is now on the decrease, there being much less of it than twenty years ago.

Dr. Hitchcock was a dyspeptic in the palmy days of dyspepsia, when the disease was a name of dread. His work made a great sensation. I can recollect hearing it talked of in early youth. I remember well the astonishment and horror with which we heard that every man, woman, and child in the United States ate on an average at least twice as much as he, she, or it ought to eat. Another statement I remember was, that somebody had sustained life a year on a hen's egg *per diem*. Anything more than this, it was implied, tended to evil. They may have drawn the argument from the Roman description of dinner, as proceeding *ab ovo usque ad mala*.

The name more commonly associated with the vegetarian movement in the popular mind is that of Sylvester Graham. His abilities, not inconsiderable, were perhaps more than equalled by his own estimate of them. If any man ever lived and died in assured confidence of posthumous fame, it was he. Though neglected, he said, by contemporaries, posterity would do him justice. There was really some good reason for hope. His name will be in many mouths, along with his bread and crackers. These articles are favorites with not a few who neutralize their virtues by the deleterious decoctions of coffee and chocolate, and the poisonous poultry or pastry, swallowed at the same time. He had some ground of complaint against his contemporaries and neighbors, who did not always treat him with proper respect. One of them, passing his house one morning, saw the doctor picking up a basket of chips: "Ah," said he, "baking-day at your house?" Dr. Graham was much offended, but without remedy.

Prominent among dietists is Dr. Alcott, the author of several pleasantly written books, and conductor of the monthly Library of Health. In the latter, I remember an article on mince-pie, showing that, if its component parts were to arrange themselves in the stomach each by itself according to its specific gravity, there would be no less than eighteen layers or strata in the stomach. As it was not shown that they do assume any such stratification, or that, if they did, harm would come of it, the argument was a little inconclusive.

The most learned man among vegetarians was Dr. Mussey, of Dartmouth, afterward of Cincinnati. It is said that he made himself dyspeptic by high living, and then cured himself by abstemious regimen—abstemious in quality, I mean; for the quantity of potatoes he consumed was astonishing to ordinary eaters. His dietetic lectures I had the pleasure of hearing. They were very capital lectures: quiet, clear, and finished, with plenty of anecdote and illustration, and with a certain dry, quaint, subdued, but caustic humor, peculiar to himself. His wit and wisdom were too much for a youth of sixteen, and I must confess myself to have been carried away for a time. I gave up tea and coffee, beef and butter, mince-pie, even, for a month, perhaps; possibly for two; quite up to the average length of his conversions—and then went back to the old way, adapted my principles to my appetites, and have so continued to this day. I need not be ashamed of being converted to vegetarianism by Dr. Mussey, for it is said that the Doctor himself was later converted from vegetarianism by an Orang Outang. Two of those mock humanities were put on shipboard for this country, and fed of course on vegetable food, as being that which they have in their native woods. One fell sick, and, in spite of all therapeutics, died. The other also sickened, and seemed to be going the same way as his companion. One day, however, his chain being loosened, he made a spring for a table not far off, on which was a roasted chicken. He devoured the chicken with the greatest eagerness, and, instead of languishing, seemed to feel the better for his meal. The hint was taken, the same diet was continued, and the fellow reached this country at length in capital health and spirits. Dr. Mussey laid great stress on the dietetic habits of Orang Outangs, Chimpanzees, and the other nearest congeners of man; and it is said that, hearing these facts, he gave up his opposition to flesh meats—whether permanently, I am not informed.

Two faults of reasoning are to be observed in Dr. Mussey's lectures. He assumes, first, that if a thing is injurious in a large quantity, it is injurious also in a small quantity, though in a less degree; if a pound will do injury, an ounce will do a sixteenth of the same injury. Dr. Mussey, so asserting in the American Temperance Convention, was opposed by Bishop Potter of Pennsylvania, with a parallel case. An atmosphere of carbonic acid gas would kill you; and hence the minute fractional part which is always and necessarily present in the atmosphere must be proportionally deleterious. Second, to determine the wholesomeness of an article of food, he looks at its effect on a weak stomach. Again and again in his lectures, he says of a particular article of food that a weak stomach cannot digest it, and therefore it should not be used. He might as well say that, as weak persons cannot take long walks, long walks are fatiguing and exhausting to the physical energy; and therefore long walks should not be taken. He might as well say that the blacksmith should not use his sledge-hammer, because a little boy would break down in the attempt to wield it. That the weak should rule the strong, the healthy stomach submit to the unhealthy, is against the law of nature. Let dyspeptics legislate for themselves, but let them not seek to establish a dyspeptic despotism over the eupeptic world.

The principal argument of the vegetarian is that man's physical organization is analogous to that of herbivorous, not carnivorous animals. There is no doubt that our teeth, our stomach, and our alimentary canal are widely different from those of the dog or wolf; and it is a fair inference that dog's meat is not proper for us. But what is a dog's meat, adapted to his teeth and stomach, adapted to his active habits and instinct? It is raw flesh. The dog wants flesh, and cannot cook it; he will take it raw; and for this he is fitted by his physical organization. The vegetarians resolutely ignore the effects of cookery, not noticing that a similar argument could be used against their favorite diet. For we might say that, as raw potatoes are unwholesome, the use of potatoes as food should be discarded.

Examples are brought to show that the highest degree of physical vigor can be maintained without animal food. The strongest case is the story told by traveller Buckingham, of powerful fellows from Nepaul, the lower slopes of the Himalaya, who had come down to Calcutta to exhibit feats of strength. They were matched against British sailors, and were always superior. The Indian athletes are restrained by their religion from eating flesh meat, of which the British sailor makes free use. There is, perhaps, some room for doubt, but two things may be said of the comparison: first, the inclination and necessity for meat is far less within the tropics than without; and second, warm climates are far more enervating to men of northern origin than to the native of India.

The Scripture argument which the vegetarians bring forward is, that in the grant to Adam only vegetable food is named, no animal. The omission is probably not accidental, for the idea of maintaining life by the slaughter of animals is repugnant to our conceptions of the Paradisiac state; but the whole condition, physical, spiritual, and moral, of the Paradisiac world is so different from that of the actual, that no argument can be drawn from it. In the grant to Noah, animals are allowed as food; but, as the vegetarians say, only because men would have it—like divorce in the Mosaic law, allowed on account of the hardness of men's hearts. Only, cookery is required; since this is supposed to be meant by "flesh with the life thereof, which is the blood, thou shalt not eat." Still, though cookery diminished the evil, human life, under the deleterious diet, fell off from Methuselah's nine hundred and sixty-nine years to the threescore and ten of the Psalmist.

The hope is that, by going back to Methuselah's Graham bread and potatoes, we shall gradually, in the course of generations, get back to his longevity—the new millennium of life on earth.

We have never been much troubled with vegetarian fanaticism here, but in some places it has been mischievous. It has often happened that a young man has got an idea that the less he eats, the better for him, and so has confined himself to brown bread, and a minimum allowance even of that. If very strong, he bears up under it, until he overlives his delusion, or is brought by appetite, example, or custom, into the ordinary way. But, if not strong, he sinks under it, and especially if he has any tendency to constitutional disease; which there is nothing more likely to develop. I have in mind the case of an excellent young man, who in my belief hastened, if he did not cause, his own death in this way.

Students need animal food not less than laboring men; rather, more; they do not need more of it, but they have more need of it. A man who can digest a peck of potatoes at a time can live upon potatoes alone, for he can get enough nutriment to sustain life and vigor. But the less hardy stomach requires more concentrated diet, so as to have nutriment enough without being overloaded.

If I were to legislate on diet and regimen, my rules would be few and simple. In regard to exercise, take a good deal of it, unless from early days accustomed to a very sedentary life; but not too soon after eating a hearty meal.

In regard to eating—eat what you want; eat nice things, eat as much as you want of them, unless you find by clear experience that something disagrees with you; but eat only at meal times, and take no meals, edible or potable, late at night. And, last not least, trust to your stomach; do not be continually watching over it and criticising it, but believe it will get along without your help; and, above all, think as little as possible about your diet.

XIX.

ON THE HEBREW CHRONOLOGY FROM MOSES TO SOLOMON.

1857.

WE find in the first book of Kings, sixth chapter and first verse, a definite chronological statement, assigning the interval in years between the departure of the Israelites from Egypt and the commencement of work in the erection of Solomon's temple. "And it came to pass in the four hundred and eightieth year after the children of Israel were come out of the land of Egypt, in the fourth year of Solomon's reign over Israel, in the month Zif, which is the second month, that he began to build the house of the Lord." In this passage, however, the Septuagint version, the oldest and beyond comparison the most important of the versions, presents us with a different number—four hundred and forty years, instead of four hundred and eighty. This is a remarkable variation, and we shall have occasion to return to it in the sequel. At present, it is enough to observe that the number of our Hebrew text is unquestionably ancient, since it appears in other ancient versions; it appears, indeed, in all the other ancient versions which were made directly from the Hebrew; we may therefore fairly conclude that in the early centuries of our era, when those versions were made, the number four hundred and eighty was the general and current reading of the Hebrew manuscripts. Whatever discrepancy may have existed among MSS. in the earlier period of the LXX. translators, the number four hundred and eighty had apparently become the approved and established reading.

It is a well-known fact, however, that this number, four hundred and eighty years, for the interval between the Exodus and the building of the temple, is at first view inconsistent (and the smaller number of the LXX. would still more be inconsistent) with the particular designations of time scattered through the earlier historical books of the Old Testament.

Let us look at these numbers, in the order of the Biblical history. First, for the prolonged desert wanderings under the lead of Moses, which followed the Exodus from Egypt, the Pentateuch assigns a period of forty years. Next, the book of Joshua (xxiv. 31) informs us that "Israel served the Lord all the days of Joshua and all the days of the elders that overlived Joshua," but does not assign any definite term of years for the days of Joshua himself, or for those of the surviving elders. After those unassigned periods, the chronology of the book of Judges opens with the first apostasy of the Hebrew people—or rather, with the punishment which followed that apostasy. In this book we find the following series of numbers, which, according to the obvious appearance and natural impression of the work, if not according to its real intent, denote successive periods of time:—

	YRS.
Servitude under Chushan Rishathaim, king of Mesopotamia....	8
Deliverance by Othniel, son of Kenaz, and subsequent rest....	40
Servitude under Eglon, king of Moab....	18
Deliverance by Ehud, son of Gera, and subsequent rest... ...	80
Ascendency of Shamgar, son of Anath, time not stated........	..
Oppression of Jabin, king of Canaan, who reigned in Hazor....	20
Deliverance by Deborah and Barak, and subsequent rest.......	40
Oppression by the Midianites..............................	7
Deliverance by Gideon, and subsequent rest..................	40
Reign of Abimelech, son of Gideon.......	3
Tola, son of Puah, a man of Issachar, judges Israel..........	23
Jair, a Gileadite, judges Israel............................	22
Oppression by the Ammonites...............................	18
Deliverance by Jephthah the Gileadite, who judges Israel... ..	6
Ibzan of Bethlehem judges Israel..........................	7
Elon, a Zebulonite, judges Israel...........................	10
Abdon, son of Hillel, a Pirathonite, judges Israel............	8
Oppression by the Philistines.......	40
Samson, son of Manoah, judges Israel......................	20

In regard to this last number, it is not certain that the writer intended to represent the twenty years of Samson as succeeding the forty of Philistine oppression: for his language is, Samson "judged Israel in the days of the Philistines twenty years." It is possible, therefore, that he conceived of Samson's twenty years as included in the forty of Philistine oppression. However this may be, it is the only instance in which the language of the book lends any plausible color to the assumption that the times above stated are not to be regarded as successive each to the preceding. Let us suppose for the present that the twenty here was thought of as following the forty; and let us add together the whole series of numbers presented by the book, from the invasion of Chushan-rishathaim to the death of Samson. We obtain an aggregate of four hundred and ten years, with an uncertain blank for the time of Shamgar, the successor of Ehud. If, now, to this four hundred and ten we add forty years for Eli, who according to I. Samuel iv. 18 judged Israel forty years, we have a total of four hundred and fifty years for the period of the Judges, as reckoned from the first chronological indication in the book of that name on to the opening of Samuel's judgeship. Now in Acts xiii. 20, we find Paul in the synagogue of Antioch, while describing in brief outline the early history of his people, saying that God "gave unto them judges about the space of four hundred and fifty years until Samuel the prophet." This is an important passage, not only as showing that the numbers which now appear in the book of Judges stood there in the first century of our era, but also because it proves that they were then regarded as designating consecutive periods of time. For, according to the only natural and unforced interpretation of the apostle's words, they assign the duration of a period during which God was giving judges to his people, a period beginning at the time when he began to give them judges, and ending with the accession of the prophet Samuel. And the duration assigned for this period, viz. four hundred and fifty years, is precisely that which results from the numbers in Judges and Samuel, on the supposition, which is strongly favored if not absolutely required by the language of those books, that the numbers stand not for contemporaneous but for successive times.

The death of Eli was followed by the judgeship of Samuel and the kingship of Saul. For these, no term of years is assigned in the Old Testament narrative. Paul, however, in the address just quoted, says (Acts xiii. 21) that when the Israelites desired a king, "God gave unto them Saul the son of Cis, a man of the tribe of Benjamin, by the space of forty years." It is possible that this term of forty years may have been intended to cover the whole interval from the close of the four hundred and fifty years mentioned just before to the accession of David, which is mentioned directly after. If so, it would include the time of Samuel's ascendency, as well as that of Saul's dominion. To David, the Old Testament itself ascribes a reign of forty years. If we add this forty and the forty years of wandering in the desert to the sum of four hundred and fifty before obtained for the Judges, we have an aggregate of at least five hundred and thirty years between the Exodus and Solomon, or fifty years more than the four hundred and eighty named in I. Kings vi. 1. We might, indeed, avail ourselves of the doubt in regard to Samson, and, by reckoning his twenty years of judgeship under the forty years of Philistine oppression, might reduce our aggregate to five hundred and ten. But even this is thirty years beyond the mark of I. Kings; and it must be still further increased, when we come to consider the two certain and important gaps in our series, one for Joshua and the elders after him, the other for Samuel and Saul.

The statement in the book of Acts gives forty years apparently to Saul alone, though meant possibly both for Samuel and Saul. At all events, we could not allow less than fifty years to Joshua and the elders, Saul, and Samuel together. We should thus swell our aggregate to an amount exceeding by eighty or one hundred years the interval assigned by the writer in I. Kings. A discrepancy at once so obvious and so large could not fail to attract attention. Much effort and ingenuity have been expended in harmonizing the discordant statements. The methods which have been suggested for this purpose, though considerably numerous, rest for the most part upon the same leading assumptions. These are: 1. that the number four hundred and eighty years given in I. Kings must be accepted as the true and exact statement of the interval in question; and 2. that the period apparently included in the book of Judges must be shortened by making the times in that book, not all successive, but more or less contemporaneous. I do not propose to criticise these schemes, or any one of them, in detail. But two or three remarks may be made which are applicable to all: 1. In itself it is not by any means improbable, but rather, considering the disordered state of Palestine after the Hebrew conquest, the imperfect subjugation of the old inhabitants, the isolation of the different tribes, the want of national centres, of common government and of concerted action—considering these facts, I say, we must acknowledge it as not improbable that the different parts of the country were subject to different fortunes, that they were oppressed at the same time by different assailants, were delivered by the heroic conduct of different chiefs, and recognized the authority of different judges. In itself, it is not improbable that the oppressions, deliverances, authoritative judgeships, described in the book of Judges, were partial and not general; confined each to particular sections of the people, and going on contemporaneously in different portions of the land. To such an extent might we concede this, without any violation of historic probability, as to reduce the period of the Judges even more than is required to harmonize its chronology with the statement in I. Kings. 2. Nevertheless, this view of the events recorded in the book of Judges, as if they were partial and contemporaneous, seems scarcely consistent with the conception of the writer. From beginning to end, from the oppression of the Mesopotamian king to the heroic death of the Danite champion, he treats the people as a whole. As a people they apostatize from the Lord, as a people they are punished by oppressive invasion, as a people they return to the Lord with repentance and confession, as a people they receive deliverance from the foreign yoke and submit to the authority of the deliverer. The more we read the book, and the more attentively we study its plan as announced in the second chapter and carried out in the sequel, the more strong becomes our impression that the writer in his own view is recording a series of national judgments, which fall successively for good and for evil on the whole Hebrew nation, the children of Israel. In passing from one to another, he almost invariably uses language which implies succession. The only exception is at the beginning of the sixth chapter, where he says: "and the children of Israel did evil in the sight of the Lord." Though, even here, the connection would seem to show conclusively that he views this evil-doing as subsequent to the rest which, according to the previous verse, the land (that is, the whole land—there is nothing to suggest the idea of a part) had enjoyed for forty years. But everywhere else he says "and the children of Israel did evil *again* in the sight of the Lord;" thus marking their conduct as a succeeding and later instance of apostasy. So he says: "And after Abimelech there arose—Tola;" "And after him arose Jair;" "And after him (Jephthah) Ibzan judged Israel;" "And after him Elon;" "And after him Abdon." We cannot be surprised, therefore, when we find St. Paul assigning as the period of the Judges a number of years equal to the aggregate of all the numbers contained in this book (increased, of course, by Eli's forty years), as if the events and conditions to which they belong were all successive. 3. The schemes referred to rest upon no positive foundation, and have no absolute probability. At most, we can only say of them, it is possible that things may have taken place in this way. The completeness with which they solve the problem, and cut down the chronology of the Judges to a dimension consistent with the statement in Kings, is far from being decisive as to their truth. For the problem, by the nature of its conditions, is essentially indeterminate—indeterminate we might say in algebraic language, because there are more unknown quantities than fixed relations between them; it admits, as the facts show, a considerable variety of solutions, and might equally well be solved in several different ways, if the standard number were as given in the Septuagint, four hundred and forty years, instead of four hundred and eighty.

But 4. I remark, in regard to these attempts at reconciliation, that they overlook a very important feature in the chronological statements which they propose to harmonize, and must therefore of necessity fail to give satisfaction. By taking this into account, we may hope, not indeed to arrive at the solution of the problem, but at least to throw light upon its nature and conditions.

If we recur to the series of numbers which we before gave, as belonging to the period from Exodus to Solomon, and examine them attentively, we cannot fail to be struck with the frequent repetition of the number forty. It stands for the wandering in the desert, the rest under Othniel, the rest under Deborah and Barak, the rest under Gideon, the oppression of the Philistines, the judgeship of Eli, and the kingship of David—that is, seven times in a series of twenty-one numbers, or once in every three numbers. Now this circumstance alone is enough to show that there is something peculiar in the chronology we are dealing with. Let us compare it with some other chronological series—*e.g.* the reigns of Solomon's descendants, the kings of Judah. Among these we may omit two or three reigns of a year or less—numbers so small could hardly find place in the more sketchy history of the earlier times. There remain seventeen designations of time, of which we find forty years for Jehoash and forty-one for Asa: only two in the seventeen which are anywhere in the vicinity of forty. Or, let us look at the sovereigns of England from the Norman Conquest—thirty-four in number extending through eight centuries, and including an uncommonly large proportion of long reigns: here we find no reign of forty years; one (Henry VI.) of thirty-nine, one (Henry VIII.) of thirty-eight; and only six out of the thirty-four which come within a half-dozen of the forty, on one side or the other. But the case as regards the use of forty in this early Hebrew chronology is not yet fully stated. The only large number beside forty which occurs in the series, the only other number which rises above five and twenty, is that given for the rest which followed the deliverance by Ehud; and this is eighty years—that is, twice forty. Now this relation may be accidental: I mean, there is no absolute impossibility in the supposition that the periods of time referred to should have had this precise ratio to each other. But it must be owned, I think, that the chances are very greatly against it. That a series of historic times given with historical exactness, or nearly so, should contain seven forties in twenty-one numbers, is exceedingly improbable; but that the only remaining number which is more than twenty-five should be twice forty, adds much to the improbability. We may fairly say that the appearance of twice forty in this place is, under all the circumstances, a fact as surprising and as much requiring explanation as if forty itself had been the number; and consequently, in estimating the character of this chronology, we may fairly consider this as another repetition of the number forty. But yet again, we find twice forty years assigned (Ex. vii. 7) for the life of Moses prior to the Exodus, and this a New Testament passage (Acts vii. 23, 30) divides into two periods of forty years each. It is an education of forty years at the Egyptian court, followed by a wandering life of forty years among the Midianites of the desert, that prepares him to act during another forty years, at once as the law-giver of his people and the leader of their desert wanderings. And lastly, as David, the great national hero and conqueror of the Hebrews, has a reign of forty years, so we find forty years assigned to the peaceful but splendid reign of his successor, the builder of the temple and the last monarch of the united people. And we have already noticed in the book of Acts a statement, resting perhaps on a tradition as ancient as the Old Testament, which gives the same period to the first in the great triad of national Hebrew sovereigns, the warlike but unfortunate founder of the Hebrew monarchy. We find thus in the chronology from Moses to Solomon inclusive no less than eleven repetitions of the number forty; or twelve, if the eighty after Ehud's deliverance be reckoned, as it fairly may, in this category.

Now the view here presented of the facts seems to suggest —and not only that, but almost to require—the conclusion that we have in this narrative traces of an artificial chronology, proceeding by periods of forty. I should call that a natural chronology which, in stating known times, should give them with exactness, or nearly so; and, in regard to others, should estimate them as nearly as it knew how, if there were means for estimating them, and if not, should leave them undetermined, either expressly or tacitly confessing ignorance.

On the other hand, I call that an artificial chronology in which the times, instead of being stated thus or left unstated, are determined in whole or in part by assumptions or allowances of an arbitrary or systematic character. Thus, if forty years should be assumed as a general expression for any period of considerable length—as for instance the reign of a king who remains some time upon the throne, or the duration of a peace which has some degree of permanence: a chronology proceeding on this assumption, and assigning forty years to particular facts or states of such a character, would be to that extent an artificial chronology. Or, if forty years should be assumed as the length of time for a generation, a chronology proceeding upon this assumption, and assigning this period to the public activity of particular individuals who should take their place in a series of generations, would again be so far forth an artificial chronology. These modes I suggest merely by way of illustration. Whether the chronology we are considering involves either of these assumptions, or whether its peculiar character is to be explained in some different way, I do not at present undertake to decide, nor is it necessary to do so. That it has traces of something different from a precise historical chronology results from the extraordinary predominance of the number forty, and results equally, whether we can find a plausible explanation for it or not. The best explanation we can suggest may be encumbered by serious difficulties: but those difficulties will not affect the evidence which seems to force upon us the conclusion already stated—that this series of numbers in the early Hebrew history from Moses to Solomon, nearly half of them forties, bears traces of what may be called in the sense just explained an artificial chronology, proceeding in some way by forties. It is not easy to see how this result can be avoided except by supposing a kind of miracle, by assuming a special divine interference, which gave to an extraordinary proportion of early Hebrew times the exact or approximate length of forty years. It is hardly necessary to add that I use the term artificial here in no invidious sense, and without in the least meaning to imply any unjustifiable deviation from historic accuracy; much less any purpose of concealing their own ignorance, or of misleading others, on the part of the ancient Hebrew chroniclers. It may have been observed that, in speaking of this series of numbers, I do not say it *is* a chronology proceeding by forties, but that it contains traces of such a chronology. For, mixed up with the forties in the book of Judges, we find other numbers of a definite and apparently historical character—thus, for the oppressions by the Mesopotamians, Moabites, Canaanites, Midianites, and Ammonites, we have the numbers eight, eighteen, twenty, seven, and eighteen years. For Abimelech we have three years, for Tola twenty-three, for Jair twenty-two, for Jephthah six, for Ibzan seven, for Elon ten, for Abdon eight, for Samson twenty. And even in regard to the forty, I would not be understood as saying that it is in every instance unhistorical, or that it is so in any particular instance; but only that the concurrence of so many forties in a chronological series of this extent can hardly be looked upon as historical.

Let us proceed now from what seems nearly certain to that which is more doubtful. We started at the outset with a particular chronological number in I. Kings, and, in comparing this with a series of numbers scattered through the earlier history, we found a discrepancy between them. We then examined the discrepant series, and discovered in it the traces of a peculiar chronology, proceeding by forties. It becomes then a fair question whether the discrepant number in I. Kings may not itself have the same character. Now, singularly enough, the number in question (four hundred and eighty years) is the precise aggregate of twelve forties. Of course this fact alone would be of little weight, if in the remaining chronology the number forty had no special prominence. In that case, the fact that four hundred and eighty consists of twelve forties would be no more important than the fact that it contains sixteen thirties or thirty sixteens. The significance of the fact lies in the coincidence that four hundred and eighty should be an exact multiple of the particular number which figures so largely in the detailed chronology. Such a coincidence is *à priori* improbable. The chance that two events remote in time should be found to be separated from each other by a number of years which is divisible by forty is only one chance in forty, if the interval is given with exactness. And the present case is one in which we should expect that the writer, if the precise number of years had been present to his mind, would have stated it precisely, instead of contenting himself with a loose approximation. For the statement is not a casual one, suggested in passing; it stands prominently forward at the opening of the section, and appears to be regarded by the writer as fixing the relation in time between the two grand eras of Hebrew history. Moreover, the expression is peculiarly distinct and circumstantial; not "Solomon began building the temple four hundred and eighty years after the Exodus;" but "it came to pass in the four hundred and eightieth year after the children of Israel were come out of the land of Egypt, in the fourth year of Solomon's reign over Israel, in the month Zif, which is the second month," etc. But, waiving this point, and supposing that the writer might have contented himself here with a loose statement of the interval, with giving it in round numbers by the nearest ten, still the *à priori* chance that the number even as thus stated should be an exact multiple of forty is but one in four.

We cannot help thinking, therefore, that the relation of four hundred and eighty to forty is calculated to suggest the conjecture (and that with some degree of force) that the statement in I. Kings may be founded on a chronological method, such as we have before been criticising. And this conjecture receives some color of plausibility from the various reading of the LXX. (four hundred and forty for four hundred and eighty) to which we have already adverted: at least, that variation makes it apparent that a similar idea was entertained as early as the time of the Septuagint translators. For, in the first place, this must be regarded as an intentional, not an accidental variation. That is, whichever of the two was the original number, the other was the result of a conscious and calculated alteration. As it will make no difference in the argument, we may assume, what appears to be most probable in itself, that four hundred and eighty was the original reading, and four hundred and forty either a change made by the LXX. translator or one which he found already made by some one else, and represented in the MS. from which he rendered. It is true that Winer and Thenius explain the variation as arising by accident from a confusion between the Hebrew letters eighty and forty. But there are these two things to be said against This : 1. That the letters in question, though a good deal like each other in the present Hebrew square character, have much less resemblance in the ancient forms of the Phœnician inscriptions and the Maccabean coins, and therefore, so far as we can judge, were not particularly liable to be confounded in MSS. of older date than the LXX. versions. 2. Aside from such a special resemblance, we must hold it in a high degree improbable that a purely accidental variation should preserve the extraordinary characteristic of the original number—that of being exactly divisible by forty. The chances against it can hardly be less than six to one. We think it highly probable, therefore, that we have here an intentional variation—such as are well known to exist on a larger scale in the patriarchal chronology of Genesis, ch.v. and xi. ;—where there is no doubt that the difference is the result of calculation on one side or the other, and perhaps on both. But if any one designedly reduced the number from four hundred and eighty to four hundred and forty, he must have regarded the four hundred and eighty as made up by the addition of forties, and have satisfied himself in some way that too many forties by one had been allowed in the calculation : in other words, he must have regarded it as belonging to an artificial chronology proceeding by forties. Now it is certainly quite supposable that the author of this variation was mistaken in his view of the original number ; but, at any rate, it is a remarkable circumstance, to which we can hardly refuse some degree of weight, that the possible relation (as we have presented it) between the four hundred and eighty of I. Kings and the forty of the detailed chronology was observed not more than three centuries, and perhaps much less, after the completion of the books of Kings.

But there is an important circumstance which lends a further degree of plausibility to the supposition that the number in I. Kings vi. 1 is to be regarded as an aggregate of so many forties. We have reason to believe that the most complete and exact genealogical registers preserved among the Hebrews gave eleven or twelve generations for the interval from the Exodus to the building of the temple. If among the family lists for that period which we find in the book of Chronicles we had to choose the one which could with most probability be relied upon for exactness and completeness, we should have no hesitation in taking that which gives us the descendants of Aaron, the family which inherited the preëminent dignity and consequence of the high-priesthood. Now here we find (I. Chron. vi. 50-53) twelve generations enumerated, beginning with Aaron and closing with Ahimaaz the son of Zadok. Ahimaaz, it will be remembered, was a contemporary of David, though certainly a younger contemporary, since his father Zadok was still living at the commencement of Solomon's reign. If therefore—I present it merely as a supposition—if on the basis of this genealogy one should undertake to assign the number of generations between the Exodus and the building of the temple, he would give twelve or eleven, according as he included or excluded Ahimaaz, the last in the series. But in the same connection we find two other genealogies, commencing with Levi and ending respectively with Asaph the Gershomite and Ethan the Merarite, whom "David set over the service of song in the house of the Lord, after that the ark had rest." In the former of these we find from first to last fifteen generations. Now in the high-priestly series just mentioned, the fourth from Levi is Aaron. If, then, in the lineage of Asaph we suppose the one named fourth from Levi to have been a contemporary of Aaron, we find here twelve generations subsequent to the Exodus. The lineage of Ethan gives us, on the same supposition, eleven generations. It is true that the lineage of Heman the Kohathite, a third chief of the temple singers, which we find in the same chapter of I. Chronicles, appears to give us twenty-two generations from Levi, or nineteen from the Exodus to the time of David. It is also true that the remaining genealogy which spans the chasm of the Judges, I mean that of David's ancestors, assigns only eleven generations from Juda the brother of Levi to David himself, which on the same supposition as before would give eight generations from the Exodus. Whatever may be thought of these series, either absolutely or in their relation to each other, the interesting fact remains, that a majority of the whole number, and among them that one which would seem most likely (judging *à priori*) to be exactly and completely given, make either eleven or twelve generations between the Exodus and the erection of the temple. Now it is a well-known fact that among the Hebrews the number forty was used as a score is with us, for a large indefinite number. It would not be surprising, therefore, if a Hebrew author, in making a chronological estimate, should allow forty years for a generation, though this is certainly beyond the real mark ; the true average for a generation being probably not much more than thirty years. In this manner we might find a plausible explanation for the four hundred and eighty of our Hebrew text, and a plausible explanation at the same time for the four hundred and forty, the early and remarkable variation of the LXX. The difference of those numbers would be accounted for by the recognition either of twelve or of eleven generations, both of them naturally suggested by the genealogical series, for the interval in question.

But if the number four hundred and eighty may have been founded on a reckoning of twelve generations at forty years each, we can hardly doubt that in the view of him who first assigned it, whether the compiler of I. Kings or some one before him, it would be connected with the forties of which so many are found in the Pentateuch, Judges, and Samuel. The forty years' wandering under Moses, the forty years of Othniel, the twice forty of Ehud, or perhaps Ehud and Shamgar together, the forty of Deborah and Barak, the forty of Gideon, the forty of Philistine oppression, including perhaps the deliverance of Samson, the forty of Eli, and the forty of David, would give nine forties. It can hardly be doubted that forty more would be allowed for the generation of Joshua and the elders who survived him ; and again, forty more for the generation of Samuel and Saul. This would make eleven forties or four hundred and forty years, the number of the LXX. As for the remaining forty of the Hebrew text, it might be made by allowing two generations for Joshua and the elders, or by allowing two for Samuel and Saul. Both of these suppositions, however, appear improbable. The elders who overlived Joshua would most naturally be viewed as belonging to the same generation; and Samuel would appear to have continued his prophetic activity until late in the reign of Saul. Another supposition is suggested by the contents of the book of Judges. The principal figures of this book are Othniel, Ehud, Deborah and Barak, Gideon, Jephthah, Samson. These alone deliver Israel from an actual subjugation by foreign oppressors. Their actions receive a prominence in the narrative, and are rehearsed for the most part with a minuteness, altogether in contrast with the brief and passing notices of the remaining judges. Each one of these is introduced with a statement that the children of Israel did evil in the sight of the Lord; that the Lord in consequence delivered them into the hands of a particular enemy, to whom they were subject for a specified time; that the people then, in their distress, cried unto the Lord (this particular is omitted only in the case of Samson), and that an individual hereupon appeared to act with divine sanction as the deliverer and judge of his people. None of these particulars is found in the case of Shamgar, Tola, Jair, Ibzan, Elon, Abdon. Now it is a curious fact that the number forty occurs only in connection with the former class of judges, and it is found in connection with all of them excepting Jephthah. This coincidence in a large number of particulars may warrant the suspicion that there was once complete coincidence where we now find a single exception. It seems not unlikely that the minute account of the six heroic deliverers may have come from a source in which only they appeared, with a chronology by forties for all of them, Jephthah not excepted; while the brief notices of the remaining six judges, and perhaps all the precise numbers of the book, are derived from other sources. The number four hundred and eighty then may have come, not from our present book of Judges, but from the source referred to, with its chronology of forties only. I am aware how little certainty can attach to conjectures of this kind, even when suggested by the obvious features of the works to which they relate. But the object is not to show how the four hundred and eighty actually was connected with the forties of the earlier narrative—for this we could hardly hope to render certain—but only to show how it may have been connected.

Another argument which has its bearing upon the subject is founded upon a connection with Egyptian history. It is well known that Manetho, in a long extract quoted by Josephus c. Apion, i. 26, describes a great removal of leprous and unclean persons from lower Egypt under Osarsiph, an apostate priest of Heliopolis, who afterwards (he says) assumed the name of Moses. This transaction is referred by Manetho to the reign of Menophis or Amenophis (as the name stands in the text of Josephus), who is identified by what appear to be convincing proofs with Menephta, a king of the XIXth Egyptian dynasty. His reign, according to Lepsius, extended from 1328 to 1309 (acc. to Bunsen, 1325–1307); and, if so, preceded the building of Solomon's temple by little more than three centuries—a period much less than the four hundred and eighty or four hundred and forty years which we have been criticising, though sufficient to allow about eleven generations of the ordinary or average length, and possibly not incompatible with twelve generations in a particular case, where the average may have chanced to be rather smaller than usual. But into this argument I do not propose to enter. To determine the degree of weight which should be given to it would require an extended discussion, demanding at once more Egyptological science than I can lay claim to, and more time than my hearers could well afford me. I shall content myself with having stated the considerations which appear to be suggested by a critical view of the Hebrew sources; and will only add a word in conclusion, to guard against a possible misconception of my meaning.

When pointing out in the detailed Chronology from Moses to Solomon the extraordinary repetition of the number forty, and inferring thence the peculiar character of this chronology, I represented the conclusion as one which it seemed to me not easy to avoid. As to the other point—that the same peculiar character may perhaps belong to the four hundred and eighty of I. Kings—I am far from intending to speak with anything like equal confidence. I have aimed to represent this as a conjecture, to which a number of circumstances lend more or less of plausibility, but by no means as a proved or ascertained result. It is no doubt much more difficult to establish any such conclusion as to a single number, which overleaps centuries at a bound, than for an extended series, where the disproportionate frequency of one designation furnishes evidence hardly to be resisted. But the intrinsic difficulty of obtaining evidence in regard to the historical exactness of the four hundred and eighty does not justify us in asserting that it is inexact or unhistorical without sufficient evidence to prove it so. And I confess that the evidence in this case—apart from that which may be furnished by the Egyptian history, for that I do not feel myself prepared to criticise—the evidence to be derived from biblical sources alone, does not appear to me by any means decisive against the historical character of the number. At the same time, I am free to acknowledge that I cannot look upon it as I should if the circumstances here brought together had no existence; and that my faith in the commonly received chronology of the early ages, which relies on this number as a bridge to overpass the chasm that separates historical from patriarchal times, is far from being clear and confident.

One word more, in acknowledgment of obligations. The idea that the period of four hundred and eighty years in I. Kings was determined by a series of generations reckoned at forty years each is said to have been suggested by Gehringer, in a program *Ueber die biblische Aere*, published at Tübingen in 1842. This I have not seen: its author appears to have maintained, nevertheless, the historical exactness of the number, and to have rearranged the chronology of the Judges in order to make it harmonize with this statement. The same idea is developed with much clearness and caution by Bertheau of Göttingen, in the introduction to his Commentary on the Judges, published in 1845, as a part of the *Exegetisches Handbuch* for the Old Testament. It is controverted by Thenius, in his Commentary on Kings published in 1849 as a part of the same manual. It is taken up and carried out still further, with abundance of learning, by Lepsius, in his great work, *Die Chronologie der Ægypter.* These are the sources from which I have derived in great part the materials for this article.

XX.

ON THE LANGUAGE OF PALESTINE AT THE TIME OF CHRIST.

1868.

THE subject of this article is not the language used by the writers of the New Testament, but the language of its speakers, the actual language of the discourses and conversations which stand reported in the Greek of the New Testament.

On the question, *What was the prevailing language of Palestine in the time of our Saviour?* there has been great difference of opinion and much earnest controversy. Some have maintained that the mass of the people spoke Aramaic only; others that they spoke Greek only; and yet others that they were acquainted with both languages, and could use this or that at pleasure. To understand the merits of the case, the simplest way will be to take up each of the two languages in question, and trace the indications of its use among the Palestine Jews of the first century.

We begin then with THE ARAMAIC (the Jewish-Aramaic or Chaldee, in distinction from the Christian-Aramaic or Syriac dialect). It is not unlikely that the long intercourse, friendly and hostile, between the Kingdom of Israel and its Aramæan neighbors on the north, especially the Syrians of Damascus, may have produced some effect on the language of the northern Israelites. But the effect must have been much greater when the Kingdom of Israel was overthrown by the Assyrians, the higher classes carried into other lands, and their places filled by importations from tribes of Aramæan speech. In the siege of Jerusalem by the Assyrians, a few years later, it appears from the proposal of the Jewish chiefs to Rabshakeh (II. K. xviii. 26) that the Aramæan language was understood by the leading men of the city, though unintelligible to the people at large. The course of events during the next century must have added to the influence of the Aramaic in southern Palestine, until at length the conquest by Nebuchadnezzar and the Babylonian captivity gave it a decided preponderance. Surrounded for two generations by speakers of Aramaic, the Judæan exiles could not fail to acquire that language. It may be presumed that many, perhaps most of them, still kept up the use of Hebrew in their intercourse with one another; but some, doubtless, forgot it altogether. After the return to their own land the Aramaic was still required for communication with many brethren out of Palestine or in it, and with the officers or agents of the Persian government, which seems to have made this the official language for the provinces between the Tigris and the Mediterranean (comp. Ezra iv. 7, 8). The progress of the change which made the Hebrew a dead language, and put the Aramaic in its place as a living one, cannot be distinctly traced for want of literary monuments. But the result is certain; it was complete at the Christian era, and may have been so two or three centuries earlier. It is true that the New Testament in several passages speaks of the Hebrew as if still in use; but in some of these (John v. 2; xix. 13, 17) it is evident from the form of a word described as Hebrew (*Βηθεσδά*, *Γαββαθᾶ*, *Γολγοθᾶ*) that the Aramaic is meant, the current language of the Hebrew people. In many other cases, where words of the popular idiom are given in the New Testament, but without being called Hebrew, they can only be explained from the Aramaic: thus Matt. v. 22, *ῥακά*; vi. 24 (Luke xvi. 9, 13), *μαμωνᾶς*; xvi. 17, *βὰρ Ἰωνᾶ*; Mark v. 41, *ταλιθὰ κοῦμι*; vii. 34, *ἐφφαθά*; xiv. 36, *Ἀββᾶ*; John i. 43, *Κηφᾶς*; Acts i. 19, *Ἀκελδαμά*; I. Cor. xvi. 22, *μαρὰν ἀθά*—to which add the words *ῥαββί*, *ῥαββουνί*, *μεσσίας*, *πάσχα*, and proper names beginning with Bar ('son'). By Josephus, too, the name Hebrew is often used to denote the popular Aramaic: thus *ἔδωμα*, 'red' (Ant. ii. 1, § 1), *χαναίας*, 'priests' (iii. 7, §1), *Ἀσαρθά*, 'Pentecost' (iii. 10, § 6), *ἐμίαν*, 'priest's girdle' (iii. 7, § 2), all of which he designates as Hebrew, are evidently Aramaic.

That this Jewish-Aramaic was not confined to a fraction of

the people, but was in general and familiar use among the Jews of Palestine in the first century, is proved by a variety of evidence, outside of the New Testament as well as in it. Josephus speaks of it repeatedly (B. J. pr. § 1, v. 6, § 5, v. 9, § 2) as *ἡ πάτριος γλῶσσα*, the tongue of the fathers and fatherland, or, as we should say, the mother tongue, the native, vernacular idiom. As such he contrasts it with the Greek, which he describes (Ant. pr. § 2) as *ἀλλοδαπὴν ἡμῖν καὶ ξένης διαλέκτου συνήθειαν*, 'a mode (of expression) alien to us and belonging to a foreign language.' From Josephus we learn (B. J. v. 6, § 3) that, in the siege of Jerusalem, when the watchman on the towers saw a heavy stone launched from the Roman catapults, he cried in the native tongue "the missile is coming;" he would, of course, give warning in the language best understood by the citizens at large. Josephus himself, when sent by Titus to communicate with the Jews and persuade them to surrender, addressed the multitude in Hebrew (B. J. v. 9, § 2), which he would not have done if the language had not been generally intelligible and acceptable. For further proof we might appeal to the Targums or Chaldee paraphrases of parts of the Old Testament, of which the oldest, that of the Pentateuch by Onkelos, was probably written not far from the time of Christ; but it is possible that these Targums may have been composed, not for the Jews of Palestine, but for those of Babylonia and the adjacent countries; as Josephus states (B. J. pr. § 1) that the first edition of his own history was composed in the native tongue (*τῇ πατρίῳ*) for the Barbarians of the interior (*τοῖς ἄνω βαρβάροις*). Of more weight as proof of a vernacular Aramaic in Palestine is the early existence of a Hebrew gospel (*i. e.* an Aramaic, or, as Jerome calls it, Syro-Chaldaic gospel, "*Chaldaico Syroque sermone conscriptum*"), commonly ascribed to the Apostle Matthew. Papias, bishop of Hierapolis, who flourished in the first half of the second century, speaks of such a book, and holds it for the composition of the Apostle. He may have been mistaken as to the authorship; but as to the existence of an Aramaic gospel at a very early period, there is no sufficient ground to discredit his testimony. It appears then that there was a body of people in Palestine during the first century to whom it seemed desirable to have the gospel in Aramaic, perhaps not solely as being more intelligible, but as recommended also by patriotic or sectarian feeling.

Turning to the New Testament, we find it stated (Acts i. 19) that when the catastrophe of Judas became known to the inhabitants of Jerusalem, the place where it occurred was called Ἀκελδαμά, 'field of blood,' a name clearly Aramaic; and that it was called thus τῇ ἰδίᾳ διαλέκτῳ αὐτῶν, 'in their own dialect.' This does not imply that the Aramaic belonged to the inhabitants of Jerusalem exclusively, so as to be spoken by no other population; nor that it belonged to them as their only language, so that no other tongue was spoken in the city; but that it belonged to them more properly than any other tongue which might be spoken there, which could only be true of the native vernacular, ἡ πάτριος γλῶσσα. A strong light is thrown on this whole subject by the account of Paul's address to the people of the city (Acts xxi. 27 ff.). The Apostle, having been rescued by the chief captain from a mob who sought to kill him, was about to be taken to the castle; but was allowed at his own request to address the multitude. "And when there was made a great silence, he spake unto them in the Hebrew tongue." "And when they heard that he spake in the Hebrew tongue to them, they kept the more silence." (Acts xxi. 40; xxii. 2.) It is plain that he took them by surprise. If they did not know him for a native of the Greek city Tarsus, they had heard him charged with bringing Greeks into the temple; and they expected him to use the Greek. When they found him speaking Aramaic, they showed by their greater attentiveness that they were not only surprised but gratified; not that a Greek address would have been unintelligible, and perhaps not on account of any prejudice against the language, but because the speaker, by adopting an idiom that was peculiarly their own, evinced his respect for their nationality, his sympathy with their feelings, and, as it were, made himself one of their number.

Of our Lord himself it is expressly stated that on three occasions he made use of the Aramaic: when with the words ταλιθὰ κοῦμι he raised the daughter of Jairus (Mark v. 41); when with ἐφφαθά he opened the ears of the deaf man (Mark

vii. 34); and when upon the cross, paraphrasing the first words of Psalm xxii., he cried ἐλωΐ, ἐλωΐ, λαμᾶ σαβαχθανί (Mark xv. 34; in Matt. xxvii. 46, ἠλί, ἠλί, λημὰ σαβαχθανι). It is hardly supposable that among all his utterances recorded in the Gospels these three were the only ones for which he used the native idiom of the country. Yet it is not easy to say why out of a larger series these alone should be given in the original form. In the last case it seems probable that the Aramaic words actually uttered by our Lord were given by the writer, to explain how it was that some of the bystanders conceived him to be calling on Elias. As to the other two, it is noteworthy that they appear in only one of the Evangelists. The miracle wrought with the word ἐφφαθά is found in Mark alone: the miracle wrought with ταλιθὰ κοῦμι is found in Luke also, but the words ascribed to our Lord (viii. 54) are Greek, ἡ παῖς, ἐγείρου—showing how unsafe it is in other cases to conclude that he spoke Greek because he is not said to have spoken Aramaic. It is not an unlikely supposition that in these two instances the narrative of Mark reflects the impressions of an individual, whose mind was peculiarly struck by the stupendous effect instantly following, and seemingly produced by, the utterance of one or two words, so that the very sound of the words became indelibly fixed in his memory. That the same subjective impression was not made in other cases of the same kind, or that being made it did not find its way with uniformity into the narrative, are both easily conceivable. There is, however, yet another instance in which our Lord is expressly stated to have spoken Hebrew (Aramaic): in his appearance to Paul when journeying to Damascus. Of this event there are three narratives (Acts ix., xxii., xxvi.); and here again it is worth noticing that among the parallel accounts only one (xxvi. 14) alludes to the fact that the language used was Hebrew. An able writer, who holds that Christ seldom spoke Hebrew, suggests that he used it on this occasion to keep his words from being understood by Paul's companions. But if these companions failed to hear or to understand the voice (Acts ix. 7; xxii. 9), it is not safe in an event of this nature to infer their ignorance of the language. And it is quite supposable that the use of Hebrew here belonged to the verisimilitude of the manifestation, Jesus appearing to this new apostle not only with the form in which he was known to the Twelve, but with the language in which he was accustomed to converse with them.

The influence of THE GREEK in Palestine began with the conquest by Alexander. The country fell under the power of Macedonian rulers, the Ptolemies of Egypt, and afterwards the Seleucidæ of Syria, with whom Greek was the language of court and government. It was used for the official correspondence of the state; for laws and proclamations; for petitions addressed to the sovereign, and charters, rights, or patents granted by him. The administration of justice was conducted in it, at least so far as the higher tribunals were concerned. At the same time, commercial intercourse between the countries under Macedonian rule came into the hands of men who either spoke Greek as their native tongue or adopted it as the means of easiest and widest communication. Partly for purposes of trade and partly as supports for Macedonian domination, colonial cities were planted in these regions, and settled by people who, if not all of Hellenic birth, had the Greek language and civilization, and bore the name of Greeks. Such influences were common to the countries about the eastern Mediterranean; and their effect in all was to establish the Greek as the general language of public life, of law, of trade, of literature, and of communication between men of different lands and races. It did not in general supplant the native idioms, as the Latin afterwards supplanted those of Gaul and Spain: it subsisted along with them, contracting but not swallowing up the sphere of their use. Its position and influence may be compared with those possessed, though in a much inferior degree, by the French language in modern Europe. The sway of the Greek extended to lands never conquered by Alexander. To a language so capable, so highly cultivated, so widely diffused, so rich in literature and science, the Romans could not remain indifferent, especially when the regions where it prevailed became part of their empire. Long before the Christian era a knowledge of Greek was an indispensable element in the training of an educated Roman. In the reign of the Emperor Tiberius, under whom our Lord suffered, we are told (Val. Max. ii. 2, 3) that speeches in the Roman Senate were often made in Greek. The emperor himself, acting as judge, frequently heard pleadings and made examinations in it. (Dion. Cass. lvii. 15.) Of the Emperor Claudius, a few years later, it is said (Sueton. Claud. 42) that he gave audience to Greek ambassadors speaking in their own tongue, and made replies in the same language.

The people of Palestine were subjected to Hellenizing influences of a special character. Their Seleucid rulers, not content with the natural operation of circumstances, made strenuous efforts to impose upon them the Greek culture and religion. The great national reaction under the Maccabees, provoked by these efforts, was of no long duration. The Romans became masters of the country; and must have given new force to the Greek influences to which they had themselves yielded. It cannot be doubted that the Roman administration of state and justice in Palestine was conducted in the Greek, not the Latin language. The first Herod who reigned for many years under Roman supremacy was manifestly partial to the Greeks. Cæsarea, which he founded, and made, after Jerusalem, the greatest city in the land, was chiefly occupied by Greek inhabitants. Of many other cities in or near the Holy Land, we learn, mostly from incidental notices, that the population was wholly or partly Greek. Thus Gaza, Ascalon, Joppa, Ptolemais, Dora, as well as Cæsarea, on the western sea-coast; Tiberias and Sebaste in the interior; and on the east and northeast, Hippos, Gadara, Scythopolis (or Bethshan), Pella, Gerasa, Philadelphia, and perhaps the remaining cities of the Decapolis. It is obvious that the Jews must have been powerfully affected by so many Greek communities established near them and connected with them by manifold political relations, and especially the Jews of Galilee, surrounded as they were and pressed upon by such communities.

While many Greeks were becoming settled in Palestine, Jews in yet larger number were leaving it to establish themselves in all the important places of the Grecian world. Without losing their nationality and religion, they gave up their

Aramaic mother-tongue for the general language of the people round them. Had the Jews of Egypt retained the native idiom, the first translation of the Scriptures would probably have been made in Aramaic, and not in Greek. Even Philo of Alexandria, an older contemporary of our Lord, gives no evidence in his voluminous and learned writings of an acquaintance with either Hebrew or Aramaic. But these Jews of the dispersion frequently returned to their fatherland; they gathered in crowds to the great national festival; and in personal communication with their Palestinian kindred, did much to extend the use of their adopted language. In many cases they continued to reside in Palestine. Thus we hear (Acts vi. 9) of one or more synagogues of Libertines (Jewish freedmen from Italy), Cyrenians, Alexandrians, Cilicians, and peoples from western Asia Minor. That many would content themselves with their familiar Greek, as being sufficient for the ordinary purposes of communication, without taking the trouble to learn Aramaic, is a fact which can hardly be doubted. It is generally believed that the Hellenists mentioned in Acts ix. 29, and (as converts to Christianity) in Acts vi. 1, were persons of this sort—separated from those around them not by speaking Greek (for most others could do so), but by speaking only Greek. The satisfaction which Paul gave by his use of Aramaic (Acts xxii. 2) makes it easy to understand how such persons, who being settled in Palestine disdained to acquire the native idiom, might be looked upon with coldness or disfavor as a class by themselves, especially if they showed, as may often have been the case, a weakened attachment to other features of the national life.

The Greek version of the LXX. did much to make the Greek known and familiar to the Jews of Palestine. The original Hebrew was an object of scholastic study; a learned acquaintance with it was highly valued in popular estimation (Jos. Ant. xx. 11, § 2); and the number of scribes, lawyers, etc. who possessed such knowledge was probably not inconsiderable; but to the mass of the people the Hebrew Scriptures were a sealed book. Nor was there, so far as we know, prior to the Christian era, any Aramaic version. To the common man—the man of common education—if he had any knowledge of Greek, the most natural and easy way to gain a knowledge of the Scriptures was by reading the Greek translation. That such use was made of it by great numbers of the people cannot well be doubted. Of the quotations from the Old Testament made by the writers of the New, the greater part are in the words of the LXX. Comparatively few give any clear evidence that the writer had in mind the Hebrew original. This familiarity with the Greek version makes it probable that it was used not only for private reading, but in the public services of the synagogue. In many places there may have been no one sufficiently acquainted with the ancient Hebrew to read and translate it for the congregation ; but in every community, we may presume, there were persons who could both read the Greek and add whatever paraphrase or explanation may have been needed in Aramaic. It is apparent in the case of Josephus, that even men of learning who had studied the Hebrew were familiar with the version of the LXX. ; in his Antiquities Josephus makes more use of the latter than of the former. To the influence of the LXX. must be added that of a considerable Jewish-Greek literature, composed mainly in the last two centuries before Christ, the so-called Apocrypha of the Old Testament. It is true that one of these books, the Wisdom of Jesus the son of Sirach, is declared in its preface to be the translation of a work composed in Hebrew (*i.e.*, not improbably, in Aramaic) by the grandfather of the translator. There is much reason for believing also that the First Book of Maccabees was written in Hebrew ; and the same may perhaps be true of some other apocryphal books. The fact, however, that no one of them is extant in that language seems to show that in general use (except in countries east of the Syrian desert) the Hebrew (or Aramaic) original was early superseded by the Greek version. A case nearly parallel is seen in Josephus's History of the Jewish War. It was composed (according to the statement of the preface) in the native tongue for the barbarians of the interior, *i. e.* beyond the Syrian desert, the limit of the Roman power. But for those under the Roman government he translated it into Greek (*τοῖς κατὰ τὴν Ῥωμαίων ἡγεμονίαν τῇ Ἑλλάδι γλώσσῃ μεταβαλών*). And this translation has so thoroughly superseded the original work that, but for the statement of its author, we should not have known, or perhaps even suspected, its existence.

That Greek was generally understood by the people of Jerusalem is evident from the circumstances of Paul's address in Acts xxii. The multitude who listened with hushed attention while he spoke to them in Aramaic were already attentive when expecting to hear him in Greek. It does not follow that all understood him in the former language, or that all would have understood him in the latter. To gain attention it would be enough that a large majority could understand the language of the speaker; those who could not might still get some notion of the speech, its drift and substance, by occasional renderings of their fellows.

The Greek New Testament is itself the strongest proof of the extent to which its language had become naturalized among the Jews of Palestine. Most of its writers, though not belonging to the lowest class, to the very poor, or the quite uneducated, were men in humble life, in whom one could hardly expect to find any learning or accomplishment beyond what was common to the great body of their countrymen. We are not speaking of Saul or Luke or the unknown writer of the Epistle to the Hebrews; but of Peter, Jude, James, John, and Matthew, if (as is most probable) we have his gospel in its original language. Yet we find them not only writing in Greek, but writing in a way which proves that they were familiar with it and at home in it. They do not write it with elegance or with strict grammatical correctness; but they show a facility, a confidence, an abundance of apt and forcible expression, which men seldom attain in a language not acquired in early life. Some have found in the Hebrew idioms which color their style an indication that they thought in Hebrew (or Aramaic), and had to translate their thoughts when they expressed them in Greek. But similar idioms occur in the compositions of Paul, who as the native of a Greek city must have been all his life familiar with the Greek language. When Greek began to be spoken by Hebrews, learning it in adult years, they had to go through a process of mental translation; and the natural result was the formation of a Hellenistic dialect, largely intermixed with Semitic idioms, which they handed down to their descendants. The latter, as they did not cease to speak an Aramaic idiom, were little likely to correct the Aramaic peculiarities in the Greek received from their fathers. Josephus speaks with emphasis of the difficulty which even a well-educated Jew found in writing Greek with idiomatic accuracy. The Greek style of a Jew, especially when writing on religious subjects, was naturally affected by his familiarity with the LXX., which copied from the original many Hebrew forms of expression, and kept them alive in the memory and use of the people.

In view of these proofs, the conclusion seems unavoidable that, as a general fact, the Palestine Jews of the first century were acquainted with both languages, Greek and Aramaic. It is probable, indeed, as already stated, that some were not acquainted with the Aramaic; and it is by no means improbable, though the proof is less distinct, that some were not acquainted with the Greek. Of both these classes the absolute number may have been considerable. But apparently they were the exceptions, the majority of the people having a knowledge more or less extended of both languages. Other instances of bilingual communities, of populations able for the most part to express themselves in two different tongues, are by no means wanting. One of the most striking at the present day is to be found in a people of Aramæan origin with a firmly held Aramaic vernacular, the Nestorian Syrians or Chaldee Christians. "In Persia most of the Nestorians are able to speak fluently the rude Tatar (Turkish) dialect used by the Mohammedans of this province, and those of the mountains are equally familiar with the language of the Koords. Still they have a strong preference for their own tongue, and make it the constant and only medium of intercourse with each other." (Stoddard's Preface to Modern Syriac Grammar; in Journal of Amer. Oriental Soc., vol. v.)

It is a common opinion that by the pentecostal gift of tongues (Acts ii.) the Apostles were miraculously endowed with a knowledge of many languages and the power of using them at pleasure. But this gift would seem from the tenor of the accounts to have been a kind of inspiration under which the speaker gave utterance to a succession of sounds, without himself willing, or perhaps even understanding, the sounds which he uttered. It does not appear from the subsequent history that the Apostles in their teaching made use of any other languages than Greek and Aramaic. It is not necessary to suppose that Paul spoke Latin at Rome, or Maltese in Melita (Acts xxviii.), or Lycaonian at Lystra (Acts xiv.). In the transactions at Lystra it is pretty clearly implied that Paul and Barnabas did not understand the speech of Lycaonia, and therefore failed to perceive and oppose the idolatrous intentions of the people until they had broken out into open act.

In choosing between the two languages which they undoubtedly possessed, the Apostles were of course guided by the circumstances. Outside of the Holy Land they would generally, if not always, make use of the Greek. In Syria, indeed, a considerable part of the people—the same for which the Peshito version was made in the next century—would probably have understood an address in the Aramaic of Palestine ; but in Antioch, the capital where the disciples were first called Christians, Greek must have been the prevalent language. Even in Palestine, Paul's addresses to the Roman governors Felix and Festus would naturally be made in Greek. This is not so clear of the address to Agrippa, who had enjoyed a Jewish education. In the meeting of apostles and elders at Jerusalem (Acts xv.), occasioned by events in Antioch and attended by delegates from that city, the proceedings were probably in Greek, as also the circular letter which announced its result to "the brethren which are of the Gentiles in Antioch and Syria and Cilicia." When Peter on the day of Pentecost addressed the multitude of Jews gathered from many different countries, he would naturally use the language which was most widely understood. It is true that the "Parthians and Medes and Elamites—and Arabians," if no others, would have been most accessible to an Aramaic address ; so we judge from the fact that Josephus, writing for readers in these very lands, composed his history in the native tongue. Still, when we consider the "dwellers in Cappadocia, in Pontus and Asia, Phrygia and Pamphylia, in

Egypt and in the parts of Libya about Cyrene, and strangers of Rome," it is probable that more would have understood Greek than Aramaic; so that if there was only one address in one language (which perhaps the terms of the narrative do not require us to suppose), it was probably made in Greek.

The difficulty of determining the language used for each particular discourse is even greater in the Gospels than in the Acts. It seems reasonable to suppose that conversations between kindred and friends, and the familiar utterances of Christ to his disciples, were in Aramaic; the native idiom of the country, if not wholly given up, would naturally be employed for occasions like these. Yet as long as speakers and hearers had another language at command, there always remains, in the absence of express statements, a possibility that this, and not Aramaic, may have been used for any given conversation. And if, on the other hand, it seems reasonable to suppose that our Lord in his more public discourses spoke Greek, there is a similar difficulty about being sure in particular cases that he did not use the other language which was familiar to him and to the mass of his hearers. A recent writer assumes that every discourse which, as reported to us, contains quotations from the Old Testament in the words of the LXX., must have been pronounced in Greek; and this criterion, were it trustworthy, would decide many cases. But if an Aramaic speech containing Scripture quotations were to be reported in Greek by a writer familiar with the LXX., who seldom (if ever) read the Scriptures in any other form, is it not probable that he would give the quotations for the most part according to the LXX.? Sometimes, it is likely, he would depart from it, because he did not correctly remember its phraseology; and sometimes because he remembered that the Aramaic speaker gave the passage a sense varying from that given by the LXX. As the writers of the Gospels were probably in this condition—of persons familiar with the LXX. who seldom (if ever) read the Scriptures in any other form—it is unsafe from the way in which they give the Scripture quotations to infer anything as to the language used by the speakers who quoted them. There are instances, however, in which the circumstances of the case afford some indications on this point. Thus in communicating with the people of Gadara, which Josephus calls a Greek city, our Lord would use the Greek language. Among the crowds who followed him before the Sermon on the Mount and who seem to have stood about the mountain while he was speaking, were some from Decapolis (Matt. iv. 25). As already stated, the ten cities of that region were (most, if not all, of them) Greek. As our Lord had thus in the surrounding multitude of his auditors some who probably were unacquainted with Aramaic, there is plausible ground for believing that on this important occasion he made use of the Greek language. In the closing scenes of his life, when he was brought before the Roman governor for judgment and execution, it is nearly certain that Greek was used by Pilate himself and by the various speakers about his tribunal.

It is stated in the Mishnah (Sotah, c. 9, n. 14) that, when the war of Titus broke out, an order was issued in which fathers were forbidden to have their sons instructed in Greek. Whether this is true or not, it would be only natural that the excited patriotism of such a time should cause the Jews to set a higher value on their national tongue. Perhaps those who spoke Greek and Aramaic were now inclined as far as possible to discard the use of Greek; the Targums, which seem to have made their first appearance or to have assumed a permanent shape about this time, would be a help in doing so. At all events, there is reason for believing that after this period there was a considerable population in Palestine who did not understand Greek. The general opinion of the Fathers (from Clement of Alexandria down), that the Epistle to the Hebrews was composed in Aramaic, had probably no other foundation than the belief that it would otherwise have been unintelligible to the Jews of Palestine for whom it was designed. This belief is of little weight as regards the original language of the epistle; but as regards the prevailing language of Palestine in later times it may not be without value. Eusebius of Cæsarea, a native and life-long resident of Palestine, declares (Dem. Evang. lib. iii.) that the Apostles before the death of their Master understood no language but that of the Syrians; this he would hardly have done if Greek had been generally spoken by the Galilæans of his own day.

The discussion as to the language of Palestine in our Saviour's time has been quite generally connected with the question whether Matthew wrote his Gospel in Hebrew or in Greek. Most defenders of the Hebrew original (as Du Pin, Mill, Michaelis, Marsh, Weber, Kuinoel, etc.) have maintained that this was the only language then understood by the body of the people. And many champions of the Greek original (as Cappell, Basnage, Masch, Lardner, Walæus, etc.) have made a like claim for the Greek. For a full list of the older writers, see Kuinoel in Fabricius, *Bibl. Græca*, ed. Harles. iv. 760. We add the names of some writers who have treated the subject more at large. Isaac Vossius (*De Oraculis Sibyllinis*, Oxon. 1680), though a staunch believer in the Hebrew original, held that Greek was almost universal in the towns of Palestine, and that the Syriac still spoken in the country and in villages had become so corrupted as to be a kind of mongrel Greek. He found an opponent in Simon (*Hist. Crit. du Texte du N. T.*, Rotterd. 1689), who allowed that Greek was the common language (*langue vulgaire*) of the country, but contended that the Jews, beside the Greek, had preserved the Chaldee which they brought with them from Babylon, and which they called the *national* language. Diodati of Naples (*De Christo Græce loquente*, 1767; reprinted, London, 1843) went further than Vossius, asserting that Greek in the days of our Lord had entirely supplanted the old Palestinian dialect. Replies to this work were put forth by Ernesti (*in Neueste Theol. Bibl.*, 1771) and De Rossi (*Della Lingua propria di Christo*, Parma, 1772). De Rossi's work was adopted by Pfannkuche as the basis of his essay on the Aramæan language in Palestine (in Eichhorn's *Allgem. Bibl.*, 1797), translated by E. Robinson (in *Am. Bibl. Repos.*, 1831) with an introduction on the literature of the subject. Another translation (by T. G. Repp) is given in Clark's *Biblical Cabinet*, vol. ii. Against Pfannkuche, who is one-sided in his advocacy of the Aramaic, Hug (*Einl. in d. N. T.*, 4th ed., 1847; 3d ed. translated by Fosdick, Andover, 1836) maintained the concurrent use of

27

Greek. His position—which is nearly the same with that of Simon—is held substantially by most later writers, as Credner (*Einl. in d. N. T.*, Halle, 1836) and Bleek (*Einl. in d. N. T.*, Berlin, 1862). A somewhat more advanced position is taken by Dr. Alex. Roberts (*Discussions on the Gospels*, 2d ed., London, 1863), who, while admitting that both languages were in general use, contends that our Lord spoke for the most part in Greek, and only now and then in Hebrew (Aramaic).

INDEX.

www.ingramcontent.com/pod-product-compliance
Lightning Source LLC
LaVergne TN
LVHW021142110826
845150LV00005B/1105

* 9 7 8 1 4 2 5 5 4 7 3 0 1 *